The Sports Doping Market

Letizia Paoli • Alessandro Donati

The Sports Doping Market

Understanding Supply and Demand, and the Challenges of Their Control

Springer

Letizia Paoli
University of Leuven Faculty of Law
LINC, Leuven Institute of Criminology
Belgium

Alessandro Donati
Libera
Roma, Italy

ISBN 978-1-4614-8240-6 ISBN 978-1-4614-8241-3 (eBook)
DOI 10.1007/978-1-4614-8241-3
Springer New York Heidelberg Dordrecht London

Library of Congress Control Number: 2013943595

Printed on acid-free paper

Springer is part of Springer Science+Business Media (www.springer.com).

For our children: Letizia's Maddalena, Isabella and Leo and Alessandro's Francesco and Matteo

Acknowledgments

Many people have supported us in this study and without the help of some of them this book would have literally not been possible.

In Italy, Dr. Luciana Magrì supported us with invaluable assistance, by constructing the entire Database on NAS Investigations, patiently typing in an Excel sheet all the data received by NAS in a pdf file, researching on the internet the prices of hundreds of doping substances, and assisting us in all the calculations.

Prof. Paoli was also helped by the capable research assistance of Bertrand Fincoeur and Evelien van Dun. The latter, in particular, played a key role in revising and formatting the references. David Schmitter proofread the entire manuscript, correcting the English style as needed. Ellen Wauters from the KU Leuven Financial Department competently took care of the project finances. At the World Anti-Doping Agency (WADA), Julien Sieveking, senior manager of Legal Affairs, was our reliable contact person throughout the study for all practical and legal matters. We are grateful to all of them.

We also would like to acknowledge the role of Victoria Greenfield (U.S. Naval Academy and RAND). She developed with us the project proposal, double checked and improved our calculations in Chap. 2, and improved substantively and stylistically the first chapters of the manuscript.

We also appreciate the help received from Dr. Giusy Muratore, Dr. Claudio Caterino, and Dr. Isabella Corazziari from the Italian Statistical Office (Istat), who provided data about proceedings initiated, the persons charged and the verdicts issued for several doping-related offenses. At our request, they extracted for the first time the data concerning the Italian anti-doping act (Act 376/2000) from the Istat database on criminal statistics. Likewise, we recognize the support received from Dr. Elisabetta Simeoni and her staff from the Dipartimento Politiche Antidroga of the Prime Minister's Office, who provided us the data on the use of steroids among Italy's adults, which had been collected through a population survey but had never been published. Many thanks also go to Kristin Smolka (German Central Office of Customs Investigation Service) who provided Paoli with valuable data about the profit margins of the trade in doping substances and information about recent German anti-doping investigations.

We received insightful comments and data from a number of other scholars and thank them all for their important contributions. Dr. Pasquale Bellotti and Dr. Roberta Pacifici (Higher Institute of Health) proofed our 100 consumption profiles and discussed them with us in detail; thanks to their in-depth experience in the fields of doping and anti-doping, they have considerably helped increase the profile validity. Prof. Caterina Pesce (University of Rome Foro Italico) shared with us the raw data of a survey she had conducted with several colleagues about doping consumption patterns among a sample of high school students in Rome. Prof. John Hoberman (University of Texas at Austin) furnished Paoli with some unpublished material on the use of doping products among law enforcement and other officers of the public and private security sector, confirming our own findings. Prof. Wolfgang Jelkmann (University of Lübeck), a world-renowned specialist for EPO, double checked our analysis of the use and production of this drug. Prof. Ulrich Haas (University of Zurich) shared with Paoli insights on the positive repercussions of Italy's anti-doping law enforcement on sports arbitration, based on his experience as judge at the Court of Arbitration for Sport (CAS). Dr. (PD) Markus Parzeller (University of Frankfurt) provided Paoli with the yet unpublished report of his comparative analysis of anti-doping legislation and criminal prosecution in five European countries (France, Germany, Italy, Spain, and Switzerland), including all five case studies. Prof. Wilhelm Schänzer (Cologne Sports University) provided data about the costs of anti-doping tests at the Cologne Anti-Doping Laboratory and his colleague, Prof. Hans Geyer, transmitted Paoli useful information on gonadorelin testing. Prof. Perikles Simon (University of Mainz) made useful comments on our literature review, also sharing some unpublished material and some comments he had received from Prof. Harrison Pope (Harvard University). Dr. Andreas Singler (Center for Doping Prevention, Heidelberg) commented on our analysis of the history of anti-doping and drug prevention programs. Dr. Erkki Vettenniemi (University of Jyväskylä) shared with Paoli his deep knowledge of the Finnish Ski Federation's doping program in the 1980s and Prof. Conconi's contacts with the Finnish researchers involved in that program.

Prof. Arne Ljungqvist (WADA and International Olympic Committee, IOC) provided Paoli with background information about the doping scandal at the 2006 Turin Olympic Games, which helped us better understand the relevance of that episode in the history of anti-doping. More generally, Paoli profited extensively from the informal exchanges of ideas she had with Prof. Arne Ljungqvist and Dr. Richard (Dick) Pound (IOC) at the margins of a symposium on "Sports Medicine and Doping in Europe" which she organized in September 2011 in her capacity as president of the Evaluation Commission for Sports Medicine in Freiburg on behalf of the Freiburg University. The insights and trust of these two key policy-makers in contemporary anti-doping have been highly appreciated.

This study would have also not been possible without the extensive cooperation granted us by the Comando Carabinieri per la Tutela della Salute (Carabinieri Command for Health Protection), better known as NAS, the acronym of the original name. In particular, we would like to thank the Captains Pietro Della Porta, Francesco Saggio, and Dario Praturlon. In their respective capacity as heads of

NAS Operations and Analyses Departments, Captains Della Porta and Saggio were extremely helpful in retrieving precious information for us, developing and administering a questionnaire to the heads of all NAS branch offices and arranging our interviews with officers in the field. We are also very indebted to the latter officers from nine branch offices, some of whom we met or talked to on the telephone several times. These officers made time available for us, answered our numerous, sometimes probably bothersome, questions and shared with us their reports, prosecutor's charges and/or verdicts in numerous closed criminal proceedings.

Likewise, we are grateful to our other respondents and specifically to the six prosecutors who shared with us their reflections on their own investigations and anti-doping policy more generally, and provided us with charges and verdicts: Dr. Luigi Bocciolini (Florence), Dr. Gianfranco Colace (Turin), Dr. Vincenzo Condorelli (Mantua), Dr. Paolo De Angelis (Cagliari), Dr. Raffaele Guariniello (Turin), and Dr. Benedetto Roberti (Padua). In particular, we owe special thanks to Dr. Guariniello, who volunteered to check the status of several key anti-doping proceedings in the internal database of the Italian Ministry of Justice and then requested a paper copy of the highest-level verdicts available from the relevant courts. We highly appreciate the several open conversations we had with him, in which he shared his assessment of the doping problem in Italy and Italian anti-doping policy. We also would like to thank Dr. Lorenzo Gestri from the Bologna Prosecutor's Office, who promptly followed up on our request and sent us a verdict concerning an important case.

We had the unique opportunity to discuss the key findings of our study and the resulting policy implications with a selected set of policy-makers, practitioners, and scholars at a workshop organized by the WADA at its office in Lausanne in January 2013. We would like to thank Frédéric Donzé Director of the WADA European Regional Office and Oliveri Niggli, Legal Coumsel at WADA, for organizing the workshop and the workshop participants for their very constructive and helpful feedback.

With their commitment to anti-doping, generosity and trust, two individuals made this study possible—and that's why we would like to thank them most warmly at the very end. One of them is General Cosimo Piccinno, the Head of NAS. Piccinno authorized the extensive and—for Italian law enforcement standards—unprecedented sharing of data and reports of anti-doping criminal investigations with us, as well as the many candid interviews and informal conversations we had with NAS officers.

The other, David Howman, the WADA Director General, decided to fund our work in a very quick, reactive manner. When one of us (Paoli) first talked to Howman on the phone about our proposal, asking whether we could submit it through the regular WADA application channels despite their current focus on doping prevention, he immediately answered: "We need this study. Period!" and secured funds.

Grazie!

Leuven, Belgium
Roma, Italy

Letizia Paoli
Alessandro Donati

Contents

Prologue: Three "Antipasti"

We begin this book with three summaries of some of the most momentous anti-doping criminal investigations in Italy. The summaries are meant to serve as appetizers, or "antipasti," as we say in Italian, for the subsequent analysis. They exemplarily show the high-level doping cases and related supply and protection networks that can be identified and dismantled, when a country has adequate criminal laws, specialized police units, and independent prosecutors. The three summaries, however, also indicate the inefficiency of the Italian criminal justice system and its difficulty of securing convictions for doping and other offenses.

Although antipasti are usually eaten at the start of a course, the first of these three investigations, which shattered the 2006 Winter Olympic Games in Turin, bears the name of a famous Viennese chocolate dessert, "Operation Sachertorte." In an interview-based biography, Prof. Arne Ljungqvist, who coordinated that case in his capacity as Vice-President of the World Anti-Doping Agency (WADA) and President of the Medical Commission of the International Olympic Committee (IOC), recounts:

> "It was a couple of days after I arrived in Turin that I learned that WADA had attempted to carry out an out-of-competition drugs test on the Austrian cross-country skiing and biathlon teams before they set off for Turin. According to the official whereabouts report that WADA had received, the skiers should have been stationed at a training camp in Austria. But when the doping control officers arrived at the given address, a guest house, no skiers were there.
>
> However, in the guest house's cellar they found what looked like a hematological laboratory. It really *felt* of blood doping. The doping control officers were quickly ushered away by the owner of the guest house, who turned out to be the wife of the Austrian ski trainer Walter Mayer[1]—the same Walter Mayer who had received an unprecedented ten-year ban from the IOC at Salt Lake City four years earlier, when he had been found with an array of transfusion equipment which suggested that he was tampering with the blood of the Austrian ski team.

[1] As a rule, in this book we only mention the names of well-known elite athletes and public figures who have been involved in anti-doping investigations when the doping allegations have been reported in a publicly available source, such as a publication in a book or in a legitimate, verifiable media report. We respect, instead, the anonymity of all other persons, suspected or even convicted of doping-related sports violations or criminal offenses.

On that occasion no skier had been caught testing positive. But this time, news came through that Walter Mayer had been spotted in the Turin area in the vicinity of the Austrian camp, even though he was not accredited by the Olympics. As Italy has a very strict doping law, and doping offenses can be treated as criminal offenses, we felt obliged to inform our Italian hosts."

On the morning of Thursday February 16, a meeting was held in the hotel suite of IOC President Jacques Rogge. Present was Rogge, Arne and two other representatives from the IOC, together with the Italian sports minister [Mario Pescante] and the chief of the Italian anti-doping organization. The IOC delegation handed over to the Italians the information that they had got from WADA, then outlined their own observations about Mayer's presence and revealed that they intended to carry out a surprise test of the Austrian cross-country skiers and biathletes on Saturday evening.

"We were forced to give the Italians some time to consider the information. At the same time, I was scared that something would be leaked giving the Austrians time to prepare before Saturday evening. Perhaps they would make themselves unavailable.

But the Italians kept quiet. They got back to us on Saturday morning and informed us that they regarded the case as so serious that they were thinking of raiding the Austrian camp. They suggested that we should co-ordinate a raid that evening."

Arne found himself heading the investigation with a group of "troops." The IOC's doping control officers and the *carabinieri*, set off at the same time for the Austrian camps in Sestriere and Pragelato. Apart from a few red traffic lights that slowed them down, it went like clockwork, with both raids happening simultaneously.

"Medical instruments and other material were thrown out of the window and the Austrians tried to get away. Walter Mayer disappeared in his car towards the Austrian border, but was stopped at a police roadblock. He ended up in hospital, apparently with excessive alcohol in his blood.

Two biathletes returned home to Austria, from where they announced their immediate retirement. Several other Austrian skiers and biathletes were tested."

The events made big news. Arne was forced to hold a press conference and explain what had happened. He was fiercely questioned, especially by the Austrian media. More press conferences took place. The Italians didn't say much about what had happened, but Arne was forced to admit at a press conference that all the drug tests had proved negative.

"It wasn't that surprising. They had, of course, planned the tampering with the blood so it would test negative at the upcoming events. But we were forced to act as we did. At the press conference, I was sarcastically asked by Austrian journalists why I had made such a fuss: everyone was negative, so it wasn't doping, they said.

I replied that doping is not just about testing positive. For example, there's possessing doping medication and doping equipment."

There was a long wait for the report from the Italians. The matter had ended up on the desk of the Turin's notoriously aggressive public prosecutor Raffaele Guariniello. "I visited Guariniello in Turin. He was a friendly but very determined gentleman. We were in contact for a long time."

As late as October 2008, Guariniello gave notice that he intended to charge a long list of Austrian officials and athletes for breaking Italy's doping laws. But before this, the IOC received enough information from Guariniello confirming that blood doping equipment had been found as well as banned doping substances in the Austrian camp. It was sufficient for the IOC to act.

Several cross-country skiers as well as team managers were banned from competing in future Olympics. The Austrian Olympic Committee was fined a US$1 million by the IOC for failing to monitor the team sufficiently. The international ski federation banned the athletes in question and the team leaders for two years. Some athletes appealed to CAS [Court of Arbitration of Sport, the highest sports court] against their conviction, without success. In June 2009, the Italian prosecutors indicted ten Austrian officials and skiers for having violated the Italian doping law.

"Sure it was a successful case. Internally we referred to it with a touch of gallows humour as 'Operation Sachertorte,' but the Austrians probably don't like that. It is really tragic for sport that something like this needs to happen. At the same time, the events are a good example of having an effective law in place in the country that is arranging a major international event. It was because they had the law on their side that the Italians could carry out such a raid and find what they did. If the Italian anti-doping law hadn't existed, the cheating being done by the Austrians would never have been discovered. All the tests were negative, after all.

At the IOC session in Guatemala in June 2007, I met the Austrian premier, Alfred Gusenbauer. He was there because Salzburg was a candidate to host the 2014 Winter Olympics, but he wanted to meet me. I felt a little embarrassed and apologized a bit for what we had done in Turin.

But he wanted to thank me for the effective action we had taken which had revealed the unacceptable cheating. It had made it possible for the Austrian parliament to pass a law in record time with strong anti-doping rules" (Lager and Ljungqvist 2008: 178–180; see also Fisher and Macur 2006; Macur 2006; Zinser 2006; IOC 2007; Mayer 2010).

Ironically, the much-praised Carabinieri raid took place only because the IOC (but not WADA) had been defeated in its effort to persuade the Italian government to impose a moratorium on its anti-doping act during the Turin Games. Mario Pescante, the then undersecretary for sport, as well as the Italian government supervisor for the 2006 Games and an IOC member, had also insistently, but unsuccessfully, called for such a moratorium but his and the IOC's request found little public and political support in Italy (Vinton 2005). "Members of Parliament consider this moratorium a sign of weakness," Pescante finally had to admit (ibid.). When Ottavio Cinquanta, the only Italian member of the IOC's executive board, was asked if Italy's Prime Minister, Silvio Berlusconi, could help persuade the country's judges to tread delicately at the Games, Cinquanta was reported saying "that it was difficult to pressure a judge" (ibid.). Almost foreseeing Guariniello's involvement in the raid, *The New York Times* noted that "one judge in particular, Raffaele Guariniello, has gained a reputation for his hard-nosed investigation of widespread doping in Italian soccer. Guariniello is based in Turin." (ibid.)

In July 2012, the Turin court finally issued a verdict on the case and convicted two athletes and the trainer of the Austrian cross-country ski team of doping. It could not convict two other athletes because the Italian anti-doping legislation does not criminalize the mere possession of doping products. The court also did not find sufficient evidence to condemn Walter Meyer. Lacking the evidence for the latter, the court also acquitted three other officers of the Austrian Ski Federation, including the federation president, despite "the omissions in controls and the carelessness with which the top hierarchy of the Austrian Ski Federation had dealt with the risk of repeating the grave doping cases ascertained in 2002 at the 2006 Turin Olympic Games" (Tribunale di Torino, 2012).[2]

The second investigation had taken place 7 years before the Turin Olympic Games, in 1999. With it, the Italian law enforcement authorities questioned—perhaps even more aggressively than in Turin—the integrity of the Italian and world

[2] Unrelated to the Turin events, Mayer was later sentenced to 15 months of imprisonment for repeated violations of the Austrian anti-doping law (*Wiener Zeitung* 2011).

sports system, by raising charges against Prof. Francesco Conconi, head of Centro di studi biomedici applicati allo sport (Centre for Bio-Medical Studies Applied to Sports) at the University of Ferrara and rector of the same university. Conconi and his staff were accused of administering blood-boosting erythropoietin (EPO) to, and practicing blood doping on, leading cyclists and other top athletes from 1992 to 1997, at the same time as Conconi was a member of the IOC's Medical Committee, the President of the Medical Commission of the Unione Cycliste Internationale (UCI), and received large amounts of funding from the IOC and the Italian National Olympic Committee (CONI). (The IOC's funding was meant to develop an EPO test, which Conconi, however, never delivered.)

Pierguido Soprani, the first prosecutor in charge of this investigation, had to fend off the opposition of the University of Ferrara and public opinion, local and national politicians, and his own Chief Prosecutor, who tried to stop his investigation. The latter also prevented Soprani from opening a parallel financial investigation by refusing to allow him to collaborate with the Guardia di Finanza. Disgusted by these undue pressures, Soprani asked to be relocated after he had filed the charges against Conconi and his staff with the judge for preliminary investigations, and left the judiciary soon afterwards. When the judge for preliminary investigations finally considered the case, he modified the charges so that the court judge had to send the proceeding back to another prosecutor. The judge for preliminary investigations also commissioned a new, unnecessary, expert report from a hematologist connected with Dr. Ferrari, one of Conconi's closest collaborators (see below), who skillfully reduced the evidence available against Conconi (Int-NAS-26 and Int-Oth-2). When the trial finally started, Judge Franca Oliva had no choice but to apply the statute of limitations, despite "the seriousness and convergence of all the evidence" (Tribunale di Ferrara 2003: 46).[3] Relying on 70,000 pages of documentation collected by the prosecutors (*NZZ* 2004), the Court of Ferrara left no doubt that Prof. Conconi and two members of his staff were guilty of sporting fraud. As Judge Oliva later stated in an interview, "Conconi was guilty. It is obvious that the defendants were perfectly aware of the EPO-doping that was administered at their institute in Ferrara. … The defendants have supported for years athletes in their EPO-doping and through the continuous medical controls they have also encouraged the athletes to make to use of EPO" (*NZZ* 2003; see Chap. 3).

In a related proceeding, Ferrara Prosecutor Soprani investigated the protection and support that high-level CONI officials, including three Presidents, had given Conconi for decades. After reconstructing the relationships between CONI and Conconi since late 1970s, in fact, Soprani came to the conclusion that

> Franco Carraro (CONI President from 1981 to 1986), Arrigo Gattai (CONI President from 1987 to 1994), Mario Pescante (CONI Secretary General from 1981 to 1994 and CONI

[3] We will explain the reasons why the statute of limitation applied to this and several other—more or less prominent—anti-doping criminal proceedings in Chap. 7. To summarize here, the extensive use of the statute of limitation in Italy is not a peculiarity of the anti-doping sanctioning but is due to some general characteristics and the resulting inefficiency of the Italian criminal justice system.

> President from 1995 to 1998), Gianfranco Carabelli (head of the Research and Documentation Section of the CONI School of Sport) and Francesco Conconi, as partner responsible for the studies funded by CONI, were the promoters of a criminal organization ([article 416 CP]; Procura della Repubblica di Ferrara 2000: 42).

This criminal association was allegedly set up to distribute drugs in a dangerous way to public health (article 445 CP) and active throughout the 1980s (ibid.; see also Capodacqua 2000a). Pescante and Conconi were regarded as the promoters of the criminal organization.

As too much time had elapsed between the alleged activities and the prosecution, Soprani had to dismiss the case but insisted that his request "does not diminish the social and criminal non-value of the activities proved" (Procura della Repubblica di Ferrara 2000: 56) and that "one could not reasonably recognize good faith of those who approved the deliberations while they were the top managers of the public body CONI. Instead, the contents of the investigative materials … have shown several elements of opposite direction" (ibid.: 43). Despite "a multiplicity of circumstantial evidence" (ibid.: 52), the prosecutor found, instead, no conclusive proof of the existence of a criminal organization between Conconi and the CONI top leaders after 1989.

Barely half a year after being accused by the Ferrara Prosecutor's Office, Pescante was elected a member of the Italian Chamber of Deputies in Silvio Berlusconi's Forza Italia (now Partito delle Libertà) party. From 2001 to 2006 he served as undersecretary of the Ministry of Cultural Heritage and Activities under Prime Minister Silvio Berlusconi and from 2004 to 2006, was the Italian government supervisor for the 2006 Winter Games in Turin. From 2008 until early 2013, he was the president of the European Union Affairs Commission of the Chamber of Deputies. His international career did not suffer either: Pescante has been without interruption an IOC member since 1994 and was the first Italian to become an IOC Vice-President in 2009 (see Chap. 5).[4]

The third investigation occurred in 1998 and led to the temporary closure of CONI's anti-doping laboratory in Rome and the withdrawal of its IOC accreditation. Searches ordered by the Turin Prosecutor Raffaele Guariniello demonstrated that the lab did not carry out proper tests for steroids[5] in 70 % of the urine samples of Italy's football league players. Positive tests were covered up and documents were destroyed (Evaluation Team 2002: 13; Travaglio 1998). A Commission of inquiry established by the government concluded that "the number of violations recorded in the mechanisms to ascertain prohibited substances specifically in football was so large as to compromise the whole anti-doping policy pursued by CONI." The latter was accused of failing to exercise properly its duties of vigilance on the

---

[4] Pescante stepped down from the Vice-Presidency in early 2012, when the cabinet headed by Mario Monti refused, for austerity reasons, to back Rome's bid for the 2020 Summer Olympics, which Pescante had headed. See http://www.olympic.org/mr-mario-pescante.

[5] Anabolic–androgenic steroids are a family of hormones derived from cholesterol that includes the natural male hormone, testosterone, together with numerous synthetic testosterone derivatives (Pope and Brower 2009).

laboratory, and the Italian Football Federation and the Italian Federation of Sports Physicians were deemed to be "co-responsible" "of the violations of the duty to establish urine Ph and density when the samples were taken" and regarded as "protagonist of a non-linear affair concerning anti-doping rules" (*Adnkronos* 1998). Under the pressure of public opinion, CONI President, Mario Pescante, stepped down (Longman 1998b; Travaglio 1998; Italy 2002: 13).[6]

[6] The investigation was initiated by the detailed report of a member of our research team (Donati) and of a chemist who worked at the lab.

Introduction

Italy's anti-doping criminal investigations not only distinguish themselves for the many high-level athletes, suppliers, and protectors they have pursued but also have few parallels in the world for their number and extent. Perhaps more than in any other country, actions under Italian anti-doping criminal law have shed light on the many different aspects of the problem of doping and specifically of the supply of doping substances and methods (hereafter referred to jointly as "doping products"), such as the emergence of an illegal market to supply large numbers of noncompetitive sportsmen and sportswomen (above all, visitors of gyms and fitness centers), the misuse of veterinarian drugs for animals and humans, the theft of medicines from trucks and the storehouses of hospitals and pharmaceutical companies and the falsification of medical prescriptions.

As discussed in more detail in the following pages, three main factors have enabled Italy's exceptionally intense anti-doping action:

1. Adoption of an anti-doping law in 2000, the Act No. 376/2000, that established the criminal offenses of doping and trade in doping products (article 9) and set up the Commissione per la vigilanza ed il controllo sul doping e per la tutela della salute nelle attività sportive (Commission for the Vigilance and Control on Doping and the Protection of Health in Sports Activities, known under the acronym CVD).
2. Existence of a police force specialized in public health, the Comando Carabinieri per la tutela della salute (Carabinieri Command for Health Protection), better known as NAS, the acronym of the original name, Nuclei Antisofisticazioni e Sanità (Anti-Sophistication and [Public] Health Units).
3. Autonomy of the public prosecutors from the government: In Italy public prosecutors are career magistrates with the same status and career path of judges and are not subordinated to the Minister of Justice. Exploiting this autonomy, several Italian prosecutors have repeatedly dared to press charges against high-level government representatives, politicians, sports body officials, and businessmen

not only in the field of anti-doping but also in the fight against corruption and organized crime (see Chap. 7).[7]

Even though some of the illegal practices revealed by the three above-mentioned proceedings may appear uniquely Italian, the Executive Committee of the World Anti-Doping Agency (WADA), the body that has been responsible for coordinating the prevention and control of doping worldwide since 2001, has repeatedly praised the Italian criminal legislation and investigations for their effectiveness, presenting them as a model to follow in other countries (e.g., WADA 2009b, 2010c). At the 2011 UNESCO "Conference of Parties to the International Convention against Doping in Sport,"—the treaty constituting the foundation of the current international anti-doping regime—Ljungqvist again referred to what had happened in Turin, stressing that the existence of anti-doping legislation is no longer a cause of concern for the IOC but a requirement for being selected as host of the next Olympic Games:

> In emphasizing the importance of appropriate legislation I usually take the incident at the Olympic Games in Torino in 2006 as an example. Had the existing anti-doping law not been in place in Italy, the organized and systematic blood doping that was practiced by part of the Austrian skiing team would have never been revealed. The IOC could only test the suspected athletes, and they all tested negative. But the Italian police found doping substances and equipment, which made it possible for the IOC to identify not just a number of involved athletes but also the people in their entourage …. May I also inform you that since I last spoke to you [in 2009], the IOC has decided to make the existence of appropriate domestic anti-doping legislation an important element when it comes to the evaluation of candidate cities for hosting the Olympic Games (Ljungqvist 2011; see also Lager and Ljungqvist 2011: 177–80).

The recent appreciation of Italy's criminal law and investigations is part, and indicative, of a broader change in anti-doping policy. As addressed in more detail below, WADA and several national anti-doping bodies are increasingly shifting emphasis from athletes' testing to law enforcement action and intelligence sharing between law enforcement agencies and national anti-doping organizations. In recent speeches, WADA President John Fahey described the latter two activities as "the future of anti-doping" (UK Antidoping 2011). WADA Director General, David Howman (2011a), elaborated the point in a 2011 speech, by making reference to the case of Marion Jones:

> One only has to remind people that Marion Jones competed for seven years, was tested on many many occasions, was never found to have an adverse analytical finding, but cheated throughout. She insisted she was a clean athlete, "look at how many times I have been tested!!"—*I have been tested more often than any other athlete and never been found positive. What does that mean*? She even wrote it in her book and sued those who suggested otherwise. It was only during the investigation process that led to her lying to a grand jury and the eventual charge of perjury against her, that she confessed most and went to prison.

---

[7] It is enough to refer here to the numerous charges raised against Silvio Berlusconi when he was Italy's Prime Minister (see *Economist* 2011a).

If criminal law action against athletes, their suppliers and protectors is to become "the future of anti-doping," then it becomes crucial to consider what can be learnt from the Italian seminal experience in this field.

Aims and Objectives

In this study we have examined Italy's anti-doping criminal law experience with the general aim of analyzing the production and distribution of doping products and understanding how anti-doping criminal provisions and their enforcement can contribute to the control of doping within and outside the sports worlds.

Seven objectives of this study support that aim:

1. To assess the size of the market for doping products, by estimating, at least for some key products and classes of users, the demand.
2. To identify the types of actors involved in the production and trade of doping products (the "suppliers"), assess the extent of their involvement in either the legal or illegal segments of the market, and consider their *modus operandi*, in particular, the extent to which different types of suppliers engage in violence, corruption, or other illegal activities as a business practice and, aware of the illegality of their market participation, take any other precautions to protect themselves from law enforcement and judicial actions.
3. To assess the relative importance of different sources of products to the doping market (e.g., diversion vs. black market; domestic vs. foreign).
4. To map the distribution system of doping products from producers to final users, by identifying and characterizing the levels or stages of the market that link producers and importers to final users for different doping products as is done in a large literature on illegal drug markets (e.g., Preble and Casey 1969; Paoli 2003a; Dorn et al. 2005; Paoli et al. 2009).
5. To estimate the financial dimensions of the sports doping market, including the revenues and profits of different types of suppliers of doping products.
6. To account for and assess anti-doping law enforcement and judicial activities (e.g., reports, arrests, convictions), identifying the challenges they face, particularly but not exclusively in the field of international cooperation.
7. To draw policy implications from the analysis.

Although the current study focuses exclusively on Italy, we would argue that our analysis and the related policy implications hold value beyond Italy's borders for both research and policy-making purposes. We explain the reasons for our conviction in the following chapter. Before that, however, we turn our attention to matters of vocabulary and provide some information about the research design and structure of the book.

Definitions of Key Concepts

To reduce the potential for misunderstanding among our readers we discuss in this section the vocabulary of doping as it appears in this manuscript. Many key—recurring—terms, including the word "doping," are used ambiguously or inconsistently in public forums and, occasionally, in the academic literature.

In the World Anti-Doping Code, which constitutes the cornerstone of the current international drug control regime and entered into force in 2004, "doping" is defined formally as the occurrence of one or more anti-doping rule violations that can be committed by an athlete or support personnel.[8] Although the Code does not make an explicit statement, the ultimate aim of such violations is assumed to be the enhancement of an athlete's performance (WADA 2009c: 14, 18–25; see also Teitler and Ram 2008). In this manuscript, we have adopted a slightly broader definition of "doping" and consider the production and trade of the substances and methods prohibited by the Code, whenever these substances and methods will be used for nontherapeutic purposes. Not all nontherapeutic users of doping products are athletes and not all users take them to enhance their performance in sports competitions. As we show in more detail in Chap. 2, a considerable share of the users of some doping products (even excluding traditional illegal drugs prohibited by WADA, such as cannabis, cocaine, and heroin) does not seek to increase their athletic performance but uses them for broader lifestyle or psychoactive purposes, such as enhancing muscle growth, reducing body fat or boosting aggressiveness (see literature review below). As a corollary, we use the expression "doping substances" to mean "performance and image enhancing substances/drugs," an expression that is increasingly common in both the scientific literature (e.g., Graham et al. 2009) and government reports (e.g., Anti Doping Denmark et al. 2012).

We also define "trade" broadly, to include producing, importing, wholesaling, retailing, prescribing, administering, and delivering doping products, including both doping substances and methods. We have purposely chosen the word "trade" rather than the more pejorative word "trafficking," to avoid exercising any judgment *ex ante* on the legal status of such activity.[9]

---

[8] Having "athletes" (see definitions below) and their support personnel in mind, the Code singles out the following eight violations: (1) presence of a prohibited substance or its metabolites or markers in an athlete's sample; (2) use or attempted use by an athlete of a prohibited substance or a prohibited method; (3) refusing or failing without compelling justification to submit to sample collection; (4) violation of applicable requirements regarding athlete availability for out-of-competition testing; (5) tampering or attempted tampering with any part of doping control; (6) possession of prohibited substances and prohibited methods; (7) trafficking or attempted trafficking in any prohibited substance or prohibited method; and (8) administration or attempted administration to any athlete of prohibited substances and methods or assisting, encouraging, aiding, abetting, covering up or any other type of complicity involving an anti-doping rule (WADA 2009c: 18–25).

[9] This choice also reflects the words used in Italy's anti-doping act, which does not speak of trafficking (see Chap. 7). NAS also speaks of the "illegal trade" of doping substances or products and use the expression "trafficking" only with reference to illegal drugs (Int-NAS-26; see Chap. 7).

With the expression "sports ruling bodies," we mean all bodies governing sports at the national or international level: i.e., the IOC, national Olympic Committees, international and national sports federations and associated disciplines. We use the expressions "sports governing bodies" and "sports bodies" as synonyms. We use instead the expressions "organized sports world" or "sporting organizations" more broadly to refer not only sports ruling bodies but also to all clubs and teams affiliated with a sports federation.

In meeting the first objective, we distinguish the several categories of users and largely focus on the sportsmen and sportswomen, collectively "sportspeople," in Italy who engage regularly or occasionally in sporting activities. For reasons of data consistency, particularly with regard to surveys and anti-doping testing,[10] and because we believe them to be less heavily involved in doping, we do not include individuals under age 15 in our assessment; nevertheless, we acknowledge that some such young people are doping or at high risk of future doping (see the findings of literature review carried out by Backhouse et al. 2007: 47). Among sportsmen and sportswomen, we distinguish between "athletes," those who engage in competitions at some level, and noncompetitive sportspeople.

Following the literature (e.g., Stirling and Kerr 2006), we further distinguish "elite" athletes from "recreational" athletes. We define the former as those athletes who take part in national or international competitions, oftentimes as a member of a team but in some instances individually (e.g., professional tennis players). Elite athletes also include professional athletes, that is, those who receive regular remuneration for their participation in elite sporting activities.[11] We define "recreational" athletes as those who compete only subnationally.[12]

Among noncompetitive sportspeople, we distinguish body-builders, most of whom are gym patrons,[13] from other sportspeople. Admittedly, some body-builders might be considered "elite" according to our criteria. However, body-building is not recognized as an Olympic sport by the IOC,[14] Italy's body-building associations are

---

[10] As discussed in the following chapter, Italy's anti-doping authorities, CONI and CVD, do not routinely test youths for evidence of doping, except in rare and specific cases (Int-Oth-2).

[11] Whereas we regard all professional athletes as elite athletes, it is important to recall that not all elite athletes are professionals. Until the 1990s the IOC nominally only allowed amateur athletes to participate in the Olympic Games (Teetzel, 2011) and some sports federations (e.g., International Boxing Association) still only allow amateurs to participate in the Olympic Games. As the concept of amateur athlete entails some "baggage" and is interpreted in different ways in different contexts (e.g., in Italy an amateur is understood primarily as a nonelite athlete), we avoid using the term in this book.

[12] Our distinction between elite and recreational athletes, made on the basis of the competitions they participate in, parallels the division of competencies between CONI and CVD in anti-doping testing (Ministero della Salute 2007; see Chap. 2).

[13] We speak of gyms (shortening of "gymnasia") rather than fitness centers, because gyms are not always distinguished from fitness centers in Italy. Gym is a broader category than fitness center. Whereas all fitness centers have a gym, gyms are multivalent sporting venues, and not all of them have the body-building machines that are instead typical of fitness centers.

[14] See http://www.olympic.org/sports.

not recognized as official sports federations by CONI (2008)[15] and some observers even question whether body-building must be regarded as a sport at all (see Littman 2010). While we reject the latter position as too extreme, we do not include body-builders in the category of athletes, following the IOC and CONI's stances, but consider them as a separate subset of sportspersons. Our choice can also be justified on pragmatic terms, as body-builders have different doping consumption patterns than athletes.

The remainder, whom we refer to simply as other sportsmen and sportswomen, or collectively as other sportspeople, does not participate in competitions, but nevertheless engages in regular or occasional physical exercise and may have some connection or susceptibility to doping for other lifestyle purposes. In Chap. 2 we also note that doping products also may be used rarely by other people who do not engage in any sport for lifestyle or pseudo-medical reasons.

While these definitions are necessary for market estimation, we are aware of the fact that the distinctions between different types of athletes and sportspeople and between sporting and nonsporting activities are far from being rigid or clear-cut. As Houlihan notes (2002: 98 and 99), there is a "continuum of sporting contexts for drug use" and "the boundary between what might be referred to as mainstream sports (Olympic and major team sports) and fringe sports (such a body-building, and exhibition/novelty sports events) is frequently indistinct with athletes often crossing the boundary more than once in their lives."

Research Design

Our data collection focused on four issue areas: suppliers, their relationships and *modus operandi*, products and markets, and control efforts. For each area, we identified a comprehensive set of items that together would have constituted an ideal dataset (see Appendix A). In the case of suppliers, for example, we sought information on gender; age at the time of investigation; ethnicity, nationality, and country of residence; background and possible role in elite or recreational sports; criminal records; "criminal career"; and motivation. As expected, we were not able to find data for all of these items but we have been able to draw a detailed picture of the sports doping market, with specific reference to the supply of doping products, and of actions under the anti-doping criminal law in Italy. In order to fulfill the first objective, i.e., to assess the size of the market for doping products, we relied on secondary sources and official data published by CONI and CVD.

[15] A few, albeit not precisely known, number of body-builders are former members of Italy's Weightlifting Federation. Between 2000 and 2011, this was called Federazione Italiana Pesistica e Cultura Fisica, with the expression "cultura fisica" (i.e., physical culture) referring de facto to body-building. To stress the difference between weightlifting and body-building, the federation changed its name in 2011 and is now called simply Federazione Italiana Pesistica (see FIPE 2012).

The data collection in the four issues areas would not have been possible without intensive collaboration with NAS. In particular, the NAS Headquarters in Rome provided us with a detailed database (in the form of a "pdf") of 73 major anti-doping investigations conducted by NAS between 1999 and 2009 that included information about the suspects, their backgrounds, the doping production and trade activities, and the products sold.[16] During the course of the current study, the NAS Headquarters then requested its 38 branch offices to update the database with information on the investigations carried out until 2011. Details on seven more investigations were added to the original 73; therefore, in total, we had summary data on 80 investigations. In a very labor-intensive process, we inserted these data in an Excel spreadsheet, made the quantities of doping products seized in the different investigations comparable, and added, for each product seized, the official price, as established by the Agenzia Italiana per il Farmaco,[17] and, when available, the unofficial internet price.[18] We refer to this database as the "Database on NAS Investigations" or "NAS Investigations Database." The database has been a most useful source of information because it gives a detailed overview of all the anti-doping investigations conducted by NAS from 1999 to 2009, which represent the vast majority of the anti-doping criminal investigations conducted in Italy.

To achieve a fuller picture of the doping substances seized in Italy, we also collected the seizure data from the websites of the Agenzia delle Dogane (i.e., customs), Guardia di Finanza (i.e., tax police), and Polizia di Stato for the period January 1998 through February 2012.[19] For the same time period, we also conducted an extensive review of all the doping-related news launched by the three main Italian news agencies—*Ansa*, *Agi*, and *Adnkronos*.

In addition to the summaries of the proceedings contained in the database, we analyzed official documents related to 46 different criminal investigations carried out by NAS or other police forces. In some cases, the documents analyzed were the extensive summaries of the investigations written by NAS officers and submitted to the Prosecutor's Office; in other cases, the charges pressed by the prosecutors, the arrest warrants issued by the judges for preliminary investigations, or first-, second-, or third-degree verdicts. We refer to these cases generically as "investigations" (from NAS's perspective) or "proceedings" (from a judicial perspective) or with the specific name of the document (e.g., verdict, charges).

---

[16] Not all investigations initiated or ongoing in 1999 are inserted in the NAS Investigations Database.

[17] See http://www.agenziafarmaco.gov.it/it/content/farmaci-autorizzati.

[18] Prices have been looked up, for example on a variety of websites, including the following: http://www.mesomorphosis.com/; http://www.eurobolic.info/; http://it.steroidset.com/; http://www.que.es/ultimas-noticias/sucesos/201203102001-decomisan-toneladas-marihuana-cocaina-suroeste-efe.html?anker_3. *It is important to note, though, that these websites change continuously.*

[19] For the Agenzia della Dogane, see http://www1.agenziadogane.it/ed/motore_ricerca/? XML=/Agenzia_Dogane/_C=eJyLz2HILGGIL8tjcExPzavKTIx3yU9PzEtliC9kS MxLTMrPyayqSswry WSIz8gscSvNyWEwNGAAAPwEEjY_/_s=0&param_query=anabolizzanti; for the Guardia di Finanza, see http://www.gdf.gov.it/ricerca/ricerca.asp?testoRicerca=anabolizzanti&ok=ok; for the Polizia di Stato http://poliziadistato.it/search/sh/.

Contrary to our original intention, we have not been able to reconstruct the entire judicial path for the main criminal proceedings on doping (that is, from the prosecutor's charges to the final verdict), except for a few cases. In fact, NAS or the Prosecutor's Offices do not collect information systematically about the proceedings originating from their investigations. Moreover, due to procedural rules regarding geographical competence and the defendants' right to request a bargaining agreement (see Chap. 8), the criminal proceedings are often split in different streams and, if the offenders are resident in different judicial districts, assigned to different courts so much so that it becomes very difficult to ascertain the final outcome of the proceedings. We have been able to reconstruct such outcomes for only 24 proceedings, primarily thanks to the personal commitment of a particular prosecutor, Dr. Raffaele Guariniello from the Turin Prosecutor's Office.

The other crucial source of information has been experts. In total, we interviewed 26 NAS officers at the Headquarters and in nine NAS branch offices as well as seven prosecutors, one policy-maker, and one other expert. In some cases, we talked to our interviewees more than one time. We refer to these interviews with the following codes: Int-NAS-1 to 26 for the NAS officers, Int-Proc-1 to 7 for the prosecutors and Int-Oth-1 and 2 for the two others. Together, with the two officers coordinating NAS's anti-doping activities, we also developed a short questionnaire to collect information on the human and financial resources, priorities and anti-doping activities, which the NAS Headquarters then sent to the all 38 branch offices.

To fulfill the study objectives, we also collected different types of statistical data, including some that had never been published before. We obtained data on the use of steroids among Italy's adults (15–64-year-old) from the Dipartimento Politiche Antidroga (Drug Control Department) of the Prime Minister's Office, which had been collected through a population survey but had never been published before (Dipartimento Politiche Antidroga 2012a). To better assess overall anti-doping actions, we also requested and obtained statistical data on the number of police reports to the Judicial Authority and court verdicts for doping and other related offenses during 2001–2010, which the Italian Statistical Office (Istat) calculated explicitly for this study.

To strengthen our conclusions, we triangulated the findings from the different sources, including an extensive media analysis.

Structure of the Book

The present manuscript is organized as follows. The first chapter briefly reviews the literature on doping and anti-doping and describes the current international policy context, illustrating the value added of the present study. It also singles out the latter's conceptual framework.

The second chapter summarily lists the doping products available in Italy and then provides some key data on Italy's sportsmen and sportswomen and the numbers of athletes who have tested positive in anti-doping tests. On the basis of these and other data, the chapter then attempts to estimate the number of users of doping products and the quantities they consume, thus addressing the first objective of the study. The second chapter also outlines the main trends in the development of Italy's sports doping market to provide necessary context for assessing the supply of doping products.

The third chapter focuses on the suppliers of doping products, largely fulfilling the second objective of the study. It identifies the different categories of suppliers on the basis of some general characteristics, builds a typology of illegal suppliers on the basis of their profession or occupation, and singles out their motives. The fourth and fifth chapters address the third and fourth objectives of the study. The fourth begins by singling out the sources of different doping products (e.g., pharmaceutical companies vs. illegal labs) and the different distribution chains. It then analyzes the suppliers' relationships and *modus operandi* and the overall structure of the market for doping products, including changes over time. The following chapter, the fifth, discusses the complicity of the Italian and, in a few cases, international sports bodies that have either tolerated or sometimes even explicitly favored illegal doping practices and considers the role of organized crime.

The sixth chapter fulfills the fifth objective of the study: It evaluates the data available on illegal suppliers' revenues and profits margins and attempts a preliminary estimate of the revenues associated with doping.

The seventh chapter examines Italy's anti-doping laws and their evolution and highlights the two key elements of the broader institutional framework that have made Italy's unprecedented anti-doping criminal law actions possible, namely the existence of a police force that is specialized in public health issues and the independence of the public prosecutors. It then presents some statistical data about the outcomes of Italy's anti-doping criminal law actions (e.g., reports, arrests, convictions) and identifies the challenges such actions face, particularly but not exclusively in the field of international cooperation. In such a way, the seventh chapter fulfills the sixth objective of the study.

The final chapter summarizes our main findings and draws generic conclusions and lessons for policy-making from the analysis, thus addressing the seventh study objective.

Chapter 1
What Is Known About Doping and What Can This Study Add to It?

Abstract In this chapter we briefly review the literature on doping and anti-doping to illustrate the value added of the present study beyond Italy's borders. We conclude that, while the demand for doping products has been addressed in numerous studies, the supply side of the market has hardly been examined yet. The lack of research of the supply side of the market also reflects the fact these activities have not been investigated systematically by many law enforcement agencies and, hence, the "supply" of research-worthy criminal justice data is also scant. As such criminal justice data are uniquely available in Italy, a study of the supply of doping products in Italy may be considered illustrative—or at least indicative—of what remains unexplored elsewhere, even if similarities and differences must be ascertained empirically in future projects.

In the chapter we also consider the international policy context to demonstrate the policy relevance and timeliness of the study and, on the basis of literature review and current anti-doping policies, we then single out the study conceptual framework. We conceptualize doping in terms of a market, with its demand and supply. A market approach is "bread and butter" in the field of illegal drugs and other illegal goods and services but, to our knowledge, but has not yet been applied to doping. In particular, we conceptualize the doping market as a semi-illegal market, at least from the point of view of criminal law. We stress that the legal status of doping products suffers the burden and ambiguity of contextual specificity; that is, in some contexts, the products, including their supply, are "legal" and in others they are not.

In this chapter we briefly review the literature on doping and anti-doping to illustrate the scientific value added of the present study beyond Italy's borders. We also consider the international policy context to demonstrate the study overall policy relevance and timeliness. On the basis of literature review and current anti-doping policies, we single out the study conceptual framework.

L. Paoli and A. Donati, *The Sports Doping Market: Understanding Supply and Demand, and the Challenges of Their Control*, DOI 10.1007/978-1-4614-8241-3_1,

1.1 Literature Review

Since the 1970s, a relatively broad scientific literature has developed on the history, prevalence, and promoting factors of the use of doping products in sports, on anti-doping policies, rules, and testing, with scholarly contributions from numerous disciplines. On the topic there is also—both in the press and on the Internet—a bourgeoning nonscientific literature, including reconstructions of major scandals and investigations and firsthand accounts written by elite athletes (e.g., Bassons 2000; Gaumont 2005; Hamilton and Coyle 2012; Millar 2012; Riis 2012) and other individuals involved in cycling doping scandals, such as masseurs and physicians (e.g., Voet 2000; D'Hont 2007). An unprecedented insight into doping in elite cycling was given by the US Anti-Doping Agency's (USADA) 2012 reasoned decision against Lance Armstrong, who had won seven Tours de France from 1999 to 2005 and was finally stripped of these seven and other titles and banned for life from all major competitions because of doping.

1.1.1 The Use of Doping Products: Trends and Prevalence

According to several historians and sociologists, there has been a "growing demand for illicit drugs by athletes" in the post-Second World War period (Waddington and Smith 2009: 64; see also Hoberman 2005; Yesalis and Bahrke 2005), which can be explained by some key trends in sports and the broader society sometimes dating back to the nineteenth century:

1. The "de-amateurization" of sports, with an increasing emphasis being placed on winning (Dunning 1986; Bette and Schimank 2006: 62), as the shift from premodern to modern society favored inter-area sports competition.
2. The medicalization of sports, as exemplified by the development, since the 1960s, of what is now called sports medicine (Waddington and Smith 2009: 66–101).
3. The politicization of sports—particularly during the Cold War, sports became an extension of the rivalry between the West and the Soviet bloc (Singler and Treutlein 2010).
4. Its commercialization, meaning the development of both sports sponsorship and global audiences, via television, for all major sports events (e.g., Hoberman 2001: 245; Coackley and Pipe 2009: 384–425). The sports industry is now estimated to be an US$800 billion a year business (Howman 2011a).

At its core, as Coakley and Pipe (2009: 205–214) stress, the use of illegal performance-enhancing substances and methods in sports is due to overconformity, that is, athletes' uncritical acceptance of the norms of the sports ethic not only to win but more fundamentally to play the game, gain the respect of their peers, and maintain their identity as elite athletes. Overconformity is the motivation not only for doping but also for risky behaviors, such as playing with broken bones and torn ligaments or using painkilling drugs to stay in the game. It is often encouraged by coaches, sponsors, administrators, and fans and, according to Coakley, "is grounded in the culture and organization of sports and the social dynamics that exist in the social worlds that are created around sports" (ibid.: 198).

Whereas elite competitive athletes have since the 1950s used steroids and other doping substances to improve performance, since the 1980s the use of steroids has spread out of the elite athletic community and into the general population (e.g., Buckley et al. 1988; Kanayama et al. 2001, 2008, 2009). This trend has been partially stimulated by the appearance of progressively more sophisticated underground guides on how to self-administer steroids (Kanayama et al. 2009). Western cultural developments have also likely contributed to the increased prevalence of steroid use, as media images have increasingly focused on male muscularity. According to Pope et al. (2000), males suffer under an Adonis complex, i.e., impossible ideals of beauty and body that favor the use of dangerous steroids and "supplements" as well as compulsive behaviors, chronic depressions, and eating disorders. Over the last few decades, even children's action toys have begun to acquire the bodies of steroid users (Pope et al. 1999). Others connect the impossible ideals of beauty with the current society's culture of performance (Quaglio et al. 2009) and its medicalization (Swedish National Institute of Public Health 2010: 66). As a result of the latter trend, aging, being overweight, sexual performance, hair loss, shyness, and tiredness are some of the events that have been redefined as medical issues and treated with drugs (Conrad 2007). In particular, as many people do not have time to live healthily and to train in order to achieve a more attractive body, medical preparations, including doping substances, appear to be increasingly seductive and effective solutions (Harth et al. 2008), and lucrative markets for health, beauty, and achievement are created at the same time. The market for doping products thus partially overlaps with the market for human enhancement drugs, i.e., drugs that have the potential to improve human attributes and capabilities (see Savulescu et al. 2011; Singler 2012).

Steroids, in particular, are used only to build muscles but also to promote aggressiveness, courage, and the feeling of omnipotence (e.g., Thiblin et al. 1997; Thiblin and Parlklo 2002; Kindlundh et al. 1998; Chantal et al. 2009; Swedish National institute of Public Health 2010: 56–57). As such, they are particularly loved by action-oriented males, who, according to John Hoberman (2012), belong to an interrelated set of subcultures and compose a "global anabolic universe." Among these males, there are police and military personnel, firefighters, mercenaries, action film stars, body-builders, bouncers, motorcycle gangsters, professional wrestlers, martial arts fighters, private security guards, and militia members. For Hoberman, in particular, steroid use is now "epidemic" among police officers in the United States, as indicated by, as one case among many, the steroid scandal involving hundreds of New Jersey police officers and firefighters that erupted in December 2010. Even the Norwegian mass murderer Anders Behring Breivik took steroids to increase his aggressiveness and determination before the 2011 attacks and in his manifesto gave detailed instructions about the use of steroids and ephedrine, claiming that "the use of anabolic steroids will significantly increase your agility, speed, strength and endurance" (Berwick 2011a, b).

Perhaps as a result of these trends, illicit steroid use has now grown into a widespread public health problem in the United States (Buckley et al. 1988; Yesalis et al. 1993; McCabe et al. 2007) and many other Western countries (Melia et al. 1996; Handelsman and Gupta 1997; Nilsson et al. 2001; Pallesen et al. 2006; Wanjek et al. 2007; Kokkevi et al. 2008). Although epidemiologic studies in these various countries have produced a wide range of prevalence estimates, most have reported a lifetime prevalence of steroid use of at least 3 % in young men, suggesting that some tens of millions of individuals worldwide have used these drugs (Kanayama et al. 2009). By contrast, steroid use in women is uncommon, since women are less likely to want to become very muscular and are also vulnerable to the masculinizing effects of steroids (Kanayama et al. 2007; see below). Many steroid users are visitors to gyms, who are thought to be the largest consuming group. Estimates of steroid users in several western countries range from 5 to 13.5 % of gym visitors (Korkia and Stimson 1997; Kanayama et al. 2001; Simon et al. 2006; Striegel et al. 2006; see also Kläber 2010).

Ranges are even broader for elite athletes. While about 1 % of official doping tests yield positive results on average worldwide (World Anti-Doping Agency 2009a, 2010a, 2011a, 2012a), scientific studies using the randomized response technique,[1] currently considered the least biased nonanalytical data collection method, show that at least 7 % of elite athletes admit having practiced doping (e.g., Striegel et al. 2010). In an early survey carried out in Italy in 1989, over 10 % of the 1,015 athletes interviewed indicated a frequent use of amphetamines or anabolic steroids at national or international level, while fewer athletes mentioned blood doping (7 %) and beta-blockers (2 %) or other classes of drugs. These proportions were 2–3 times higher for occasional use, and similar opinions were expressed by the 216 coaches, doctors, and managers who were also interviewed (Scarpino et al. 1990). Surveys targeting athletes engaging in power sports or weightlifting report even higher prevalence estimates of steroid use with estimates ranging from about 20 % to more than 50 % (Beel et al. 1998; Kanayama et al. 2009). A 2011 analysis of 7,289 blood samples from 2,737 athletes from all disciplines and countries concluded that the prevalence of blood doping ranged from 1 to 48 % for subpopulations of samples and a mean of 14 % for the entire study population (Sottas et al. 2011).

According to some sports physicians, the real rate of elite athletes engaging in doping may be as high as 40–60 % (Simon 2010). Anecdotal reports—and repeated scandals—lend credence to, or even go beyond, the latter perceptions. Several elite athletes, coaches, and physicians have admitted that doping practices, especially but not only the use of anabolic steroids, were widespread in different sports disciplines, including weightlifting, rugby, discus and hammer throwing, and other track-and-field sports during the 1960s, 1970s, and 1980s (see the numerous events and declarations reported in Todd and Todd 2001; de Mondenard 2004; Singler and Treutlein 2010). According to Hoberman (2011b), all the female world records

[1] The randomized response technique is a data collection method used in interviews or in surveys that offers a high degree of perceived protection to interviewees, because the latter can give responses to sensitive questions according to a randomized procedure (e.g., Striegel et al. 2010).

achieved in the 1980s and 1990s in the 100–10,000 m (without hurdles), discus throw, and shot put as well as the male records in discus and hammer throw and shot put are suspicious and were–certainly or most likely—achieved with the help of doping (see also Singler and Treutlein 2010; Simon 2011). The Festina scandal at the 1998 Tour de France demonstrated that drug use in cycling was not a matter of few individual riders acting on their own initiative, but that it was widespread, systematic, and organized. As Hanstad et al. (2008: 227) note, "drug use was institutionalized within the structure of professional cycling." Lance Armstrong's candid confession in his 2013 interview with Oprah Winfrey finally confirmed what many experts (e.g., Brissonneau et al. 2008; Christiansen 2005; Hoberman 2002; Møller 2008; Singler and Treutlein 2010) and a few former riders (e.g., Bassons 2000; Gaumont 2005; taz 2011) had been reporting for years: until very recently doping "was part of the job" in top elite cycling (The Telegraph 2013).

1.1.2 A Brief History of Doping Products and Anti-doping Tests

Doping deaths and scandals have been the main factor promoting the development of the contemporary anti-doping control regime. Although several international sports federations had banned doping before the Second World War, the world's sports ruling bodies came under pressure to introduce drug testing after the doping-related death of two cyclists—the Dane Knud Enemark Jensen and the Englishman Tom Simpson—who abused stimulants and died during competition. (Jensen died at the 1960 Olympic Games in Rome and Simpson died during the 1967 Tour de France.) The IOC did not take any direct measures after Jensen's death and did not mention it in the final report of the XVII Olympic Games (de Mondenard 2004: 76). Instead, it was forced to react to Simpson's death, which had taken place under the eyes of millions of people watching the Tour on television. In 1967, the IOC Medical Commission became fully operational and set up its first list of prohibited substances, introducing drugs tests at the Olympic Winter Games in Grenoble and at the Olympic Games in Mexico in 1968 (Henne 2009).

Effective tests became available only in the early 1970s. In 1973, the London anti-doping laboratory developed the first test capable of detecting the metabolites of anabolic steroids in urine samples. After being refined further by the Cologne anti-doping laboratory, the test was used for the first time at the 1976 Olympic Games in Montreal—but only in eight disciplines, because the other sports federations refused to cooperate (de Mondenard 1984: 127–129; Houlihan 2002).

In the meanwhile, athletes and their coaches knew when to stop taking anabolic steroids to avoid testing positive or to alternate anabolic steroids with testosterone, which gave similar performance-enhancing results but could not be detected with regular tests (de Mondenard 1984: 130). The IOC tried to obviate to this problem by setting maximum limits between testosterone and epitestosterone, a natural steroid that is not affected by the exogenous administration of testosterone. However, the initial ratio between testosterone and epitestosterone of 8:1 was set so high that, according to some critics (e.g., Ferrara 2004: 279), it would only serve to reduce the numbers of positive test results and legal conflicts. When the IOC lowered the ratio to 6:1, athletes began taking epitestosterone together with testosterone.

By the time the laboratories could distinguish between natural and artificial testosterone, other drugs had been developed that could stimulate the endogenous production of testosterone and could not yet be detected by chemical analyses. Among them, the most powerful is gonadorelin, a manmade protein that is like the natural gonadotrophin-releasing hormone and is used in the treatment of dysfunctions of the pituitary gland and other pathologies. [2] In the criminal proceedings against Prof. Conconi in 1996, Dr. Luigi Pressi (1996), who was the chief physician of the national Italian cycling team, reported the frequent use of gonadorelin among professional riders. Allegedly they used this undetectable hormone in order to enhance their performance without testing positive and to obtain evidence of a naturally high level of testosterone from the official anti-doping laboratories.

In the early 1970s, Finnish sports officials started harvesting blood red cells from elite athletes and then transfusing them back into the athletes' circulatory systems prior to endurance competitions (the so-called *autologous transfusions*). With the aid of this practice, the Finnish athletes succeeded in dominating the international competitions of 1,500–10,000 m tracks in track and field and cross-country skiing. Soon this practice spread in endurance disciplines of other countries, above all, East Germany, the United States, and Italy (see Chap. 3). The Italian Ministry of Health banned blood transfusions for nontherapeutic purposes in early 1986 (Donati 2012: 46–48); the IOC followed closely on that in the same year. In the late 1980s, an advance in medicine led to an entirely new form of blood doping involving EPO, a naturally occurring hormone that stimulates the formation of red blood cells. Many doping doctors—including in Italy, Prof. Conconi (Procura della Repubblica presso il Tribunale di Ferrara 2000)—shifted from blood transfusion to EPO doping or at least began combining the two approaches. No direct test exists yet for autologous blood transfusions, and the direct testing of EPO use has proven very difficult despite the existence of a urine test (Lundby et al. 2012). Moreover, due to financial restrictions, not all urine samples are tested for EPO (Howman 2011a).

Gonadorelin, chorionic gonadotrophin, and EPO belong to the group of peptide hormones. Among them there are also somatotropin and its recombinant version, somatropin (both known as "growth hormone" or "GH"), the latter being a prescription drug used to treat children's growth disorders and adult growth hormone deficiency. At the beginning of the 1980s, the suspicion was widespread that growth hormone was routinely extracted from the pituitary gland of cadavers for performance-enhancing purposes (de Mondenard 2004: 627–629). In 1987,

[2] Gonadorelin is otherwise known as peptide gonadotrophin-releasing hormone (GnRH) or luteinizing hormone-releasing hormone (LH-RH). A test for its detection was first detected in 2008 (e.g., Thomas et al. 2008).

somatropin was produced by recombinant DNA technology and began to be sold on a commercial basis (Houlihan 2002: 84–87).

The IOC banned both the natural and chemical versions of GH in 1989[3]; however, the ban long remained unenforceable, because traditional urine analysis could long not detect doping with either variant of GH. Before the 1984 Olympic Games, the US endocrinologist, Dr. Robert Kerr, admitted to treating more than 4,000 athletes from 20 countries with GH and other peptide hormones and after the Olympics he claimed that many of his "patients" had won medals (Todd and Todd 2001: 78–82; Crowe 2001). In the early 1980s one of Kerr's assistants, Dr. Guillermo Laich, went back to Spain and his consulting room became a purported "pilgrimage" goal for sports directors, coaches, and athletes of different countries (Donati 1989: 142). Blood tests that could distinguish between natural and artificial GH began to be developed during the early 2000s but they did not become a standardized protocol. Even in the present day, urine tests can only detect GH, if taken in the hours before the test.

The latest stage in doping history is represented by gene doping, which the WADA (2009c: 7) defines as "the non-therapeutic use of cells, genes, genetic elements, or of the modulation of gene expression, having the capacity to improve athletic performance." Gene doping undoubtedly has the potential to become a threat to public health, as it is possible that genetic mutations in athletes could spread to the rest of the population. The extent to which gene doping already represents a common practice rather than a potential threat is yet unclear, though (Simon 2010).

The literature also indicates a strong connection between the use of doping agents, narcotics, alcohol, dietary supplements, and pharmaceuticals (among others, DuRant et al. 1994; Sjöqvist et al. 2008). In a US Internet study (Parkinson and Evans 2006), for example, 96 % of the 500 respondents reported using other substances such as stimulants, fat burners, GH, and insulin in addition to steroids, either to increase the effects of steroid use or to mitigate or master their side effects (see also Hildebrandt et al. 2006; Swedish National Institute of Public Health 2010: 45–49).

Whereas the IOC banned narcotics in 1967 and cocaine in 1971 (de Mondenard 2004: 784, 269), the prohibition of cannabis is much more recent. Only after the 1988 Olympic Games in Seoul did the IOC place cannabis in the category of "substances undergoing certain restrictions," while international sports federations continued to maintain different rules that were more or less restrictive. Roughly 15 years later, the 2004 World Anti-Doping Code issued by WADA, the new world anti-doping agency set up in 1999 after the Festina scandal at the 1998 Tour de France, fully banned cannabis (ibid.: 223–225) in competition.

Within the IOC and WADA and among the general public worldwide, there has long been a debate about whether cannabis, and to a lesser extent also cocaine,

[3] Realizing the performance-enhancing potential of GH, UCI had intervened much earlier than the IOC. UCI initially inserted GH in its prohibited list in 1968. However, it took it out in 1971, on the grounds that GH could not be detected in urine samples (de Mondenard 2004: 635–636).

should be on the banned substances list.[4] Numerous observers do not regard cannabis as a performance-enhancing drug, while others note that cocaine may have performance-enhancing effects in some sports but it is used by athletes primarily for recreational rather than for doping purposes (e.g., Waddington and Smith 2009: 44–47; Smith 2012; contra, see Blackshaw 2012).[5]

The disqualification of athletes testing positive to cannabis has stirred controversy and in some instances elicited the opposition of team members and sports federations.[6] WADA has long defended its policy on the grounds that cannabis and cocaine are illegal and represent a serious threat to the athletes' health (see the statements of WADA President Fahey in Read 2010; Huestis et al. 2011).[7] However, in partial contradiction of both arguments, it prohibits the two drugs only in competition. Accounting for 8–10 % of all substances detected, cannabis constitutes the second or third most frequently tested group of doping substances worldwide after anabolic steroids and, in 2010, stimulants. Cocaine represents, instead, a much smaller percent of the so-called *adverse analytic findings* (i.e., positive test results; see World Anti-Doping Agency 2009a, 2010a, 2011a, 2012a).[8] In May 2012, WADA President Fahey announced that WADA might consider revising the generalized ban on cannabis and maintaining it only for certain disciplines, such as pistol shooting and golf, where the drug has clear performance-enhancing effects (Lane 2012).

In 2004, WADA took all caffeine products off the prohibited list, regardless of the fact that some caffeine products, such as Animine, can cause serious heart problems and even death if taken in high dosages (de Mondenard 2004: 184–201). In doing so, it seemed to confirm its predominant interest in guaranteeing the fairness of competitions as separate from the health of athletes. Other scholars, however, approve WADA's decision given the general availability of caffeine in medical

[4] The prohibition of opioids, however, has been uncontroversial. As a matter of fact, athletes hardly ever use heroin, morphine, or other opioids through systemic routes of administration, because these substances would depress their athletic performance.

[5] For a review of that debate and a list of the main cases of elite athletes testing positive to one of the two substances, see de Mondenard (2004: 207–226, 253–269).

[6] For example, the case of the Canadian snowboarder at the Nagano 1998 Olympics, who was stripped of his gold medal because he tested positive for marijuana (i.e., cannabis); see Longman (1998).

[7] The use of cocaine, in particular, can be harmful when it is coupled with heavy training, which might be prescribed by coaches who are not aware that their athletes use cocaine. The use of this strong stimulant can also further perturb the psychological equilibrium of the athletes, who may already experience the ups and downs of exaltation and dejection as a result of their participation in competitions and other pressures from the organized sports world (de Mondenard 2004: 253–269).

[8] Given the purported recreational use of these drugs, sports ruling bodies sometimes try to impose lighter sentences on athletes testing positive to either cocaine or cannabis. For example, in 2008 CONI gave a reduced sentence to a tennis player who had tested positive to cocaine, on the grounds "that the type of substance ingested did not increase his athletic performance capability" (Court of Arbitration for Sport 2008: 6). However, WADA successfully appealed against CONI's decision at the Court of Arbitration of Sport (ibid.).

products and the limited risks associated with this substance (e.g., Waddington and Smith 2009: 33).

Pursuant to article 4.3.1 of the Code, WADA currently decides to include a substance or method in its prohibited list if it determines that the substance or method meets any two of the following three criteria: (1) potential health risk, (2) performance-enhancing potential, and (3) violation of the "spirit of sport" (World Anti-Doping Agency 2009c: 32).[9] As reflected in the debate about cannabis and cocaine, several scholars and policy-makers object to the fact that a drug may be banned on the grounds that it damages the health of athletes and that it is contrary to the "spirit of sport," even though the substance has no performance-enhancing effect (e.g., Schneider and Butcher 2001; Waddington and Smith 2009: 44–47, who also report critical comments of several policy-makers). Even those, such as the authors of this report, who prioritize health protection note that WADA should clarify the reasons and criteria for banning or not banning some substances or methods, with particular reference to the vaguely defined concept of "spirit of sport" (see also Coakley and Pipe 2009 and Chap. 8).

Increasingly aware of the limits of testing, WADA Executive Committee introduced the Athlete Biological Passport Operating Guidelines on December 1, 2009. The fundamental principle of the athlete biological passport is based on the monitoring of an athlete's biological variables over time to facilitate indirect detection of doping on a longitudinal basis, rather than on the traditional direct detection of doping (World Anti-Doping Agency 2013f). The passport builds on the experience of a few international sports federations, above all the Union Cycliste Internationale (UCI) and the Federation Internationale de Ski (FIS). The latter had introduced as early as the late 1990s markers of blood doping to deter the abuse of recombinant EPO that was undetectable by direct means at that time (Lundby et al. 2012). The 2009 guidelines are the product of lengthy negotiations organized by WADA among key sports federations (World Anti-Doping Agency 2013f). The UCI has been most aggressive in implementing the passport and has sanctioned several riders for committing an anti-doping rule violation on the basis of the passport data (McQuaid 2011).

While the biological passport represents an important step forward, WADA recognizes that "in some ways, [it] had been the author of its own misfortune, by introducing the passport and other techniques that had really driven sophisticated dopers to be more sophisticated" (World Anti-Doping Agency 2010d). The latter increasingly resort to micro-dosing, manipulation, blood doping, and other methods that were very hard to detect. In a recent study, for example, Ashenden et al. (2011) concluded that the software on which the Athlete Biological Passport is based is not capable of detecting micro-dosing of EPO. WADA itself admits that "dumb dopers … probably" represent "the vast number of those who tested positive" (World Anti-Doping Agency 2010d).

[9] The Code then adds a fourth criterion in the following article (article 4.3.2): the masking potential of a substance or method (see Teitler and Ram 2008).

The 2012 London Olympics again demonstrated the limits of athletes' testing: despite the 6,000 tests conducted, only two athletes tested positive during the Olympics, whereas seven others were "caught" in the preceding 2 weeks, which are also considered official testing period for the games (Associated Press 2012; Niggli 2013, personal communication; see also AFP 2011). At the previous summer Olympic Games (2000 in Sydney, 2004 in Athens, and 2008 in Beijing), a total of 10,796 tests were carried out, yielding only 53 positive results. The IOC's miserable success rate of 0.5 % is still much higher than that obtained by the International Football Federation (FIFA): at the latest four World Cups not a single case of doping has been discovered (Hoberman 2012: 1). According to some back-of-the-envelope calculations by Simon (2010), a leading German sports physician, an elite athlete who is doping may undergo tests 150 times before he or she tests positive, implying that each detection costs approximately US$300,000 (see also Hoberman 2001).

1.1.3 *The Harms of Doping Products*

Knowledge of the harmful effects of doping agents has increased in the past 20 years, but studies have so far focused on the harms associated with steroids, which are thought to be the most frequently abused substance class. Steroid use is associated with a range of adverse medical effects, including dyslipidemia, cardiomyopathy, and prolonged suppression of the hypothalamic–pituitary–gonadal axis (Kanayama et al. 2008). In some individuals, steroids may also cause serious psychiatric effects, especially mood syndromes, which may sometimes be associated with aggression or violence (Thiblin and Parlklo 2002; Perry et al. 2003; Kanayama et al. 2008; Pope and Brower 2009). According to the Swedish National Institute of Public Health (2010: 55–56), depressive symptoms are currently viewed as the most common, most widespread, and probably the most serious side effect after discontinued steroid intake, becoming a risk factor for both violence and suicide. Moreover, steroid dependence is documented in about 30 % of illicit steroid users in various field studies (e.g., Kanayama et al. 2009).

Women are affected by side effects similar to those in men and the risk of exhibiting them is higher (Kindlundh et al. 1998; Quaglio et al. 2009). Use also often entails a masculinizing effect that does not automatically return to normal after discontinued use. Some of the reported side effects are larynx growth, beard growth, substantial body hair growth and simultaneously raised hairline, menstruation disturbances, clitoris growth, and regression of the breasts (Kanayama et al. 2007; Swedish National Institute of Public Health 2010: 53).

A number of Swedish studies have shown that steroid use entails an elevated risk of premature death (Thiblin et al. 1999; Thiblin and Petersson 2005; Petersson et al. 2006). This may be due to physical complications such as cardiac death, suicide, or death resulting from the individual exposing himself to risk taking in connection with use (Pärssinen et al. 2000; Petersson et al. 2006).

The harmful effects associated with other substances have been studied less systematically, but this does not mean that they are less serious or frequent (for a review, see Peters et al. 2002). As a matter of fact, some scholars regard some of these substances, such as those taken by body-builders in addition to steroids, as more dangerous than steroids themselves (Evans 2004; Parkinson and Evans 2006). Health risks are further increased by the fact that a growing, albeit often not precisely known, share of the doping substances on the international market are counterfeited. A study in the Netherlands (de Hon and van Kleij 2005) has shown that at least 50–60 % of the products illegally obtained do not contain what is declared on the label. As de Hon and van Kleij (2005: 7) note, "the dosages of these products are completely unpredictable, which means that the side effects that are encountered are likewise unpredictable. In some instances, the lack of hygiene surrounding the places where these products are processed poses an additional health risk."

Even greater risks are likely to arise from doping users' frequent polypharmaceutical practices, i.e., the unsupervised use of different doping substances, but the increased health risks associated with these practices have been hardly studied yet (Parkinson and Evans 2006; Swedish National Institute of Public Health 2010).

1.1.4 The Supply of Doping Products: A "New" Topic for Inquiry

Unlike use, the topic of the supply of doping products has received little scientific attention, represented in just a handful of scientific publications. Two seminal studies based on interviews, Koert and van Kleij (1998) and Oldersma et al. (2002), examined the illegal distribution networks of doping substances in gyms in the Netherlands. In 2007 Donati sketched out the *World Traffic in Doping Substances* on behalf of the WADA, analyzing secondary sources and firsthand documents retrieved online.

A few other—quantitative (e.g., Kindlundh et al. 1998; Lambert et al. 1998; Striegel et al. 2006) and qualitative (e.g., Brissonneau 2007; Fincoeur 2009)—studies that focus on doping use and government or sports federation reports on use (e.g., Australian Senate Standing Committee on the Environment and Recreation and the Arts 1989; Dubin 1990; Mitchell 2007) occasionally reveal information on the athletes' sources of doping products. Research on the state doping programs of the former East Germany (e.g., Berendonk 1992; Franke 1995; Spitzer 1998) also documents that doping athletes may not need to buy doping products on the black market but, at least in some extreme circumstances such as a nondemocratic country, may be supplied directly by state officials. A few biochemical analyses have also focused on doping drug seizures (e.g., Lüdke et al. 2007; Thevis et al. 2008). Isolated but interesting observations can also be found elsewhere: Bette and Schimank (2000), for example, stress that, contrary to the media representation of doping as a deviant behavior of single individuals, drug-using athletes are not working alone without the assistance and support of others. They speak of a "constellation of actors," not limited to the world of elite sports but also including the public, mass media, and economic and political actors. In his turn, Waddington (2000: 159) points to a "doping network" surrounding the athletes.

Aside from these few publications, we know of no study focusing on the supply of doping products. A search on the Criminal Justice Abstracts (CJA), PubMed, and Web of Science databases (they are, respectively, the largest and most authoritative database for criminology, the largest medical database, and one of the largest databases of any kind worldwide) in April of 2012 revealed only four relevant publications on the topic, using "doping" and "trafficking," "trade," and "supply" as keywords. In PubMed, the two relevant publications consisted of a one-page letter in the *British Medical Journal* describing the ease of obtaining insulin from UK pharmacies (Elkin et al. 1997) and a biochemical article indicating that black market copies of drug candidates are easily available via the Internet (Thevis et al. 2011). In CJA, we found an article written in Slovenian and another one about the use and trafficking of steroids among body-builders in the United States (Kraska et al. 2010). In particular, criminology as a discipline has yet to discover the problem of doping (Paoli 2012). The 2012 search on the CJA found 85 other publications listing "doping" as a keyword but the overwhelming majority of them consisted of forensic articles or treated the topic of doping only marginally.

1.1.5 Literature Review Implications

What have we learned from this necessarily brief literature review? The demand for doping products exists in most countries and has been addressed in numerous studies. Although there is no consensus on its extent, doping constitutes a public health problem. At 3 % of the world young male population, the prevalence of steroid use alone is comparable to that of some illegal drugs, such as heroin (United Nations Office on Drugs and Crime 2012). In addition to steroids, doping involves a plurality of substances and methods that are not used only for performance-enhancing purposes.

If there is a demand, there must surely also be a supply; however, the supply side of the market has been examined by very few studies. None of these studies has tried to identify the different actors and channels of supply in a given country. The lack of research of the supply side of the market also reflects the fact these activities have not been investigated systematically by many law enforcement agencies and, hence, the "supply" of research-worthy criminal justice data is also scant. As such criminal justice data are uniquely available in Italy, a study of the supply of doping products in Italy may be considered illustrative—or at least indicative—of what remains unexplored elsewhere, even if similarities and differences must be ascertained empirically in future projects. Indeed, we hope that this study may convince researchers and policy-makers in other countries and multilaterally of the scientific relevance of our approach.

1.2 International Policy Context

Research on the supply of doping products and on supply-oriented policy interventions is not only scientifically innovative but also policy relevant.

1.2.1 The Three Pillars of Anti-doping Policies

As already mentioned, an international anti-doping regime began to take shape during the 1960s through the interaction of the IOC, international sports federations, and national governments. Among the latter, France was the first to enact anti-doping legislation. Other governments followed later on, but their involvement in anti-doping remained largely symbolic and international cooperation was long restricted to the Council of Europe, whose Anti-Doping Convention entered into force in 1990 (Houlihan 2002). According to numerous scholars and observers, the international sports bodies, and in particular the IOC, also did not make a credible effort to implement their own sports rules and anti-doping tests at least until the new century. Houlihan (2002: 184), for example, notes that for a long time there was a "lack of enthusiasm among senior members of the IOC for an intensive anti-doping programme." Even Dick Pound (2011b), former IOC Vice President and founding President of WADA, is very critical.

> The response to doping in sport, on the part of sports authorities and governments, did not come until long after the phenomenon was recognized as a serious problem in virtually every sport. Years and years and years of endemic doping in cycling passed almost without notice and, when it was noticed, it was denied or passed off as an isolated aberration. The growing use of anabolic steroids, stimulants and other doping methods in other sports were met with institutional denial, individual lies and inconsequential sanctions. Testing was introduced with enormous reluctance and testing programs were normally limited to in-competition tests, in which a positive test was, in effect, failure of an intelligence test as much as a doping test.

In particular, it has been suggested that the IOC's longstanding neglect of doping was driven by its growing concern with commercial issues, since effective controls would expose numerous famous athletes and alienate Olympic corporate sponsors (Hoberman 2001: 245; see also MacAloon 2001: 213). This critical view of the IOC was reinforced by persistent allegations of suppressed positive test results at several Olympic Games during the 1980s (Hanstad et al. 2008: 230). At the Moscow Olympics in 1980, for example, no positive test results were reported, but the urine samples were retested after the Games by the German drug-testing expert Prof. Manfred Donike, who found that 20 % of the samples were positive for testosterone (Teetzel 2011 quoted in Hanstad et al. 2008: 231).

Driven by growing skepticism toward the IOC's and international sports federations' self-regulation, during the 1980s and 1990s governmental agencies increased their participation in anti-doping, but until the end of the twentieth century, there were no harmonized policies nor standardized power-sharing agreements between international sports bodies and the national government agencies. As a result, the doping sanctions imposed by sports federations and the IOC were often disputed and sometimes overruled in civil courts. The 1998 Tour de France scandal provided a window of opportunity to establish, 1 year later, the WADA, a nongovernmental international agency to unify standards for, and provide coordination in, anti-doping action (Hanstad et al. 2008).

Aiming at harmonizing anti-doping sports rules, sanctions, and testing procedures in all sports and countries, the WADA soon produced a World Anti-Doping Code, which entered into force in 2004. The Code primarily concerns elite athletes and nowadays constitutes the first and by far most developed pillar of anti-doping policies. As governments cannot be legally bound by a nongovernmental document such as the World Anti-Doping Code, they have implemented it by individually ratifying the UNESCO International Convention against Doping in Sport, the first global international treaty against doping in sport, which was adopted in 2005 and came into force in early 2007.[10]

Embodying the governments' growing responsibility for anti-doping, WADA is funded on an equal basis by governments and by the IOC, and its governing bodies, the Council and the Executive Committee, both have equal representation from governments and the IOC. Government interventions have also led to the development of two other pillars of drug policies. These are governmental as opposed to the disciplinary and private law orientation of the sports movement and concern not only elite athletes but also recreational athletes and sportspeople. They are also much less harmonized than the first pillar.

The administrative pillar, ruled by public and administrative law, operates from a public health perspective and is primarily focused on the prevention of doping, but also carries out testing and involves administrative actions such as rule making and administrative adjudication of its own and sports rules. This pillar is primarily entrusted to the National Anti-Doping Organizations (NADOs), which all countries signatory to the Code have committed themselves to set up. Despite the lack of systematic analysis, there seems to be considerable variance in the NADO's institutional bases, composition, and powers. Depending on the countries, other bodies with broader competencies, such as the Ministries for Sport, might also play a role in the administrative pillar, especially in the launch of preventive initiatives.

The third pillar is inspired by criminal law and aims at prosecuting the suppliers of doping products and, in a few countries such as Italy, even the athletes. This is the least developed pillar and the largest differences persist, despite the fact that article

[10] Some scholars still see considerable differences in the implementation of the WADA and UNESCO rules by the anti-doping panels of the national sports federations and courts (see Hendrickx 2008; Henne 2009). Some national policy-makers are worried that some National Anti-Doping Organizations (NADOs) and anti-doping laboratories are more efficient than others, thus de facto giving an unintended advantage to the athletes of less efficient countries (Sportausschuss des Deutschen Bundestages 2011: 24–25). Olivier Niggli, WADA Legal Counsel, admitted that WADA "has at the world level problems to obtain conclusive data [from the laboratories]. There is no reporting according to the same rules. The data we receive do not state always the same" (ibid.: 28).

8 of the 2005 UNESCO Convention against Doping in Sport calls on State Parties to "adopt measures against trafficking to athletes." As the law enforcement officers of numerous countries note, the lack of harmonization of national criminal laws on doping represents a big hurdle to an effective international cooperation in the control of the supply of doping products. For example, Andreas Holzer (Sportausschuss des Deutschen Bundestages 2011: 14), head of the Special Commission Doping of the Austrian Federal Criminal Police Office (BKA), recently stated: "Different legal bases and provisions in the countries make international cooperation relatively difficult: the trade in doping products works like the trade in drugs, and there should also be international cooperation in the fight against the former [as there is in the fight against the latter]."

According to survey conducted by the Asser Institute in 2010, the trade and distribution of doping products is a criminal offense prohibited by and sanctionable under:

- Criminal law in Cyprus, the Czech Republic, Finland, Hungary, [Italy], Lithuania, the Netherlands, and Slovenia
- Anti-drug laws in Austria, Belgium, Denmark, Germany, Ireland, the Netherlands, Portugal, Romania, Sweden, and the UK
- The Sports Act in France, Greece, Luxembourg, and Spain

At the time of the survey, Bulgaria, Latvia, Malta, Poland, and Slovakia had no existing laws and regulations relating to trade and distribution of doping products.

In a more in-depth comparison of the anti-doping legislation of five European countries (France, Germany, Italy, Spain, and Switzerland), Parzeller and his colleagues (2009:10, Parzeller et al. 2009:10) noted efforts in all selected countries to fight doping in sports with criminal law means and to address also the athletes' support personnel and therefore heterogeneous doping. They concluded, however, that the relevant criminal law provisions had been often included in special laws (such as the anti-doping act or act regulating the sale and administration of medical drugs), and there were significant differences in sanctions (see also Houlihan and García 2012).

Even broader differences exist with regard to the possession of substances prohibited under the UNESCO Convention, as shown by another survey carried out in 2009 by the German Federal Ministry of the Interior among 20 EU Member States. The conclusion was as follows:

> Member States have very different opinions in particular on the penalties under sport and criminal law. Views range from strict bans against the possession of doping agents to an outright rejection of criminal liability. Between these poles there are various approaches which only partly penalize the possession of doping agents. In many countries the possession of some substances listed in Annex 1 of the UNESCO Convention is not punishable. Many substances are, however, subject to general provisions, e.g. laws on medicinal products, which also ban the possession of these substances. Other countries impose bans on the possession of doping agents only if it can be established that the accused intended to pass them on or sell them (e.g., in Denmark, Finland and the Netherlands). In some countries it is not punishable to possess doping agents, but athletes may be required to pay fines and lose their license (Spain).

The German survey also uncovered significant differences regarding the banned substances. While some countries ban all prohibited substances listed in Annex 1 of the UNESCO Convention, others only refer to certain substances or groups of substances. "There is no general trend in this field," concluded the German Federal Ministry of the Interior (2009: 3).

Although no study has yet systematically examined the issues, crucial differences also seem to persist in the institutional arrangements called to implement the national criminal law provisions. According to Hoberman (2011a: 100), for example, the seminal 1965 French anti-doping law "remained essentially irrelevant for decades." In Germany there is not yet an anti-doping law and, according to Rössner (2011: 420), there is an "implementation deficit" even of the criminal controls that are already available (see also Rechtskommission des Sports gegen Doping 2005).

1.2.2 An Ongoing Shift from the First to the Third Pillar?

In the anti-doping policy community, awareness is growing that the first pillar of anti-doping policies has "focus[ed] squarely on the athlete[s]" (World Anti-Doping Agency 2013d) and their testing and is not effective. As we have seen in the previous pages, anti-doping tests detect a very limited number of offenses. As each test costs between 300 and 500€ depending on the products tested (Evaluation team 2002; Schänzer 2012 personal communication), there are also growing concerns about the costs of testing. On the contrary, several large-scale criminal investigations carried out by the US Drug Enforcement Administration and other national law enforcement agencies since 2000 have demonstrated the potential of anti-doping criminal prosecution (e.g., Balco case, Operations "Gear Grinder" and "Raw Deal" in the US; see Fainaru-Wada and Lance 2006; Dohrmann and Llosa 2006; U.S. Drug Enforcement Administration 2007, respectively; and for Europe, see Bundeskriminalamt 2011).[11]

The legitimacy of the first pillar of anti-doping policies is also being questioned. Some critics go as far as to challenge the ethical justifications of the "war on doping" and call for the liberalization of enhancement practices in sports within a framework of medical supervision (e.g., Savulescu et al. 2004a, b; Kayser et al. 2007; contra, Wiesing 2011). Even those who have no principled objections to the anti-doping regime point to numerous critical issues. One of them is the

[11] Most shockingly, parallel investigations undertaken by the USADA and the federal prosecutors revealed that the Bay Area Laboratory Co-Operative (Balco) in California had marketed for several years prior to 2002 an until-then undetected designer anabolic steroid ("the Clear") as well as GH and other drugs to a number of high-profile elite athletes from the United States and Europe (Fainaru-Wada and Lance 2006). In 2011, a joint operation of the Austrian and German police and customs led to the closure of what is believed to have been the oldest and most renowned underground laboratory for doping products in Europe, International Pharmaceuticals, and the seizure of over 5,000,000 units of steroids, hormones, and stimulants (Bundeskriminalamt 2011).

overreliance on nongovernmental forms of policy-making and adjudication, which are not bound to respect constitutional guarantees (Jacobs and Samuels 1994, 1995: 581–583; Peterson 2010: 322–323). Sports federations are private bodies and the Court of Arbitration for Sport (CAS), the sports law highest court, is based on private law under the jurisdiction of the Swiss legal system—a problematic fact in light of human rights law, particularly as regards fair trial and due process principles (Soek 2006; Rudolph 2009, 2010). The strict liability principle, which Hard (2010: 225) defines as "the most scrutinized feature, and the hallmark of the Code," is also questioned. It implies that, in the event of a doping offense, in principle, the athlete's "good faith" or "good intentions" are not taken into account and de facto reverses the burden of proof (see also Blumenthal 2010: 228). The new whereabouts requirements and testing methods are also disputed (e.g., Hanstad and Loland 2009; Mitten 2009) and are considered by some scholars (Groleau 2009) to be a violation of the athletes' rights to privacy.[12]

Against this background, there is a growing consensus among national and international policy-makers (e.g., European Commission 2007; Department for Culture and Media and Sport 2009; UK Antidoping 2011; World Anti-Doping Agency 2011b, c, 2013d, g) and many scholars (e.g., Bannenberg and Rössner 2006; Rössner 2009, 2011; Howman 2011a, b; Houlihan and García 2012) that a broader approach is needed, including the more frequent use of criminal law instruments and, specifically, the repression of "trafficking." Already in its 2007 White Paper on Sport, "the [European] Commission (2007) recommend[ed] that trade in illicit doping substances be treated in the same manner as trade in illicit drugs throughout the EU." Having acquired specific legal competencies on sports with the Lisbon Treaty, which entered into force in late 2009, the Commission does not rule out presenting a binding law-making initiative to criminalize "trafficking" in doping substances throughout the EU, if a political consensus were to emerge (Kornbeck 2009; Krejza 2009). According to the UK government, which hosted the 2012 Olympic Games in London, it is necessary to shift from a "'traditional' approach to testing athletes" to a "new paradigm of anti-doping" to tackle those who supply and administer doping substances (Department for Culture and Media and Sport 2009: 5). Reflecting this approach, the UK government established a new organization, referred to simply as "UK Anti-Doping" in 2009, which it presents as an "intelligence-led organization" that works closely with law enforcement partners, such as the Serious Organised Crime Agency (SOCA), customs, pharmaceutical companies, and the usual sports stakeholders.[13]

According to the WADA (2013d) too, "it is imperative that additional strategies be combined with testing, research and education to ensure an efficient and effective anti-doping fight." Testing alone cannot tackle five of the eight core violations listed in the revised WADA Anti-Doping Code, which entered into force in 2009, including trafficking in, and possession of, prohibited substances and methods.

---

[12] The Belgian sport union, Sporta, legally challenged them, arguing that they violate European privacy laws (BBC 2009).

[13] See http://www.ukad.org.uk/what-we-do/intelligence/.

Drawing on all these insights, WADA (2013g) lists the following as the third of eight key objectives in the 2011 version of its Strategic Plan: "Generate universal involvement of public authorities and public leaders in the campaign against doping in sport, and in particular encourage national laws to allow the sharing of evidence gathered or collected through investigations and inquiries by appropriate bodies." Moreover, WADA (2013f) now considers "cooperation with law enforcement" as its second priority right after its core mission of monitoring the code compliance, specifically indicating that "in collaboration with UNESCO, [it] works with individual governments to persuade them to have laws in place that allow to combat manufacturing, supply and possession of doping substances on their territories." To achieve such an objective and priority, WADA (2011d) has in recent years formalized cooperation agreements with Interpol and the World Customs Organization. In 2011 it also released guidelines designed to enhance judicial investigations and the cooperation between National Anti-Doping Organizations (NADOs) and law enforcement agencies (World Anti-Doping Agency 2011e). In those guidelines WADA again refers to the Italian experience as a model, along with the Balco investigation. Despite the fact that the IOC long insisted on having the Italian anti-doping law suspended during the Turin Olympic Games (Vinton 2005), WADA now considers exemplary the close cooperation the IOC and WADA had with the Italian law enforcement agencies that lead to the discovery of systematic doping practices at the Austrian biathlon and cross-country teams (World Anti-Doping Agency 2011e).

1.3 Conceptual Framework: A Semi-illegal Market

We conceptualize doping in terms of a market, with its demand and supply. A market approach is "bread and butter" in the field of illegal drugs and other illegal goods and services but, to our knowledge, has not yet been applied to doping. We are aware of the fact, though, that there is not necessarily a monetary transaction between the final users of doping products and their suppliers (e.g., when these are team staff members).

In particular, we conceptualize the doping market as a semi-illegal market, at least from the point of view of criminal law. We stress that the legal status of doping products suffers the burden and ambiguity of contextual specificity; that is, in some contexts, the products, including their supply, are "legal" and in others they are not. In that way they are more like typical diverted pharmaceutical products and less like traditional illicit substances, such as cocaine, heroin, and cannabis. By and large society treats the latter as "inherently" illegal: most countries prohibit trafficking and possession of cocaine, heroin, and other illegal drugs for nonpersonal use because, with few exceptions, these drugs have been deemed dangerous to public health and lacking therapeutic value. Instead, most doping products are also legitimate, well-established pharmaceutical products.

The ambiguity of doping products has repercussions on both demand- and supply-side activities. Even in Italy, which has some of the world's most stringent anti-doping criminal legislation, the users of the same doping products may or may not commit a legal offense, depending on the goals of their use. In fact, only athletes using such products "in order to improve [their] competitive performance" (article 9 of Act No. 376/2000) are held liable. The same ambiguity can be found in the application of the world anti-doping sports rules. According to the WADA Anti-Doping Code, the users of the same doping products may or may not violate a sports rule, depending on whether or not they have a therapeutic use exemption (see World Anti-Doping Agency 2013h). A further complication is held by the superimposition and occasional mismatch of national laws and sports rules. Minor athletes who test positive for a certain doping substance clearly violate sports rules but cannot be held liable by a criminal court, not even in Italy, if they were administered the doping substance by their parents or physician (Int-Pro-2).

The legal status of many supply-side activities also varies contextually; in particular, it varies along the distribution chain and, for the same activity, from country to country. Even within each country, differences depend on the products exchanged, the final uses of the products, the applicable offenses, and the good faith of some suppliers. We consider each of these variations in legal status.

A drug may begin its "life" as a legal product at one end of the supply chain and conclude its "life" as an illegal product at the other. Many drugs, which are used illegally as doping products are produced by legitimate drug manufacturers[14] or by pharmaceutical companies that may not meet the regulatory requirements of western developed countries but can operate lawfully in their own countries.

Given the lack of harmonization of the relevant criminal law legislation even within the EU, the same supplying activities are likely to have different legal statuses in different countries. Body-builders in Germany can legally obtain anabolic steroids through regular physicians and pharmacies (Striegel et al. 2006), whereas physicians and pharmacists cannot legally prescribe or sell the same drugs to body-builders in Italy and The Netherlands (Koert and van Kleij 1998). In a comparative perspective it is also necessary to ascertain the effective degree of enforcement of the existing regulations and prohibitions (for the concept of "effective illegality," see Paoli et al. 2009). As already mentioned, even the existing sports rules and criminal law provisions have not always been implemented effectively.

Even within the same country, some doping products, with very restricted therapeutic uses, may be "more" illegal—at least from the point of view of criminal justice rather than sports authorities—than others. Leaving aside "traditional" illegal drugs, such as cocaine and cannabis, which are also on the WADA Prohibited List, nandrolone is a good case in point. In 2010, the Italian Ministry of Health added nandrolone, an anabolic steroid, to the list of psychoactive substances to be controlled under Italian drug law (DPR 309/1990 and later amendments), therefore sharply reducing the possibility of its legal sale and consumption and allowing a

[14] A note on vocabulary: we distinguish drug manufacturers from drug distributors in those instances in which it is possible and important to make the distinction; in other instances, we refer to both with the expression "pharmaceutical companies."

whole range of special investigation methods (e.g., controlled delivery[15]) that are not allowed by Italy's anti-doping act (Ministero della Salute 2010b).

According to the Italian legislation, many actors frequently involved in the supply of doping products, such physicians or pharmacists, may or may not commit a crime depending on the therapeutic needs of their customers and clients. Specifically, the legality or illegality of their decisions and actions depends on whether their customers and patients are athletes consuming certain products "in order to improve [their] competitive performance" (article 9 of Act No. 376/2000). At one extreme, prescribing or materially supplying a performance-enhancing product to an athlete taking part in competition always constitutes a crime according to the Italian anti-doping act. At the other extreme, supplying the same product to a patient, including an athlete, who needs it for therapeutic reasons never constitutes a crime. Between these two extremes, there is an ambiguous continuum where the legal status of the physicians' or pharmacists' decisions and actions depend on whether offenses other than those foreseen by the anti-doping act are applicable and on the physicians' assessment of patient's psychophysical conditions and needs.

The potential applicability of multiple offenses to doping contributes to the ambiguous legal status of supply-side activities. As apparent in the NAS investigations and related criminal proceedings, the supply of doping products has been criminalized and punished in Italy with reference to various offenses, beyond that of doping. In our analysis of the supply of doping products, we refer to all these different applicable offenses as "doping-related" offenses and in Chap. 7, we consider in detail the offenses that have been concretely charged.

In fully illegal markets, both parties in a transaction are usually aware of the illegal nature of the exchange, even if, as might occur in Italy, the drug user does not necessarily commit an offense if buying drugs solely for personal consumption. In the case of doping, one of the parties to a transaction involving doping products may be ignorant of any illegality or rule breaking, reflecting the "embeddedness" of doping exchanges in legitimate social networks and professional activities. This is, for example, the case of a pharmacist who sells a doping product on the basis of a fraudulent or stolen prescription.

Thus, illegality cannot be presupposed, but must be ascertained empirically for each level of the distribution chain, country, product, and supplying activity; for the goals of each transaction; and for each party to the transaction.

[15] This is defined by Article 1g of the 1988 United Nations Convention against Illicit Traffic in Narcotic Drugs and Psychotropic Substances as: "(…) the technique of allowing illicit or suspect consignments of (…) drugs (…) or substances substituted for them, to pass out of, through or into the territory of one or more countries, with the knowledge and under the supervision of their competent authorities, with a view to identifying persons involved in the commission of offences." See http://www.unodc.org/pdf/convention_1988_en.pdf.

Chapter 2
Doping Products and Their Demand

Abstract In this second chapter we provide context for the analysis of the supply of doping products, by considering the products available in Italy and by assessing, at least roughly, the demand. Despite the lack of specific historical or cross-country studies, we draw from the assumption that the use of doping substances and methods in Italy has followed the same broad lines of development known from studies in other countries. On the basis of NAS seizure data and anti-doping investigations we show that the entire palette of doping substances and methods is currently available on the Italian market. Exploiting the available data, we then estimate the size of the two main groups of users of doping products, athletes and body-builders, and demonstrate that a significant minority of the nearly 14 million Italians, aged 15 and older, who regularly engage in sports has consumed doping products at least occasionally, generating a market that is comparable to that of heroin.

In this second chapter we provide context for the analysis of the supply of doping products, by considering the products available in Italy and by assessing, at least roughly, the demand. Despite the lack of specific historical or cross-country studies, we draw from the assumption that the use of doping substances and methods in Italy has followed the same broad lines of development known from studies in other countries. On the basis of NAS seizure data and anti-doping investigations we show that the entire palette of doping substances and methods is currently available on the Italian market. Exploiting the available data, we then estimate the size of the two main groups of users of doping products, athletes and body-builders, and demonstrate that a significant minority of the nearly 14 million Italians, aged 15 and older, who regularly engage in sports has consumed doping products at least occasionally, generating a market that is comparable to that of heroin.

L. Paoli and A. Donati, *The Sports Doping Market: Understanding Supply and Demand, and the Challenges of Their Control*, DOI 10.1007/978-1-4614-8241-3_2,

2.1 Doping Substances and Methods Available in Italy

The substances seized by NAS between 1999 and 2009, as reported in the NAS Investigations Database, demonstrate that the Italian market encompasses the full range of doping substances and methods.

The NAS seizures data constitute the best available source of information concerning the doping substances that are available on the Italian market, but their analysis requires preliminary methodological attention. From NAS, we received a detailed list of all the substances seized, including, for about 90 % of the cases, the number of pills, vials, or ampoules contained in each package. To aggregate the seizures correctly and meaningfully, we have relied on the internal guidelines established by the NAS Headquarters in close cooperation with Donati (NAS 2011) and used the "dose" as our unit of measure.

2.1.1 Doping Doses

The US Drug and Enforcement Administration (DEA) was the first agency to introduce the concept of a dose to this arena, but—to our knowledge—the agency applies the concept without drawing distinctions between pills, ampoules, and other packages of anabolic steroids,[1] regardless of the fact that, for example, ampoules of steroids and some corticosteroids usually contain four to ten times more of the active ingredient than a pill of the same product.[2] The same problem also applies to stimulants and testosterone, which are available both in pills and ampoules. To properly account for these considerable differences, the NAS Headquarters and Donati defined the key term of "dose" as the quantity of active ingredients contained in a single administration, even if more than one dose is taken daily and then undertook a three-part effort to establish the dose of each of the different products, in which they:

1. Recorded the active ingredients of each product seized, regardless of the differences in packages (e.g., pills, ampoules, spray). Only by considering the active ingredient can drugs seized in different packages be meaningfully aggregated and different packages of the same substance compared.
2. Retrieved information on recommended doses from the pharmaceutical companies' instructions and/or specialized Web sites and from the Web sites of the

[1] This procedure was described by DEA officials to Donati during a symposium organized by WADA in 2007 to enhance cooperation in the fight against doping in sport. See http://www.wada-ama.org/en/News-Center/Articles/Symposium-calls-for-increased-co-operation-in-fight- against-doping-in-sport/.

[2] For example, a Web site offered both steroids in pills for 10–25 mg and ampoules for 100–250 mg. See http://www.steroid4u.eu/compra-iniettare-steroidi/winstrol-depot?language=It. Accessed March 13, 2012.

Table 2.1 Doping doses for the main types of doping substances seized by NAS

Doping substances	1 dose
Anabolic agents	10 mg
Peptide hormones, growth factors and related substances, of which	
EPO and other similar peptide hormones	200 IU or 1 mcg
GH and other similar peptide hormones	1 IU or 0.333 mg
Chorionic gonadotrophin	1,000 IU
Gonadorelin	1.2 mg
Adrenocorticotropic hormone (ACTH) and other corticotrophins	0.25 mg
Insulin	10 IU
Beta-2 agonists	2 mcg
Hormones and metabolic modulators	10 mg
Diuretics and other masking agents	25 mg
Stimulants	25 mg
Narcotics	50 mg
Glucocorticosteroids	25 mg
Beta-blockers	5 mg

Source: NAS Headquarters (2012)

Agenzia Italiana del Farmaco[3] and Pagine Sanitarie.[4] The latter Web site provides detailed information about the different drugs available on the Italian market to pharmacists, physicians, and the public.

3. Compared the official doses, e.g., those of the pharmaceutical companies, with the dosages revealed by different athletes or their suppliers in wiretapped conversations, seized documents, or in official questionings or known to Donati through his previous experience as coach of several national Italian teams in track and field and other sports (fencing, rowing, Alpine and Nordic skiing, volleyball, basketball, water polo, and equestrian sports) and CONI official.

Table 2.1 below summarizes the quantities of active ingredients that constitute a doping dose for the doping substances seized by NAS and listed in the NAS Investigations Database. The classification of doping substances corresponds to that made by WADA (2012b) in its Prohibited List. However, we exclude cannabinoids, a separate category in the WADA Prohibited List, and cocaine, which is included in the category of stimulants, for both substantive and practical reasons. Whereas we will explain the substantive reasons in the following pages, the practical reasons are striking: no seizure of cannabis or cocaine is reported in the NAS Investigations Database.[5]

[3] See http://farmaco.agenziafarmaco.it/index.php.

[4] See http://www.paginesanitarie.com.

[5] In the case of both "narcotics" and "hormones and metabolic modulators," we have adopted WADA designations, but we only refer to the subsets of substances that have been seized by NAS. The category "narcotics" thus exclusively consists of local anesthetics. As already mentioned, athletes hardly ever use systemic narcotics, such as heroin or morphine, and no seizure of such drugs is reported in the NAS Investigations Database. Within the second category of "hormones and metabolic modulators," we refer exclusively to antiestrogens, the main products included into that category and the only product of that category for which positive tests were recorded in Italy. "Local anesthetics" and "antiestrogens" were also the two labels used by CVD until 2008 (see Ministero del Lavoro, della Salute e delle Politiche Sociali 2009).

Given the purposes of the exercise, criminal justice sources and Donati's direct experience were given priority vis-à-vis the pharmaceutical indications. As a result, the doping doses established by the NAS Headquarters and Donati sometimes differ significantly from the doses advised by pharmaceutical companies (see also Parkinson and Evans 2006; Swedish National Institute of Public Health 2010: 44). In the case of steroids, testosterone, or stimulants, in fact, doping athletes often exceed the official doses indicated by pharmaceutical companies and government bodies. The reverse is true in the case of EPO. The mean dose in renal failure patients on dialysis in Italy or Germany is 8,000 IU per patient and week.[6] As a matter of fact, the doping dose that the NAS Headquarters and Donati suggest for EPO is also considerably lower than the usual doping doses of, say, elite riders reported in the literature (up to 700–1,000 IU two or three times a week; see Lundby et al. 2011). The NAS Headquarters and Donati have specified the lower dose because Italian investigations (e.g., NAS Brescia 2011) confirm the trends to "micro-dosing" highlighted by WADA (2010d) and the scholarly literature (Ashenden et al. 2011; Lundby et al. 2012). Namely, doping athletes and particularly elite riders increasingly tend to fragment the dosage to avoid unnecessary shocks to their bodies and now often take 200 IU several times a day. Smaller EPO doses also have the advantage to look more natural and to be even more difficult to detect with anti-doping tests (Int-NAS-15 and 16).

2.1.2 NAS Seizures

Table 2.2 provides key data on the seizures reported in the NAS Investigations Database and presents the results of our calculations, made on the basis of the previous parameters. In the 11-year time frame covered by the database, NAS seized 7,176,780 packages of doping substances. Most of these packages belonged to 1 of 495 different packages of substances for which we had or could reconstruct precise information about the active ingredients they contained. For about 10 % of the packages, though, we did not have enough information to determine the active ingredient contained in them. To include such packages in our estimates, we have calculated the average active ingredients contained in the packages seized of the same product (or classes of product) and assumed that the packages with no additional information contained the average doses. In such a way, we estimate that the substances seized by NAS between 1999 and 2009, as reported in the database, correspond to 1,042 kg of active ingredients[7] and to 88 million doses. Thus, on average, each year, NAS seized

[6] This figure was indicated by Prof. Wolfgang Jelkmann, an authority on EPO (personal communication, 2012 June 18).

[7] This sum does not include the active ingredients of peptide hormones, because they are not comparable to each other and to the other doping substances.

Table 2.2 Substances seized by NAS between 1999 and 2009, as presented in the database on NAS Investigations

Type of substance	Pills, ampoules, and other packages seized	Active ingredients seized (mg)	No. of doping doses	% of total doses
Anabolic agents	3,531,232	745,476,230	74,547,623	83.16
Peptide hormones, growth factors and related substances, of which:	45,812	Not comparable	1,604,608	1.79
EPO and similar hormones	12,430	Not comparable	626,335	0.70
GH and other growth factors	20,482	Not comparable	928,335	1.04
Related substances[a]	12,900	Not comparable	49,938	0.06
Beta-2 agonists	640	9,780	4,890	0.01
Hormones and metabolic modulators	35,561	355,610	35,561	0.04
Diuretics and other masking agents	13,339	340,125	13,605	0.02
Stimulants	3,373,570	291,379,175	11,655,167	13.00
Narcotics	1	6,750	135	0.00
Glucocorticosteroids	130,802	4,549,125	181,965	0.20
Beta-blockers	11	55	11	0.00
Total	7,176,780	1,042,116,850	88,043,565	100.00

Source: our calculations on the basis of the NAS Investigations Database
[a]This category includes all other substances related to peptide hormones and growth factors, such as chorionic gonadotrophin, gonadorelin, ACTH and other corticotrophins, and insulin, which we had listed separately in Table 2.1

652,434 packages of doping substances, corresponding to 95 kg of active ingredients and to eight million doping doses.[8]

Given the focus of NAS investigations on body-building (see Chap. 7), these seizure data tend to overestimate the share of anabolic steroids, which are typically consumed by body-builders. With almost 75 million doses, steroids account for 85 % of the doses seized. On the other hand, NAS seizure data under-assess the relevance of peptide hormones, growth factors, and related substances,[9] which constitute only 1.8 % of the drugs seized because they are used by athletes of speed and endurance disciplines rather than body-building. Under this broad category, NAS seized 626,335 doses of EPO and 928,335 doses of GH, accounting respectively

[8]It must be taken into account, however, that NAS conducted only a handful of anti-doping investigations and seizure before the year 2000 and the adoption of a specific anti-doping law, while some of the earlier investigations, e.g., that concerning Prof. Conconi, are not inserted in the database.

[9]This is a complex category that, as noted in Table 2.1, includes various types of EPO, GH, and other growth factors, such as insulin-like growth factor-1 (IGF-1), chorionic gonadotrophin, gonadorelin, adrenocorticotropic hormone (ACTH) and other corticotrophins, and insulin; see WADA (2012b).

for 38.6 and 52.3 % of the doses seized in that category. After steroids, the second largest category of substances seized involves stimulants, which account for 13 % of all the doses. All other categories of doping substances account for small fractions of the doses intercepted.

The substances reported in the NAS Investigations Database are not the only doping substances that have been seized in Italy. Other law enforcement agencies have also seized doping substances over the years and the NAS itself has carried out a few seizures during the period 1999–2009 that are not included in the database and several others afterwards. We will discuss these data in more detail in Chap. 6, when we try to assess the financial dimensions of the market. For the moment, we use seizure data merely to demonstrate the availability of all doping substances included in the WADA Prohibited List (2012b) in Italy.

As noted previously, anti-doping investigations also reveal the frequent administration of doping methods and particularly of autologous and heterologous transfusions. In addition to the criminal proceeding against Conconi and his staff, other, more recent closed and ongoing investigations indicate that transfusion remains a frequent practice among elite athletes of endurance disciplines and particularly cycling (e.g., NAS Firenze 2005; Int-Pro-4). A recent investigation coordinated by the Mantua Prosecutor's Office has, for example, identified several specialized centers in Italy and abroad that are willing to carry out transfusions on elite riders, showing that the latter visit one or another center depending on their location (NAS Brescia 2011).

2.1.3 *Harmful Consequences of Doping Products*

Albeit inadvertently, Italy's anti-doping investigations also persuasively indicate the harmfulness of the use of doping products. Our sources indicate that several key investigations originated from the suspicious death of a young athlete or body-builder. The large "Oil for Drug" investigation conducted by the Florence NAS Branch Office on behalf of the Rome Prosecutor's Office, for example, drew from the death of a recreational rider who was suspected of using stimulants and had a heart attack while training at the periphery of Rome (NAS Firenze 2005). The investigation, known as "Flebo," of the Padua Branch Office took off when another young rider was admitted to a nearby hospital, after he fainted during an analogous transfusion carried out by the sports director of a cycling team known in the cycling world as "the wizard" (NAS Padova 2009). The Rome Carabinieri launched another large-scale investigation after the death of a female competitive body-builder in 2004. She died in her sleep as a result of a brain aneurism, provoked by her abuse of anabolic steroids. Initially, her fiancé and manager was convicted and sentenced to a 6-year prison sentence for the abusive exercise of a profession and the administration of dangerous drugs (article 348 and 445 CP); however, the verdict was subsequently canceled by the appeals court because of the territorial incompetence of the Rome first-degree court and the whole proceeding was annulled because the statute of limitations had run out in the case (La Gazzetta di Modena 2012).

Several interview partners at NAS also reports smaller investigations concerning the suspicious deaths of body-builders. Since 1997, at least five body-builders are known to have died of sudden heart failure solely in the regions of Emilia Romagna and Tuscany (Int-NAS-2, 3, 5, 6, 8, and 23). At least two other cases of body-builders' suspicious deaths were reported by Cagliari and Rome Branch Offices. The NAS officers, however, also report that many doping-related deaths go undetected. According to our interviewees, most emergency room admissions or sudden deaths that could be associated with abuse of steroids are not reported by the hospitals to NAS or other law enforcement agencies (Int-NAS-16 and 24).

Several other cases of sudden cardiac death of Italian body-builders (Camoni et al. 1997; Fineschi et al. 2007) are also reported in the scientific literature and, albeit with less degree of certainty, in the Italian media as a consequence of steroid use.[10]

Risks are obviously not related only to steroids. In the following, a professional rider, who decided to become a witness after the 2001 raids at the Giro d'Italia, describes the spread of very dangerous doping habits in the world of professional cycling:

> The first time I tried to make myself an injection on my bottom, I pricked myself eight times. Then it became a habit, a fantastic habit. All of a sudden, the bike starts going by itself, you no longer feel fatigue. I took EPO, GH, Sinacten,[11] Depo (i.e., Depo-Medrol, a powerful corticosteroid). Whatever came into my hands … We did not ask ourselves questions. The important thing was to go faster and faster. There is a well-known drug called Igf3 (insulin-like growth factor 3). On the instructions it is written: "not for human use." We thought: "Wau, if it is good for horses, you can imagine what its effect on us will be." We read newspapers to remain updated about new drugs; when we read that a big champion had been caught with Actovegin,[12] we ran to buy it as well, in Chiasso [Switzerland], there was not even an ampule left. … [To avoid controls] we slept with Emagel on the bedside table, it lowers the [blood] levels, or we shoot half a liter of physiological solution to dilute our blood. At the end of a competition we immediately took Andriol [testosterone undecanoate], which tests positive for 7 days, but the following Sunday we were already clean … A day I risked dying for an injection that did not function well, I was even admitted to the hospital in Milan … (Fazzo and Mensurati 2002b).

---

[10] See http://radiomosaici.blogspot.com/2010/03/palermo-culturista-muore-in-palestra.html; http://www.ivg.it/2010/01/morte-culturista-dopo-incidente-si-attende-referto-su-autopsia/; http://nl-nl.facebook.com/note.php?note_id=374070606228; http://qn.quotidiano.net/1999/08/11/149085-Morto-un-culturista-anabolizzanti-sul-tavolo-.shtml; http://qn.quotidiano.net/1999/08/11/149085-Morto-un-culturista- anabolizzanti-sul-tavolo-.shtml; http://archiviostorico.corriere.it/2004/dicembre/23/Doping_blitz_nelle_ palestre_ucciso_co_9_041223052.shtml; http://www.bodyweb.com/forums/threads/139057-culturista-24enne-morto-nel-bergamasco; http://www.chimica-oggi.it/archives/0002902.html; http://www.vivisicilia.com/index.php?option=com_content&view=article&id=1421%3Apalermo-culturista-muore-dopo-gli-allenamenti&catid=1%3Aultime&Itemid=2.

[11] Synacthen®, the brand name of tetracosactide is a synthetic analogue of the naturally occurring ACTH. Whereas Synacthen should be used for diagnostic purposes only, some professional cyclists also take it for prohibited performance-enhancing purposes.

[12] Actovegin® is a highly filtered extract obtained from calf blood that enhances aerobic oxidation in mammals. This improves absorption of glucose and oxygen uptake in tissue, which may enhance physical performance and stamina (see Pacifici and Donati 2011: 54 and 55 and Maillo 2008).

Body-builders and athletes may suffer harm not only as a direct consequence of the use of doping substances but also because of the misuse of illegal and additional drugs that may accompany doping (often cocaine and alcohol, as in the case of the Belgian 2005 world champion of cycling, Tom Boonen, who tested positive twice for cocaine; see BBC 2009), hazardous injection techniques (e.g., Baker et al. 2006) and, in the case of elite athletes, the depressions that follow the abrupt, doping-related end of their sports careers. Exemplary of the latter problems is the life history of Marco Pantani, who won both the Tour de France and the Giro d'Italia in 1998 and was considered one of the best climbers in road bicycle racing. Despite the fact that Pantani never tested positive, his career was beset by doping allegations. In the 1999 Giro d'Italia, he was expelled due to his irregular blood values. Although he was disqualified for "health reasons," it was implied that Pantani's high hematocrit was the product of EPO use. Following later accusations and more frequent doping tests of Pantani, this went into a depression from which he never fully recovered. He died of acute cocaine poisoning in 2004 (Jones and Maloney 2004).

Altering the users' mood, steroids may not only cause harm to the users but also to others. In 2009, for example, a former competitive body-builder, who suffered from depression (a frequent consequence of steroids use) stabbed his wife to death. When he later turned himself in to the police, he admitted that he could not remember what he had done (Il Corriere della Sera 2009).[13]

2.2 Italy's Sportsmen and Sportswomen and the Groups at Risk of Doping

According to a 2006 Istat population survey, in Italy there are over 13,780,000 "adults," defined for our purposes as individuals aged 15 or older, who participate regularly or occasionally in one or more sports, corresponding to 27 % of Italy's population of the same age (Istat 2007: 3). Of the nearly 14 million adult sportspeople in Italy, about 3,090,000 take part in official competitions and about 1,600,000 in unofficial competitions, for a total of almost 4,690,000 adult sportspeople (ibid.: 14). Although we do not include them in our market assessment, the Istat data indicate that 3,460,000 Italian youths, ages 3–14, also participate in sports regularly or occasionally, of which 1,590,000 engage competitively, suggesting that the total number of competitive sportsmen, sportswomen, and young people might amount to almost 6,280,000 (ibid.: 3 and 14).[14]

[13] In a WADA Foundation Board meeting, Mathieu Holz, an Interpol officer specialized in anti-doping investigations reported data of the Swedish police, according to which, in 25 % of cases of domestic violence, the husband was on steroids (World Anti-Doping Agency 2010d).

[14] As addressed in Chap. 1, we do not include youths in our calculations for reasons of data consistency and because we do not believe them to be as heavily involved in doping as their adult counterparts; however, we acknowledge that some may be doping already or at high risk of future doping (see DuRant et al. 1994 and the findings of literature review carried out by Backhouse et al. 2007: 47). Note that preadolescent and adolescent Italians, ages 11–14, constitute about 1,480,000 and 780,000 of the total and competitive youth figures, respectively, and would be more likely to engage in doping than children ages 3–10 (Istat 2007: 3 and 14).

In scoping the market for doping products, we regard the 4,690,000 adults who compete in sports as Italy's "athletes." Among them, as noted previously, we distinguish between "elite" athletes, on the one hand, and "recreational" athletes, on the other, even though we are aware of the fact that there is continuity and even two-way flow between the two groups. Consistent with the scientific and nonscientific literature, we regard elite athletes to be at a higher risk of doping than recreational athletes, because elite athletes devote greater time, energy, and personal commitment to sports and typically experience more competitive pressures than do recreational athletes. Within the category of noncompetitive sportsmen and sportswomen—again on the basis of the literature—we single out gym visitors, and specifically body-builders, as groups that are also at high risk of doping.

2.2.1 *Members of Sports Federations, Associated Disciplines, and Enti di Promozione Sportiva*

As of 2008, 4,186,752 people of all ages, here the data do not allow an age-based distinction, were enrolled in at least one of the 45 National Sports Federations (4,002,040) or in one of the 16 Associated Disciplines (184,712) recognized by CONI (2008: 6 and 9). Three team sports—football (27 %), basketball, and volleyball (8 % each)—account for 43 % of this group (ibid.: 10).

In Italy, membership in a sports federation, associated discipline or one of the 15 Enti di Promozione Sportiva (see below) is regarded as the discriminating criterion to distinguish the pool of athletes who (are supposed to) take part in competitions from the mere casual and noncompetitive sportspeople. The Enti are associations intended to promote sports in different social contexts, for example, among university students; some of them were originally linked to a political party or union, although they have now become largely autonomous.[15] The members of these three sets of sporting organizations are also targeted by CONI and CVD for the anti-doping tests. While we have exact data on the athletes enrolled in sports federation and associated disciplines, there are only partial data on the Enti membership—and therefore it is impossible to estimate the entire pool of athletes on the basis of this criterion. In fact, only 8 of the 13 Enti publish the number of their associated athletes or members (see Table 2.3).

Moreover, not all Enti are equally involved in competitions; some speak of members rather than athletes and report only approximate numbers, suggesting that only a minority of their members take part in competitions; the athletes of some associations at least partially overlap with those enrolled in a sports federation

[15] For example, Centro Sportivo Italiano (CSI) was once linked to the Christian Democracy Party and the Italian Bishop Conference (CEI), the Unione Italiana Sport per Tutti (UISP) was originally linked to the Italian Communist Party, and the Unione Sportiva ACLI (US ACLI) was originally linked to the Catholic unions.

Table 2.3 Sportspeople enrolled in the 15 Enti di Promozione Sportiva

	Number of members
Associazione di Cultura, Sport e Tempo Libero (ACSI)	n.a.
Alleanza Sportiva Italiana (ASI)	150,000
Attività Sportive Confederate (ASC)	n.a.
Centro Nazionale Sportivo Libertas (CNS Libertas)	861,567
Centro Sportivo Educativo Nazionale (CSEN)	820,000
Centro Universitario Sportivo Italiano (CUSI)	n.a.
Movimento Sportivo Popolare Italia (MSP Italia)	503,896
Unione Sportiva ACLI (US ACLI)	600,000
Associazione Italiana Cultura Sport (AICS)	n.a.
Centri Sportivi Aziendali Industriali (CSAIN)	n.a.
Centro Sportivo Italiano (CSI)	953,789
Ente Nazionale Democratico di Azione Sociale (ENDAS)	300,000
Polisportive Giovanili Salesiane (PGS)	n.a.
Organizzazione Per l'Educazione allo Sport (OPES)	n.a.
Unione Italiana Sport Per tutti (UISP)	1,250,000
Total	5,439,252

Source: our calculations on the basis of the data retrieved from the Enti Web sites
The data were collected from the following Web sites
Associazione di Cultura Sport e Tempo Libero (ACSI) at http://www.acsi.it/
ASI at http://www.alleanzasportiva.it/web/asi/i-numeri
Attività Sportive Confederate (ASC) at http://www.ascsport.org/
Centro Nazionale Sportivo Libertas (CNS Libertas) at http://www.cnsl-libertas.it/
Centro Sportivo Educativo Nazionale (CSEN) at http://www.csen.it/
Centro Universitario Sportivo Italiano (CUSI) at http://www.cusi.it/home.aspx/
Movimento Sportivo Popolare Italia (MSP Italia) at http://www.mspitalia.it/
US ACLI at http://www.usacli.org/chi-siamo
AICS at http://www.aics.info/
Centri Sportivi Aziendali Industriali (CSAIN) at http://www.csain.it/.
CSI at http://www.csi-net.it/numeri?PHPSESSID=7ca6a107b53b36977d83c26e38d82cc0
Ente Nazionale Democratico di Azione Sociale (ENDAS) at http://www.endas.it/htm/ita/home.html/
Polisportive Giovanili Salesiane (PGS) at http://www.pgsitalia.org/index.asp
Organizzazione Per l'Educazione allo Sport (OPES) at http://www.opesitalia.it/
UISP at http://www.uisp.it/nazionale/index.php?idArea=163&contentId=453

or an associated discipline, and, even in the cases of Enti publishing good data, only an undetermined fraction of their "athletes" really takes part in races. Given all these caveats, knowing as we do that 5,439,252 people are enrolled in Enti is not particularly helpful. We note, however, that if we assumed that only half of the known Enti members (i.e., 2,709,626 people) take part in competitions without being also enrolled in a sports federation or associated discipline and add them to the over four million who are enrolled in a sports federation or associated discipline, we would reach the figure of 6,906,378 — a figure rather close to the 6,280,000 competitive sportsmen, sportswomen, and youths found in the Istat data. [16] Rather than trying to estimate the overall number of athletes through the membership in a sports federation, associated discipline or Ente, we work with the more robust Istat data.

2.2.2 *Elite Athletes*

There are no official data on the number of the elite athletes in Italy and it is difficult to develop an estimate because elite athletes merely represent an upper tier of a much wider pool of would-be or former elite athletes who would like to participate in national or international competitions. The borders between the elite, would-be elite, and former elite are fluid and blurred. Athletes rise or fall in the official ranks and therefore can be included in, or excluded from, national and international competitions; some retire, while others emerge; they may or may not be allowed by their federations to take part in some competitions or may be supplemented by foreign athletes who play for Italian clubs. In the wider pool of elite athletes, we can more easily identify the uppermost or "super" elite, that is, those who participate or have very good chances of participating in international competitions and are therefore most likely to be targeted by CONI's anti-doping tests. While a secretary of the CONI's Scientific Commission, a member of our project team (Donati) was responsible for identifying the—de facto "super"—elite athletes to be targeted by the CONI's anti-doping tests. Relying on the same criteria that were then (and are still) used by CONI (Int-Oth-2), we estimate that the total number of super elite athletes in Italy participating or likely to participate in international competitions is about 10,000 people, most but certainly not all of whom are likely to be "adults" as defined above (see Table 2.4).

Even if the super elite athletes represent only a minute share of the 6.2 million athletes, they are those most under pressure to use doping products. Moreover, they play a crucial role in the market for doping products for at least three other reasons.

---

[16] A different estimation procedure has been suggested by Alfredo Cucciniello, who was for many years the coordinator of all the Enti. According to him, the real number of Enti members is approximately 6,100,000 units, of which 4,100,000 of them effectively engage in sports. About 40 % (i.e., 1,640,000) of the actively engaged group is also associated with a sports federation or associated discipline and therefore need to be excluded from the calculation because otherwise we would count them twice. The remaining 60 % (i.e., 2,460,000 athletes) is only associated with an Ente. According to Cucciniello, about 10 % of the sports federation members rarely takes part in competitions or stops taking part in them during a given year. Therefore, only 3,750,000 out of the 4,186,752 sportspeople officially enrolled in a sports federation or associated discipline effectively take part in competition. By adding the former figure to the 2,460,000 Enti athletes, we reach an estimate of 6,210,000 athletes, which is very close to the 6,280,000 athletes aged 3 and older estimated by Istat.

Table 2.4 Estimate of the "super" elite athletes active in Italy: 2011–2012

Members of the male football teams playing in the first and second leagues (Serie A and B) and the members of the female football teams playing in the first league	1,800
Members of the first- and second-league male and female volleyball teams	1,600
Members of the first- and second-league male basketball teams and members of the first-league female basketball teams	1,400
Members of the first-league male and female water polo teams	600
Members of the first-league male and female hockey teams	600
Members of the first-league rugby male teams	400
10–15 best male and female athletes playing individual sports and specifically:	0
Cycling (including professionals and under 23 athletes)	600
Swimming	500
Track and field	500
Winter sports	400
Rowing	200
Canoe/kayak	200
Ice skating	100
Weightlifting	100
Combat sports	
Other sports	1,000
Total	10,200

Source: our own estimates based on Donati's personal experience (the estimate of super elite athletes corresponds to the number of athletes considered eligible by CONI for its anti-doping tests. It is an approximate estimate, as CONI controls are sometimes extended to minor leagues or to teams and athletes ranked after the first 15)

1. With their illegal behavior, even if it is only suspected or if it is not consistently sanctioned by either sports law bodies or criminal justice agencies, they constitute negative role models for the millions of other elite, would-be elite, and recreational athletes and occasional sportspeople. Almost paradoxically, the doping super elite athletes who are left unscathed may be particularly harmful, because their experience suggests that great sports successes can be achieved by cheating and with impunity.
2. Super elite athletes significantly contribute to the economic "success" of some suppliers of doping products, in particular, a few prominent physicians and pharmacists. As some NAS investigations show, these suppliers build up a "reputation" by treating famous super elite athletes and then "monetize" this reputation, by selling their services or drugs to a larger number of lower-level sportsmen and sportswomen (NAS Firenze 2005; Int-Pro-4). An ongoing investigation focuses on a famous sports physician, who has been linked since the late 1990s to several champions of different sports disciplines and who more recently also "treated" a wide clientele of recreational athletes (Int-Pro-6).
3. Several super elite athletes have gone on to become coaches or officials of sporting organizations and, therefore, if they were able to enhance their performances

with doping products and avoid harm or detection, they are likely to socialize future generations of promising athletes to such illegal practices, thus perpetuating a vicious circle.[17]

Our sources provide a number of examples of known super elite athletes who failed drug tests or were involved in anti-doping criminal investigations during their active sports careers and later became coaches or sports body officials. Manuela Di Centa, a cross-country skier who won several Olympic medals, for example, was 1 of the 33 professional athletes explicitly mentioned in the 2005 verdict of the Tribunale di Ferrara and indicated to have been treated with EPO by Conconi and his staff (see also Capodacqua 2003). Like the other 32 athletes, Di Centa was not charged with doping because the facts addressed in the Conconi proceeding antedated the adoption of Italy's anti-doping law. Despite proof of what would have been illegal doping practices under current standards, Di Centa became CONI Vice President and a member of the IOC (Moresco 2005a, b). The case of the football player and manager, Josep Guardiola, is even more recent. In 2001, Guardiola tested positively twice to nandrolone, while he was playing for Brescia football team (Capodacqua 2002a). Consequently, he was suspended by the Italian Football Federation (FIGC) and convicted by a first-degree court in Brescia. After retiring as a player, Guardiola became the team manager of Barcelona FC, leading the team to win the Spanish League, Spanish Cup, and Champion League in his first season and numerous other prestigious trophies afterwards.[18] Seven years after the positive tests, in 2009 Guardiola was able to question the procedure used by the Rome Anti-Doping Laboratory in analyzing his samples and to obtain the reversal of the verdicts issued by the FIGC and the Brescia first-degree court (Int-NAS-9). In early 2012 Guardiola received the FIFA World Coach of the Year for Men's Football award.

Last but not least, many super elite athletes—with the exception of 2 or 3,000 professional athletes in football, basketball, volleyball, and cycling—are dependent on government funding for their sports careers. Therefore, the athletes themselves, their coaches, and the officials of sports federations are under a particular obligation to make sure that taxpayers' money is not spent on doping practices that violate the laws of the funding government.

The super elite athletes represent only the very topmost segment of a much wider pool of elite athletes who take part in national competitions. These include, for

[17] In 2011 the UCI Management Committee approved the introduction of a new article in the regulations aiming to prevent anyone found guilty of an anti-doping violation during his cycling career from obtaining a license authorizing him to take on a role in cycling as a member of a team's staff. However, the measure is not applied retroactively. Therefore, the new rule does not affect numerous current managers, such as Bjarne Riis, who admitted to doping during his active sporting career, including 1996 Tour de France victory, and now runs an elite cycling team (The Telegraph 2011 and Velonews.com 2011).

[18] For details, see http://www.fcbarcelona.com/football/first-team/staff/coaches/guardiola/biography.

example, in football, the players of Serie C (Italy's third league) and the first and second category and in other sports such as track and field or swimming, elite athletes of different age groups who take part in national competitions but are excluded for different reasons from the international ones. Among them, there are the best athletes of the younger age groups who still take place in lower-level (national) competitions than the adult elite athletes but are considered promising as well as older athletes who have passed their best performing age or started late their sporting activities but still want to, and can, compete at a national level.[19] The ratio between super elite and other elite athletes may be 1:30 or 1:50, but, having no means of precisely estimating the overall number of elite athletes, we cannot precisely establish the ratio between them.

It is important to stress, though, that many non-super elite athletes as well as the even broader range of would-be elite athletes train all day, every day, and devote a considerable amount of energy and personal commitment to sports. Thus, they should also be considered at high risk of doping.

2.2.3 Recreational Athletes

Even if we have no means to precisely estimate the number of elite athletes, there is no doubt that recreational athletes constitute the bulk of the almost 6,280,000 athletes of all ages and the 4,690,000 adult athletes that we identified earlier (Istat 2007: 3, 14). With the exception of the would-be elite athletes among them, most recreational athletes are less committed to sports than elite athletes and are therefore less at risk of doping. However, given their sheer numbers, they are likely to constitute a very large share of the demand for doping products.

Despite the lack of reliable longitudinal data, we hypothesize, on the basis of the scientific literature (see Chap. 1) and a few NAS investigations, most notably "Oil for Drug" (NAS Firenze 2005), that the recreational athletes' demand for doping products has grown steadily from very low levels since the 1970s as a consequence of the broader range of drugs and changes in sports and society. In turn, this growth has led to a significant expansion of the market for doping products and, therefore, also an increase in the recreational athletes' market share. Probably until 2000, the demand for doping products largely consisted of two separate segments: elite and would-be elite athletes, on the one hand, and body-builders, on the other. The sports successes of elite athletes suspected of or proven to be using prohibited performance-enhancing products and even the scandals and police investigations involving some of them, such as Pantani, have fostered the demand for and consumption of doping products

[19] For example, the Italian Athletics Federation (FIDAL), which includes the track and field disciplines, recognizes the following categories of competitive athletes and organizes national competitions for each of them: ragazzi (age group 12–13); cadetti (age group 14–15); allievi (age group 16–17), juniores (age group 18–19), promesse (age group 20–22), seniors (23 and older), amatori (age group 23–34), and masters (35 and older; see FIDAL 2012).

also among the masses of recreational athletes. As we will describe in more detail in Chap. 3, the investigation "Oil for Drug" (NAS Firenze 2005) and the investigations concerning Dr. Michele Ferrari (Tribunale di Bologna 2004; Int-Pro-4; MacMichael 2011a, b; U.S. Anti-Doping Agency 2012c) document that several physicians have built up a "doping" reputation by treating a few super elite and elite athletes but then gone on to make the bulk of their earnings by selling their services to a much larger number of unknown recreational athletes.

2.2.4 *Body-Builders*

In addition to elite athletes, the other group of sportsmen and sportswomen most at risk of doping practices are body-builders, as is well known from the literature (see Chap. 1). In Italy, there are no official figures concerning this group of sportspeople who usually attend gyms and, with few exceptions, do not belong to an official sports federation recognized by CONI or take part in competitions. In order to estimate its dimensions, we can rely on the results of a survey of the gyms of the regions Apulia, Emilia Romagna, Latium, Trentino Alto Adige, and Veneto, which was conducted in 2007 by the Ministries of Sports and Social Solidarity. The two ministries collected data from the Camera di Commercio (Chamber of Commerce), Confartigianato, and three main Enti di Promozione Sportiva (CSI, ACLI, e UISP). (Many gyms are enrolled in an Ente in order to obtain a more favorable tax regime.) The study identified about 1,350 gyms with at least one room fully devoted to body-building equipment or machines and estimated the number of sportsmen and sportswomen attending these gyms as approximately 423,000 people (Ministero dello Sport and Ministero della Solidarietà Sociale 2008). As the five above-mentioned regions account for about 33 % of the Italian population,[20] we can estimate that there are 4,050 gyms with at least one room for body-building machines in the whole of Italy serving almost 1,270,000 potential body-builders. We refer to them as "potential" body-builders, because some or even many individuals may frequent gyms with rooms dedicated to body-building machines or equipment without being, themselves, body-builders. In this subset of gym patrons, there are also a considerable number of athletes especially those, such as weightlifters, discus and hammer throwers, and rugby players who visit gyms to increase their muscle mass and strengths. In other words, despite the formal separateness between athletes and body-builders, gyms often become a meeting point for different groups at high risk of doping who exchange advice on training methods, diets and, last but not least, doping products. They are also a venue where athletes and body-builders meet other sportspeople

[20] In total, 20,226,933 out of 60,626,442 residents in Italy. See http://www.comuni-italiani.it/regioni.html.

and the former two groups may become a model or a source of advice on doping and other matters for the latter.

2.3 The Results of Anti-doping Tests

Italy's Anti-Doping Commission (CVD) and the Italian National Olympic Committee (CONI) are jointly responsible for conducting anti-doping tests in Italy, with CONI effectively sharing its competence with the Italian sports federations and, at least in principle, with the WADA and the international sports federations.[21] An agreement signed in October 2007 by the then Minister of Health, the Minister of Youth Policies and Sports, and the CONI President formalized an official division of labor that had taken shape since CVD's establishment in 2000. In the cited agreement, the three parties "agreed … to regard the national and international competitive sports activities as the prevalent object of CONI's anti-doping activities." At the same time, the agreement restricted CVD's competencies to recreational athletes. The parties to the agreement also "agree[d] to consider the non-competitive activities and the competitive activities having no national relevance as the prevalent object of the anti-doping activities of the Commission" (Ministero della Salute 2007). According to some observers, including Bellotti (2009) the former head of the CONI Scientific Commission and a former member of the CVD, the 2007 agreement overrules the Italian anti-doping law, Act 376/2000 (see Chap. 7). Neither authority routinely tests youths, although, given cause, one or the other may do so in a specific case (Int-Oth-2).

2.3.1 CONI's Tests of Elite Athletes

As formalized in the 2007 agreement, CONI and the national sports federations target only elite athletes with their anti-doping tests. CONI oversees the data collection on all such tests carried out in Italy but has not published the data for 2006 and since 2008 (see Comitato Olimpico Nazionale Italiano 2012).[22] As shown in Table 2.5, CONI and the national sports federations carried out an average of about 9,400 anti-doping tests over the past 5 years for which data are available (2002–2005

[21] Due to funding constraints, WADA tests, on average, only seven or eight athletes per day all over the world and therefore the chance that an Italian elite athlete is targeted by a WADA control is very small. As a rule, international sports federations carry out most testing during the most important sports competitions, such as World Championships (Int-Oth-2).

[22] The Rome Anti-Doping Laboratory, which carries out the tests on behalf of both CONI and CVD, does submit the results of its tests to WADA, which then publishes them in an annual report (e.g., World Anti-Doping Agency 2011a). However, these data are not helpful to determine the number of positive results in CONI's tests because WADA merely reports "analytical adverse findings" and, as WADA itself notes (2011a: 1), these "may not be identical to sanctioned cases, as the figures … may contain findings that underwent the Therapeutic Use Exemption (TUE) approval process."

Table 2.5 Anti-doping tests carried out in Italy by CONI and the National Sports Federations: years 2002–2005 and 2007

	2002[a]	2003	2004	2005	2007	Average
Total tests	7,823	9,431	9,950	8,791	11,154	9,430
Positive results	48	62	65	52	69	59
Percent of positive results on total tests	0.61	0.66	0.65	0.59	0.62	0.63

Source: our calculations on CONI (2012) (for further details, see http://www.coni.it/index.php?dati_statistici)
[a]Tests analyzed, not carried out

and 2006), thus potentially reaching many or most of the elite athletes in Italy at least once each year.[23] However, the rate of positive test results is only about 0.63 % on average with very little variation after 2002. On average, about 59 elite athletes fail a drug test each year.

Among the elite athletes that have tested positive, some are well known in Italian sports. To give just an example, ten professional football players in addition to Guardiola—including Edgar Davids, who was then a Juventus midfield; Fernando Couto, then a Lazio stopper; Francois Gillet, gatekeeper at Bari; and several other less known players—tested positive to nandrolone in 2001, the year in which the official anti-doping laboratory in Rome started to operate again after the 3-month suspension resulting from the scandal mentioned in the introduction (La Repubblica 2002). These players were suspended by the Italian football authorities (The Telegraph 2001). At least Davids, Couto, and Gillet were also convicted by a regular court for the offense of doping foreseen by article 9 of Act. 376/2000 (La Repubblica 2005).

Judging by CONI's positive tests, one might conclude that the problem of doping hardly exists in Italy. CONI's data can be complemented with results of the anti-doping criminal investigations carried out by NAS and other police forces. With few exceptions, the elite athletes involved in these investigations did not test positive for doping products. At least 100 different riders, for example, have been involved collectively over the years in some of the largest anti-doping investigations, such as the proceeding against Prof. Conconi (20 or more riders; see Tribunale di Ferrara 2003), the "Campioni senza valore" proceeding run by the Bologna Prosecutor's Office (another 20 or more riders; Tribunale di Bologna 2000), the so-called "Oil for drug" case coordinated by the Rome Prosecutor's Office (another 30 or more riders; NAS Firenze 2005), and the recent investigation in Mantua concerning a local pharmacist (another 40 or more riders; see NAS Brescia 2011 and Pacifici and Donati 2011), with several others implicated in smaller cases (e.g., NAS Firenze 2002). At least 50 other elite athletes of different disciplines have also been suspected of illegal doping practices in the investigations conducted by NAS.

The abuse of legitimate drugs and the extensive use of doping substances were also documented by the charges pressed by Dr. Guariniello from the Turin Prosecutor's Office against Antonio Giraudo and Dr. Riccardo Agricola, respectively the manager and the chief sports physician of the Juventus football club. According

[23] See http://www.coni.it/index.php?dati_statistici.

to Guariniello, "the drugs seized from the Juventus' inventory would have been sufficient to supply an entire town" (Hartmann 2003). The prosecutor's charges were confirmed by a 2007 verdict of the Corte Suprema di Cassazione (2007; see also Travaglio, 2007 and chapter 3). No negative consequences were drawn from this verdict by the Italian sports authorities. However, if the Juventus team manager and chief physician were found guilty by the Court of Cassation of sporting fraud for purchasing and administering illegal performance-enhancing substances, such as corticosteroids, the logical implication of the Corte di Cassazione's verdict is that some if not all the Juventus players were administered illegal performance-enhancing substances. Moreover, the Corte di Cassazione (2007) concluded that the two defendants committed the same offense of sporting fraud when they administered legal drugs not included in the list of banned performance-enhancing substances, if these are used off-label, i.e., for purposes different than those officially foreseen. These practices seem to be widespread in the elite football world, as reported by the judge who wrote the first-degree verdict in the Juventus case: "up to the end of the trial the defense lawyer repeatedly argued that Agricola's behaviors were enormously widespread in the sports world and that in practice all physicians of professional football teams behaved in the same way" (Tribunale di Torino, 2004: 46).

Rather than reflecting the above-average "cleanness" of Italian elite athletes, the low percentage of positive samples in CONI's anti-doping tests might testify to the difficulty of detecting doping substances and methods in urine samples, the testing method used almost exclusively. CONI's rate of positive tests or "detection" is further hampered by fact that CONI conducts few out-of-competition, hence, genuinely surprise, tests (Int-Oth-1). Already in 2002, the Council of Europe team that evaluated Italian anti-doping policies came to the conclusion that "the proportion of out-of-competition controls provided for by the [1989 Council of Europe] Convention … as being the most effective appears rather low. Moreover, advance warning of these controls seems in actual fact to be quite lengthy (at least 24 h), which means that they cannot be regarded as unannounced controls within the meaning of the Convention" (Evaluation Team 2002: 34). Judging on the basis of the data available and the opinion of some respondents with detailed knowledge of these issues (Int-Oth-2 and Int-NAS-26), we conclude that the problems noted by the Council of Europe evaluation team in 2002 do not yet seem to have been solved.

2.3.2 CVD's Tests of Recreational Athletes

Although the recreational athletes overseen by CVD might be expected to have less interest in taking performance-enhancing drugs than the elite athletes targeted by CONI, CVD has been considerably more effective than CONI with its doping tests.

Table 2.6 Anti-doping tests carried out in Italy by CVD: years 2003–2011

	2003	2004	2005	2006	2007	2008	2009	2010	2011	Simple average, 2003–2011	Simple average, 2008–2011
Total tests	740	1,556	1,875	1,511	1,607	955	1,328	1,115	1,676	1,303	1,374
No. substances detected	n.a.	n.a.	n.a.	40	52	n.a.	52	97	80	n.a.	76.3[a]
Positive results	20	42	37	37	46	39	42	53	52	40.9	46.5
Percent of positive results on total tests	2.7	2.7	2.0	2.4	2.9	4.1	3.2	4.8	3.1	3.4	3.8

Source: our calculations on Ministero del Lavoro, della Salute e delle Politiche Sociali (2009), Ministero della Salute (2010a, 2011b), and Ministero della Salute and Istituto Superiore di Sanità (2012: 11)

[a]Average 2007–2011

CVD has been considerably more effective than CONI with its doping tests.[24] CVD has been testing recreational athletes since 2003 and, as shown in Table 2.6, between 2003 and 2011, CVD carried out on average 1,365 tests each year, about one seventh of the tests conducted yearly by CONI. With 3.4 % positive tests on average, CVD has a five-time higher positive rate than CONI. Moreover, since 2008 the effectiveness of CVD's tests has considerably improved, with 3.8 % positive tests on average, six times higher than CONI's average rate. In 2 recent years, 2008 and 2010, the rate of positive tests exceeded 4 % (with a record 4.8 % in 2010), but the number of tests was below average (there were 26 % less tests in 2010 than in 2006).

A lack of financial means constrains CVD's, more so than CONI's, ability to conduct tests out of competition. However, given that more than four million people within CVD's jurisdiction and the seemingly countless numbers of recreational sports competitions, CVD's tests represent in most cases a surprise for the selected athletes. A crucial factor in improving the CVD's testing performance was also the fact that for the period 2009–2010 its tests were coordinated by Dr. Pasquale Bellotti, a sports physician and sports teacher and former head of the CONI Scientific Commission, who has an in-depth knowledge of different disciplines and training methods and who could therefore more effectively select the dates and events to control (see Chap. 6). Throughout the years, many more male athletes have tested positive than their female counterparts: in 2011, for example, the rates were 84.6 % versus 15.4 %, and the ratio is not significantly different in the previous years (Ministero della Salute and Istituto Superiore di Sanità 2012: 11). Older athletes tend also to dope more frequently than younger ones. As shown in Table 2.7, the age classes older than 30 consistently record

[24]The CVD's controls are representatives for geographic areas and sports disciplines, considering also the number of sportsmen and sportswomen practicing the different disciplines (Ministero della Salute 2011b; see also Bellotti 2009).

Table 2.7 Percent of athletes testing positive by age on the total of tested athletes: 2008–2011

	2008 (%)	2009 (%)	2010 (%)	2011 (%)
<19	0.0	0.9	0.4	1.2
19–24	3.1	3.7	2.1	1.1
24–29	3.3	2.5	5.0	4.8
29–34	6.8	4.3	6.9	2.1
34–39	5.7	3.0	8.0	3.2
39–44	8.2	2.7	6.7	3.9
>44	13.2	5.2	7.1	7.7
Total	4.1	3.2	4.8	3.1

Source: Ministero della Salute and Istituto Superiore di Sanità (2012)

higher rates of positive tests than the younger age classes and, in 3 out of the 4-year period 2008–2011, the category of over 44-year-olds registered the highest positive rates (Ministero della Salute and Istituto Superiore di Sanità 2012: 13).

Excluding the sports federations, associated disciplines, and Enti, in which only a few controls were carried out, the highest rates of positive athletes were found in natural body-building (12.8 %),[25] followed by weightlifting (7.6 %), motorcycling (6.2 %), and ex aequo cycling and sailing (5.9 %). Other sports with above-average rates were also rugby (5.1 %), golf (5.0 %), boxing (4.9 %), and squash (4.6 %; Ministero della Salute and Istituto Superiore di Sanità 2012: 15).

The substances identified in the CVD's anti-doping tests from 2003 to 2011 are listed, in percent values, in Table 2.8. In assessing the table it needs to be taken into account that, as the tests are exclusively conducted during competitions, they tend to over-assess the use of stimulants and diuretic agents, while they provide only a limited view of the use of anabolic steroids, which are commonly used in training. Moreover, as the CVD's (and CONI's) tests only involve urine samples, they cannot detect a wide range of peptide hormones. In particular, urine tests cannot detect GH, unless this drug has been taken a few hours before the test—which obviously athletes hardly ever do.

Analyzing the time series of CVD's positive samples with these caveats in mind, we observe, nonetheless, considerable changes in the relevance of different substances. Between 2003 and 2004 and 2010–2011,[26] the share of samples in which stimulants have been detected has decreased 14.7 % points, from 30.5 % in the earlier period to 15.8 % in the later period. The share of samples containing traces of cannabis has also decreased considerably: whereas cannabis was found in 26.7 % of all samples in 2003–2004, it was found in only 12.4 % in 2010–2011. On the contrary, no peptides or other hormones were detected in 2003–2004, whereas they

[25] The Natural Body-Building Federation is a small federation of recreational body-builders, which is not recognized by CONI but is part of an Ente, the ASI (Alleanza Sportiva Italiana, ASI; see Ministero della Salute and Istituto Superiore di Sanità 2012: 30).

[26] As the percent of positive results by substance in anti-doping tests are partially due to several not fully predictable factors, we have considered the average value of the first 2 years and the last 2 years of the overall time span under consideration in calculating the differences.

Table 2.8 Doping substances ascertained in CVD's anti-doping tests in percent values: years 2003–2011

Substances	2003	2004	2005	2006	2007	2008	2009	2010	2011	Average 2003–2011	Averages 2003/2004 (1)	Averages 2010–2011 (2)	Differences (1)–(2)
Anabolic agents	20.0	10.4	6.4	7.5	5.8	25.4	7.7	37.1	20	15.6	15.2	28.6	13.4
Peptide hormones, growth factors and related substances[a]	0.0	0.0	2.1	5.0	5.8	25.4	7.7	10.3	3.8	6.7	0.0	7.1	7.1
Beta 2-agonists	4.0	4.2	2.1	7.5	5.8	4.0	5.8	6.2	5	5.0	4.1	5.6	1.5
Hormones and metabolic modulators	0.0	0.0	0	2.5	0.0	0.0	0.0	0.0	0.0	0.3	0.0	0.0	0.0
Diuretics and other masking agents	16.0	16.7	19.1	20.0	17.3	3.4	15.4	12.4	25	16.1	16.4	18.7	–2.3
Stimulants	36.0	25.0	19.2	12.5	17.3	16.4	23.1	10.3	21.3	20.1	30.5	15.8	–14.7
Narcotics	4.0	0.0	0	0.0	0.0	0.0	3.8	2.1	0.0	1.1	2.0	1.1	–1.0
Cannabinoids	16.0	37.4	42.6	32.5	42.3	16.9	28.8	7.2	17.5	26.8	26.7	12.4	–14.4
Glucocorticosteroids	0.0	4.2	6.4	10.0	3.8	8.5	5.8	14.4	12.5	7.3	2.1	13.5	11.4
Beta-blockers	4.0	2.1	2.1	2.5	1.9	0.0	1.9	0	0.0	1.6	3.1	0.0	–3.1

Source: our calculations based on Ministero del Lavoro, della Salute e delle Politiche Sociali (2009), Ministero della Salute (2010a, 2011), and Ministero della Salute and Istituto Superiore di Sanità (2012: 11)

Note: totals may not match sums because of rounding

[a]GH and other growth factors are not included as they hardly can be detected and were indeed never detected so far in the urine tests ordered by CVD

were found in 7.1 % of all samples in 2010–2011, and the shares of anabolic steroids and glucocorticosteroids also increased considerably, by 13.4 % and 11.4 %, respectively.

CVD's data also clearly document the medicalization of sports (see Harth et al. 2008; Waddington and Smith 2009). In fact, the athletes selected for CVD's testing are also asked to fill in a questionnaire about the legal drugs (including homeopathic products) and health products (vitamins, mineral salts, amino acids, creatine, and other dietary supplements) they have taken in the 15 days before the test. In 2011, out of 1,676 athletes tested, 64.9 % admitted using at least one of the above-mentioned products and out of these, 36.9 % declared using three or more products. The most frequent class of products used are anti-inflammatory drugs, which amount to 26.2 % of all the declared products and to 42.6 % of all drugs taken (Ministero della Salute and Istituto Superiore di Sanità 2012: 29–31). Similar rates were also recorded in the previous years (Ministero della Salute 2011a).

2.4 Estimates of the Users of Doping Products

To estimate the demand for doping products in Italy, we can use several datasets, none of which, however, provides a full or unbiased picture.

2.4.1 IPSAD Data on the Use of Steroids in the Adult Population

There is only one partial estimate concerning the whole Italian population and this relates exclusively to the consumption of anabolic steroids. In 2007, the lifelong, past-year, and past-month prevalence of anabolic steroid use were collected in a sample of 85,000 respondents of the Italian population aged 15–64 by researchers of the Consiglio Nazionale delle Ricerche (National Research Council, known under the acronym of CNR) through the Italian Population Survey on Alcohol and other Drugs (IPSAD).[27] Almost 1 % of the sample admitted using anabolic steroids at least once in their lives; 0.30 % of the sample reported having used steroids in the 12 months preceding the interview, and 0.23 % of the sample reported the use of steroids in the past 30 days (Dipartimento Politiche Antidroga 2012a; see Table 2.9).[28] If the sample was representative of all Italians aged 15–64, then those

[27] The survey was repeated in 2010 but the questions concerning steroids were not asked (Dipartimento Politiche Antidroga 2012b).

[28] These rates are roughly comparable with those recorded in other countries. A nationwide population survey conducted in 2008 in Sweden found a 0.9 % lifetime steroid prevalence among men aged 15–54, thus lower than the almost 1.0 % found in Italy for both sexes (Swedish National Institute of Public Health 2010: 21). However, population surveys carried out five times since 1997 in the Netherlands have found lifetime prevalence rates between 0.7 and 2.7 % for a variety of performance-enhancing drugs (Anti Doping et al. 2012: 14–15). Although these drugs are broadly defined in the Dutch surveys as to include all the most frequent doping substances as well as cocaine and amphetamines, steroids are likely to be an important component of them.

Table 2.9 The lifelong, past-year, and past-month prevalence of anabolic steroid use in the Italian population aged 15–64: year 2007

	Rate (%)	Total population aged 15–64	Estimated users
Lifetime	0.995	39,306,261	391,054
Past year	0.300	39,306,261	117,907
Past month	0.225	39,306,261	88,436

Source: author's calculations from unpublished data provided bythe Dipartimento Politiche Antidroga (2012a), based on the 2007 IPSAD survey

Table 2.10 Estimated number of users of doping substances among athletes

Year	Number of athletes	Users of doping substances
2010	4,685,257	222,707
2011	4,685,257	145,243
Average	4,685,257	183,975

Source: our calculations on the basis of Istat data, as reported in Istat (2007), Ministero della Salute (2011a, b), and Ministero della Salute and Istituto Superiore di Sanità (2012)
Note: we do not have separate estimates for the total number of athletes for 2010 and 2011

percentages would implicate a total of 391,054 such Italians as lifetime users; 117,907 such Italians as past-year users; and 88,436 such Italians as past-month users. Given the well-known biases of these surveys (e.g., Zhao et al. 2009), which usually have low response rates and are administered at home in condition of limited anonymity, the forgoing figures can be considered low-end estimates of the numbers of users. The researchers in charge of the IPSAD survey explicitly speak of a "systematic effect of underestimation of the phenomenon" (Ministero della Solidarietà Sociale 2006: 55), albeit with reference to the 2005 IPSAD survey that did not contain questions on steroids.[29]

2.4.2 *Estimates of Doping Athletes*

Another route for estimating the use of performance-enhancing drugs is to apply the rates for positive test results recorded by CDV in recent years, such as 2010 and 2011, to the approximately 4,690,000 adult athletes in Italy. This might also be treated as a low-end estimate of the users because positive results in anti-doping tests, even if they are as high as those of the CVD, unavoidably under-assess the true extent of doping, not least because many current doping products cannot be detected by the tests (see Chap. 1). As shown in Table 2.10, with this method, we find that the

[29] This under-assessment is confirmed by the comparison between the IPSAD data, for the 15–19-age group, and the data collected with the EPSAD survey. The latter exclusively targets 15- to 19-year-old students but has a very high response rate, because it is administered in class (for details, see Donati 2005).

Table 2.11 Number of substances detected in CVD's controls in 2010 and 2011 and estimated numbers of users of doping products, by substance

Substances detected	Cases in 2010	Cases in 2011	Total number of cases	Users of doping substances based on 2010–2011 data
Anabolic agents	36	16	52	87,292
Peptide hormones (growth factors) and related substances,[a] of which	10	3	13	21,823
EPO	4	4	5	8,392
Chorionic gonadotrophin	6	2	8	13,431
Beta-2 agonists	6	4	10	16,787
Hormones and metabolic modulators	0	0	0	0
Diuretics and other masking agents	12	20	32	53,718
Stimulants, of which	10	13	23	38,610
Cocaine	3	4	7	11,751
Narcotics	2		2	3,357
Cannabinoids	7	14	21	35,253
Glucocorticosteroids	14	10	24	40,289
Beta-blockers	0	0	0	0
Total substances/users	97	80	177	297,130

Source: our calculations on the basis of Ministero della salute (2011a, b) and Ministero della Salute and Istituto Superiore di Sanità (2012)

[a]GH and other growth factors are not included as they were never detected in the urine tests ordered by CVD

number of users of doping products for the most recent 2 years, i.e., 2010 and 2011, would average about 184,000 persons.

On the basis of CVD's data, we can also estimate the number of users of the different substances. By simply considering the number of substances detected on average in the 2,791 tests carried out in 2010 and 2011, we reached the following estimates (see Table 2.11): there are about 87,300 users of anabolic agents among elite and recreational athletes. Reflecting the location of CVD's tests (i.e., in competition), the second largest group of users consists of those using diuretics and other masking agents (53,700), followed by about 45,325 using stimulants and 40,300 athletes using corticosteroids. With an estimated number of 35,253, users of cannabis represent the fourth largest group, followed by 21,800 users of peptide hormones and related substances (13,431 users of chorionic gonadotrophin and 8,392 users of EPO)[30] and 16,800 users of beta-2 agonists.

The sum of the estimated number of users of the different categories of substances is higher than the total number of users, as many athletes use more than one prohibited substance at a time (for example, they use a diuretic just before the competition, to mask the use of a performance-enhancing substance). As a matter of fact, CVD often detects more than one substance per sample. In 2010, for example, 19 athletes out of 52 tested positive for more than one substance: in particular, 11 tested positive for two substances, four athletes for three, three for four, and three other athletes

[30] As mentioned earlier, GH and other growth factors, which also belong to this class of substances, cannot be detected in tests, unless they were taken a few hours before the tests.

Table 2.12 Number of substances detected in samples taken during CVD's anti-doping controls: 2010–2011

	Positive athletes in 2010	Positive athletes in 2011
Number of substances	No. (%)	No. (%)
1	32 (60.4)	33 (63.5)
2	11 (20.7)	16 (30.8)
3	4 (7.6)	1 (1.9)
4	3 (5.6)	0 (0.0)
5	1 (1.9)	0 (0.0)
6	1 (1.9)	2 (3.8)
8	1 (1.9)	0 (0.0)
Total	53 (100.0)	52 (100.0)

Source: Ministero della Salute (2011b) and Ministero della Salute and Istituto Superiore di Sanità (2012)

tested positive for five, six, and even eight substances, respectively (Ministero della Salute 2011b: 30; see Table 2.12).

Although cannabis and cocaine are on the WADA's Prohibited List (2012b), we do not regard them as part of the market for doping products for both substantive and practical reasons. Substantively, it is not always clear if the athletes testing positive to cannabis and cocaine used them for performance-enhancing or for recreational purposes. Moreover, these two illegal drugs are probably smuggled and distributed in Italy through separate channels than those supplying the doping market, despite the occasional, but growing, overlap between the doping and illegal drug markets (e.g., Paoli 2000). Practically speaking, we have no matching information for these drugs on the supply side, as the NAS investigations do not target them. For 2011, it is possible to separate those who exclusively used cannabis and cocaine from the rest, as exact data are provided about the combinations of the active ingredients found. In particular, we know that 13 users exclusively tested positive for THC, the active ingredient of cannabis, one for cocaine alone and a further person for cocaine and THC (Ministero della Salute and Istituto Superiore di Sanità (2012: 10). If we subtract these 15 cases from the 52 athletes who tested positive to tests in 2011, we are left with a positive rate of 2.3 % and therefore with 103,000 users of doping substances other than cannabis or cocaine (see Table 2.13). We do not have such detailed data for 2010, and therefore we have resorted to an alternative procedure. As shown in Tables 2.6 and 2.10, CVD detected in 2010 cannabinoids seven times and cocaine three times out of a total of 97 substances detected in 53 positive tests (Ministero della Salute 2011b: 30–32). Through use of a simple rule of proportionality (i.e., 10:97=x:53), we calculate that almost 5.5 of the positive tests pertained to either cannabis or cocaine. Subtracting them from the total of 53, we reach a rate of 4.26 % positive test results, excluding cocaine and cannabis, and therefore arrive at an estimate of 199,592 athletes using doping substances other than cannabis or cocaine.[31] Making an average between the 2010 and 2011 estimates, we identify about 150,000 users of doping products other than cannabis or cocaine.

[31] In both cases, we have assumed a one-to-one correspondence between the number of tests and athletes. With over 4.6 million recreational athletes, the chances of being tested twice are extremely low.

Table 2.13 Estimated number of users of doping substances among athletes, including and excluding cocaine and cannabis: 2010–2011

Year	Number of athletes	Users of doping substances	Percent of positive results on total tests w/o cannabis and cocaine	Users of doping substances other than cannabis and cocaine
2010	4,685,257	222,707	4.3	199,592
2011	4,685,257	145,243	2.2	103,076
Simple average	4,685,257	183,975	–	151,334

Source: our calculations on the basis of Istat data, as reported in Istat (2007), Ministero della Salute (2011b), and Ministero della Salute and Istituto Superiore di Sanità (2012)
Note: we do not have separate estimates for the total number of athletes for 2010 and 2011

2.4.3 *Estimates of Doping Body-Builders*

Whereas the above-mentioned estimates also include elite athletes, the first group at substantial risk of doping, they almost entirely exclude the second group, i.e., body-builders. With few exceptions, they do not participate in competitions and, hence, are not, technically speaking, "athletes."

To estimate the number of body-builders that engage in doping, we have combined the data from the survey of gyms carried out in 2007 by the Ministries of Sports and Social Solidarity with the findings of the many NAS investigations that have targeted gyms (e.g., Tribunale di Bologna 2000; Tribunale di Ravenna 2004; Tribunale di Forlì 2009; NAS Bologna 2000; NAS Firenze 2005; Tribunale di Siracusa 2010). These investigations have been conducted in seven different Italian regions (Valle d'Aosta, Piedmont, Trentino Alto Adige, Veneto, Liguria, Emilia Romagna, Toscana, Latium, Campania, Apulia, Sardinia, Sicily) and concluded that at least 130 gyms were involved in the distributions of doping out of the 800 different gyms with body-building equipment screened over about a decade (that is, 16.25 % of the total). Applying this rate to the earlier estimates of 4,050 gyms with at least a room for body-building equipment or machines, one could argue that since the late 1990s nearly 660 such gyms have participated in illegal doping practices. As the 4,050 gyms currently serve about 1,270,000 patrons, we can apply the same 16.25 % rate and further conclude that the gyms involved in doping practices might attract about 206,000 potential body-builders. The above-mentioned judicial investigations also provide circumstantial evidence that approximately one third of these visitors—that is, just under 69,000—use on an occasional or habitual basis doping products, primarily anabolic steroids alone or in combinations with other doping substances (such as stimulants and GH).

Some further supporting evidence for the 69,000 estimate as well as for the range of substances misused emerges from a survey carried out in 2011 in Emilia Romagna among 86 managers of gyms, including those not specialized in body-building. These managers believe that 38 % of their male customers use anabolic steroids, 31 % stimulants, and 21 % growth hormones. They indicate much lower prevalence estimates for female visitors: 26 % are purported to be using anabolic steroids, 14 % stimulants, and 8 % growth hormone (Leone 2010a: 21). The survey coordinator (Leone 2010a: 19) has acknowledged that the managers' perceptions are exaggerated, all the more so that they refer not only to visitors of gyms specialized in body-building but to the visitors of all kinds of gyms. To give an idea of the unrealistic perceptions, it is enough to state that one out of four respondents believes that anabolic steroids are used by more than 60 % of the male athletes visiting the gyms (ibid.). Despite the apparent exaggerations, the managers' perceptions unequivocally confirm that the use of anabolic steroids constitutes a widespread problem in gyms.

Another interesting element emerging from anti-doping investigations concerns the users themselves. Apparently, many users of anabolic steroids attending gyms work in the public or private security sector. Twenty-one police agents, for example, were reported to buy anabolic steroids from other policemen in a recent case handed in by the Tribunale di Torino (2012a; see also Numa 2010). US soldiers located in a military base in Sicily were reported to be users–importers of steroids in an investigation coordinated by the Prosecutor's Office in Siracusa (Tribunale di Siracusa 2010). Two other soldiers, one belonging to the US Army, also emerged from the NAS Investigations Database as buyers and consumers of anabolic steroids. Another criminal case handled at the Tribunale di Forlì documented the sale of anabolic steroids to several "bouncers" working in discos on the Adriatic Coast and in Bologna (Tribunale di Forlì 2009: 20 and 103). An investigation conducted by the Bologna Branch Office also documented the shipment of hundreds of steroids-containing packages to US soldiers in Iraq (Int-NAS-13).

Our respondents at several NAS branch offices (Int-1, 3, 8, 16, 17, 20, 22, and 24) also confirmed the frequent involvement of law enforcement officers and private security guards in their anti-doping investigations. Their widespread perception is that most of these officers and guards purchase anabolic steroids and other drugs solely for their own consumption; a few of them, as we will see in Chap. 3, are also active as traders or suppliers. The spread of anabolic steroids among this group confirms Hoberman's (2012) findings about steroid use among US law enforcement and military personnel and is particularly worrying. In fact, all Italian policemen and many Italian private security guards have access to weapons and are entitled to the use of force while they perform their professional functions. Given the aggressiveness and sudden mood changes stimulated by anabolic steroids, public and private security staff taking these drugs can provoke harm not only to themselves but also to uninvolved victims.

2.4.4 Doping Use in the Rest of the Population

Anti-doping investigations and other sources reveal that doping products are also used occasionally by a small fraction of those who participate in sports without taking part in competitions or visiting a gym with body-building equipment—about 7.8 million people in Italy[32]— and by an even smaller fraction of those who do not

[32] We reached the 7.8 million figure by subtracting the nearly 4.7 million sportsmen and sportswomen taking part in competition and the almost 1.3 million visitors to gyms with body-building equipment (whom we called earlier potential body-builders) from the approximately 13.8 million adults who practice regularly or occasionally one or more sports estimated by the Istat (2007: 5).

engage in any sport. Anti-doping investigations and particularly the "Artificial Body" investigation conducted by the Bologna Branch Office at the turn of the century (NAS Bologna 2000) indicate that these two residual groups of users resort to doping products for a variety of reasons. Performance enhancement is still an important motivation for some recreational sportspersons, even if they do not take part in competitions; weight loss appears to be a frequent reason for consuming stimulants, whereas many users of steroids among both noncompetitive sportspeople and those who do not engage in any sport want to look "healthy" or to speed up the recovery from a trauma. This variety of motives for taking performance- or image-enhancing drugs even by those who do not take part in competitions or are body-builders also emerges from surveys conducted in several countries among fitness center visitors and managers (see Anti Doping Denmark et al. (2012): 19–23) and the growing literature on human enhancement (Savulescu et al. 2011; Evans-Brown et al. 2012; Singler 2012).

A survey carried out among a sample of 952 high-school students in Rome, aged 14- to 19-year-old, sheds some light on doping consumption patterns among recreational sportspersons and people who do not undertake physical exercise, demonstrating that the use of doping products is spread not only among competitive athletes and gym visitors but also these other two groups of consumers (Lucidi et al. 2004).[33] Thirty-one students (3.25 % of the sample) admitted using doping products in the 3 months preceding the survey and 29 declared that they were going to use these same products also in the subsequent 3 months. Interestingly, 13 of them reported using doping products, even if they did not take part in competitions. Of these thirteen, four were gym visitors, seven engaged in sports independently, and two admitted using doping products without participating in any sports. Out of the seven who engaged in sports independently, three took stimulants (other than cocaine), three took steroids, and one took steroids with EPO. The two nonphysically active students both used stimulants.

These limited insights, however, are not sufficient to quantify properly the number of users of different doping products among noncompetitive sportspersons and physically inactive people in Italy. Despite the lack of clear evidence, we hypothesize that the consumption of doping products in the latter two groups has grown in recent years, as a result of the general medicalization of society and the growing emphasis on performance (e.g., Ehrenberg 1991; Gasparini 2004; Hoberman 2005; see Chap. 1). The latter emphasis is also reflected in the rapid expansion of the consumption of cocaine and other illegal stimulants, such as ecstasy, since the early 1990s in Italy and elsewhere (e.g., European Monitoring Centre on Drugs and Drug Addiction 2012)[34]: even though their consumption is mostly unrelated with sports, these stimulants are also doping, i.e., performance-enhancing, drugs.

---

[33] We are grateful to Prof. Caterina Pesce (Rome University, Foro Italico) for giving us the raw survey data, so that we could make our own calculations.

[34] See the trends in past-year prevalence of cocaine use among young adults (aged 15–34) in numerous European countries published by the European Monitoring Centre for Drugs and Drug Addiction on its Web site: http://www.emcdda.europa.eu/stats11/gpsfig14b.

Table 2.14 Estimated number of users of doping products in Italy

Among	Users of doping products	Percent of total	Users of doping products excluding cannabis and cocaine	Percent of total
Athletes	185,000	73	150,000	69
Body-builders	68,700	27	68,700	31
Total	253,700	100	218,700	100

Source: our calculations on the basis of the data presented earlier
Note: totals may not match sums because of rounding

As noted earlier, successful super elite athletes, who have tested positive to doping products or have been suspected of taking such products but have never been caught, also constitute powerful negative models.

2.4.5 Concluding Estimates

Table 2.14 summarizes our estimates of the number of users of doping products in Italy. If we consider all substances included in the WADA Prohibited List, we estimate 253,700 users of doping products in Italy. If we exclude cannabis and cocaine, we reach the lower estimate of 218,700 users. This estimate supports that doping is not limited to elite athletes and poses a serious threat to greater public health.

Even the lower figure of 218,700 users is comparable to the number of heroin misusers estimated in Italy for 2010: 218,425 people were estimated to need an opiate detox or substitution treatment based on a prevalence rate of 5.5 per thousand among residents aged 15–64 (Dipartimento Politiche Antidroga 2011: 78).[35] However, both figures are somewhat lower than the estimated number of cocaine users (353,000 people based on a 2010 past-year prevalence rate of 0.9 %) and dramatically lower that the estimated number of cannabis users estimated on the basis of the last population survey (Dipartimento Politiche Antidroga 2011: 8).[36,37]

[35] Our estimate of the number of users of doping products is more than twice as large as the estimated number of heroin users emerging from the last population survey (98,000 people based on a 2010 past-year prevalence rate of 0.25 %; see Dipartimento Politiche Antidroga 2011: 8).

[36] On the basis of the past-year prevalence rate recorded in the 2010 population survey, there were over 350,000 current users of cocaine (last-year prevalence rate of 0.9 % out of over 39 million people aged 15–64) and over two million users of cannabis (last-year prevalence rate: 5.2 %). The differences would become even bigger, if the results of the 2008 population survey were considered, which were considerably higher than those recorded in 2010 (Dipartimento Politiche Antidroga 2011: 8).

[37] In what seems to be a back-of-the-envelope calculation, Prof. Botré, the head of the Rome Anti-Doping Laboratory, reaches much higher estimates. In fact, according to him, there are over 400,000 Italian sportspeople who use prohibited doping products. Botré reaches this estimate by applying the rate of positive tests found in his laboratory (the average of CONI's and CVD's test results) to the whole population of Italian sportspeople, which he estimates at 16 million people. Instead, we have applied CVD's rate of positive results only to the 4,690,000 sportspeople aged 15 or older who engage in competitions. Given the lack of data, we have refrained from estimating doping use among the much broader set of noncompetitive sportspeople. As discussed earlier, these are likely to use doping products less frequently than athletes (Il Nuovo ciclismo 2007).

It is worth remembering that not all users of doping products commit an offense for the mere fact of using doping substances. Even if Italy's anti-doping legislation is rightly considered to be some of the strictest in the world (Evaluation Team 2002), article 9 of Italy's anti-doping act (Act 376/2000) punishes athletes for using doping products only if they want "to improve the[ir] competitive performance." Noncompetitive sportspersons and those who do participate in sports but use doping products for lifestyle purposes are not liable on the basis of the Act 376/2000. All users, however, can be indicted of "receiving," if they buy doping substances that have been stolen, fraudulently imported, or represent the proceeds of any other crime. For example, the 18 officers of the Italian Polizia di Stato who were body-builders and bought steroids from their colleagues were charged by the Turin Prosecutor's Office of receiving an illegal product (Numa 2010; Tribunale di Torino, 2012b).

The same ambiguity can be found in the application of the world anti-doping sports rules. According to the WADA Anti-Doping Code, the users of the same doping products may or may not violate a sports rule, depending on whether or not they have a therapeutic use exemption.

2.5 A Preliminary Estimate of the Size of the Market

Given the number of doping products available and the preferences of the different users and their advisors, it is an almost impossible exercise to assess the quantities of the different products consumed and therefore the size of the market for doping products in Italy. As shown in Tables 2.8 and 2.11, the substances detected by CVD in its anti-doping tests provide a first, albeit partial and possibly or even likely biased indication of the products chosen by doping athletes. No such detailed statistical data exists for body-builders and therefore we have had to rely on less solid data, explained in detail below.

In a preliminary attempt to scope the quantities consumed, we have developed average consumption profiles of 100 hypothetical users of doping products (see Appendix B). In developing such profiles, we have started from the understanding that the market for doping products consists of a multiplicity of substances and methods, some complements and some substitutes, and users mix them up for performance-enhancing or lifestyle purposes. Whereas the markets for illicit drugs are usually considered separately for the purposes of estimation (e.g., United Nations Office on Drugs and Crime 2005; Paoli et al. 2009), this approach is intractable and undesirable in the case of doping.

The specific combination of doping products used and the related dosages also vary widely depending on a variety of factors, including the users' motivations and qualifications, the sports disciplines they engage in, and, in the case of athletes, the upcoming competitions. A sprinter needs different products than a boxer or a rider and an elite athlete taking part in many high-level competitions is likely to use performance-enhancing substances more frequently than a recreational one.

The extent and type of doping also depends on the perceived legitimacy of doping and specifically performance-enhancing practices in the wider social contexts in which the users operate. A recent WADA-funded study on doping practices in French, Swiss, and Belgian elite cycling, for example, shows that, whereas doping was considered a de facto legitimate practice in elite cycling until the 1998 Festina affair, the repeated scandals, intensified control activities as well as the moral and occasionally also legal condemnation of doping have decreased the legitimacy and probably also the prevalence of doping practices among recreational and non-super elite riders. Several elite and would-be elite riders interviewed by Brissonneau and his colleagues (2009) stressed that they were committed to staying clean even if that commitment meant that they would give up successful career prospects (no super elite riders were included in Brissonneau et al.'s sample. The fact that both the winners and the other riders of the Tour de France have increased their average speed since the 1998 Festina scandal leads Hoberman (n.d.) to conclude that doping has remained widespread among super elite riders).

Given the multiplicity of doping products and patterns of use, we have opted for the definition of 100 profiles, covering the two broad categories of users identified in the previous sections, i.e., athletes and body-builders. Reflecting their percent of the total number of users of doping products in Italy (see Table 2.11, above), athletes account for 69 % of these profiles and body-builders account for 31 % (see Table 2.14). For athletes we have developed the profiles, in such a way that the share of the substances consumed corresponds to the percentages of the substances detected by the CVD in 2010 and 2011.

For body-builders, we have, above all, relied on the data emerging from the anti-doping investigations and in particular from the at least 15 investigations in which Donati has been a consultant at over the years. The latter task, included among others, reading hundreds of pages of wiretapped conversations, in which body-builders, other users, and their suppliers discuss dosages. For body-builders, we have also analyzed the consumption suggestions given in numerous Web sites.[38]

Except for GH, our estimates of body-builders' consumption profiles are comparable with the data collected by Parkinson and Evans (2006) in a 2004 anonymous Internet survey of 500 steroid users, a large majority of whom (78.4 %) were non-competitive body-builders and nonathletes. Parkinson and Evans' study constitutes the most recent study and one of the rare studies of consumption levels of doping products (see also Perry et al. 1990; Pope and Katz 1994; Evans 1997; Bolding et al. 2002). Almost all of their respondents (95 %) practiced polypharmacy, taking other drugs in addition to steroids, with one in four users taking GH and insulin. Parkinson and Evans' respondents reported using between 70 and 6,000 mg of testosterone and other steroids per week for "cycles" ranging between 4 and 20 weeks. Converting Parkinson and Evans' data to annual average dosages by using 10 mg as a dose, we conclude that the 500 respondents had an average annual consumption of 28,810 mg or 2,881 doses of steroids. The latter figure is only slightly lower than the 2,525

[38] For example, http://www.bodybuilding.com/fun/drobson221.htm and http://www.anabolicsteroids.com/steroids-deca.html.

doses of steroids consumed on average by the 31 hypothetical body-builders of our model (78,300 doses/31 body-builders). By applying the same conversion method, we also conclude that Parkinson and Evans' respondents consumed about 10,500 mg or 420 doses of 25 mg of stimulants on average on an annual basis—a figure almost coinciding with the 393 average doses we estimate in our model. Only our assumptions concerning GH consumption are significantly lower than the data recorded by Parkinson and Evans. In fact, reflecting the findings of Italian investigations, we estimate that our 31 hypothetical body-builders consume on average 55 doses of GH on a yearly basis, whereas the average GH consumption in Parkinson and Evans' study would correspond to 315 doses (each corresponding to 1 IU or 0.333 mg) of GH. Together with a few other hormones, GH is one of the most expensive doping substances available. Reflecting the official price of GH in Italy, we estimate that each dose of GH costs 13.90 € (see Chap. 7).[39] Italian body-builders' lower GH consumption can perhaps be partially explained with the lower purchasing power of Italian body-builders' vis-à-vis their US counterparts.

To increase the profiles' validity, we have also discussed them in detail with two Italian experts. The first is Dr. Bellotti, whose qualifications and key role in improving CVD's testing performance we have already mentioned. The second expert is Dr. Roberta Pacifici, director of the Observatory on Smoking, Alcohol and Drugs at the Higher Institute for Public Health in Italy, President of the Italian Society for Clinical Biochemistry and Clinical Molecular Biology and the Higher Institute for Public Health's representative within CVD. As part of the latter role, Pacifici coordinates the writing of CVD's yearly reports. Except for Bellotti and Pacifici's feedback, though, we are fully aware of the fact that our consumption profiles lack external validation, and we present them as a work in progress, hoping to obtain feedback and suggestions for improving them from other experts worldwide.

By applying the average quantities of the different products consumed by the two classes of users, we estimate that on a yearly basis over 371 million of doping doses are consumed annually in Italy (see Table 2.15). Among them, steroids represent the lion's share with 58.9 % of the market, followed by stimulants with 13.9 %. Three other classes of substances have similar shares: diuretics and other masking agents represent 8.7 % of the market, followed by glucocorticosteroids with 5.8 %, and peptide hormones, growth factors, and related substances with 6.4 %. All other classes of substances are marginal.

Our calculations also indicate that body-builders, although they represent only 31 % of the users, account for a very large share of the market (55.2 %). Body-builders, in fact, consume steroids and other doping products continuously throughout the year and some of them take very large dosages, whereas athletes are usually more selective in their choices of doping products and, depending on the products, take them only during training, for a few weeks or months, or just before a

[39] The cost of a GH dose in the United States is comparable. We have checked the prices of GH packages sold by seven leading drug manufacturers on a US Web site (see http://www.somatropin.net/hgh-brands.html) and conclude that a dose of 1 IU of GH currently costs US$17 or 13.60 €.

Table 2.15 Estimated doses of doping substances consumed in Italy, by type of users and classes of substances

Substances	Athletes	Body-builders	Total dosesper class	Percent of total
Anabolic agents	45,304,348	173,522,903	218,827,251	58.93
Peptide hormones, growth factors and related substances[a], of which	19,956,522	3,767,419	23,723,941	6.39
EPO	7,675,907	0	7,675,907	2.07
GH[b]	n.a.	3,564,001	3,767,419	0.96
Chorionic gonadotrophin	12,280,615	203,418	12,484,033	3.36
Beta-2 agonists	13,130,435	11,081	13,141,515	3.54
Hormones and metabolic modulators	0	132,968	132,968	0.04
Diuretics and other masking agents	32,391,304	55,403	32,446,708	8.74
Stimulants	24,739,130	27,036,774	51,775,905	13.94
Narcotics	7,000,000	0	7,000,000	1.89
Glucocorticosteroids	21,130,435	531,871	21,662,306	5.83
Beta-blockers	2,608,696	0	2,608,696	0.70
Total doses	166,260,870	205,058,419	371,319,290	
Percent of total	44.78 %	55.22 %	100.0 %	

Source: our estimation on the basis of the data presented earlier and the consumption profiles developed in Appendix B

[a]In the 100 consumption profiles we make detailed estimates for each user only in terms of the general category of substances belonging to this class. In fact, whereas we have considerable information on the dosages of EPO and GH, we have no basis to hypothesize the annual doping doses for other substances included in this class, such as chorionic gonadotrophin, ATCH, gonadorelin, or insulin. However, we distinguish among the EPO, GH, and chorionic gonadotrophin (the three main substances belonging to this class that have been either detected in CVD's tests or seized by NAS; see Tables 2.2 and 2.11) in aggregate terms, for each set of users, i.e., athletes and body-builders. This differentiation is necessary for the subsequent estimate of the financial size of the market, given the considerable differences in prices among the substances included in the category of peptide hormones, growth factors, and related substances (see Chap. 6). For this differentiation we have relied, for athletes, on CVD's positive test results. In 2010 and 2011 there were 13 positive tests for this class of substances, five for EPO and 8 for chorionic gonadotrophin. We have thus split the total number of doses on the basis of the same proportion. For body-builders, we relied on NAS seizure data to estimate the consumption of GH and chorionic gonadotrophin—this focus is made plausible by the focus on NAS investigations on body-building (see Chap. 7). In doing so, we have excluded EPO seizures, as NAS investigations have never delivered any proof of EPO being consumed by body-builders: in other words, we have assumed that the EPO seized by NAS is entirely bound for athletes. We have also excluded other substances belonging to this class, as we cannot estimate their consumption. Moreover, these other substances represent only a negligible share of the substances seized by NAS. Reflecting the relative share of GH and chorionic gonadotrophin in NAS seizures, we have hypothesized that GH accounts for 94.6 % of the total doping doses of this class consumed by body-builders, whereas peptide hormones, growth factors and related substances, and chorionic gonadotrophin account for 5.4 %

[b]We have no estimate of GH consumption by athletes because our estimates are based on the results of CVD's anti-doping tests and GH has never been detected in such tests

competition. Therefore, it is plausible that athletes account for only 44.8 % of the market, even if they represent 69 % of the users.

We would like to point to two biases in our estimates of the doping substances consumed by athletes. As we rely on the results of CVD's anti-doping tests, we underestimate the use of other doping substances consumed out of, rather than in, competition. CVD's data were, however, the only way to anchor our estimates to objective data. For the same reasons, we do not factor in the use of GH and other hormones that have never been detected in CVD's tests.

A 2000 analysis of the blood parameters of athletes preparing for the Sydney Olympic Games, which was carried out by CONI Scientific Committee, gives some hint about the spread of GH misuse among Italy's elite athletes. Such an analysis anticipated the current blood passport and was intended to determine 10 % variations from the athletes' average parameters of hematocrit, hemoglobin, GH, testosterone, IGF-1 (insulin-like growth factor), and others. Between May and July 2000, CONI Scientific Committee carried out 538 controls among athletes of 20 different disciplines, identifying numerous anomalous values and specifically 61 anomalies in the case of GH. The GH anomalies were concentrated in just a few sports. Among females, 32 of the 36 cases concerned swimming, volleyball, track and field, canoeing, and weightlifting; among males, 20 out of 25 cases involved swimming, rowing, cycling, and canoeing. Seven of the athletes with these blood anomalies won gold medals at the Sydney Olympics, and several others won silver and bronze medals (see Chiusano 2000). The results were later confirmed by a commission of experts set up by the Turin Prosecutor Raffaele Guariniello, which reanalyzed 250 of the 538 samples and found 43 subjects with GH/IGF-1 anomalies (Müller et al. 2002; see also Toti 2002 and Donati 2012: 211–213 and 219–223).

As GH can be used in many different sports disciplines, a conservative assumption would be to hypothesize that it is used as least as frequently as blood-boosting EPO, the main hormone detected by CVD in the category of peptide hormones, growth factors, and other related substances, which is attractive only for the athletes of endurance disciplines. As shown in Table 2.11, EPO was detected in 2.82 % of CVD's 2010 and 2011 anti-doping tests corresponding to 8,392 athletes using that drug and 1,116,501 doping doses of 200 IU or 1 mcg each. On the basis of such data, we could conservatively assume that athletes also use a comparable amount of GH doses.

Other data collected by CVD also suggests the extensive misuse, presumably for doping purposes, of gonadorelin, which is also included in the classes of peptide hormones, growth factors, and related substances. Gonadorelin is a hormone of very limited therapeutic use, capable of freeing chorionic gonadotrophin and thus stimulating the endogenous production of testosterone with the related anabolic effects. Until 2008 it could not be detected in anti-doping tests. In 2008 Cologne anti-doping laboratory validated a method for the detection of gonadorelin from urine samples (e.g., Thomas et al. 2008). However, the analysis for gonadorelin is not automatically included in the standard screening procedures; it is an additional analysis that has to be requested by the federations or the NADOs. As of December 2012, there had been no positive test yet for gonadorelin in Italy (Ministero della Salute and Istituto Superiore di Sanità 2012) or Germany (Geyer 2012, personal communication).

Through Federfarma, Italy's federation of pharmacies, CVD collected data about 2009 gonadorelin pharmacy sales from 16,669 pharmacies corresponding to 96.7 % of all Italian pharmacies. These reported selling 101,310 packages of gonadorelin.[40] Whereas there was considerable difference in the dosages contained in different types of packaging, each package contained on average 5.75 doses of 1.2 mg of gonadorelin. The data reveal gross differences in the territorial distribution of sales, which cannot be justified on the basis of gonadorelin therapeutic use. As shown in Table 2.16, the provinces of Novara (1,184), Ferrara (669), Salerno (561), Caltanissetta (949), and Palermo (434) and the whole region of Calabria (763) reported very high sales per 100,000 inhabitants. Leaving aside these provinces and the respective regions, the sales ranged from a maximum of 1.3 packages per 100,000 in Umbria to 134 in Friuli. Sometimes the differences between neighboring provincial and regional contexts are striking. Whereas 669 gonadorelin packages per 100,000 inhabitants were sold in Ferrara province, the neighboring provinces of Bologna and Modena recorded rates of 1 and 10 per 100,000, respectively. Likewise, Calabria reported 792.5 packages sold per 100,000 inhabitants and the neighboring region of Apulia 3.4 per 100,000.

Given gonadorelin's very high price, the "aberrant" provinces and regions report much higher expenditures than the rest. Although they account only for 9 % of the total population, their share of gonadorelin pharmacy sales and expenditures in 2009 was about 35 %. If we apply the average rate of 119.4 packages of gonadorelin sold per 100,000 inhabitants to these provinces and region and then subtract the results from the packages effectively sold, we come to the conclusion that 24,408 packages at a value of over eight million euro were abnormally sold in these provinces and region, corresponding to 24 % of the packages sold in all of Italy and 30 % of the total market value, respectively. Thus, we can hypothesize that about a quarter of annual gonadorelin sales is diverted for nontherapeutic, most probably doping purposes.

In short, we do not claim to have ironclad bases for all our assumptions, and we are aware that our model underestimates the consumption of some substances and sets of users. Nonetheless, we believe that this first estimate of the size and the different shares of the Italian market for doping products may provide relevant insights to policy-makers. In Italy, the problem of doping is still largely conceptualized as a problem of the elite sports world and, except for a few projects such as the Palestra Sicura project mentioned earlier, most resources are still focused on the prevention and control of doping in sports and particularly in elite sports. One just has to consider the number of annual tests carried out by CONI (approximately 10,000 for about 10,000 super elite athletes) with those conducted by CVD (on average 1,313 between 2006 and 2010), even though the latter targets a much wider, albeit not precisely determined, number of athletes. By singling out the users who consume doping products more abundantly, namely, the body-builders, our estimate can help (re-)focus resources on this rather neglected group of users who are likely to suffer most harm. "What is at stake," Turin Prosecutor Guariniello (2011) pointed out "is not only protecting the health of top athletes, of the privileged individuals that make up the sporting élite. What is at stake is first and foremost protecting the health of the many people, young and not so young, who engage in any sport or go to fitness clubs."

---

[40] Pharmaceutical companies also sell gonadorelin directly to hospitals and other health care centers, but CVD collected no data on these sales.

Table 2.16 Gonadorelin pharmacy sales in Italian regions and selected provinces in 2009

Region/province	Inhabitants	Packages sold	Total value	Packages sold per 100,000	Total value per 100,000
Piedmont	4,432,571	28,178	7,342,211	635.7	165,642
Novara province	343.040	4,063	1,113,759	1,184.4	324,673
Aosta Valley	127,065	28	8,106	22.0	6,379
Trentino Alto Adige	1,018,657	97	26,557	9.5	2,607
Venetium	4,885,548	5,675	1,661,377	116.2	34,006
Friuli	1,230,936	1,645	507,734	133.6	41,248
Liguria	1,615,064	814	235,196	50.4	14,563
Emilia Romagna	4,337,979	2,942	758,387	67.8	17,482
Ferrara province	357,980	2,396	623,474	669.3	174,164
Tuscany	3,707,818	851	203,713	23.0	5,494
Umbria	894,222	12	1,576	1.3	176
Marche	1,569,578	867	242,723	55.2	15,464
Latium	5,626,710	872	233,825	15.5	4,156
Abruzzo	1,334,675	42	5,211	3.1	390
Molise	320,795	401	147,955	125.0	46,121
Campania	5,812,962	12,311	2,921,818	211.8	50,268
Salerno province	1,106,099	6,207	1,508,804	561.2	136,408
Apulia	4,079,702	157	35,247	3.4	864
Basilicata	590,601	270	89,674	45.7	15,184
Calabria	2,008,709	15,317	4,297,389	762.5	213,938
Cosenza province	733,508	7,049	2,024,430	961.0	275,993
Sicilia	5,037,799	8,542	2,266,027	169.6	44,980

Caltanissetta province	272,289	2,583	748,339	948.6	274,833
Palermo province	1,244,680	5,406	1,393,428	434.3	111,951
Sardegna	1,671,001	431	78,859	25.8	4,719
Total	60,045,068	101,310	26,727,207	168.7	44,512
Selected provinces and region	5,332,797 (8.9 %)	35,972 (35.5 %)	9,685,193 (36.2 %)	674.5	181,616
Rest of country	54,712,271	65,338	17,042,014	119.4	31,148
Hypothetical sales in selected provinces and region at average rate	5,332,797	11,564	1,661,081	119.4	31,148
Difference between effective and hypothetical sales	n.a.	24,408 (24.1 %)	8,024,112 (30.0 %)	n.a.	n.a.

Source: CVD (2010) and Istat, for the population data

Chapter 3
The (Illegal) Suppliers of Doping Products

Abstract In the third chapter, we first consider the main characteristics of the illegal suppliers of doping products in Italy, develop a typology of them based on their profession or occupation, and single out their motives. As we draw our information almost exclusively from law enforcement sources, we speak of illegal suppliers—that is, people who import, distribute, or administer doping products and have been at least suspected of a doping-related offense under Italian law. As will become clear in the course of this and especially the following chapters, however, there is a very thin and ambiguous line between illegal and legal suppliers, so much so that we will drop the adjective "illegal" in the following chapter, when we consider distribution chains and market relationships. On the basis of Italy's anti-doping investigations, we conclude that illegal suppliers of doping products are predominantly male Italians and have a legitimate profession or occupation. Many of them, in particular, belong to the world of gyms, health care or human, and horse sports. For most of them, the primary motive for engaging in the supply of doping products is private (or, more rarely, institutional) profit. Staff members of sports teams and sports federations are however often motivated by the same overconformity to a sports ethic that also drives elite athletes to dope (Sport in society: Issues and controversies, Boston, 205–214).

Although the chapter only analyzes empirical data on Italy, the findings here presented can be considered illustrative of the suppliers of doping products in other countries, even if similarities and differences must be ascertained empirically in future projects.

In this chapter we first consider illegal suppliers' main characteristics, develop a typology of them based on their profession or occupation, and single out their motives, thus fulfilling the second objective of the project. As we draw our information almost exclusively from law enforcement sources, we speak of illegal suppliers—that is, people who import, distribute, or administer doping products and

L. Paoli and A. Donati, *The Sports Doping Market: Understanding Supply and Demand, and the Challenges of Their Control*, DOI 10.1007/978-1-4614-8241-3_3,

have been at least suspected of a doping-related offense under Italian law. As will become clear in the course of this and especially the following chapters, however, there is a very thin and ambiguous line between illegal and legal suppliers, so much so that we will drop the adjective "illegal" in the following chapter, when we consider distribution chains and market relationships. On the basis of Italy's anti-doping investigations, we conclude that illegal suppliers of doping products are predominantly male Italians and have a legitimate profession or occupation. Many of them, in particular, belong to the world of gyms, health care or human, and horse sports. For most of them, the primary motive for engaging in the supply of doping products is private (or, more rarely, institutional) profit. Staff members of sports teams and sports federations are however often motivated by the same overconformity to a sports ethic that also drives elite athletes to dope (Coackley and Pipe 2009: 205–214).

3.1 Key Sociodemographic Characteristics

To draw an overview of the actors involved in the supply of doping products and highlight their gender, nationality, criminal records, and profession, we start by considering the Database on NAS Investigations, which contains data on about 71 supply-related investigations carried out by NAS from 1999 to 2011.[1] In total, these investigations have led to the arrest of 74 individuals and the reporting of 359 individuals to the judicial authorities for different doping-related offenses.[2] Whenever possible and appropriate, we integrate the data from the database with information drawn from the different police and judicial documents that we collected (e.g., police reports, charges, or verdicts) and the expert interviews that we conducted.

3.1.1 Gender

No explicit data are provided in the database about the gender of the suspects; however, as the Italian language has different, female and male, endings for most words, the impression that emerges from the database analysis is that the overwhelming majority of the suspects are male. The analysis of the police and judicial documents collected also confirms this gender disproportion. The few women who are

[1] The Database on NAS Investigations contains data on 80 closed investigations. However, nine of them concern athletes' consumption of doping products, which is criminalized in Italy, and we have therefore excluded them from the current analysis. Through the interviews, we have also become aware of several, mostly ongoing, investigations that are not included in the database.

[2] A higher number of arrests and reporting emerges from the answers to a questionnaire filled in by all the 38 NAS branch offices at the request of the NAS Headquarters. For the comparison between the two datasets and a detailed analysis of the offenses, see Chap. 7.

suspected of a doping-related offense are linked by blood, marriage, or love ties with the male suspects and mostly play ancillary functions in the illicit businesses.

For example, in the so-called “Anabolic Web” investigation, the main defendant, a body-building instructor who ran a distribution ring in Emilia Romagna and other regions, was supported by his mother, sister, and fiancé. The three women sent packages of doping products, primarily anabolic steroids, to customers located in several Italian regions and received money transfers from them on their own bank accounts (Tribunale di Ravenna 2004). In another case, a woman whose partner was both a supplier and co-owner of a gym was not actively involved in the trade but was fully aware of her partner’s illicit actions and gave him advice on how to protect himself from law enforcement investigations (Tribunale di Bologna 2000: 63–64). Sometimes, business relationships are stronger than those of affection: the former wife of L.S. kept on cashing the checks he received from the illegal sale of anabolic steroids and other products, even after their marriage failed (Tribunale di Bologna 2000: 67).

We are aware of only a few cases of women who have taken up active, managerial roles. In a proceeding of the Siracusa Prosecutor’s Office, for example, the wife of the principal suspect—both of them body-builders—was fully involved in the importation of illegal performance-enhancing drugs from abroad and the latter’s distribution among the clients of their gym (Tribunale di Siracusa 2010: 23–29).

3.1.2 Nationality

Although nationality is not a required or explicit element in the database, the case summaries included in the database—as well as the defendants’ lists of the 46 criminal proceedings analyzed—indicate that most suspects are Italian. The preponderance of Italians is largely due to the fact that NAS investigations usually stop at the borders of Italy. The NAS officers and the prosecutors whom we interviewed complained (Int-NAS-5, 6, 9, 10, 16) that they are rarely able to identify and charge the foreign suppliers of the Italian traders in doping products because of the lack of effective international cooperation (see Chap. 7).

Notwithstanding these limitations, the NAS investigations document that very few foreign residents in Italy, in particular members of ethnic minorities, are involved in the trade in doping products in Italy. In a few criminal cases, some foreign residents in Italy are reported as users or “users–dealers” of the products. In the latter case, they buy the doping products, primarily anabolic steroids and stimulants, largely for their own consumption and then re-sell part of the total purchase amount to others. For example, a Sudanese and a Bulgarian man and a Ukrainian woman were involved in the so-called “Take Away” investigation: the first two bought steroids and the third stimulants from the main suspect (Tribunale di Forlì 2009). We are aware of only one case in which a foreign resident was a wholesaler. In the above-mentioned Siracusa proceeding, one of the two main suspects was a Nigerian-US woman, who exploited her US citizenship to have the doping products shipped to a nearby US military base (Tribunale di Siracusa 2010).

The very limited role played by foreigners on the Italian market constitutes a major difference vis-à-vis the market for illicit drugs, where migrants, mostly undocumented, now occupy the lowest and most dangerous levels in the distribution system, by selling drugs on the street (e.g., Paoli and Reuter 2008). This difference appears to be a consequence of the semi-illegal nature of the doping market and points to the persistent "embeddedness" of the supply networks into legitimate social networks and specifically professional affiliations and relationships.

Nevertheless, the Italian market for doping products is not insulated from its foreign counterparts. Just as in the case of traditional illegal drugs, Italian suppliers of doping products are often part of large international networks: They often receive their products from abroad, and occasionally, they also sell them to foreign clients. We discuss the foreign sources in more detail below, but here it is worth referring to the charges recently filed by the Mantua Prosecutor's Office to understand how "multiculti" the network of an Italian supplier of doping products can be (Int-Pro-4). Whereas his core customers were Italian professional riders, the main suspect of that case, Guido Nigrelli, a pharmacist, also sold doping products to a Danish professional rider and a foreign consul, who was a recreational rider; exchanged drugs and therapies with a like-minded Spanish doctor; provided advise to the sports director of a professional US cycling team; and received regular data from Italian, Spanish, and Swiss hematological centers that were visited by the (Italian) riders to undergo blood doping (NAS Brescia 2011; Pacifici and Donati 2011).

Italian suppliers are also occasionally full-time participants in large international criminal organizations. A 2009 investigation of the Brescia NAS Branch Office, for example, identified one of these organizations, which was headed by a former high-level employee of a US drug manufacturer. The Italian employee of this criminal organization was a former nurse of a Turin hospital, who produced himself anabolic steroids in a laboratory close to Brescia and marketed them through a Web site (Int-NAS-9).

3.1.3 Criminal Records

The NAS Investigations Database provides no detailed information on the suspects' criminal records. However, the NAS officers and prosecutors interviewed unanimously confirmed that most suspects of doping-related offenses have no criminal records, again reflecting the embeddedness of doping supply in legitimate professional affiliations and relationships. In other words, most suspects have not had a traditional "criminal career," one that would typically start in youth with petty thefts or violent crime and move on with advancing age to more serious crime (e.g., Laub and Sampson 2003).

In face-to-face interviews (e.g., Int-NAS-9 and 16 and Int-Pro-2) and in the questionnaire distributed by the NAS Headquarters to the 38 NAS branch offices, however, the officers also pointed out four sets of exceptions to the general finding of clean records. First, there is a small group of former or current gym managers and owners

Table 3.1 Leading relevant professions of the suspects reported in the NAS Investigation Database—1999–2011

Profession	Number of suspects
Gym owners or managers and body-building instructors[a]	158
Veterinary physicians, breeders, horse drivers	140
Owners or managers of dietary supplement shops	64
Pharmacists[b]	20
Physicians[c]	17
Staff members of cycling teams[d]	12
Sports federation officials	10
Law enforcement and military staff	10
Hospital employees (including 5 nurses and 2 former employees)	10
Employees and salesmen of (para)-pharmaceutical companies[e]	6
Staff of private security companies	2

Source: our calculations on the basis of the Database on NAS Investigations

[a]An unspecified number of gym owners or managers and body-building instructors was reported in ten investigations

[b]An unspecified number of pharmacists was reported in five other investigations

[c]An unspecified number of physicians was reported in three other investigations, and an unspecified number of vets in another

[d]An unspecified number of staff members of cycling teams was reported in two other investigations

[e]An unspecified number of employees of pharmaceutical companies was reported in another investigation

who have been involved in the trade of doping products since the 1990s and have therefore been charged and convicted several times with doping-related offenses. Second, some bouncers have criminal records for fights and similar violent offenses. (Bouncers are, as a rule, mere users of doping products or at most users–retailers and play no role in the upper echelons of the market.) Third, a few suppliers, especially at the retail level, have criminal records for dealing with illegal drugs. Fourth, the robbers of trucks and storehouses containing legitimate drugs with potential doping effects often have criminal records for robberies. Together with veterinary physicians, breeders, and horse drivers involved in horseracing, they are also the only group of suppliers of doping products who have links, and sometimes are even affiliated, with Southern Italian mafia-type organized crime, most notably the Neapolitan camorra (see below).

3.1.4 Profession

The legitimate professional positions held by most of the persons suspected of doping-related offenses lend further weight to the embeddedness of doping supply in legitimate activities. To get a first overview, we classified the suspects mentioned in the NAS Investigations Database according to their profession and report in Table 3.1 the most frequent and relevant professions of note. In analyzing these data, it is important to keep in mind that the survey on which the database is drawn was not meant specifically to collect the suspects' profession, and therefore, not all NAS branch offices provided detailed information on this matter. The figures presented in Table 3.1, therefore, must be regarded as indicative, as they provide only a partial and approximate idea of the different professional categories involved in the supply of doping products.

Gym owners, gym managers, or body-building instructors constitute by far the largest group among the suspects targeted by NAS investigations. Their preponderance reflects the persistent focus of NAS investigations on body-building and, more generally, the gym world (see Chap. 7). In total, 158 such characters were reported as traders in doping products in 28 of the 71 supply-related investigations contained in the NAS Investigations Database. In 1 of these 28 and 9 other cases, an unspecified number of gym owners, managers, or instructors were also reported to be involved.

The second largest category of suspects belongs to the world of horseracing. One large-scale investigation involved 140 veterinary physicians, breeders, and horse drivers (25 individuals were arrested and 115 were merely reported by NAS to the judicial authority; no specific data about the professions of the suspects were given). Other sources, reviewed below, provide evidence of several other investigations.

Less surprisingly, given the focus of NAS investigations on body-building, the third most frequently recurring profession in the database is that of owner or manager of a dietary supplement shop. Sixty-one suspects with such qualifications are reported in the database in eight different investigations.

The fourth largest professional category involved in NAS investigations is composed of pharmacists. In total, 20 pharmacists are suspected of doping-related violations in nine different investigations. Moreover, an unspecified number of pharmacists were reported in five other investigations. The database on NAS Investigations also lists 17 accommodating or corrupt physicians, who constitute the fifth largest professional group mentioned in the database.

Twelve staff members of cycling teams and ten members of sports federations are also suspected of illegal doping practices according to the NAS Investigations Database, with an imprecise number of staff members of cycling teams reported in two other investigations. In the same data set, ten law enforcement or military officers and two staff members of private security companies have been suspected of trading and selling performance-enhancing drugs. Last but not least, ten employees of public hospitals, including five nurses, have been suspected of doping-related offenses according to the database, along with six employees or representatives of pharmaceutical and dietary supplement companies.

3.2 A Typology

On the basis of the most frequent professions and occupations listed in the database and criminal proceedings, we have identified ten main types of illegal suppliers of doping products in Italy and grouped them in five main categories. A note on

Table 3.2 Categories and types of illegal suppliers of doping products in Italy

Category	Type
Gym	Gym managers or owners and body-building instructors
	Managers or owners of dietary supplement shops
Health care	Pharmacists
	Physicians
	Hospital, health clinic, and nursing home employees
	Employees or salesmen of (para-) pharmaceutical companies
(Human) organized sports world	Staff members of sports teams
	Staff members of sports federations
Horseracing	Veterinary physicians
	Breeders
	Drivers
Use	Athletes
	Body-builders
Other	People with no distinctive profession or occupation

vocabulary: We use the expression "supplier" broadly, fully aware of the fact that some suppliers do not sell, but merely administer, or provide a prescription for, a doping substance to the final users.

The first category, "gym," consists of the two types of illegal suppliers that are the largest numerically in the NAS Investigations Database: gym managers or owners and body-building instructors, on the one hand, and managers or owners of dietary supplement shops, on the other hand. The second category, "health care," consists of four other types: pharmacists, physicians, hospital employees, and employees or sale representatives of pharmaceutical and para-pharmaceutical companies (including not only manufacturers but also distributors). Two other types, staff members of sports teams and federations, compose the third category, which we refer to as the "organized sports world." The fourth category refers to the world of horseracing and includes breeders, veterinarians, and drivers. The fifth category, which we term "use," consists of athletes and body-builders and their close relatives. Athletes could easily also belong to the category "organized sports world" and body-builders to that of "gym." However, we have created for them a separate category of "use," to stress that their involvement in the illegal supply of doping products is linked inherently with, and facilitated by, their own consumption. In creating such a category, we also stretch the definition of "occupation" to include sporting and body-building activities. Finally, we include an "other" category for those suppliers who cannot be distinguished on the basis of a specific profession or occupation.

We list these types and categories in Table 3.2 and discuss each of the types in the following subsections.

3.2.1 *Gym Managers and Owners and Body-Building Instructors*

Gym owners or managers and body-building instructors work most often as retailers, selling doping products (primarily anabolic steroids but also stimulants) to gym patrons. Some of these individuals, though, are also wholesalers, selling to retailers, who are often other gym managers, instructors, or body-builders. R.F., the manager of a gym in Forlì, for example, supplied not only several visitors of his gym but also the managers of at least four other gyms with anabolic steroids and other drugs (Tribunale di Forlì 2009: 16–19). So did O.P., the owner of a gym specialized in body-building in Naples, who also distributed steroids and other drugs through a small network of accomplices (NAS Napoli 2003). D.P., another body-building instructor, was able to distribute anabolic steroids in several regions, including Emilia Romagna, where he was based, Lombardy, Latium, Apulia, and Sardinia (Tribunale di Ravenna 2004: 123). The NAS investigations reconstructed a wide network around him, which was composed—in addition to his mother, sister, and girlfriend—of the following people:

- At least two "partner–customers," including the owner of the gym where he worked, who were actively looking for new customers
- Twenty-one customers who served as distributors in other regions, including six people who sold the products in Sardinia, one person responsible for the area of Rome, two persons based in Milan and its province, and the other 12 distributing the steroids in the region of Emilia Romagna
- Numerous users, who were primarily body-builders (Tribunale di Ravenna 2004: 124)

In 22 investigations listed in the NAS Investigations Database, some gym owners or managers and body-building instructors also turned out to be importing doping products from abroad (e.g., Tribunale di Ravenna 2004: 125–126; NAS Napoli 2003) and, in six partially overlapping cases, obtaining doping products from pharmacies with fraudulent methods or with the help of a corrupt pharmacist (Tribunale di Bologna 2000).

According to the experts interviewed, three (former) gym owners surpass all other known steroid suppliers for the length and scope of their illegal businesses. The first one is P.B., the owner of a Bologna gym, who has been the largest known wholesaler in the Bologna area over a period spanning 3 decades, serving numerous other gym owners, including the above-mentioned R.F., as well as the visitors of his own gyms. Since the late 1990s, P.B. has been arrested five times for the sale of doping products. In the last proceeding against him, P.B. was aided by two employees of his gym. Through a trusted couple, both body-builders, originating from Sardinia but resident in Bologna, he was able to sell steroids also in Sardinia (Tribunale di Forlì 2009: 16–19; 173–175). In a previous investigation, his distribution network was even wider, extending to other Italian regions (NAS Bologna 2000). Moreover, at the turn of the century, P.B. not only bought steroids from the two other major Italian suppliers (see infra) but also imported these drugs and their raw materials from third countries, received drugs from a Bologna Hospital employee, and, most likely, also counterfeited medicine in laboratories, which were however never identified (ibid., 2000: 142, 408–412, and 428–435).

An even bigger trader in anabolic steroids is L.S., the owner of gyms in Campania and Milan, who like P.B. has been repeatedly involved in anti-doping investigations since the late 1990s (Tribunale di Forlì 2009: 93; see also Spezia 2009; Cascella 2008). Since then at least, L.S. supplied P.B. and numerous other customers through Italy. In the late 1990s, he bought most of his merchandise from V.G.F., who was then Italy's largest importer of anabolic steroids and GH and with whom L.S. had a very close working relationship. Since the beginning of the present century, L.S. also began importing large quantities of drugs from abroad on his own. Additionally, throughout his career, he also received doping products that had been stolen from trucks in Southern Italy (Tribunale di Forlì 2009: 93, NAS Bologna 2000: 148). L.S. was arrested for the last time in July 2008 in front of P.B.'s gym, when he was trying to get rid of a big garbage bag containing a large quantity of anabolic steroids. In 2011, he was involved in another investigation conducted by the Milan Branch Office and accused, among others, of supplying steroids, through intermediaries, to a famous body-builder. To escape the new arrest, he went on hiding (Il Giorno 2011).

As already noted, the third large-scale supplier is V.G.F., who was described in 2000 by the Bologna Branch Office as the "'big father' of national and international trafficking in anabolic steroids" (NAS Bologna 2000: 233). This former employee of the Pesaro tax collection office, body-builder, and gym owner was first reported for the illegal import of anabolic steroids in 1993. In the late 1990s, V.G.F. supplied both L.S. and, through L.S. and directly, P.B., who was one of their major customers. In V.G.F.'s notes, the NAS officers discovered the names of seven Italian pharmaceutical companies, two pharmacies and a private hospital, which were considered to be the sources of some of the drugs distributed by V.G.F.[3] In addition, the agenda revealed contacts with pharmaceutical companies in Greece, Spain, and Portugal, the three countries from which most of the products seized originated, as well as in Eastern Europe, Colombia, the Dominican Republic, and Albania and numerous international couriers (NAS Bologna 2000: 268–272). In addition to the gyms supplied through P.B. and L.S., V.G.F. also had direct contacts with at least 27 other gyms located in Piedmont, Lombardy, Trentino Alto Adige, Friuli Venezia Giulia, Emilia Romagna, Tuscany, Marche, Umbria, Latium, Campania, Apulia, and Sicily (ibid.: 243–244 and 267–268).

V.G.F. was arrested again in August 2011 in Ancona for the illegal importation of very large quantities of doping products (Frezzi 2011). In a storehouse under his control, the Ancona Branch Office seized over 45,000 ampoules and 50,000 pills of

[3] The NAS officers state that they would focus on the exact relationship between V.G.F. and these health care bodies in a "possible later phase of the investigation" (NAS Bologna 2000: 269). However, this was never done, given the very scarce chance of finding evidence backing charges against the pharmaceutical companies in the absence, back in the 1990s, of anti-doping criminal provisions.

somatropin, testosterone, nandrolone, ephedrine, and methadone with an estimated market value of over one million euro. The drugs were produced in clandestine laboratories in Spain, the Netherlands, and the UK. V.G.F. had them shipped via unsuspecting couriers to several addresses in Italy, using several false identities. He then collected the drugs by car or truck; had local typesetters and carton companies produce the packages, blisters, labels, and instructions; and packaged himself the drugs with a few collaborators (Frezzi 2011; Il Resto del Carlino 2011).

3.2.2 Managers of Dietary Supplement Shops

Managers and owners of dietary supplement shops also figure prominently in NAS investigations and related proceedings. An investigation conducted by the Parma Branch Office focused on N.P., a former body-builder and the owner of two gyms, and his associate A.P. Together, they ran a dietary shop in Cesena and a related Web site to sell their products via Internet. The two imported steroids from Bulgaria, Romania, Turkey, and Greece and sold them to a wide clientele throughout Italy, using C.P.'s body-building reputation and a catalogue of dietary supplement to attract new clients. According to the two officers in charge of the investigations, these illicit businesses produced revenues of about two million euro (Int-NAS-13 and 15). In another investigation, the manager of a dietary supplement shop, himself a former professional body-builder, occasionally sold anabolic steroids but most often gave advice to other body-builders, including some participating in competitions, on the specific product combinations and quantities to use and the tricks necessary to avoid testing positive in anti-doping tests (Tribunale di Forlì 2009: 234–254).

3.2.3 Pharmacists

Two examples illustrate the role of corrupt pharmacists in the doping market. Over a period of several years in the 1990s, the owner of a central pharmacy in Bologna, P.L., provided illegal performance-enhancing products, primarily stimulants, and other drugs to many elite athletes, ranging from riders to Serie A football players, from volleyball players to track-and-field athletes. P.L. was skilled in preparing Galenic products, but he also sold prepackaged performance-enhancing drugs, including some that were unavailable in Italy. Prominent physicians—some of them repeatedly suspected of doping practices, such as Michele Ferrari (see infra)—sent their patients to buy drugs at P.L.'s pharmacy and occasionally also bought the drugs themselves (Tribunale di Bologna 2004; Capodacqua 2001). In a wiretapped phone conversation, P.L. was heard saying that "Michele Ferrari passed by and emptied my pharmacy" (La Repubblica 2001). Among P.L.'s customers, there were also the sports physicians of the Italian football and track-and-field teams as well as those of several Serie A football teams, including Parma Calcio (Int-NAS-10). Two of these physicians were indicted but later acquitted of any wrongdoing by the Bologna Court in 2001. In the same trial, P.L. pleaded guilty and received a 2-year imprisonment sentence for illegally acting as a pharmacist and adulteration and counterfeiting of food products (La Repubblica 2001). In an interview, the prosecutor in charge of the case regretted that P.L. could not be convicted of doping because the latter's criminal activities predated the introduction of Italy's anti-doping law (Spezia 2001).

In a more recent, still ongoing investigation, another pharmacist, Guido Nigrelli, in the nearby province of Mantua is accused of treating the riders of the professional cycling team Lampre-ISD, including the 2008 World Champion Alessandro Ballan. Detailed wiretapped conversations and police observations document that Nigrelli administered the athletes a variety of illegal performance-enhancing drugs, including EPO, ephedrine, testosterone, and corticoids and also arranged analogous transfusions for some of them. Although this pharmacist had no formal position within the team, he had a very close relationship with the team manager, the former World Champion, Giuseppe Saronni[4] and de facto acted as a team physician (NAS Brescia 2011; Int-Pro-4; Ryan 2011).[5]

Pharmacists may also be involved unwittingly in the sale of performance-enhancing drugs, that is, without being aware of the illegal goals of the purchases. Most frequently, these "non-guilty" pharmacists sell doping drugs on the basis of false or stolen prescriptions or on the basis of prescriptions written by accommodating or corrupt physicians (e.g., Tribunale di Ravenna 2004: 122, Int-NAS-17 and 19). The line between the deceived and corrupt pharmacist is sometimes difficult to draw, though. A pharmacist involved in an anti-doping investigation explained the sale of some anabolic steroids in the following way: "It happened a couple of times and I would have never thought that a person I knew was linked to the trafficking of doping substances. He came to me asking me Testovis, a hormone which is useful for weakened animals. He told me that it was for his dog and that he would have brought the prescription later. I made a mistake but I have nothing to do with these problems" (Spezia 2009). According to official charges, however, the pharmacist sold different performance-enhancing products in addition to Testovis and at a price higher than the official one—facts that indicate that he was likely aware of the illegal nature of the business (Tribunale di Forlì 2009).

3.2.4 Physicians

Several NAS investigations point to the role played by physicians in the supply of doping products. In the "Bianchi" case of the Bologna Branch Office summarized in the NAS Investigations Database, for example, a specialist in endocrinology

[4] See also http://en.wikipedia.org/wiki/Giuseppe_Saronni.

[5] Several other corrupt physicians, who delivered performance-enhancing drugs, were also involved in the investigation "Flebo" of the Padova Branch Office (NAS Padova 2009) and in "Anabolandia" of the Bologna Office (Tribunale di Rimini 2011).

and sports medicine prescribed stimulants and anabolic steroids to at least 14 recreational athletes practicing cycling, swimming, and triathlon. In another recent investigation of the Brescia Branch Office, which is not included in the database, a local anesthetist issued void prescriptions and assisted an illegal producer of steroids in exchange for drugs and specifically a suntan cream, which he used in great dosages (Int-NAS-9).

The most insightful investigation in the database is, however, "Oil for Drug," which details the prescriptions and sale of illegal performance-enhancing drugs to at least 146 elite and recreational athletes of different sports in 29 Italian provinces and led to the seizure of large quantities of doping products, totaling to 38,059 doses and blood-doping equipment. In such a case, two physicians played a key role not only in prescribing these drugs to the athletes but also in convincing them of the need to take these drugs. As a rider stated in an interrogation, "[the physician] told me that I was at a crossroads: I either decided to take some prohibited substances to enhance my sports performance or I would have keep on having no results" (NAS Firenze 2005: 454). As reported in the press (Brown and Abrahams 2007), the most prominent of the two physicians was Carlo Santuccione, an Italian sports doctor, who is allegedly known as *Ali the Chemist*.[6] A former assistant of Prof. Conconi's at the University of Ferrara (see infra), Santuccione had been suspended from acting as a sports physician from 1995 to 2000 by CONI for a previous doping offense. In the "Oil for Drug" investigation, he was suspected of coordinating the whole network of suppliers of illegal performance-enhancing drugs and of connecting the athletes with their suppliers. In December 2007, Santuccione was given a lifetime ban by CONI as a result of these charges (Brown and Abrahams 2007). The main tranche of the criminal proceeding is still pending at the Rome Court.

The two most prominent Italian physicians linked to doping are not mentioned in the NAS Investigations Database because the investigations concerning them started in the mid-1990s, prior to the inception of the database.

The "father" of Italy's doping physicians is undoubtedly Prof. Francesco Conconi, professor of biochemistry at the University of Ferrara since 1967, current head of its Centro di Studi Biomedici applicati allo Sport, and rector of the same university from 1998 to 2004.[7] Professor Conconi is most famous for having "prepared" Francesco Moser for his successful attempt to break the world hour record in Mexico, 1984, among other things, by using blood doping, as Moser himself would later admit (La Repubblica 1999). In the late 1970s, Conconi started providing a variety of doping products to Italian elite athletes, primarily in track and field, cycling, swimming, pentathlon, rowing, and ski sports, with the tacit support of CONI (see infra). In particular, Conconi's most effective application consisted of blood doping or analogous transfusions, a doping method that was allegedly applied in those years also in other countries (e.g., Finland). Conconi augmented it, for

[6] Although not a credible academic citation or claim to legitimacy, the entry under his name in Wikipedia provides evidence of the mere existence of an allegation. See http://en.wikipedia.org/wiki/Carlo_Santuccione.

[7] See his personal webpage at http://docente.unife.it/francesco.conconi/curr.

example, by preserving and re-injecting only blood plasma and by selecting and re-injecting only the younger red blood cells.[8] Starting in the early 1990s, he began using EPO and increasingly substituted "EMO doping" with "EPO doping." With his doping "research" funded by CONI (sums corresponding to more than two million euro over the years; see Tribunale di Ferrara 2003), Conconi was able to achieve spectacular results with the athletes working with him: at the 1994 Winter Olympics, Italy sensationally emerged as a powerhouse in long-distance skiing and won 34 medals. It would later be documented that many of these athletes registered hematocrit values of greater than 50 %—a strong indication of EPO use and measurements that today would invoke suspension from competition (Akinde 2006). In their reports, the experts who supported the prosecutor of this case showed the close correspondence between the highest hematocrit values and the best performances during the competitions (Bellotti 1999). At the same time, Conconi and his collaborators published several articles in scientific journals about EPO in athletes' blood samples and the eventual possibilities of its detection (e.g., De Paoli Vitali et al. 1988; Casoni et al. 1993; Conconi et al. 1994).

By the early 1990s, Conconi started to provide systematically his services to elite riders working in private teams. In addition to assisting a few of these teams (e.g., Gewiss-Ballan and Mercatone Uno), Conconi also treated a large number of the stars of the 1990s, such as Marco Pantani, Claudio Chiappucci, and Gianni Bugno. In one of the files later seized by NAS on behalf of the Ferrara Prosecutor's Office, detailed information was found about 407 athletes monitored—and hence presumably at least some doped—by Conconi during the 3-year period 1992–1995 (Tribunale di Ferrara 2003: 6–7).[9] As already mentioned in the introduction, these searches and related investigations conducted by the Bologna and Firenze Branch Offices and the Ferrara Prosecutor Soprani lead to the indictment of Conconi and two of his assistants of the crime of sporting fraud. Despite "the seriousness and

[8] Analogous transfusions were not prohibited in Italy until 1985 when they were banned by a Decree of the Italian Ministry of Health. Even before that decree, it was clear, though, that analogous transfusions were not a standard therapeutic or research practice and that they might de facto constitute doping, as recognized by Conconi himself. In an interview quoted in an official document of the Ferrara Prosecutor's Office, Conconi stated: Analogous transfusion "may be doping but before classifying it as such we need to analyze the reasons why the technique of analogous transfusion is carried out on an athlete. If one aims to treat a subject who has a hemoglobin level lower than average and to raise that level to the average, then an analogous transfusion performs only a therapeutic function, because it 'normalizes' an anomalous situation. If instead, one deals with a subject with normal hemoglobin values and adds up blood to enhance performance, then this operation can be seen as doping"" (Donati 2012: 37–38).

[9] According to the prosecutor's charges, Conconi himself was listed in the database under a pseudonym—and took EPO too. On one occasion in September 1994, his hematocrit was recorded as recorded as high as 57. In that period, Conconi raced together with Francesco Moser, whom Conconi was preparing to break the hour record a second time, ten years after Moser's success. Under Conconi's guidance, Moser, who was then 43 years of age and had already retired from professional cycling, eventually rode 51.840 km in 60 min, thereby riding 689 m beyond his record set in 1984 (Josti 1994). Even more surprisingly, Conconi, who was then 59 years old, finished only two minutes behind Moser in a mountain race in South Tyrol (cyclingnews.com 2000).

convergence of all the evidence" (Tribunale di Ferrara 2003: 46), however, the inefficiency of the Italy judicial system and the defendants' procedural tactics (e.g., Toti 2003) left the Ferrara judge no other choice but to dismiss the case in 2003 due to the statute of limitations (see also Donati 2012: 12–38).

Even more than Santuccione, the most famous of Conconi's pupils is Michele Ferrari, who split from Conconi in the late 1990s and later specialized in attending to high-level riders. While the most prominent among his clients was Lance Armstrong (see U.S. Anti-Doping Agency 2012c), Ferrari helped many other athletes to succeed. In April 1994, for example, the Gewiss team, for which Ferrari worked as team physician, dominated a classic cycling race, the Flèche Wallonne, taking all three podium spots. After that race, Ferrari gave a candid interview to the French newspaper *L'Equipe*. Among other things he stated: "You are doped, if you test positive in a test," "As an elite athlete, I would take anything that improves my performance, as long as I remain within the rules" and "EPO is not dangerous, it's the abuse that is. It's also dangerous to drink 10 L of orange juice" (Bergonzi and Kindhauser 2001).

Like Conconi, Ferrari eventually became the target of a criminal investigation. On the basis of that investigation, he was sentenced to 1 year of imprisonment and 900 € fee by the Bologna Court for the offenses of sporting fraud and illegal exercise of the pharmaceutical profession, while he was acquitted of the charge of distributing products dangerous for public health. (As in Conconi's case, the offenses foreseen by Italy's anti-doping law could not be applied because the investigations began before the adoption of that law.) In writing his verdict, the judge concluded that

> When the best sports physicians, those trained at a center of excellence funded by CONI, such as Dr. Ferrari, get involved in doping, there is reason to fear that cheating—gross cheating no matter how sophisticated it may be from a pharmacological point of view—will offset the effective value of the athletes. There is reason to fear that a "cosi fan tutti" culture will prevail and that behind the screen of more or less sincere statements of principle, the conviction will remain widespread that it is not possible to achieve great results without pharmacological support. It is for this reason that the sanctioning of Dr. Ferrari (…) cannot be mild (Tribunale di Bologna 2004: 81).

Ferrari's case ultimately gave way to an absence of hard evidence and, like that of his one-time mentor Conconi, the statute of limitations. The Bologna Court of Appeals in 2006 acquitted him of illegally acting as a pharmacist "because the facts do not exist" and of the sporting fraud because the statute of limitations had run out, despite the existence of "an imposing series of circumstantial evidence." (Corte d'Appello di Bologna, 2006)

As a consequence of this proceeding, Ferrari was banned from practicing as a sports doctor in cycling by the Italy's Cycling Federation, but ignored the ban. In June 2012, in fact, US Anti-Doping Agency (USADA) opened a formal action against him for numerous anti-doping rule violations, including possession, trafficking, and administration of doping products along with the seven-time Tour de France winner Lance Armstrong, the team manager, coach, and physicians of Armstrong's cycling teams. In its notifying letter, USADA writes that

> numerous riders will testify that Dr. Ferrari gave to them, encouraged them to use and/or assisted them in using products and/or prohibited methods, including EPO, blood transfusion and testosterone during the period from 1999 through 2006. Riders and other witnesses will also testify that Ferrari taught them how to devoid detection of their drug use, actively working to conceal rule violations by himself and others throughout the period from 1999 to the present" (U.S. Anti-Doping Agency 2012a: 9).

Ferrari as well as physician and coach of the United States Postal Service team accepted the charges and received lifetime bans a few weeks afterwards (U.S. Anti-Doping Agency 2012b). As documented in USADA's subsequent Reasoned Decision against Lance Armstrong (U.S. Anti-Doping Agency 2012c) and confirmed in Tyler Hamilton's book, Ferrari was the mastermind of the doping and training programs followed by Armstrong and some of his team colleagues since Armstrong's first Tour de France victory in 1999: "Ferrari was our trainer," Hamilton recalls,

> our doctor, our god. … Ferrari had a knack for designing sessions that were like torture devices: enough to almost kill us but not quite. In later years we often heard Lance tell the public that Chris Carmichael was his official coach—and Carmichael built quite a business on that relationship. I know they were friends. But the truth is, during the years I trained with Lance, I don't recall ever mentioning Chris's name or citing a piece of advice Chris had given him. By contract, Lance mentioned Ferrari constantly, almost annoyingly so. *Michele says we should do this. Michele says we should do that* (Hamilton and Coyle 2012: 102).

For the documental evidence corroborating Armstrong's former colleagues' incriminating statements, USADA's decision largely built on an ongoing criminal investigation against Ferrari that is coordinated by the Padua Prosecutor's Office. According to USADA's summary, media reports (Pasqualetto 2011; MacMichael 2011a), and witnesses' testimonies (e.g., U.S. Anti-Doping Agency 2012c: 24–25), Ferrari operated a mobile clinic from a camper van to elude investigators and continued treating leading riders at different locations in Italy and abroad. Among his clients were several leading riders and triathlon athletes, as well as the Peking Olympic 50 km race walk champion Alex Schwazer, who tested positive for EPO shortly before the 2012 London Olympic (Reuters 2012). Ferrari kept contact with his "patients" through his son, who was located in Monaco (U.S. Anti-Doping Agency 2012c: 7, 88). He collected his fees through an anonymous Swiss firm: as reported in the USADA's decision, more than one million dollars in payments were transferred on the bank account of such firm by Armstrong alone (ibid: 7).

3.2.5 Hospital, Health Clinic, and Nursing Home Employees

Several investigations and related proceedings document the frequent involvement of hospital, health clinic, and nursing home employees in the supply of doping products other than the physicians who may also work in these institutions. Low-level health care employees often contribute to the supply of doping products through thefts. A 2000 proceeding of the Bologna Court (Tribunale di Bologna 2000: 64) singled out a male nurse who stole GH from the Endocrinology Division of the Bologna Hospital where he worked and EPO from other divisions. Systematic thefts of drugs from hospitals have also been documented to take place in the 1990s in Tuscany, particularly at the Hospital of Pistoia (Int-NAS-16). In a proceeding recently dealt by the Turin Court, D.F., the receptionist of a local hospital did not steal the drugs themselves but merely booklets of blank prescriptions and the stamps of several hospital physicians so that he could obtain performance-enhancing drugs from local pharmacies at reduced cost. D.F. then re-sold the drugs in the gym he visited and in other places, including the hospital itself (Tribunale di Torino 2009).

Private health clinics may also take part in the supply of doping products, by providing illegal doping methods to elite riders. The recent investigation focusing on the pharmacist Nigrelli, for example, has proven that he arranged blood doping for some elite riders in a private health clinic (NAS Brescia 2011). Not only low-level employees were involved in these illegal practices but reportedly also the physicians and the manager of the clinic. The health clinic Web site, in fact, explicitly offered several "special services" under the heading "sports medicine," including "ozone treatment," "small," and "large auto blood doping" (Pacifici and Donati 2011: 45).

3.2.6 Employees and Sales Representatives of (Para-) pharmaceutical Companies

The last type of health care professionals playing a role in the supply of doping products consists of employees and sales representatives of pharmaceutical and dietary supplement companies, who sometimes work independently and sometimes on behalf of a company. D.F. constitutes the example of a salesman of dietary and para-pharmaceutical products who acted on his own initiative. In the late 1990s, he was proven to supply ephedrine and amphetamine products to three important wholesalers, L.S., P.B., and V.G.F., partially using his wife's pharmacy as a cover (Tribunale di Bologna 2000: 64–67).

A more concerning example emerges from a more recent investigation of the Bologna Branch Office. Three employees of the Italian branch of Swiss drug maker giant, Sandoz, including the commercial director of the Biopharmaceutical Division of Sandoz Italy, allegedly supplied large quantities of GH to the pharmacies suggested by a physician, B.H.E. The physician prescribed GH to numerous bodybuilders and elite athletes, including the female track-and-field World Champion in the master category and a football player of an elite team, Rimini Calcio (Tribunale di Rimini 2011; Il Fatto Quotidiano 2011). As it emerges from extensive wiretappings, the three Sandoz Italy employees were aware of the fact that their expensive drug, Omnitrope, was not bound to children with growth problems and even made plans with B.H.E. to transfer the seat of the physician's activity from Rimini to the nearby Republic of San Marino to better protect the latter's activities. The sale representative of Sandoz Italy held close contacts with some athletes, occasionally providing them with GH at reduced prices and with the special needle (the so-called "pen") to inject it. At the end of 2009, the three Sandoz Italy employees even paid a 4,000 € honorarium to B.H.E. to reward him for his numerous prescriptions, fraudulently justifying the honorarium as a consultancy (ibid.: 41–43). The three Sandoz Italy employees and the physician have been charged of criminal organization (article 416 CP) by the Judge for Preliminary Investigations of the Rimini Court. The case is pending.

Drug makers in Italy and abroad produce many of the doping substances consumed by Italy's users, as these substances to a large extent consist of legitimate drugs. As the pharmaceutical companies are often—largely or entirely—unaware of the diversion of their products onto the doping market, we consider their role as legal producers in the following chapter.

Lastly, employees of drug distributors are reported to be frequently involved in the diversion of legitimate drugs with potential doping effects from the storehouses or trucks of their companies—their involvement occurs through either suspicious disappearances or thefts (Int-NAS-9 and 26).

3.2.7 *Staff Members of Sports Teams*

The large-scale raids repeatedly conducted by the NAS branch offices at several editions of the Giro d'Italia and in other circumstances, such as the "Oil for Drug" investigation, and the considerable amounts of drugs seized in some of these raids[10] leave no doubt that cycling team staff members were not only aware and tolerant of the illegal doping practices of their athletes but were also actively involved in such practices. Following up on the 2001 Giro raid, for example, the Court of San Remo sentenced P.P., the masseur of the team Mercatone Uno, of both doping and sporting fraud and convicted him to 8 months of imprisonment and a 6,000 € fine, as doping products had been found in his possession during the raid (Tribunale di San Remo 2005; see also NAS Firenze 2002; 2005).

Other investigations provide even clearer evidence of the involvement of cycling team staff members in the supply of doping products. The "Muscoli e Fiale" investigation, which was conducted in the late 1990s by the Treviso Branch Office, indicates that the President and two sports directors of two Veneto cycling teams bought doping substances on the black market in Italy and abroad and delivered them to the team athletes and other customers. The illegal network also involved five pharmacists who sold illegally some of these drugs, eight sports physicians and three masseurs, including a Guardia di Finanza officer, who was the masseur of the national juniores cycling team (NAS Treviso 2009).

[10] Over 8,100 doses of doping substances were seized in the 2001 raid by the Florence NAS Branch Office at the Giro d'Italia in San Remo (Int-NAS-16, NAS Firenze 2002). Over 38,000 doses of doping products were seized in the searches conducted during the "Oil for Drug" investigation (NAS 2011; NAS Firenze 2002).

A similar investigation was prompted 2 years later in Brescia by the report of a recreational rider. The latter recalled that he had been pressured by the sports director and another manager of his cycling team to use illegal doping substances if he did not want to be excluded from the first team. The sports director of the rider's team, the director of another team, two pharmacists, several riders, as well as the manager of the Italy's national cycling team (!; see infra) were involved in this investigation (Quotidiano.net 2001; Capodacqua 2000b).

The role of sport directors emerges vividly from an interview with a professional rider-turned witness: "The stuff circulates in every way. Sports directors constitute the main supply channel; they sell it to the riders. My first supplier was a masseur from the Gewiss [a cycling team], he sold EPO at 250,000 lire per ampoule [approximately, €125]." This rider, known as a witness under the nickname of Tau, also confirms that sports directors and other team personnel are not only the retailers but also play a crucial role in initiating riders into illegal doping practices. Asked how he began doping, he answered:

> With the sports director, as almost everybody else. There are some riders who dope since they are young boys. When I started cycling, I did not even think about it. One day, my sports director explained me that he did not let me "run the race", that is, he did not select me among those bound to win, because I did not "treat myself." Still naïve, I replied,: "Why shall I treat myself, I feel perfectly well." Then I understood what he meant. The day of my first dose, the team physician smiled: "At last you also get into the world of doping" (Fazzo and Mensurati 2002b).

Suppliers of doping products can be found not only in cycling teams. An investigation of the Turin Judicial Police and Prosecutor's Office proved widespread illegal doping practices in the football club Juventus Turin from 1994 to 1998, years in which the team won three Italian Championships, the Champions League, the Intercontinental Cup, and Italy's Cup. The related criminal proceeding documented the abuse of an incredible number of drugs at Italy's leading football team, which were bought centrally by the team and administered by the sports physician and his assistants, in some cases without obtaining the informed consent of the players. Whereas the offense of doping itself could not be applied because it was established only in 2000, in 2007 the two main defendants, Giraudo and Agricola, the manager and chief sports physician of the team, were found guilty by Italy's Supreme Court, Corte Suprema di Cassazione (2007), of sporting fraud for purchasing and administering illegal performance-enhancing substances, such as corticosteroids. The Corte di Cassazione confirmed the Turin Prosecutor's Office's original thesis that the offense of sporting fraud could also be committed through the purchase and administration of legal drugs not included in the list of banned performance-enhancing substances, if these are used off label, i.e., for purposes different than those officially foreseen (Tribunale di Torino 2004).

As the verdict handed down by the Court of Cassation states, the defendants were accused, in particular, of

> being in collusion with one another with the aim of achieving an outcome other than that arising as a result of the proper and fair conduct of sporting competitions organized by the Italian Football Federation, Serie A football championship and Coppa Italia, and of having

> carried out a number of related and substantial fraudulent acts [...] in obtaining and administering medicinal products outside the indications authorized by the Ministry of Health to football players with the aim of enhancing their performance (di Cassazione and Sezione Seconda Penale 2007: 37).

While stating that the crime had expired due to the statute of limitations, the Italian Supreme Court of Cassation concluded that even "with reference to medicinal products that are not specifically banned ... the conduct of the accused amounted to the crime described in article 1 of the Act No. 401 of 1989 [i.e. sporting fraud]. In fact, the Court went on, "the trial records provide ample evidence ... that from 1994 to 1998 the administration of the drugs in question actually took place and was often carried out off label, in other words outside the scope of authorization identified by the Ministry of Health or in non-permitted forms." (ibid.).

3.2.8 Sports Federation Officials

The line between the staff members of sports teams and the officials of sports federations is often thin and blurred; however, we believe that it is an important analytical distinction, as the latter belong to sports ruling bodies. Several proceedings based on NAS investigations report the involvement of sports federation officials in doping practices, both as direct suppliers and as "protectors." We will discuss the protection-like services that officials of sports federations and other ruling bodies offer to doping athletes and their suppliers in Chap. 5. Here, we consider exclusively the sports federation officials' role as direct suppliers.

The role of supplier is well documented in the detailed diaries of Daniele Faraggiana, which became public in 1986. Faraggiana was a former decathlete and then a sports physician on the payroll of both Italy's Athletic and Weightlifting Federations. In his diaries, he listed the names of all the athletes he doped (among them, a track-and-field champion of the Los Angeles Olympics), the substances administered, the respective dosages, the negative effects on the athletes' health, and the athletes' performances. The treatment of a national thrower was, for example, described as follows:

> April 17, 1985: up to April 20, methandrostenolone, protein 2 per day; lecithin 1 spoon per day, Supradyn 1 pill per day. If he feels muscle tiredness, Berolase 2 ampules each every second day; vitamin C 3 gr oral or 1 gr intravenously per day. From April 22 Testoviron 100 mg every Monday, Wednesday, and Friday up to May 5; vitamin B12 (Benexol B12 or Epargriseovit 2 red ampules or similar), Epargrisovit 2 red ampules intramuscularly or intravenously every two days up to ....; Honey, brewer's yeast, Vitamin E (Ephinol, 1 pill per day from April 22 to ....; protein and lecithin as above and Supradyn. Diet without fats, increase starchy food in the last 10 .... If sleepiness arises, Brain 3 pack. Die; if laziness arises, Sargenor 4-6 ampoules die (Donati 1989: 78).

Faraggiana also listed the transfers of doping substances to coaches and other physicians, including Prof. Conconi, with details about the types and quantities and the dates of each transfer. On another sheet, he also summarized the philosophy of his "pharmacological strategy", writing that this had "to complement the technical strategy" and he should also "give copy of [his] strategy" to the trainer of all throwers, according to whom "50 % of the results depend on the medical therapy" (ibid: 89; see also Donati 2012: 51–60).

Donati's casual discovery of a large box of about 1,000 bottles (about 100,000 doses) of the prohibited drug methandrostenolone in the offices of the Italian Athletics substitute Federation (FIDAL) in 1985 also seems to suggest the federation's involvement in doping practices (ibid: 76). However, these discoveries and the repeated public complaints of Donati and a few other federation officials did not lead to any criminal law or sports investigations. On the contrary, as we discuss below, Primo Nebiolo, who was then the President of both the Italian and worldwide athletics federations (known as International Association of Athletics Federations),[11] ignored the reports and attempted to cover up the scandal (Donati 2012: 30–32).

More recently, in the investigation "Oil for Drugs," a high-level official of the Italian Cyclist Federation (FCI) was reported to be coordinating a group of distributors of doping substances and two controversial physicians who prescribed riders doping substances and methods. The NAS final report to the Rome Prosecutor's Office hypothesizes that the FCI official with his accomplices ran a criminal organization, which he himself headed. The official repeatedly put these suppliers in contact with potential customers and especially elite riders, misusing FCI's funds and other properties. To increase his position within the federation, the official even set up teams of doping riders, who scored well in competitions and thus helped consolidate the official's prestige and power (NAS Firenze 2005: 509–512).

Coaches—regardless of whether they are on the payroll of a private sports team or a sports federation—may play a crucial role even when they are not actively involved in the purchase or administration of doping products but merely tolerate or recommend their use. One member of our research team (Donati) recalls that, in preparation of the 1984 Los Angeles Olympic Games, all the coaches of Italy's national track-and-field teams accepted the administration of testosterone and anabolic steroids and blood transfusions to their athletes to enhance the latter's performance.[12] All athletes—other than those trained by Donati—participated in such activities, which were administrated centrally by the Athletics Federation in close cooperation with Prof. Conconi. Reflecting on this experience, Donati (2003) concluded: "It was then that I understood how, when it comes to doping, the key figure is the coach; it is not really a question of honest or dishonest athletes but of honest or dishonest coaches." The evidence that we have presented in Chap. 2 and

[11] For biographical details, See http://en.wikipedia.org/wiki/Primo_Nebiolo.

[12] Whereas the use of testosterone and steroids had already been banned by the IOC and, in Italy, by the Ministry of Health , blood transfusion was then not prohibited, although it had all the characteristics of doping—a fact that led Donati to reject it.

we present below nevertheless suggests that the athletes cannot be dismissed uniformly as "innocents," entirely lacking culpability.

3.2.9 *Veterinary Physicians, Breeders, and Drivers*

We discuss these three types of suppliers jointly, as the NAS Investigations Database and other sources do not provide specific information on each. A large 2003–2004 investigation conducted by the Naples NAS Branch Office documented how widespread doping practices were in the world of horseracing. The 140 veterinary physicians, breeders, and drivers charged exchanged doping products, which they administered to horses. One of the purposes of these practices was to "fix" the results of official competitions organized by UNIRE[13] and thus earn considerable sums of money with legal and illegal bets. An imprecise number of suspects, presumably no larger than the 25 persons who were arrested, were also charged of criminal organization (article 416 CP). Predominantly based in the area of Naples, they largely used doping substances received from robberies and especially truck robberies (see below; see also Fazzo and Mensurati 2002b).

Another 2006 investigation conducted by the Naples police flying squad, reported in the media, confirmed the administration of doping substances to horses to fix at least 50 races at some of the best Italian racetracks, especially in Campania. Both cases proved the veritable maltreatment of horses, which often had accidents as a result of the heavy stimulants and diuretics taken and were slaughtered as soon as they could not be used in competitions (De Arcangelis 2006; see also La Repubblica 2004a). Veterinarians, breeders, and drivers are often threatened by, or colluded with, members of camorra groups who have repeatedly tried to fix races particularly but not only in the Campanian racetracks. A telling detail is the fact the racetrack of Cirigliano in Aversa, a town north of Naples dominated by the powerful Casalesi clan, recorded in 2007 the highest average of bets in whole of Italy (Zunino 2007). Horses are made run not only in official racetracks but also in unauthorized ones or even on regular streets at night or at dawn, where horses are maltreated even more (Zunino 2009, Int-NAS-22 and 23).

A 2008 investigation of the Italian Polizia di Stato coordinated by the Lucca Prosecutor's Office again proved the fixing of dozen races, in several racetracks, and the maltreatment of the horses, which were routinely given doping substances. This case also demonstrated the pervasiveness of illegal practices in the world of Italian horseracing and not just in the South (La Repubblica 2008).

---

[13] UNIRE (Unione Nazionale Incremento Razze Equine) is a public body established in 1932 and charged with the promotion of horse breeding and the organization of horse races (for further information, see http://www.unire.gov.it/).

3.2.10 Athletes

NAS investigations and media reports indicate that athletes do not just use doping products to increase their performance but they or their closest family members also engage in the import and distribution of doping substances. Given their frequent trips abroad, elite athletes are in an ideal position to import doping substances. According to some of our interviewees (Int-NAS-25 and 26), it also may be the case that famous athletes are likely to be less frequently and less intensively checked at customs controls. Exploiting differences in the national regulations and enforcement, they also may be able to buy some of these products legally and then to sell amounts in excess of their consumption needs to other people.

Most athletes engage in these activities to increase their own sports performance. In 2005, for example, the Lithuanian rider, Raimondas Rumšas was arrested at his house in Lucca for smuggling banned performance-enhancing drugs into France. On the day of Rumšas' third place finish in the 2002 Tour de France, the French police had discovered corticoids, EPO, testosterone, GH, and steroids in his wife's car. She was jailed for several months before being released, despite her claim that the drugs were for her mother-in-law. In January 2006, Rumšas and his wife received a 4-month suspended prison sentences for the import of prohibited doping substances (cnn.com 2006). The wife of another rider was also arrested in 2005 at the Italian-French border because she transported EPO ampoules in her car, while her husband, an Italian rider, was taking part in the Tour de France (Il Corriere della Sera 2005).

A few athletes, however, also engage in the illicit trade of doping substances to re-sell these drugs to others. A recent investigation coordinated by the Mantua Prosecutor's Office has, for example, singled out an elite rider who imported—through undetermined channels—steroids, GH, and other products and sold them to colleagues and even a pharmacist (NAS Brescia 2011). The rider-cum-witness previously mentioned recalls that his own cycling career was, at a certain point, enhanced by his experience in supplying doping substances: "My team manager had understood, he told me: 'I keep you for another while, even if you ride slowly. The only thing you have to procure me is the stuff.'" The witness goes on recalling that many people turned to him, because it was known that he had a good supplying channel. "The list of my customers would be long"—he adds—"physicians, sports directors, colleagues" (Fazzo and Mensurati 2002b).

3.2.11 Body-Builders

As much as athletes, body-builders, too, occasionally trade in the same doping products they consume. Whereas most body-builders remain user–dealers, a few expand the scale of their businesses beyond the retail level, as proven by several NAS investigations. The main defendant of an investigation carried out by Udine

NAS Branch Office in 2004–2005, for example, was a famous body-builder, who had also been elected "Mister Universe." Based in Trieste, the body-builder imported considerable quantities of steroids and other doping products from nearby Slovenia. He then partially retailed these drugs in one of his gyms and partially sold them to a network of distributors who were located in other Italian regions, above all in Lombardy, Veneto, and Marche (NAS Udine 2009a).

Among body-builders selling doping substances, police officers and private security personnel compose a numerically consistent and particularly worrying subtype. As we have seen in the previous chapters, body-building is an attractive activity for both sets of professions, which are usually associated, especially at low levels, with an athletic and imposing physical presence (see Hoberman 2012). As other body-builders, some public and private security staff members practicing body-building sell doping products to finance their own consumption habits and, in some cases, earn extra money.

Several bouncers, for example, were reported mostly as customers but also as occasional retailers of doping substances in the investigations of the Bologna Branch Office (e.g., Tribunale di Bologna 2000; Tribunale di Forlì 2009). In an investigation carried out in Brescia, the owner of a private security firm, a former law enforcement officer, did not solely retail but also distributed large quantities of anabolic steroids, providing them to a large network of lower-level suppliers (Int-NAS-9).

Several investigations also detail the illegal supplying activities of law enforcement officers, who are themselves body-builders. A 2001–2002 investigation of the Udine NAS revealed that a Guardia di Finanza agent and his cousin, both body-builders, sold doping products in the gym they visited, in other places, and via mail. Their main supplier was the brother of one of them, a Polizia agent based in Naples. The illicit trade was hidden through the dietary supplement shop of the police agent's wife (NAS Udine 2009b). More recently in Turin, an investigation of the local NAS branch office and Prosecutor's Office revealed that a Polizia di Stato officer bought large quantities of steroids and stimulants via the Internet and then sold them to the clients of his wife's esthetical center and to several of his colleagues. Some of his colleagues further retailed the drugs to other policemen and other customers in the gyms of Turin and periphery. In total, 21 policemen were reported in different Italian regions; however, only three acted as suppliers (Numa 2010; Tribunale di Torino 2012a).

3.2.12 Other Illegal Suppliers

The final category of illegal suppliers consists of persons with no distinctive profession or occupation. There are many of them, and they are, above all, active in the thoroughly illegal segments of the market for doping products, as producers of doping substances in illegal labs, thieves, truck hijackers, or operators of specialized

Web sites. A good illustration of this type of supplier is the jobless former nurse of a Turin hospital, who produced anabolic steroids in a lab close to Brescia and marketed them through a Web site on behalf of an international criminal organization (Int-NAS-9).

3.3 The Illegal Suppliers' Motives

The primary and secondary motives of the main types of illegal suppliers of doping products are summarized in Table 3.3.

Unsurprisingly, profit provides the main and often sole motive for the nine types of illegal suppliers belonging to the categories of "gym," "health care," "horseracing," and "other" and for body-builders. Whereas the latter may also want to finance their own consumption, gym owners and managers, body-building instructors, managers of dietary supplement shops, hospital employees, and other people with no specific professional or occupational background have no other, discernible motive than profit to enter the trade in doping products. As illustrated by the case of Dr. Ferrari (Tribunale di Bologna 2004) and the Bologna pharmacist involved in the "Campioni senza valore" investigation (Int-NAS-10), many pharmacists and physicians administering or selling doping products are also driven by profit. As the Sandoz Italy case points out, though, in some cases the main gain may not be personal but possibly institutional (Tribunale di Rimini 2011). Most of Prof. Conconi's financial earnings, too, did not consist of private money but of funds for his biochemical university center (Tribunale di Ferrara 2003).

The closer the supplier comes to the organized sports system, the more important nonfinancial motives become. The Conconi's case, for example, indicates that prestige may be an important complementary motive for the some physicians involved in illegal doping practices (Tribunale di Ferrara 2003). Physicians and pharmacists, such as Nigrelli (NAS Brescia 2011), may also break laws and the ethical codes of their professions out of a misconceived love for sports, having become fans of the athletes they treat. Whatever the exact motives, these professionals probably feel that the fame of the winning elite athletes at least partially reflects on them and may take satisfaction in giving those athletes a decisive advantage through their doping therapies and products (see also Waddington 2011).

Nonfinancial motives seem to be dominant for suppliers belonging to the organized sports world and for the athletes who trade in doping products. Staff members of sports teams and sports federation officials may receive a premium or a pay rise when some of their athletes are successful but have no other direct financial gain from the athlete's doping practices. The illegal behavior of staff members of sports teams and sports federation officials can rather be explained in terms of "overconformity" with norms and values embodied in sports, as the result of a socialization taken to extremes (Escriva 2001; Coackley and Pipe 2009). Dr. Faraggiana, a former decathlete and sports physician, who systematically treated the athletes of the Italian Athletics (FIDAL) and Weightlifting Federations with doping substances, did not

Table 3.3 Primary and other motivations of the types of suppliers of doping products in Italy

Category	Type	Motive	
		Primary	Other
Gym	Gym managers or owners and body-building instructors	Personal profit	n.a.
	Managers or owners of dietary supplement shops	Personal profit	n.a
Health care	Pharmacists	Personal profit	Prestige, sports success
	Physicians	Personal or institutional profit	Prestige, sports success
	Hospital employees	Personal profit	n.a.
	Employees, sale representatives of(para-) pharmaceutical companies	Personal or company profit	n.a.
(Human) organized sports world	Staff members of sports teams	Sports success	Personal profit/career
	Staff members of sports federations	Sports success	Career
Horseracing	Veterinary physicians, breeders, and drivers	Personal profit	n.a.
Use	Athletes	Sports success	Personal profit, group solidarity
	Body-builders	Personal profit	Own consumption
Other	People with no distinctive profession or occupation	Personal profit	n.a.

Source: our elaboration on the basis of the NAS investigations analyzed

receive a premium and had no other personal gain. Just like the trainer he quoted in his notes, he was simply convinced that a "pharmacological strategy" was unavoidable to be competitive (Donati 1989: 89). Even though they are not financial, selfish motives cannot be ruled out even in the case of many staff members of sports teams and sports federation officials. In fostering or tolerating doping practices and thus achieving sports successes, they might also aim to consolidate and extend their own positions, foster their careers, and increase sponsor or government funding for their own teams or federations.

Most athletes and competitive body-builders who import or export doping substances for personal use are probably also largely driven by overconformity to sports rules, i.e., the desire to score well competition and be accepted by their peers, as Tau's above-mentioned quote suggests. For the super elite athletes of some popular disciplines, such as cycling, tennis, and track and field, though, succeeding athletically and succeeding financially may be two sides of the same coin. A rider or tennis player, for example, might be driven by an interest in enhancing his or her performance and beating the competition, but a good result in an important event could entail new contracts with professional teams or sponsors and may sometimes result in a substantial direct payment, e.g., a large prize.

Financial motives are more clearly distinguishable among those athletes who trade in doping substances not only for their own consumption but also sell them to other sportspersons. Many athletes selling or giving doping substances to other colleagues are not exclusively driven by financial incentives, though. Tau, the earlier-mentioned rider-turned witness recalls: "Everybody knew everything. And there was even some sense of solidarity, if you had only a vial left, you shared it with those riders who were without. If a colleague was riding fast, you offered him to procure him the stuff, so that he did not stress out and focused only on winning" (Fazzo and Mensurati 2002b).

Chapter 4
Distribution Chains and Market Relationships

Abstract In the fourth chapter, we first analyze the distribution chains composed by legal and illegal suppliers of doping products in Italy, noting that the length of the chain and the legal status of the transactions vary depending on the products exchanged. Given the embeddedness of many supply-side activities in legitimate professions and exchanges, we then argue that the relationships the suppliers develop with each and their customers can often be subsumed under the broad category of white-collar crime. Tout court illegal enterprises also emerge, though, particularly among the suppliers dealing with substances that are illegally manufactured for doping purposes. Although the chapters only analyze empirical data on Italy, the findings here presented can be considered illustrative of the market for doping products in other countries, which have yet not been studied empirically. Future projects are called to ascertain empirically similarities and differences between the Italian market and what remains unexplored elsewhere.

In this chapter we first analyze the distribution chains composed by legal and illegal suppliers of doping products, noting that the length of the chain and the legal status of the transactions vary depending on the products exchanged. Given the embeddedness of many supply-side activities in legitimate professions and exchanges, we then argue that the relationships the suppliers develop with each and their customers can often be subsumed under the broad category of white-collar crime. Tout court illegal enterprises also emerge, though, particularly among the suppliers dealing with substances that are illegally manufactured for doping purposes.

L. Paoli and A. Donati, *The Sports Doping Market: Understanding Supply and Demand, and the Challenges of Their Control*, DOI 10.1007/978-1-4614-8241-3_4,

4.1 Sources, Distributions Levels, and Connections Between the Legal and Illegal Segments of the Market

Many suppliers identified in the earlier typology—e.g., physicians, pharmacists, but also members of sport teams and sports federations—operate as retailers; that is, they sell doping substances or administer doping substances and methods directly to the final users. Other suppliers are, instead, wholesalers. Employees and salesmen of (para)-pharmaceutical companies are the most obvious example of this category, as they rarely have direct contacts with users and supply pharmacies or less frequently physicians. Whereas most gym owners and managers are exclusively active at the retail level, some also operate at the middle or wholesale levels, and a few import doping drugs from abroad, particularly through Internet. Hospital employees stealing doping products or prescription forms from hospitals are also a hybrid category: they may or not be retailers depending on whether they provide users or other suppliers with the drugs they have stolen from the hospitals or bought from pharmacies using stolen prescriptions.

A peculiarity of the market for doping products is that not all the suppliers engage in market relationships with the final consumers of the doping products. A sports team or sports federation physician, masseur, or other staff member usually administers a performance-enhancing substance or method to an athlete without expecting any immediate financial reward from him or her. The sports team or sports federation staff member may even not have purchased the drug or doping equipment himself. He (or, less likely, she) either receives the drug or doping equipment directly from the team or federation, which has bought it centrally (as happened in the Faraggiana's case), or is provided with it by the athlete, who has bought the doping material independently.

To further clarify the (often variable) market position of the different types of suppliers, we need to identify the sources and distribution levels of the different doping products, and to do so, we also need to distinguish between doping substances and methods, on the one hand, and among different doping substances, on the other. In the case of doping methods, it hardly makes sense to speak of a distribution system, as these methods are administered using legitimate and often banal medical instruments. All doping substances, instead, entail a distribution system that requires close examination. However, the system can have different numbers and types of levels depending on the substances and quantities traded and the degree of entrepreneurship of the final users. In delineating the sources and distribution levels, we also establish the legal status of the sources and transactions between the different distribution levels, thus distinguishing the illegal suppliers from those who are unaware of the illegal nature of the exchanges they are involved in.

4.1.1 Doping Methods

Doping methods, such as transfusions, are the simplest case. As there is no real distribution system for them, it makes no sense to distinguish between retailers and wholesalers. Doping methods are usually practiced only on elite or professional athletes, and according to the evidence found in the NAS investigations, they are administered by physicians working in public (university) hospitals, such as Conconi

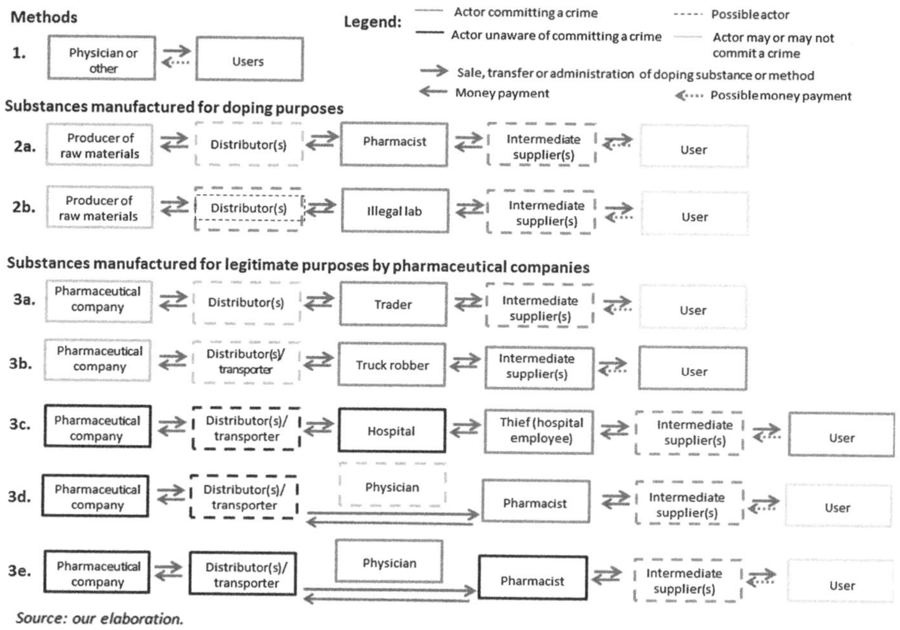

Fig. 4.1 Main distribution chains of doping methods and substances

(see Tribunale di Ferrara 2003) or private health clinics (NAS Brescia 2011) or, more rarely, by the staff members of a sports team or members of the athletes' entourage (e.g., NAS Padova 2009; NAS Brescia 2011; see case 1 of Fig. 4.1).[1]

In order to administer a transfusion, by far the most frequent doping method, the suppliers need specialized equipment. Conconi obtained it regularly from the Ferrara University Hospital (Tribunale di Ferrara 2003), and the private health clinic involved in the recent investigation coordinated by the Mantua Prosecutor's Office reportedly provided it to its staff (Pacifici and Donati 2011). In other cases, it is not clear where the equipment came from. We see two possible alternatives: the equipment can be bought legally by the supplier of the doping method or diverted from hospitals and other health care centers. The recent Mantua proceeding additionally indicates that riders have equipped themselves with portable equipment to keep their blood refrigerated so that they can re-inject it at their own convenience (NAS Brescia 2011; Pacifici and Donati 2011).

4.1.2 Substances Manufactured for Doping Purposes

Substances can be produced exclusively for doping purposes in pharmacies or in illegal labs, in Italy and abroad. NAS investigations indicate that "corrupt" pharmacists or people with access to pharmacy labs still occasionally prepare such drugs,

[1] Similar evidence emerges also from doping scandals abroad (e.g., D'hont 2007; Dopingkommission 2009).

albeit less frequently than in the past. At the end of the 1990s, for example, a Bologna pharmacist prepared stimulants and sold these and a variety of other doping products to the coaches of several Italian Olympic and Serie A football teams (Int-NAS-16; see case 2a of Fig. 4.1). A few years afterwards, another investigation of the Bologna NAS Branch Office singled out a borderline case, that is, a salesman of para-pharmaceutical products who used the lab annexed to his wife's pharmacy to prepare pills of ephedrine, clobenzorex, and caffeine, working, however, on a much smaller scale and degree of sophistication than the real pharmacist (NAS Bologna 2000: 276–303).

If pharmacists sell the substances they produce directly to the users, they are "producer–retailers." If they sell the same drugs to coaches, trainers, or other representatives of sports teams or sports federations or to other doping suppliers, as in the case of the Bologna pharmacist, they act as "producer–wholesalers." Given the explicit performance-enhancing goal of the drugs produced, the production itself and any subsequent exchange are by definition illegal, even though pharmacists are often able to hide the illegal nature of their activities under the cover of their legal profession.

The legal status of the exchange of raw materials before production varies by circumstance. As far as we could reconstruct, the Bologna pharmacist bought the raw materials from legal suppliers (Int-NAS-16). Instead, the salesman of para-pharmaceutical products who used the lab annexed to his wife's pharmacy imported raw materials illegally from Switzerland (NAS Bologna 2000: 303–306).

Doping substances can also be produced in labs under completely illegal conditions and, in this case, usually consist of counterfeited products (see case 2b of Fig. 4.1). In fact, known brands make it easier for producers and retailers to market the doping products. There is also a difference in the drugs produced and clientele served. Pharmacists producing a doping substance tend to serve elite and professional athletes. Illegal labs instead focus predominantly on body-builders and thus produce above all anabolic steroids (Int-NAS-9).

Few investigations provide evidence of the existence of such illegal labs in Italy. In the investigation "Artificial Body" of the Bologna Branch Office (NAS Bologna 2000), the existence of labs illegally producing doping products was hinted at in several wiretapped phone conversations, but the labs themselves were never identified. An indirect confirmation of the existence of such labs was given by the seizure of numerous drug labels and, in particular, Masteron, Equipoise, Goldline Nort-4 injection, Goldline Bolasterone injection, and Goldline Nandrolone from P.B. in Bologna. In a previous conversation with a client who was complaining about the quality of Winstrol ampoules, P.B. reassured him about the quality of the lab that had prepared them and was heard saying that "at most they might have been made a mistake with the labels" (NAS Bologna 2000: 226–227).

In a more recent case, the Brescia Branch Office dismantled a laboratory located near Brescia, which was part of a large network of laboratories set up by a South African national. An employee of that network, a young Israeli chemist, spent several weeks in Brescia to train the main Italian suspect, D.B. (Int-NAS-9). The South African ringleader bought active ingredients primarily from an illegal lab in Moldavia and delivered it to D.B. through a Moldavian courier service specialized in supplying Moldavian products to Moldavian migrants living in Italy. According to the estimates of the Brescia Branch Office, D.B. used 2,000–3,000 L of active ingredients and produced at least several million pills. Most of the pills were of poor quality, despite the fact that D.B.'s Web site and the other foreign Web site of the organization he was part of were guaranteed by the logo "British Dragon." This is a well-known brand in body-builders' circles and is supposed to guarantee the quality of the steroids sold (Int-NAS-9).

Illegal labs can either sell their products directly to users or to other suppliers. The lab mentioned in the Bologna investigation served primarily the latter, including some large-scale wholesalers, such as P.B. The suspect operating the Brescia lab distributed his own products and other drugs manufactured abroad through a Web site and thus reached both users and other suppliers (Int-NAS-9).

Doping substances may also have been produced exclusively for doping purposes by pharmacists or illegal labs located abroad. In the above-mentioned year-2000 investigation of the Bologna Branch Office, for example, the main suspect, P.B., purchased doping drugs, among many other channels, from a Greek physician, who prepared them for him (NAS Bologna 2000: 428–438). In another NAS investigation in Aosta, a gym manager bought anabolic steroids from a Swiss person who produced the drugs (Int-NAS-9).

As stressed by all NAS respondents, most foreign labs remain unknown to Italian police forces. These labs seem to be, however, a considerable, if not the largest, source of steroids and other doping substances used by body-builders. At the end of the 1990s, an appointment calendar seized from one of the largest importers, V.G.F., demonstrated that he had contacts with presumably illegal producers in Portugal, Albania, and Poland (Tribunale di Bologna 2000: 67). More recently, several other suppliers belonging to the category of "gym" also imported steroids produced in foreign illegal labs, with Spain being the source most often mentioned (NAS Napoli 2003; Tribunale di Siracusa 2010; Tribunale di Bologna 2004: 125–126).[2] Our sources indicate that a large share—albeit inestimable—of the steroids and other doping substances produced in illegal labs are sold via pseudo "online pharmacies" and other dedicated Web sites (e.g., Int-NAS-10, 12). These Web sites are sometimes shut down, above all by the US authorities, but they often reappear under slightly different names or with a seat in an exotic country.

A recent, very innovative investigation of the Bologna Branch Office identified a network of Web sites selling anabolic steroids and storehouses of the same substances in different countries in Europe and elsewhere. The central server of the network was based in Slovenia and was run by a Slovenian couple who lived in Austria. Once a customer placed an order on a Web site, an automated system transferred the order to one of the storehouses, making sure to pick different storehouses in the case of repeated orders by the same customers to avoid steroid deliveries from the same country. One of the storehouses was based in Northeastern Italy and was identified by the Bologna Branch Office after some packages containing steroids

[2] In some cases, though, NAS officers have difficulties to ascertain whether the doping substances they intercept have been produced by illegal labs or legitimate companies (see Chap. 7).

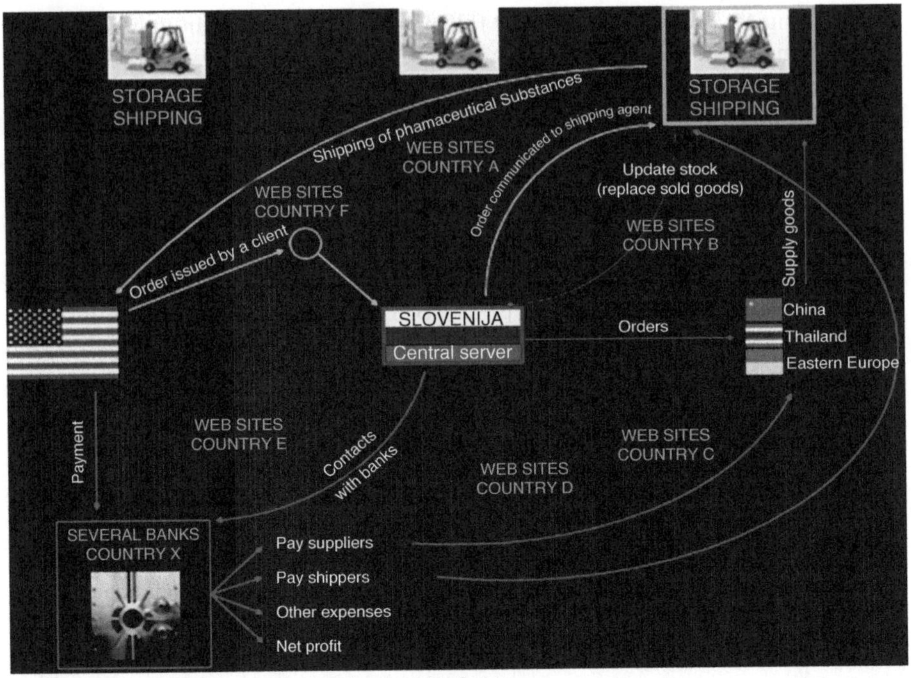

Source: Our elaboration on the basis of Int-NAS-11.

Fig. 4.2 Graphic representation of the network of Web sites and storehouses of doping products identified in the investigation of the Bologna NAS Branch Office

were seized at the border (Int-NAS-13; see Fig. 4.2). According to the Austrian police who finally arrested the Slovenian couple in December 2011 in close cooperation with NAS and the US DEA, this had earned about US$50 million with the business (Der Kurier 2011; DiePresse.com 2012).

The Bologna Branch Office was able to trace shipments of steroids ordered through the Slovenian Web site from China, Thailand, and several Eastern European countries. However, it could not collect any direct information on the producers themselves (Int-NAS-13). Whereas the Eastern European labs are likely to be at least formally illegal, we have no information on the legal status of the production centers located in China and Thailand.

As much as the substances produced in Italy, the substances produced abroad for exclusive doping purposes are likely to be counterfeited. One of our interviewees, for example, recalls that his and other NAS branch offices recently seized large quantities of nandrolone-based drugs, allegedly produced by the Greek company Norma but containing little or no active ingredient (Int-NAS-9). However, in the current project we have no elements to assess the share of the Italian doping market that is accounted for by counterfeited products. Italy's prosecutor's offices do not always order the analysis of the substances seized, and, even if they do, they rely on different laboratories for the analyses, and no centralized register is kept.

What is clear is the fact that a growing number of Italian users take advantage of Internet and order doping substances, primarily steroids, from Web sites. When those who operate the Web-based businesses are located abroad, the users buying steroids bypass the whole Italian distribution chain and become, so-to-say, "users–importers"—in the same way in which illegal drug users living in countries surrounding the Netherlands increasingly go there to buy cannabis or other illegal drugs (Paoli 2000; Fijnaut and De Ruyver 2008). However, profiting from the ambiguous legal nature of doping products, the consumers of steroids and other doping substances do not even have to physically move out of the country. From their computer desks, they simply order the drugs they need and have them delivered at home by mail. Judging from the parcels intercepted by NAS, foreign users do not behave differently than Italian users: they too increasingly buy steroids and other doping substances on the Internet, even if they may be less targeted by their respective law enforcement agencies than their Italian counterparts (Int-NAS-1, 7, and 25; see also the foreign investigations summarized in Chap. 1).

4.1.3 Substances Manufactured for Legitimate Purposes

A large, but not precisely known, share of the doping substances sold in Italy appears to have been produced by a legitimate drug manufacturer located in Italy or abroad and diverted at some stage from the legal distribution chain. The database on NAS investigations indicates that 85,086,928 doses of doping substances or 96.6 % of the total doses seized consist of "drugs authorized in Italy." Only 2,956,637 doses or 3.4 % are not authorized. For the reasons explained earlier, there is no way to know which share of the drugs authorized in Italy has been effectively produced by a legitimate drug manufacturer in Italy or abroad. The perception of NAS officers is that the large-scale shipments intercepted as a rule contain legitimate drugs and that counterfeited substances are most likely to be bought by private individuals in small quantities on the Internet (Int-NAS-2, 3, 9 10, 16, 25, 26).

At least in principle, the diversion of a legitimate drug that can be used for doping purposes may be decided by the company itself or one of its dependencies. On the basis of an in-depth study of the corporate crime in the pharmaceutical industry in the late twentieth century, the Australian scholar Braithwaite (1993: 525) concluded that "the pharmaceutical industry arguably has the worst record of serious corporate crime of any industry"; hence, we regard the involvement of pharmaceutical companies in the supply of doping products as a possibility. This possibility is also concretely suggested by three criminal investigations. First, in the early 1980s and 1990s, the Italian subsidiary of the pharmaceutical giant Boehringer delivered large quantities of EPO to Conconi for years, notwithstanding the fact that his specialization was not the treatment of anemia or cancer but biochemistry applied to sports (Toti 2003)—the company or any of its representatives were never charged, however. Second, the ongoing proceeding of the Rimini Court, involving the employees and a commercial director of Sandoz Italy, does not in any way prove that the sale of GH for doping purposes was a company policy. However, given the charges raised against the commercial director, the proceeding does suggest that the sale of GH for doping purposes was not just due to the deviant attitudes of a couple of low-level employees (Tribunale di Rimini 2011; see also Il Fatto Quotidiano 2011). The latter proceeding also confirms a finding of corporate-crime research (Gobert and Punch 2003: 30–31; Braithwaite 1985: 8): excessively ambitious sales goals set for low- and middle-level employees (and the premiums offered for robust sale increases) may have a powerful criminogenic effect, if there are no strong compliance controls within the company to make sure that the goals are reached by legitimate means.

The off-label sale of GH is by no means a uniquely Italian practice. In the United States, Pfizer, a pharmaceutical giant, agreed to pay in 2007 almost $35 million in fines to settle federal charges that a rival drug maker, Pharmacia, it had acquired 4 years earlier had inappropriately marketed another GH-based product, Genotropin, for off-label use (Reuters 2007a). In its fourth settlement over illegal marketing activities since 2002, Pfizer agreed to pay $2.3 billion in 2009 to settle civil and criminal allegations that it had illegally marketed its pain-killer Bextra. According to the *New York Times*, this was "the largest health care fraud settlement and the largest criminal fine of any kind ever" (Gardiner 2009; see also Rost 2006).

Third, a 2009 Guardia di Finanza investigation demonstrated also the involvement of the staff of a legitimate pharmaceutical company in the production of EPO and GH. After seizing some rare microdoses of EPO at a suspect's house, the Guardia di Finanza raided the drug manufacturing company and found 83 bottles containing the active ingredients of EPO and GH that would have been sufficient for the production of 10,000 ampoules of analogous doping products (Capodacqua 2009).

Rather than dealing directly with controversial subjects, pharmaceutical companies most often simply produce more drugs than can be justified on the basis of the demand for legitimate therapeutic purposes. A few years ago, the Belgian Senate (Senaat 2005) estimated that about 80 % of the global production of EPO (assessed in four billion euro) and GH ended up being misused in sports. The exactness of this estimate might be questionable—indeed some experts (e.g., Jelkmann 2012, personal communication) have expressed doubts about its accuracy—but Italian anti-doping law enforcement activities indicate how companies deal with overproduction. In a recent investigation coordinated by the Brescia NAS Branch Office, two Spanish distributors of an Italian pharmaceutical company introduced large quantities of Winstrol, an anabolic steroid, on the black market, and some of these substances were then smuggled into Italy. Only after being alerted by NAS did the Italian company interrupts the delivery of the steroids to the two Spanish storehouses (Int-NAS-9). This case illustrates a fundamental weakness in the regulation of the international drug market. Namely, each company produces and sells as much of its own drugs as possible, and there is no overarching regulatory body checking if the quantities produced worldwide correspond at least roughly to the demand for legitimate therapeutic purposes (int-NAS-26).

NAS investigations also show that Italian illegal suppliers, particularly those operating on a large scale, often receive doping substances from Spain and other countries with supposed lax regulation (see also Donati 2007: 73–75) and that these substances have been produced by local pharmaceutical companies or from branches or companies associated with Italian drug makers. Large-scale shipments of controversial substances, including those that can be used for doping purposes, seem to be often shipped from Spain via Melilla, a Spanish enclave in Morocco that is reported to enjoy particularly lax controls (Int-NAS-9). In one case, for example, large boxes of chorionic gonadotrophin and other doping substances were shipped from the Spanish storehouse of an Italian pharmaceutical company to the Italian member of the large criminal organization run by a South African national (Int-NAS-9). While they lack exact information on the senders, NAS officers believe that most diversions are due not to the employees of the drug makers themselves but to the employees and managers of the foreign drug distributors (see case 3a of Fig. 4.1).

Large-scale Italian suppliers can import substances with performance-enhancing effects that have been legitimately produced in foreign countries using their personal contacts in those countries or in transit countries (Tribunale di Bologna 2004: 125–126; Tribunale di Siracusa 2010). Internet and specifically dedicated Web sites also allow small-scale traders and users to import these substances directly.

Robberies from the storehouses or trucks of drug distributors can also serve the purpose of diverting legitimate drugs with doping properties onto the black market (see case 3b of Fig. 4.1). Several NAS investigations show that illegal suppliers of doping products, particularly in the gym world, more than occasionally receive steroids and other drugs that have been stolen or "lost" from storehouses or trucks of drug distributors (e.g., Tribunale di Forlì 2009: 153). In several cases, the thieves have been linked to the world of organized crime and particularly to the Neapolitan camorra and have a network of pharmacies and other retailers to receive the stolen products (Int-NAS-9 and 26). Two of our interviewees (Int-NAS-9 and 26) suspect that many thefts involving doping substances and other drugs are carried out on the basis of tips by employees of drug distributors or the logistic companies working for the distributors. The thieves seem often to know in advance what the storehouses or trucks contain and steal primarily drugs that can be sold at a premium on the illegal market. According to some NAS respondents (Int-NAS-9 and 26), some companies may also occasionally prefer to place controversial medicines, such as steroids, on the market through a faked robbery, in order to avoid the legal distribution channels, which are subject to many controls.

A 2001 investigation conducted by the Naples Branch Office (not included in the NAS Investigations Database) dismantled a big network specialized in truck robberies and the distribution of the stolen drugs, revealing the complicity of many employees and representatives of the health care sector. The Naples Prosecutor's Office issued 81 arrest warrants, targeting 16 pharmacists, 4 house physicians working for Italy's public health system, 6 drug wholesalers, 2 pharmaceutical salesmen, and 4 couriers in addition to the robbers and several truck drivers who were the latter's accomplices. The drugs—not only doping products but also many others, above all Viagra—were first stored in basements in very unhygienic conditions and then distributed through a network of complacent drug wholesalers, pharmaceutical salesmen, and pharmacies predominantly located in Naples, in Rome, and in Apulia.

Corrupt physicians provided prescriptions so that the drugs could be sold "legally" and the pharmacists could even claim a reimbursement for the drugs sold from the Italy's public health system (Int-NAS-26 and Marino 2001).

The NAS officer (Int-NAS-26) who coordinated that investigation recalls that truck robberies began to occur frequently in the mid-1990s reached their peak at the turn of the century and then suddenly declined in 2004, when the Decree Law 269/2003 introduced the compulsory traceability of all drugs and thus impeded the distribution of stolen drugs through legal channels. Reportedly, truck robberies of pharmaceutical drugs started again in 2007, but on a much smaller scale than in the past.

The diversion of legitimate pharmaceutical substances with performance-enhancing effects may also take place further down the supply chain. As discussed earlier, several hospital employees stole from their workplaces doping substances that had been delivered through legitimate distribution channels and then sold them on the black market, either to users or other suppliers (see case 3c of Fig. 4.1).

Diversion can also take place in pharmacies. The Mantua pharmacist recently targeted by a criminal investigation is regarded as a full accomplice of the illegal doping practices of a professional cycling team, Lampre (NAS Brescia 2011; Pacifici and Donati 2011; see case 3d of Fig. 4.1). At the opposite end, as already mentioned, the pharmacists may be absolutely unaware of the nontherapeutic purposes for which some of their customers buy drugs and sell the latter drugs on the basis either of a prescription written by a corrupt physician (see case 3e of Fig. 4.1) or of a false or stolen prescription. In other cases, the pharmacists may turn a blind eye and not ask detailed questions to his or her customers. This seems or seemed, in particular, to be the policy adopted by many Spanish pharmacies, which are allegedly subject to lax regulations and are indicated as a source of doping products in many Italian and foreign investigations. In 2002 Tau, the rider-turned witness, stated: "Another fundamental supply channel is represented by Spanish pharmacies, when the amateurs go to Spain, they stock up on doping drugs for the whole team" (Fazzo and Mensurati 2002b; see also Int-NAS-9 and 16).

The data previously shown about the sales of gonadorelin suggests that diversion can be substantive, accounting for the overwhelming majority of gonadorelin packages sold in Italy. CVD has never collected data about the legitimate sales of other doping substances from Federfarma, the Italian federation of pharmacies. As most of these substances have broader therapeutic usages than gonadorelin, estimating the share of diverted drugs would undoubtedly be more complicated. In Italy, this has been done so far in a single case. After a 1998 investigation of the Turin NAS and Prosecutor's Office proving the diversion of large quantities of EPO and GH from the local public hospitals, the Health Department of the Region Piedmont estimated that about half of the EPO sold in the region with a market value of 18 billion lire (corresponding to almost nine million euro) was likely to have been diverted for doping purposes (*ANSA* 1999 reported in Donati et al. 2011: 19).

Not only can legitimate drugs be misused for doping purposes, but the active ingredients of doping substances are sometimes included in dietary supplements sold in specialized shops or over the Internet. Several NAS interviewees (e.g., Int-NAS-25 and 26) and prosecutors (Guariniello 2011) pointed out that this is a new market that is not yet sufficiently controlled. Some users may use these dietary supplements with the conscious aim of enhancing their performance or image, while others may inadvertently take them without being aware of the fact that the supplements contain restricted substances.[3]

4.1.4 *Multiple, Variable, and Partially Overlapping Distribution Chains*

The preceding analysis shows that the distribution chains of doping products are very different from the six-level hierarchical model (from importers to end users), which was developed by Preble and Casey (1969) in the late 1960s for the New York heroin market and long considered a correct representation of illegal drug markets in Western countries and particularly in Italy (Arlacchi and Lewis 1990). More recent research indicates that contemporary illegal drug markets, too, considerably depart from that model especially in Europe, not least because the abolition of border controls in the Schengen area easily allows users to obtain cheaper drugs from neighboring countries thus reducing the number of the domestic distribution levels (Paoli 2002a).

The supply of doping products differs even more radically from Preble and Casey's model. The first and most fundamental difference derives from the fact that the market for doping products entails a vast multiplicity of products, which, unlike the heroin of their research, can be produced domestically or imported from foreign countries. Moreover, within several classes of products, and especially in the largest, anabolic agents, there are functionally equivalent products that can be easily substituted with each other, even though the final users or their advisors may have their own preferences.[4] For most classes of products, there are, therefore, multiple sources, and the links between them and the users can be established through a variety of alternative distribution chains. Hence, for example, a body-builder can order a steroid directly from an Italian or foreign Web site, buy it from a gym or dietary supplement shop manager or owner or other retailer, obtain it from a pharmacy through the collusion of a corrupt pharmacist, acquire it on the basis of a false or stolen prescription or a prescription written by a corrupt physician, or receive it from a hospital employee who stole it from his or her workplace.

Second, reflecting the multiplicity of products, sources, and distribution channels, and the increasingly important role of the Internet, the length of the distribution chain for the same products may differ radically. Whereas one user may be able to

---

[3] The NAS Headquarters and the Higher Institute of Public Health have recently launched a joint initiative to systematically analyze dietary supplements bought randomly in different shops throughout Italy with a view to prohibit those containing restricted substances (Int-NAS-25 and 26). The results of such an analysis are not known yet.

[4] If considering the larger category of "opioids," there are more but not nearly as many opportunities for substitution than if considering only opium-derived heroin.

bypass the entire domestic distribution chain by ordering a specific doping product on a foreign Web site and receiving it at home by mail, another user of the same product may buy it from a retailer after it has passed through several hands, i.e., several distribution levels. The big investigation conducted by the Bologna Branch Office in the gym world at the turn of the century reconstructed distribution chains for steroids entailing up to seven levels between the importers and users (NAS Bologna 2000).

Third, departing from typical distributional practices in traditional illegal drug markets, the same suppliers often operate in different distribution chains.[5] P.B., for example, the main suspect of the 2000 "Artificial Body" investigation of the Bologna Branch Office (Tribunale di Bologna 2000), bought different products from different channels: he bought the stimulants produced by the dietary supplement salesman at the pharmacy lab of the latter's wife, imported directly doping products produced from a Greek pharmacist and from another Greek source, and bought large quantities of steroids from a large-scale supplier, L.S., who bought it from the importer, V.G.F., as well as from V.G.F. himself. More recently, the Mantua pharmacist sold elite riders performance-enhancing drugs that had been delivered through legitimate channels to his pharmacy as well as other doping substances that he had purchased on the illegal market, administered analogous transfusions, helped the athletes arrange contacts with other providers of doping methods, and advised them on how to use performance-enhancing drugs the riders had bought for themselves (NAS Brescia 2011).

Fourth, many suppliers play different roles even in the distribution chain of the same products. In illegal drug markets, it rarely happens that an importer or wholesaler also sells small quantities of heroin or cocaine to the final users, because the former simply regard the contacts with the latter as too risky (Reuter and Haaga 1989). In the market of doping products, instead, these contacts are not unusual, particularly in the gym world. To give just one example, despite his large-scale businesses, P.B. also kept on selling steroids and other doping substances in his own gyms (Tribunale di Bologna 2000; Tribunale di Forlì 2009).

4.2 How Best to Conceptualize the Relationships Among the Suppliers?

Whereas the suppliers of doping products may or may not have collaborators or employees and constitute separate illicit enterprises, they are all part of a wider Web of relationships linking them to higher- or lower-level suppliers or users. The analysis of the different distribution chains has documented that suppliers of doping products, with the partial exception of those exclusively administering doping methods,

[5] Note that this may not be a departure from the distributional norm for other diverted pharmaceutical products, such as painkillers.

are part of wide-ranging and often cross-border networks even when they operate through small (or even one-man) enterprises. This finding is entirely consistent with the literature on illegal markets (e.g., Bouchard and Morselli 2013) and also corresponds to the reality of legitimate businesses.

However, the fact that doping products are oftentimes legitimate pharmaceutical products has decisive consequences for the relationships that the suppliers build with each other and with their customers. Unlike suppliers in fully illegal markets, such as those for traditional illegal drugs, the majority of the suppliers of doping products can hide their illegal transactions and their relationships with their "doping partners"—their own suppliers, collaborators, and customers or patients—behind the legitimate roles they play in their businesses, organizations, or professions. The embeddedness of doping-related supply-side activities in legitimate professions, roles, and institutional settings often makes unnecessary the development of separate illegal enterprises to run these activities.

As seen earlier, however, some suppliers have trouble finding a professional cover to hide their involvement in the supply of doping products. Some of them have no suitable profession—as in the case of many nonprofessional body-builders who do not work in the private or public security sector or hijackers attacking trucks to steal performance-enhancing and other drugs. For other suppliers, their profession or occupation is not sufficient to hide the full range of their activities. For many of them, professional affiliations are especially helpful to disguise contacts with users and retailers. For the suppliers working in the health care sector, these affiliations are also helpful to hide upper-level illegal transactions in doping products. Other suppliers, however—e.g., the owners or managers of gyms and fitness centers or the suppliers linked to the organized sports world—are not protected by their profession or occupation when they engage in the production, import (i.e., smuggling), diversion (which often means theft), or distribution of doping products at higher market levels. The trouble is most apparent when these supply-side activities involve anabolic steroids and other products meant for body-builders that have very limited therapeutic value and are therefore more obviously illegal than others. At the higher market levels and especially for steroids, illegal enterprises may develop that are similar to those operating in other illegal markets, such as the market for heroin, cocaine, or other illegal drugs. These are, for example, the enterprises set up by gym owners and managers to import and trade in wholesale quantities of steroids and other doping products for body-builders and those running specialized Web sites or producing doping substances in illegal labs or conducting robberies on trucks. Some illegal partnerships within or across legitimate organizations engaging in the purchase or sale of doping products may also consolidate to such an extent that they can also be regarded as illegal enterprises.

Stated slightly differently, an analytical complication of the market for doping product (but at the same time also a chance for policy-making) is that the market includes both activities that can be best understood in terms of white-collar crime and others that fit into the category of illicit enterprise, with some overlap between the two concepts.

4.2.1 White-Collar Crime

The very embeddedness of doping supply-side activities in legitimate professions, roles, and institutional settings is suggestive of white-collar crime and the related and partially overlapping concepts of occupational, corporate, and organizational crime. In 1949 Sutherland (1983) published a seminal book on white-collar crime in which he documented numerous and very serious crimes perpetrated by America's 70 largest private companies and 15 public utility corporations. Whereas the definition of white-collar crime given in that book has been rightly criticized by later scholars (for a discussion, see Braithwaite 1985; Nelken 2007), Sutherland offered a more straightforward definition in the *Encyclopedia of Criminology*, also published in 1949. In the encyclopedia Sutherland wrote that "the white-collar criminal is defined as a person with high socioeconomic status who violates the laws designed to regulate his occupational activities" (1949: 511 quoted in Geis 1992: 34). This definition suggests a clear correspondence to many of the illicit supplier types that we identified earlier. Pharmacists, physicians, high-level employees and officials of health care clinics, pharmaceutical companies, sports teams, and sports federations, veterinarians and elite athletes meet the requirements of that definition.

Gym owners and managers, managers of dietary supplement shops, breeders, horse drivers, nurses, and other low-level health care employees and staff members of sports teams also "violate laws designed to regulate [their] occupational activities," but they less typically satisfy the requirement of a high socioeconomic status. These suppliers of doping products can be understood, instead, as participants in "occupational crime," which Clinard and Quinney (1973: 188) defined in 1973 as the "violation of the criminal law in the course of activities of a legitimate occupation," to cover persons at all levels of the social structure. In a distinction that has become widely accepted in the literature about white-collar crime, Clinard and Quinney contrasted occupational crime with corporate crime, which is said to consist of "offenses committed by corporate officials for their corporations and the offenses of the corporation itself" (1973: 189). The Sandoz Italy commercial director who was alleged to be involved in the sale of GH for doping purposes might provide an example of corporate crime, depending on the basis—independent or institutional—of his actions. The actions of officials, if not staff members, of private sports teams might also be subsumed under the category of corporate crime, depending on whether the teams are "corporations"[6] and, as above, the basis of the individuals' actions. Other suppliers of doping products—such as university professors and sports federation officials—work, instead, for public institutions. Thus, we do not regard them as corporate criminals but consider them, instead, as a manifestation of the broader concept of organizational crime (e.g., Reiss and Tonry 1993).

---

[6] A "corporation" can take many different forms, generally implying the creation of an entity with its own rights and liabilities, distinct from those of its owners. For our purposes we use the term in reference to corporations that are "for-profit" business enterprises. Private teams typically constitute for-profit business enterprises but may or may not incorporate their operations.

Since Sutherland's white-collar crime book, there have been longstanding doubts whether or not all misbehaviors discussed under this rubric can be considered to count as crime. Sutherland (1945) insisted that violations of all types of law, if they are punished with a sanction, can be considered crime (see also Braithwaite 1985; Nelken 2007: 741–742). Other scholars have argued that the misbehaviors discussed by Sutherland and his followers do not always satisfy the legal criteria for crime. Rather they are violations of "regulatory" laws, as they do not lead to a prosecution in a criminal court (Tappan 1947; Gobert and Punch 2003: 9–14). Given the Italian criminal law provisions on doping, both athletes' consumption and the trade of doping products satisfy even the more restrictive interpretation of white-collar crime. In other countries, in which no criminal law provisions on doping exist, one can only apply the label white-collar crime to doping if that label is interpreted broadly to include violations of administrative laws and sports rules, the first and second pillars of the anti-doping policies reviewed in Chap. 1. However, the broader terms of corporate deviance (Punch 1996) and corporate or organizational wrongdoing or misconduct would still be applicable (Gobert and Punch 2003: 9–14).

The contested legal status of many exchanges of doping products is in itself typical of white-collar crime. As noted by Clarke (1990), all the illegal practices subsumable under the broad heading of this concept take place in a legitimate business or organizational environment during the course of legitimate activities and therefore have an inherently ambiguous nature that leads to contestability of the offenses charged. On the "bright side," however, white-collar criminals are among the most deterrable types of offenders. As Chambliss (1967) argued, they satisfy two conditions: they do not have a commitment to crime as a way of life and their offenses are instrumental rather than expressive. White-collar criminals are also more deterrable than underworld criminals because they have more of those things that can be lost by criminal conviction or informal means of stigmatization—status, respectability, money, a job, a comfortable home, and family life. As noted by Braithwaite (1985) and Simpson (2010–2011), this view is supported by some quasi-experimental time series and interview studies, which suggest that white-collar offenders are deterred by prosecution. We will come back to this issue in our policy implications.

4.2.2 *Illicit Enterprise*

The concept of the illicit or illegal enterprise is most often used to describe the producers and traffickers of illegal goods and services, such as cocaine or heroin or human smuggling, and the relationships that these producers and traffickers develop with each other (e.g., Smith 1975; Haller 1990; van Duyne 1997). As the criminological literature on illegal markets documents, illegal enterprises face specific constraints on their operations, arising from the illegal nature of the products in which they trade. These constraints have been referred to as "constraints of illegality"

(Reuter 1983). At the end of their analysis of the world heroin market, Paoli et al. (2009: 241) concluded:

> In countries with strict enforcement, traffickers and producers are obliged to operate not only without the protections of state institutions, notably the court system, but against those institutions. Illegality then means that the businesses are likely to be small, ephemeral and not vertically integrated, largely relying on preexisting social relationships, such as family ties or bonds of friendship or locality. The factors promoting the development of large firms in the legal portion of the economy—namely, to take advantage of economies of scale and scope—are outweighed in illegal markets by the threats that a strong government poses and the need to reduce visibility.

The illegal enterprises that we have identified in Italy's market for doping products are also subject to the "constraints of illegality" (Reuter 1983). Operating without the benefits of state institutions, they cannot resort to state institutions to enforce contracts. As a result, property rights are poorly protected and employment contracts cannot be formalized, discouraging the development of large, formally organized and enduring enterprises. Moreover, in operating against the state in a country with strict anti-doping enforcement such as Italy, suppliers of doping products also operate under the presumption of overt government hostility, that is, under the constant threat of incarceration and asset seizure.

Much like their counterparts in illegal markets, some suppliers of doping products tend to incorporate illegal relationships and transactions into blood or family relationships to increase the cohesion of their enterprises and reduce their vulnerability to law enforcement efforts (e.g., Reuter 1983, 1985). Hence, as in traditional illegal markets, some of the illegal enterprises set by suppliers of doping products are family businesses, that is, they are based on blood or family ties. For example, D.P. was supported by his sister, mother, and fiancé (Tribunale di Ravenna 2004: 123); the earlier-mentioned US-Nigerian female body-builder based in Sicily fully shared the management of a gym and the import and distribution of doping products with her Italian husband (Tribunale di Siracusa 2010: 23–29), and Dr. Ferrari, a prominent physician involved in illegal doping practices, allegedly held contacts with his "patients" through his son (Pasqualetto 2011; MacMichael 2011a).

Even when they are not (entirely) family-based, illegal enterprises specialized in the sale of doping products tend to be small. For example, despite being one of the largest (known) suppliers of anabolic steroids in Italy, L.S. kept on working primarily by himself, delegating menial tasks only to two or three collaborators, including his estranged wife. L.S. was described as a "lone wolf" by a NAS officer who arrested him twice (Int-NAS-9). Even in the latest 2009 investigation, L.S. was reported to travel almost weekly to the Netherlands where he bought doping products and to deliver them mostly personally by car on the way back to his house south of Naples (Int-NAS-9). Likewise, V.G.F., another longtime large-scale supplier, also preferred to carry out the most risky tasks by himself and therefore still travelled around with a van to pick up the parcels of steroids he had delivered at different addresses under fake identities in Italy (Frezzi 2011; Int-NAS-10). As known from the literature on illegal drug markets, limiting the number of people aware of an illegal business is a frequent strategy of illegal entrepreneurs to reduce their vulnerability to law enforcement efforts (Paoli et al. 2009).

We know of only one case of a formally organized criminal organization. This is the organization that was headed by the former South African employee of a US pharmaceutical company; purchased doping products, active ingredients, and drug labels in several countries, primarily in Moldavia and India; and ran a network of sales representatives and producers of anabolic steroids in different European countries. At the core, this organization also consisted of a family business, as the South African's closest collaborator was his wife. The relationships with the national sale representatives were, instead, rather formalized so much so that the latter can be regarded as true "employees" of the South African national. For example, D.B., the Italian representative of the organization, received a 2,000 € monthly basis salary from his foreign boss in addition on a percent on his sales. Further showing his subordination to the organization, D.B. hardly ever bought doping substances or active ingredients by himself but received instead regular deliveries through an informal Moldavian courier service. In the rare cases he bought some raw materials for his lab (e.g., citric acid) in local pharmacies or had postal expenses, he was reimbursed by the organization. D.B. also received ready-for-sale peptide hormones from the Spanish branch of the organization (Int-NAS-9).

4.3 The Suppliers' Modus Operandi

Except for the truck hijackers, the suppliers of doping products in Italy are rarely reported to use violence. The nonviolent nature of the trade reflects above all the white-collar background of most suppliers and the embeddedness of many supply-side activities in legitimate professional affiliations and relationships. As already mentioned, none of the suppliers considered, except for the truck hijackers and some bouncers (see Chap. 3), have criminal records for violent crime.

The analysis of NAS investigations also reveals no conflict among suppliers that the participants felt the need to solve with violence. Except for the thefts, we are aware only of an attempt to openly use violence: it occurred when a Moldavian courier working for the South African's organization tried to hit a Carabinieri officer who had stopped his car (Int-NAS-9). Even occasional disagreements about the quality of the products delivered are usually solved in a rather "civilized," nonviolent way, probably reflecting the consensual nature of the exchanges and the interest of all participants in a long-term relationship (e.g., NAS Bologna 2000).

The anti-doping investigations and our respondents also provide scant evidence of suppliers of doping products bribing or attempting to bribe public officials. Only in one case, a major supplier, P.B., invited two officers who had just seized his doping products "to pretend that nothing had happened, if I give you five million lire [approximately €2,500] each" (Tribunale di Bologna 2000: 67). As seen earlier, some law enforcement officials did engage in the distribution of such products to finance their own consumption habits and to bring in extra income, but they did it on their own initiative, not because they were bribed or in other way offered illicit favors by other suppliers. The literature on illegal markets shows that the corruption of public officials is generally limited in countries with relatively effective governments that regularly enforce the prohibitions enacted (e.g., Paoli et al. 2009: 206–207). However, the almost complete lack of evidence of (even attempted) bribery appears to be a peculiarity of the market for doping products, especially in a country such as Italy with above-average levels of perceived corruption (Transparency International 2011). Notwithstanding the fact that Italy's enforcement of anti-doping prohibitions has few parallels in the world, the lack of proof of bribery also reflects the low sanctions that are associated with doping offenses. The very fact that P.B. or L.S. has been arrested five or six times since the late 1990s seems to indicate that they were never sentenced to long imprisonment terms. As we will see in Chap. 5, though, the lack of bribery does not mean that the suppliers of doping products have never received protection from public bodies.

Just like the "regular" illegal entrepreneurs and the white-collar criminals who are aware that they are doing something illegal (e.g., Packer 2011), the suppliers of doping products take precautions to hide their activities from law enforcement agencies. Several investigations indicate that especially in the distribution chains servicing body-builders but increasingly also in the trade meant for elite athletes, most suppliers use cover names to refer to doping products or speak only circumspectly on the phone. In the recent proceeding of the Mantua Prosecutor's Office, for example, Nigrelli and the elite riders he treated referred to GH vials as *culatelli* (one of the most prestigious salami made in Italy) or as "Topo Gigio vials," allegedly a well-known nickname in elite cycling (NAS Brescia 2011: 86). The most experienced suppliers, such as L.S. and V.G.F., not only limit the number of their collaborators and customers but also avoid talking on the phone, preferring to organize instead face-to-face encounters. They also conduct no business via emails or specialized Web sites (Int-NAS-9 and 16; Frezzi 2011). Having more collaborators due to his network in several European countries, the above-mentioned South African ringleader tried to limit to the extent possible the contacts with them. Throughout the NAS investigation that lasted several months, for example, he exchanged only an email with his Italian referent, delegating instead the contacts with the latter to a trusted Spanish collaborator (Int-NAS-9).

For their operators, Web sites selling doping products also frequently represent an effective protective strategy. Our respondents (Int-NAS-9 and 11) report that they can shut down the Web sites based in Italy and often identify and pursue their operators but have little means to shut down Web sites located abroad and even less possibilities to identify the persons operating them, given the differences in the criminal legislation and related enforcement on doping matters and the resulting difficulties in international police and judicial cooperation (see Chap. 7). Reflecting these differences, Web sites specialized in doping products have no counterpart in traditional illegal markets. They constitute, however, a subset of the broader market for online pharmaceutical products, which are also to a large extent counterfeited, just like the doping products (e.g., UNICRI 2007; WHO 2012). Whereas online Web sites can be an effective smokescreen for the suppliers operating them, it is unclear whether they offer long-standing guarantees to their customers. Several investigations began following the observation of online orders or the seizures of suspected parcels shipped by other operators (Tribunale di Siracusa 2010; Int-NAS-25 and 26).

We note, however, also some considerable differences between the precautions taken by the suppliers of doping products and their counterparts in fully illegal markets. Specifically, the former take more limited precautions than the latter. Several suppliers of doping products still speak rather freely on the phone under the thin cover of implausible nicknames (e.g., NAS Brescia 2011). Many of them, including those who order doping products on Internet, use the regular postal services to have doping products delivered at home or to send them to their customers. They use their personal bank accounts to transfer or receive money for the payment of drug deliveries (e.g., Tribunale di Ravenna 2004). Moreover, in contrast to the actions of L.S. and V.G.F., no major drug trafficker would personally move large quantities of drugs, because such drugs would automatically deliver, in case of arrest and asset seizure, a very heavy imprisonment sentence. Finally, if it is true that V.G.F. has been arrested in 2011 with doping products for an estimated market value of over one million euro and his business generated monthly revenues of about 90,000€ (Frezzi 2011), we note also differences in the management of inventories. As argued by Paoli et al. (2009: 207–208), these tend to be kept at a minimum in heroin markets in countries with strict enforcement, simply because they are too risky. On the contrary, V.G.F., despite his long-time experience in the trade in doping products, still kept products with a value corresponding to his yearly revenues in a single place.

These differences in the modus operandi can only be explained with the lower sentences foreseen for doping-related offenses and possibly also the lower degree of enforcement of prohibitions. The suppliers of doping products, even when they are fully aware of the illegal nature of their activities, still perceive lower risks of imprisonment and probably also lower arrest and asset seizure rates than the suppliers of illegal goods and services.

Just like legal and illegal entrepreneurs, the suppliers of doping products sometimes aggressively market their goods and services. In a recent proceeding of the Forlì Prosecutor's Office, for example, gym managers and body-building instructors were filmed instigating the use of anabolic steroids among visitors and specifically body-builders to build muscle (Tribunale di Forlì 2009: 135, 168–170). In many other cases, no such instigation is needed as the users are willing to use these products, whether or not they are fully aware of their harmful consequences.

A peculiarity of the market for doping products, particularly in elite sports, is that these products are often proposed—prescribed, administered, or sold—to adolescent and young adult athletes by more senior and respected individuals, such as physicians, pharmacists, coaches, and sports federation officials, who abuse their positions of authority and the trust of the young athletes and the athletes' parents. Including an Olympic champion, the elite athletes treated by Daniele Faraggiana were, for example, 17 to 25 years old, and one of them had been administered steroids since he was 13 years old (Donati 1989: 85).

4.4 Changes over Time

In addition to the huge increase in Internet sales, which we have discussed earlier, we see two major interrelated changes in the Italian market for doping products: the partial integration of the market for athletes and body-builders, which has been itself enhanced by the proliferation of specialized Web sites, as well as growing competition and the almost complete disappearance of market power.

In the past, the market for doping products consisted of two largely separate segments, one targeting body-builders and another exclusive to elite, especially super elite, athletes. Until the beginning of the current century, the situation was quite clear-cut. In Bologna, the market of which has been best investigated and also had extra-regional relevance, the two segments were clearly separate from each other. P.B. and other suppliers of the gym world sold steroids and other substances to the local body-builders, obtaining them from a plurality of channels, mostly illegal (NAS Bologna 2000). A respected pharmacist provided the physicians of several elite teams and individual athletes with his own Galenic products and other drugs, mostly stimulants, which he had bought primarily through legal channels (Int-NAS-10).

Still today, some types of suppliers are primarily focusing on specific classes of users. The gym owners, managers, and body-building instructors primarily service body-builders and other gym visitors, whereas staff members of sports teams and sports federation officials target exclusively super elite athletes. Whenever they engage in supply-side activities, athletes and body-builders also tend to sell doping substances to members of their own sporting groups. Other suppliers, though—i.e., managers of dietary supplement shops, pharmacists, physicians, hospital employees, pharmaceutical companies and their employees and sales representatives, and, last but not least, the suppliers with no distinctive profession or occupation—are willing to provide their goods and services to whomever is interested in them and therefore can be considered "generalist" suppliers.

The differentiation of the market for doping products in two clear-cut markets for elite athletes and body-builders has partially faded away in recent years, as a result of three changes: the increased repression, the rise of Web sites selling doping products, and the spread of doping practices among recreational athletes. We have already described the second and third changes previously and we will fully document the second in Chap. 7. Here we note that:

- Elite athletes and their entourage still prefer as much as possible to exploit separate, better-quality channels, but as a result of the stricter enforcement of sports rule and criminal law anti-doping provisions in Italy and elsewhere, they are increasingly obliged to resort to the same sources and suppliers of other users. Due to the increased repression, sports federation officials; university physicians such as Conconi (Tribunale di Ferrara 2003); and, despite the recent case of the elite cycling team Lampre (NAS Brescia 2011), also the managers of sports teams have become more cautious in directly supplying elite athletes with doping products and, instead, leave it up to the athletes themselves to ensure that they are competitive, if necessary by doping.

- Despite the minimal quality guarantees, specialized Web sites have become an attractive alternative for all types of users vis-à-vis physical suppliers (see above).
- As argued in Chap. 2, recreational athletes constitute nowadays a much larger share of the market for doping products than in the past and help integrate the previously separate market segments of elite athletes and body-builders. Recreational athletes not only have contacts with both the former, via federations, and the latter, via gyms, but also buy from suppliers —e.g., managers or owners of dietary supplement shops, pharmacists, physicians, hospital employees, and operators of specialized Web sites—who also serve elite athletes or body-builders or both. Among these generalist suppliers, a few physicians have come to play a crucial role and serve as a connecting link between elite and recreational athletes and, more rarely, also body-builders. For example, some physicians, like Santuccione (NAS Firenze 2005) and Ferrari (Pasqualetto 2011; MacMichael 2011a), exploit the reputation they have built with super elite athletes to attract a larger pool of non-super elite and recreational athletes and thus considerable expand their revenues. Other physicians, such as B.H.E., treat indistinctly athletes, both elite and recreational, and body-builders (Tribunale di Rimini 2011).

The barriers around the market for elite athletes have not completely disappeared, though. Notwithstanding the growing market integration, doping methods and specifically blood doping are still reserved for super elite athletes, not least because of their high costs and the expertise and specialized equipment that they require (e.g., NAS Brescia 2011).

Given the growing integration of the different markets, it is not surprising to see that the relationships among many suppliers of doping products, specifically those that target primarily body-builders, recreational athletes, and other users, generally involve competition rather than collusion. The high degree of competition is not only the result of that process of integration but is also due to several other factors: the sheer amount of products available, which can be partially substituted with each other; the multiplicity of channels through which these products can reach the final users and which have incrementally expanded in the last 10 years due to the spread of specialized Web sites; and the above-mentioned constraints of illegality, which make economies of scale and scope unlikely in illegal operations and therefore discourage the development of monopolies or oligopolies (Paoli et al. 2009: 208). The best evidence of competition is the fact that the prices of many doping products, especially steroids, are very low and that many, probably most, suppliers have no ability to exclude others or to set prices, the hallmarks of market power (Katz and Rosen 1994: Chap. 13; see Chap. 6).

A large-scale investigation carried out by the Bologna Branch Office (NAS Bologna 2000) at the turn of the century suggests that, at that time, some importers and wholesalers of anabolic steroids, who were active in all of Italy, had some market power. Reportedly, L.S. and V.G.F. operated on such a large scale that in 1999 and 2000 they were able to set the market prices for some anabolic steroids and GH in different parts of Italy. This market power is hinted at in several phone calls. For example, in one of them L.S. talks to a Catania customer, and the latter complains that other local suppliers are selling steroids, such as Deca Durabolin and Testoviron, and GH, at lower prices. The Catania retailer further asks L.S. if he has been supplying other people in the Catania region. L.S. replies that he has been selling some products to another person, however at prices higher than those made to his phone partner. "At the end of the conversation," the Bologna Branch Office notes, "L.S. says that he has probably understood who the other seller was and reassures his phone partner that it will not happen again" (ibid: 217). In another conversation, P.B. receives similar complaints from a customer serving the Rome market concerning the product Testoviron. P.B. replies that "the taps have already been turned off" to the other Rome distributors, referring, according to the Bologna Branch Office, to interventions of V.G.F. and L.S. (ibid: 217). On another occasion, P.B. talks to R.F., a distributor in Tuscany, who is looking for an Australian veterinary drug, RWR Drive, for an athlete who is a client of his. However, P.B. does not have the product and reassures his business partner in the following way:

P.B.: Ah, there is no more, you will see, there is no more.
R.F.: No?
P.B.: It is finished, I am almost positive.
R.F.: But say, you say that you cannot find it in Florence, don't you?
P.B.: No, no. If I do not have it, the others do not have it either, don't worry.
R.F.: Because, because they say that they can find in Florence, I've heard it from some friends ....
P.B.: Yes, yes, you could find it, but now they no longer can find it, you can trust me.
R.F.: No? You say that if you have finished it, it is finished also …
P.B.: If I have finished it, they have also finished it as a consequence" (NAS Bologna 2000: 267).

According to the judge who issued the arrest warrants on the basis of this investigation, the three suppliers, L.S., V.G.F., and P.B., "imposed a cartel at the national level to effectively control competition" (Tribunale di Bologna 2000: 67). This market control seems very plausible in the case of the Australian veterinary drug, which was very specific, and possibly also GH, which was still rare to find at the turn of the century. It is instead more puzzling that L.S. and V.G.F. were also able to control the market for basic steroids, such as Deca Durabolin and Testoviron. From the wiretapped phone conversations, it is not positive whether the two suppliers were just boosting or they really had such a market power. What is certain is that, if market power for anabolic steroids ever existed, it has now dissipated as a result of the multiplication of distribution chains and particularly the spread of specialized Web sites.

Only a few suppliers primarily targeting elite athletes still maintain some limited market power, as the barriers around the market for elite athletes have not completely disappeared, some doping methods require specialized equipment, and expertise and some users, primarily elite athletes, put a premium on quality and are therefore willing to pay higher prices for the original products, such as doping substances stolen from hospitals or from drug distributors' storehouses and trucks, that have a guaranteed quality. Michele Ferrari is one of the few doping suppliers know to law enforcement agencies who at least until the beginning of his judicial "troubles" was able to maintain some market power. As we discuss in more detail in Chap. 6, Ferrari's market power is demonstrated by the high fees that he was able to charge to his customers, among whom there were many super elite athletes (Int-NAS-16; U.S. Anti-Doping Agency 2012c).

Chapter 5
The Role of Sports Bodies and Organized Crime

Abstract To fully understand the market relationships among the suppliers of doping products, we focus in the fifth chapter on two very different sets of actors. The first ones are officials of national sports bodies, including in this expression both the Italian National Olympic Committee (CONI) and sports federations. As seen in the third chapter, during the 1980s and 1990s, officials of sports federations occasionally distributed doping products directly to elite athletes of some disciplines, most notably track and field and weightlifting. Most often, though, CONI and sports federations officials have "merely" provided protection to doping elite athletes and the latter's suppliers of doping products or have not exercised their supervisory and control functions with due diligence. In doing so, Italian sports body officials often did not behave any differently than their foreign or international counterparts, as several examples suggest. On more than one occasion, moreover, Italian sports body officials enjoyed the support of successive Italian governments.

The second set of actors here analyzed consists of organized crime and underworld members and organizations, whose growing involvement in the market for doping products has repeatedly been denounced by high-level international sports officials in recent years. On the basis of the Italian data, however, we can only partially confirm these worried forecasts, even though they may still be applicable for other countries, especially in Asia. Southern Italian mafia organizations, such as Cosa Nostra, the 'Ndrangheta, and camorra, still seem to play a limited role in the market. Nonetheless, many supply-side activities can be also defined as a form of organized crime, as they meet all the requirements of the loose official definitions of organized crime adopted at the international level.

In the cases of both set of actors, we draw from the Italian market and consider the extent to which our findings can be generalized to other nations.

To fully understand the market relationships among the suppliers of doping products, we focus in this chapter on two very different sets of actors. The first ones are officials of national sports bodies, including in this expression both CONI and sports

L. Paoli and A. Donati, *The Sports Doping Market: Understanding Supply and Demand, and the Challenges of Their Control*, DOI 10.1007/978-1-4614-8241-3_5,

federations. As earlier mentioned, during the 1980s and 1990s, the officials of sports federations occasionally distributed doping products directly to elite athletes of some disciplines, most notably track and field and weightlifting. Most often, though, CONI and sports federations officials have "merely" provided protection to doping elite athletes and the latter's suppliers of doping products or have not exercised their supervisory and control functions with due diligence. In doing so, Italian sports body officials often did not behave any differently than their foreign or international counterparts, as several examples suggest. On more than one occasion, moreover, Italian sports body officials enjoyed the support of successive Italian governments.

The second set of actors here analyzed consists of organized crime and underworld members and organizations, whose growing involvement in the market for doping products has repeatedly been denounced by high-level international sports officials in recent years. On the basis of the Italian data, however, we can only partially confirm these worried forecasts, even though they may still be applicable for other countries, especially in Asia. Southern Italian mafia organizations, such as Cosa Nostra, the 'Ndrangheta and camorra, still seem to play a limited role in the market. Nonetheless, many supply-side activities can be also defined as a form of organized crime, as they meet all the requirements of the loose official definitions of organized crime adopted at the international level.

In the cases of both set of actors, we draw from the Italian market and consider the extent to which our findings can be generalized to other nations.

5.1 Sports Body Officials as Key Providers of Protection

Protection, here understood as immunity from criminal (or sports) prosecution, is a key resource in traditional illegal markets and is often bought by the traffickers of drugs and other illicit products with bribes in money or kind to law enforcement officials or other government representatives. As earlier mentioned, bribery has up to now played a limited role in the market for doping products in Italy. Nonetheless, our sources indicate that sports body officials have repeatedly provided protection to the market servicing elite athletes, seemingly out of shared interests in sports success rather than for private monetary gains—and this protection constitutes the most startling peculiarity of Italy's market for doping products. The difficulty is in drawing a clear line between the action of those individuals and the policies and practices of the institutions, writ large. At what point do the collective actions of enough institutional representatives of sufficient rank, de facto, speak not just for their interests but for those of the institution? Regardless of any formal or legal standing, at what point are the individuals that represent the institution and "the institution" one and the same?

As scandals and criminal proceedings indicate, the representatives of national sports bodies, including some very high-ranking officials, exercised their roles as "protectors" quite openly until the late 1990s. Since then, no cases of overt high-level complicity have come to the fore, but the national sports bodies' apparent lack of interest in a thorough fight against doping still emerges from several criminal proceedings and outright policy choices.

5.1.1 Conconi and His Protectors

A fine line might separate individuals from their institutions, but a request filed in October 2000 by the Prosecutor's Office of Ferrara in the proceedings against Conconi provides evidence of high-ranking individual involvement so much so that it might be difficult to argue against institutional complicity. As already mentioned in the prologue, the prosecutor Pierguido Soprani reconstructed the relationships between CONI and Conconi since the late 1970s and concluded that throughout the 1980s, three CONI Presidents—Carraro, Gattai, and Pescante—and a secretary general had run a criminal organization together with Prof. Conconi to distribute drugs dangerous to public health to numerous elite athletes (article 445 CP), but could not charge them because of the statute of limitations (Procura della Repubblica presso il Tribunale di Ferrara 2000). (As the offense of sporting fraud was established in 1989 and doping was not at that point a criminal offense,[1] the Ferrara Prosecutor's Office could not charge Conconi and his associates for the period before 1989 of either offense. It is important to recall, though, that the administration of the substances mentioned in the prosecutor's charges did constitute a violation of the IOC's rules and that CONI, as the Italian National Olympic Committee, was bound to respect and enforce IOC rules. Moreover, in funding doping-related research and the administration of doping products, CONI, a public body, violated its own mission, which we will describe more in detail in Chap. 7.) As too much time had elapsed between the alleged activities and the prosecution, the Prosecutor's Office had to dismiss the case, but it insisted that this request "does not diminish the social and criminal non-value of the activities proved" (ibid.: 56). Instead, Soprani found no conclusive evidence of the existence of a criminal organization between Conconi and the CONI top leaders after 1989.

The Prosecutor's Office provided detailed evidence of its statements. In particular, it showed that from the very beginning, the relationship between CONI and Conconi was meant to enhance the performance of Italian elite athletes through doping: as the Prosecutor himself wrote: "the relationship between CONI and Conconi was born and was intended to develop, in an institutional context, sports doping practices" (ibid.). According to Donati, a member of our research team,

[1] It had been introduced as an offense in 1971 but it was then decriminalized in 1981 and was not re-established as a criminal offense until the end of 2000; see Chap. 7.

Conconi proposed in the early 1980s that CONI assists selected Italian athletes of endurance sports in improving their performances—an offer that CONI accepted. Donati was then a track-and-field coach for the Italian Olympic team and was himself approached by Conconi to participate in his treatment program, which basically consisted in blood doping and the administration of testosterone (Donati 2003).

CONI and Conconi did not make any real effort, at least until the early 1990s, to hide the purposes of the covenant that CONI had underwritten with the University of Ferrara (de facto Conconi's biochemical institute) in 1981 and which was renewed first each year and then, since 1987, every 4 years.[2] According to the Ferrara Prosecutor's Office, the managers of the national sports federations and CONI were well aware of Conconi's specialization in analogous transfusions (ibid.: 23). Moreover, other doping practices were clearly mentioned in the scientific programs enclosed to the covenants and in the annual reports of activities. For example, the 1983 scientific program included "a study of the effects of anabolic steroids on various performance components, in male athletes who already take the drug" (ibid: 25, emphasis in original) and the 1983 Annual Report of Activities listed the following three items under the heading "Drugs and Aerobic Performance:"

- Item a, which deals with the effects of the administration of anabolic steroids on the alactacid anaerobic performance and on metabolic power in middle-distance athletes, double-blind study
- Item c, which deals with the effects of benzodiazepines on the shooting precision in biathlon
- Item d, which deals with the effects of benzodiazepines on trampoline jumpers (ibid.: 28)

Other similar documents provide corroborating evidence of doping, for example, showing that anabolic steroids were administered to middle-distance runners throughout the 4-year period 1982–1986 (ibid: 38). The Ferrara Prosecutor's Office noted that "CONI top managers who underwrote the Conventions were not only perfectly aware of this [and other doping practices]—we can say 'per tabulas' (i.e., by documentary evidence) as the practice was listed in Conconi's research programs—but consciously decided that the benefits in terms of competition results were higher and more convenient for CONI itself than the probable harms" (ibid: 38).

Conconi's integral role in and for CONI was further enhanced by his appointment as President of the CONI Section for the Ferrara Province in 1981 (ibid.: 8).[3] Over the years, CONI funded Conconi very generously for a total of about two

---

[2] At the same time, Conconi also underwrote similar agreements, for similar purposes with numerous sport federations (Procura della Repubblica presso il Tribunale di Ferrara 2000: 16).

[3] Conconi enjoyed high-level connections even beyond CONI. He attended to, and regularly went riding with, Romano Prodi, Italy's Prime Minister, in 1996–1998 and in 2006–2008. According to media reports, Prodi seriously considered Conconi as a possible undersecretary for sports for his cabinet in 1996 (Pontani 1996; Smargiassi 1996).

billion lire (approximately one million euro), from the early 1980s to the late 1990s.[4] CONI also invested some funds to organize several workshops with coaches and experts of the national sports federations to inform them about Conconi's progress and findings (ibid.: 29).

During the late 1980s and early 1990s, the IOC also supported Conconi and his "research" on doping activities. In fact, the IOC funded Conconi—according to media sources (cyclingnews.com 2000) with several million dollars, but the sum is probably exaggerated—to develop a test to discover EPO. Prince Alexander de Merode, who was the President of the IOC Medical Committee, went as far as to repeatedly back Conconi's claim that a urine test for EPO was ready or almost ready and other false statements (Capodacqua 1993; Eric 1999).[5,6] At the Winter Olympics in 1994 in Lillehammer, Conconi gave a talk to IOC members on his research progress and described how he had carried out controlled experiments with 23 recreational athletes with EPO treatment. The raid carried out at his office at University of Ferrara in 1998 revealed that only one of the 23 athletes was recreational (Conconi himself!), whereas the other 22 were elite professionals, including at least six professional riders (Donati 2003). In gratitude for De Merode's support, Conconi had the University of Ferrara confer an honorary degree on his patron. The latter, who was by education an art historian, was allegedly very pleased to receive a natural sciences PhD, albeit *honoris causa* (Int-Oth-2). Conconi was also well connected with UCI, the World Cycling Federation, and served during the 1990s as President of its Medical Commission. According to newspaper reports, Conconi abused that position in 1993 to avoid the disqualification of a rider who had tested positive to an anti-doping test (Toti 2003; see Donati 2012: 129–175).

[4] With the 1987 four-year long convention, for example, CONI committed itself to transfer to Conconi's institute 410 million lire for the years 1987 and 1988 and 60 million lire (approximately US$46,100 at the exchange rate of the time) for the years 1989 and 1990. In 1987 and 1988 CONI also paid 700 million lire (about US$540,000) to renovate the building where Conconi's institute was located, and for the 3 years, i.e., 1988, 1989, and 1990, it also granted each year additional 100 million lire (US$77,000) to buy new equipment and pay the salary of Conconi's staff and other ordinary expenses. Over the period 1985–1994, CONI also reimbursed Conconi and his staff of many travel costs (for a total of 120 million lire; approximately US$92,000), including many trips that fell beyond the scope of the Convention between CONI and the Ferrara University (e.g., trips to attend computer courses or congresses of scientific societies, meeting with representatives of private companies, to produce films on the IOC's behalf; Procura della Repubblica presso il Tribunale di Ferrara 2000: 6–12). Among the equipment bought, there was some that left no doubts about Conconi's doping purposes, such as refrigerated centrifuge and a lab freezer (ibid: 30).

[5] Before obtaining funds from the IOC, Prof. Conconi also submitted its project proposal to the CONI Anti-Doping Commission. Despite Pescante's insistence, the commission decided not to fund Conconi's project, because of the latter's low scientific quality and unrealistic promises (personal memory of Donati, who was then the secretary of CONI Anti-Doping Commission).

[6] It is plausible that Conconi circulated such totally unfounded rumors, which he knew would eventually taint his reputation, to discourage other teams from using EPO and thus give a further advantage to the athletes that he treated. According to Erkki Vettenniemi (personal communication, 2012), a Finnish scholar who has studied the use of EPO in Finnish elite winter sports, the Finnish national ski federation and researchers on its payroll resorted to such a strategy ahead of the 1989 Lahti (Finland) Nordic ski world championships.

None of the four CONI top officials indicted by the Ferrara Prosecutor's Office chose to appeal the latter's charges and, surprisingly, at least for outside observers, the charges did not appear to negatively impact the suspects' sports manager or political careers. Although the charges did not yield prosecutions, one might have thought the veracity of the comments of the Prosecutor's Office would have some bearing on the suspects' future success. However, Pescante became undersecretary for sports less than a year after the prosecutor's request was filed (see prologue); Carraro remained President of the Italian Professional Football League and, in the course of 2001, was elected President of the Italian Football Federation—a position that he held until he was involved in the 2006 Italian football scandal, which proved that many Serie A matches had been rigged (Crosetti 2006).[7]

Carraro's and Pescante's careers suggest that the determination to fight doping consequently in all its manifestations has long not been equally shared throughout Italy's political class, despite the lip-service declarations in the aftermath of a large doping scandal. As indicated by the persistent opposition faced by Prosecutor Soprani in his investigation against Conconi (see prologue), the will to fight doping was also lacking on the part of the judiciary (see also Chap. 7). This assessment is also shared by several interviewees (Int-NAS-10; Int-Oth-2) and other observers. After the judge sent back the charges against Conconi and his codefendants to the Prosecutor's Office for a new formulation, the largest Italian sports daily *La Gazzetta dello Sport* wrote an article entitled "What kind of justice is this?" and stated that "the judiciary is unable to pass sentence on the most scandalous case of doping in Italian history" (quoted in Der Spiegel 2003). Even according to Centamore (2011: 18), a German-Swiss legal scholar who recently evaluated Italy's anti-doping legislation, "the progress of the proceedings [against Conconi] raises suspicions that no serious effort was made to sentence such a high-ranking character as Conconi."

International sports body officials were no more impressed by the accusations of the Ferrara Prosecutor's Office than the majority of Italian policy-makers and public. While Carraro was a member of the IOC Executive Board from 2000 to 2004, Pescante has been since 1994 without interruption an IOC member and was the first Italian to become an IOC Vice President in 2009. Pescante was also first Secretary General (1989–2001) and then President (2001–2006) of the European Olympic Committees (EOC, former Association of the European National Olympic Committees) and served as Vice President of the Association of the National Olympic Committees for the period 2001–2006.[8]

The IOC and UCI also failed to distance themselves from Conconi and those who had supported him in Italy after the scandal became public. According to Internet sources (fmk 2011), in 2001 Conconi still served as a member in the IOC's medical committee and remained the President of UCI Medical Commission until 2001 with the responsibility to protect the riders' health in cycling![9]

---

[7] See http://www.olympic.org/mr-franco-carraro.

[8] See http://www.olympic.org/mr-mario-pescante.

[9] No exact data about the length of Conconi's term as a member of the IOC Medical Committee and UCI Medical Commission could be found on either his Web page or the Web sites of the two organizations.

5.1.2 *Other Cases of Complicity in the 1980s and 1990s*

The protection granted by Italian sports bodies to elite athletes and those administering doping product to them goes beyond Conconi's case. As already mentioned in the introduction, an investigation coordinated by another courageous magistrate, Dr. Guariniello from the Turin Prosecutor's Office, led in 1998 to the temporary closure of CONI's Anti-Doping Laboratory in Rome and loss of the IOC accreditation. Questioned by Dr. Guariniello, the scientific director of the laboratory later admitted that the lab carried out thorough tests for all the prohibited substances, in particular, steroids, in only 30 % of the urine samples taken from professional football players (Evaluation Team 2002: 13 and Travaglio 1998). A Commission of inquiry, which was established by the government and headed by a well-respected lawyer, Carlo Federico Grosso, stated that "practices had developed and facts were committed at the Rome laboratory of analysis and after the matches, when the samples were taken, that violated IOC and CONI rules" (Adnkronos 1998). As a result of this scandal, Pescante stepped down as President of CONI in 1998.[10]

Faraggiana's diaries, which had been made public 12 years earlier, also showed that the CONI's Anti-Doping Laboratory in Rome was not exercising its mission properly. Indeed, they went one step further than the 1998 investigation conducted by the Turin Prosecutor's Office in suggesting that the lab was used to establish the amount of time required for traces of doping substances to disappear from the urine samples of the individual athletes (Donati 1989: 84–5)—despite the fact that the IOC had formally banned a wide range of performance-enhancing substances in 1967 and added steroids to that list in 1976 (World Anti-Doping Agency 2013a). The diaries also indicated that Faraggiana was working closely, on behalf of the Italian Athletics Federation (FIDAL), with another public laboratory that was conveniently located in Pisa not far away from the main FIDAL training site and was run by the Consiglio Italiano delle Ricerche (CNR), the most prestigious public research organization in Italy as well as the main funding agency for scientific research. The Pisa lab routinely examined blood and urine samples of the athletes "treated" by Faraggiana for the same illicit purposes of the Rome lab, possibly

[10] Pursuant the principle of territorial competence, the proceeding was transferred from the Turin to the Rome Prosecutor's Office. After carrying out the necessary investigation, the latter did not pursue the case not having determined on the basis of the elements under scrutiny that a punishable crime had been committed (Evaluation Team 2002: 13). The Prosecutor's Office in Rome has been known since the 1970s with the nickname of "porto delle nebbie," i.e., "the fog port," because it did not press charges in many proceedings against high-level politicians and state representatives, which were transferred to Rome because of the rule of territorial competence.

Moreover, Rome prosecutors and judges were traditionally very close to the world of organized sports, as they often served as judges in sport justice commissions, receiving generous compensations for their services (Int-NAS-26; Int-Oth-2). This close relationship changed only when Italy's Higher Council of the Judiciary, known as CSM (see Chap. 7), forbade prosecutors and judges from accepting such extrajudicial tasks.

The Rome Prosecutor's Office has recently improved its reputation. No empirical evaluation of its decisions and output in comparison to those of other offices has ever been carried out (Sansa 2011).

documenting serious harms provoked by the doping substances administered. Nonetheless, when the diaries became public, no action was taken against either lab, and the labs were not even called to justify their practices. Exchanges of letters between the President of the Pisa lab, Dr. Federghini, and FIDAL managers document that in 1981 and 1982, the former tried, with the support of the latter, to have the Pisa lab accredited by the IOC (ibid.: 82–84).

As already mentioned, the publication of Faraggiana's diaries and the repeated public complaints of Donati and a few other Athletic Federation officials did not lead to any criminal or sports law investigation. On the contrary, Primo Nebiolo, who was then the President of both the Italian and worldwide athletics federations (known as International Association of Athletics Federations or IAAF),[11] ignored the reports and did his best to cover up the scandal in the bud (Donati 1989). In 1985 Prof. Romano Tordelli, who had been responsible for middle-distance runners for over 15 years, wrote several letters to Nebiolo to inform him of the spread of illegal doping practices within the track-and-field disciplines in Italy. Among others, Tordelli wrote that the documentation he had collected "demonstrates that the doping practices in FIDAL have reached such a seriousness to hypothesize veritable criminal offenses against the community and the athletes who have undergone such practices, with repeated violations of the sports law and the Italian criminal laws" (Donati 1989: 92). Tordelli also listed the products administered by Faraggiana, concluding that "the costs of these products, the payment of the physicians administering them, the trips necessary for the purchases, the payment (at least as a partial contribution) of the medical structures needed to control continuously the 'treated' athletes with sophisticated and expensive procedures, the cost of supporting and detox drugs are very high" (ibid.: 92–93). On this basis, Tordelli asked Nebiolo "if these expenses did not represent a demonstration of irresponsible administration of the federation resources."

Tordelli also informed Nebiolo—almost 15 years before his statements were confirmed by the Ferrara Prosecutor's Office—that "Conconi's position went beyond blood transfusions and that he appears to be active also in the administration of anabolic steroids and testosterone even to athletes who have won medals at the Olympics" (ibid.: 93). Nebiolo and the other FIDAL top managers did not even respond to the Tordelli's early letters. The former replied only when Tordelli sent a letter in copy to all the FIDAL officials. Even then, Nebiolo merely wrote that he had "forwarded the letter to the competent technical and administrative bodies to obtain the necessary clarifications" and later invited Tordelli to a meeting during which no concrete action was taken (ibid: 93–94).

Two years later, in 1986, excerpts of Tordelli's letters were published in a weekly magazine, *L'Espresso* (e.g., La Repubblica 1987). Following the scandal provoked by these letters, a few other insiders, athletes, and trainers talked openly about doping in interviews. Among others, the elite discus thrower Zerbini reported that "some federation officials before the Los Angeles Olympic Games came to my trainer and me and were very clear. Or you take some substances or you do not attend the Games" (Audisio 1986). Despite these revelations and charges, Nebiolo

[11] For biographical details, see http://en.wikipedia.org/wiki/Primo_Nebiolo.

was reported repeatedly saying: "I speak about everything but not about doping" (Audisio 1987a, c). In addition to the strategy of silence, FIDAL removed the trainers who had had the courage to denounce openly the problem of doping. For example, Carlo Vittori, the personal trainer of national hero Pietro Mennea and coach of the Italian national track team, was first prohibited to have any further contact with journalists (Donati 1989: 88) and then removed from his trainer job (Audisio 1987b see also Donati 2012: 61–67, 75–87 and 115–121).

In 1989, Pietro Pujia, the winner of 54 national titles in weightlifting, sued the Weightlifting Federation for having obliged him to take steroids since he was 13 years old, including before the 1988 Seoul Olympic Games, claiming compensation for damages to his back from the Federation and CONI. The Weightlifting Federation, CONI, and some of Pujia's physicians and trainers were prompt in denying all the charges, ostracizing and denigrating him. They did so regardless of the fact that another member of the Olympic weightlifting team, Norberto Oberburger, Olympic champion at the Los Angeles Games, had tested positive to steroids immediately after coming back from the Seoul Games—a fact that the Weightlifting Federation had allegedly tried to hide for several months—and that Pujia's and Oberburger's intake of doping substances and other drugs were detailed in Faraggiana's diaries (Capodacqua 1989a, b).

This pattern of denial and isolation of the few whistleblowers repeated itself in the following years. In 1993, an elite track-and-field athlete, Francesca Delon, filed a report with CONI Anti-Doping Prosecutor's Office that her trainer had pressured her and several other elite athletes to use anabolic steroids, enclosing also the recordings of conversations with the trainer on a tape as proof (Zambardino 1993a, b). After a series of hearings during which CONI Anti-Doping Prosecutor's Office even managed to ruin the tape, media pressure finally obliged CONI Prosecutor's Office to strike off the trainer and disqualify several athletes the latter had trained—but Delon was marginalized and treated as a traitor (Zambardino 1994).

In 1994, Donati submitted a dossier to the President and to the General Secretary of CONI, detailing the spread of EPO among professional riders and Conconi's role in such a spread, on the basis of interviews with twelve key figures of the cycling milieu, including athletes, physicians, and team officials. The dossier remained in a drawer for 2 years, while Conconi was celebrated as the great champion of the struggle against doping. Only in 1996, at the pressure of the media, was CONI forced to admit the existence of the dossier and had to justify why it had disregarded the dossier for 2 years, had not reported the detailed circumstantial evidence included in the dossier to law enforcement agencies, and had failed to review CONI's cooperation with Conconi (e.g., Capodacqua 1996b). Eventually, the dossier constituted the impetus for the judicial investigations against Conconi earlier discussed.[12]

[12] Five years earlier, Donati had published a book *Campioni senza valore* to illustrate his struggle against doping and corruption in sports and the difficulties that he and the few other whistleblowers had encountered. The book was presented to the press in a major bookshop in Rome and during the first week the sales were very successful. Then, the book was suddenly and completely withdrawn from the market—for reasons that were never fully explained by the publisher. The book is now available for free on the Internet (see also Donati 2012).

Sports body officials not only tried to ignore or isolate the few whistleblowers who challenged illegal performance-enhancing practices but occasionally also tried to discredit the whistleblowers' reputations and careers. In early 1997, a few months after the publication of Donati's EPO dossier, Anna Maria Di Terlizzi, a 100 m hurdler trained by Donati, tested positive for caffeine. However, the second sample of urine, which was tested in the presence of an expert of Donati and Di Terlizzi's choice, tested negative, indicating that the first sample had been manipulated (e.g., Capodacqua 1997; La Repubblica 1997). On another occasion, CONI officials went as far as sabotaging criminal investigations. In 1996, when NAS officers asked for the collaboration of the CONI Anti-Doping Prosecutor's Office in searching all cycling teams arriving by ferry in Brindisi after the first two stages of the Giro d'Italia in Greece, CONI officials informed the cycling team managers and even Italy's main sports daily, *La Gazzetta dello Sport*, effectively thwarting the raid (Int-NAS-16 and 26; see also Capodacqua 1996a and Donati 2012: 177–198).

As late as 2000, when the CONI Scientific Committee informed CONI President Gianni Petrucci and the sports federations about the GH anomalies found in the blood samples of 61 super elite athletes, CONI reacted by shutting down the Scientific Committee (La Repubblica 2000). Later on, when the data on the GH anomalies were leaked to the press, Petrucci filed a report against unknown persons with the Rome Prosecutor's Office, at the same time as several CONI officials actively looked for incriminating evidence against Donati, who was then a member of the Scientific Committee. Donati was later freed from all accusations. In the same period, Donati was also sued by several employees of the Rome Anti-Doping Laboratory and representatives of the Sports Medicine Federation for slandering the reputation of the lab. When Donati presented the statements of several elite athletes and physicians indicating that the lab had carried out in the 1980s tests to help the former to better tune their intake of doping products, the claimants withdrew their suit and even offered to pay Donati's legal fees (see Donati 2012: 213–236).

Episodes like these and the direct evidence emerging from the proceeding against Michele Ferrari led the first-degree judge of the Bologna Court in charge of that proceeding to conclude the following: "Doping is a topic that the world of professional sports does not yet seem to be able to deal with the necessary courage and straight back that a pitiless self-criticism would require" (Tribunale di Bologna 2004: 18).

5.1.3 *The Tolerance of National Sports Bodies Since the Turn of the Century*

In Italy as elsewhere, national sports federations and the Olympic Committee were forced by scandals to intensify the fight against doping, as the reputation, funding, and media attractiveness of the organized sports world were increasingly at stake. No open complicity with doping athletes or the latter's suppliers is possible. Nonetheless, not all officials of Italy's sports bodies, as of today, seem to be equally committed to the struggle against doping. As of 2002, for example, Tau, the previously mentioned rider-turned witness, still reported:

> The [cycling] federation knows everything. The Italian riders are selected on the basis of the values of their analyses. Those making the selections for the national teams are the first to ask the sports directors to keep certain athletes "ready" for a certain appointment. When they set up the team for the Olympics, they even gave a "reimbursement" for the drugs. As a sort of expense list. And when the whole national track team was caught with a load of stuff, they convinced the poor T[.] to take responsibility for it, promising him that they would cover him. (Fazzo and Mensurati 2002b).

There was obviously no possibility to check independently these serious allegations. What is clear is that the collaboration between sports federations and NAS is far from being optimal. Several NAS officers (e.g., Int-NAS-9, 25, 26) and prosecutors (e.g., Int-Pro-1 and 3) complain about the repeated lack of collaboration on the part of some sports federation officials, and some NAS investigations also clearly document the sports bodies' lack of anti-doping commitment. Recalling the first criminal investigations on doping, a senior NAS officer told us (Int-NAS-26): "When we started conducting the first anti-doping interventions and progressively realized with surprise how widespread and serious the phenomenon was, we were struck by the fact that no person belonging to the sports world ever came to us to denounce or at least to report facts" (Int-NAS-26). Reflecting on its own "Muscoli e Fiale" investigation concerning the world of professional cycling, for example, the Treviso Branch Office concluded that "some doping cases reported to the FCI [i.e., Italian Cycling Federation] have been blocked thanks to the omission of high-level officials belonging to the disciplinary commissions and other bodies of the sports law" (NAS Treviso 2009). In another investigation carried out by the Brescia NAS, the manager of Italy's national cycling team was wiretapped while he reassured the coach of a young athlete who was taking performance-enhancing drugs and promised his phone partner that he would take care of doping controls (Quotidiano.net 2001; Capodacqua 2000b). On another occasion, the team physician of a Serie B football team manipulated the athletes' anti-doping selection procedures and later accepted a sentence bargaining agreement (*patteggiamento*; see Chap. 7) for this charge (Int-NAS-16).

The persistent lack of commitment to anti-doping is also suggested by the continuity of the top management of Italy's organized sports, which lasted at least until the election of the new CONI President Giovanni Malagò in February 2013. This continuity is well illustrated by the earlier-mentioned Carraro's and Pescante's careers. In particular, Pescante served as undersecretary for sports for 5 years, until 2006. "Appointing Pescante to stand guard over sports is a bit like putting a fox in charge of the henhouse"—complained the journalist Marco Travaglio (2005). In his capacity of Italian government supervisor for the 2006 Winter Games in Turin, Pescante repeatedly asked, at the IOC's insistence, for the temporary suspension of the Italian anti-doping law, "because otherwise there is the risk to watch competitions reduced to half" (Tropeano 2005; see also Vinton 2005). A consequence of the IOC and Pescante's proposal, which was stopped by the determined opposition of the Health Minister Storace, would have been to wipe out all the ongoing anti-doping criminal proceedings against athletes and their suppliers (Travaglio 2005).

Continuity with the past is also reflected in the appointment of a few past members of CVD, the body responsible for doping controls among recreational athletes. Among them, for example, in the period 2001–2004, there was a FIDAL physician who had been sentenced by the Milan Court for substituting an athlete's urine sample with his own ahead of a doping test, as well as Prof. Giorgio Santilli, the former President of the Federation of Sports Physicians.[13] In the latter capacity, at the end of the 1990s, Santilli held responsibility for the Rome Anti-Doping Laboratory and in 1998 stepped down, together with Dr. Pescante, in the aftermath of that scandal. During the following CVD term (2005–2008), Felice Rosati, the Director of the Rome Anti-Doping Laboratory until 1998, served as a CVD member along with Prof. Santilli, in spite of the fact that Rosati had also been removed from his job when the laboratory was closed down because of the irregular analyses of football players' urine samples (Moresco 2005b; Int-Oth-2).

Even when there is no direct connection with the past, the appointment of other CVD members raises doubts about the anti-doping commitment of Italy's sports bodies and government, given the appointees' potential conflict of interests. To give just one example, in 2010 the last Berlusconi government appointed two high-level representatives of Italy's cycling federation, including the chief physician, as CVD members (Ministero della Salute 2012)—despite the fact that CVD is responsible for testing the vast majority of Italy's athletes and cycling is considered one of the sports most polluted by doping (Int-Oth-2; see also Chap. 1).[14]

The law enforcement agencies themselves seem to be not completely immune from potential conflicts of interests, as the sports teams of some agencies traditionally include some of the very best elite athletes in Italy. In a criminal proceeding of the Bolzano Prosecutor's Office (Procura della Repubblica presso il Tribunale di Bolzano 2002), two suppliers of anabolic steroids and other doping substances repeatedly hinted at a high-level law enforcement officer who allegedly was their customer and expressed the expectation that the officer would help them retrieve some of the substances that had been seized by another police force. However, the law enforcement officer was not identified, and the investigation on the matter was not further pursued. As the training camp of the teams of a law enforcement agency was located near Bolzano, these suspicions were regarded as worthwhile of further investigation by one of our interviewees (Int-Oth-2).

Lastly, CONI published only in the fall of 2012 the results of its anti-doping tests from 2008 onwards, as the news of our study became public. This delay obviously does not testify to a thorough commitment against doping.

In its turn, UNIRE, the public body in charge of regulating horseracing, had a very bad reputation and competed with few others for the title of being the worst managed public agency in Italy. With 111 million euro debt, in 2009 UNIRE had the

[13] See http://www.salute.gov.it/dettaglio/pdPrimoPiano.jsp?id=23&sub=3&lang=it.

[14] The names and qualifications of the two members are listed openly on the CVD's Web site—a confirmation of Italians' scarce awareness of conflicts of interest (see also The Economist 2011b): see http://www.salute.gov.it/antiDoping/paginainternaDoping.jsp?menu=commissione&lang=italiano&id=131

highest debt rate per employee. Both its top management positions and the position of race judges were often assigned to protégés—respectively of politicians and the UNIRE top management. A witness in the 2003 investigation of the Naples Prosecutor's Office allegedly reported "some UNIRE officials bet on races after the cashiers were closed; they had found ways of stopping the time" (Zunino 2009). UNIRE was transformed in July 2011 in ASSI, Agenzia per lo sviluppo del settore ippico [Agency for the Development of the Equestrian Sector), in attempt to improve management standards and revive the highly indebted world of horseracing.[15]

In the meanwhile, the few elite athletes who find the courage to become whistle-blowers keep on being harassed and marginalized, while they are punished for their violations of sports rules. Filippo Simeoni, the only rider who already at the beginning of the current century confessed to having received prescriptions of doping substances by Dr. Ferrari and who became the main witness at the Bologna trial, subsequently found employment only in small cycling teams. As late as 2007, he recounts: "Six months suspension, 100,000€ of earnings lost, my salary reduced when I came back, I no longer had any great chances. You survive, but you have to swallow a lot. Harassment and humiliations. On the one hand, I was the sinner, on the other the traitor. They held it all against me. I was isolated, a bastard, I deserved nothing." Even Lance Armstrong took time to personally harass Simeoni at the Tour de France. "Lance hated me because I had badmouthed Ferrari. I joined a group of riders in a breakaway. He came to us and said to the others: you can, he can't. He even started singing at me: 'Fool, fool.' Two other mates shouted: 'You are a disgrace, you bite the hand that feeds you.' Even Cipollini did what he could to prevent me from racing, I was dangerous, I had spoken out" (Audisio 2007).

5.1.4 The Parallels Between Doping in Elite Sports and Insider Trading

The analysis just concluded empirically confirms Bette's (2008) thesis of doping in elite sports as "a 'normal accident,' which occurs over and over due to precisely-identifiable social conditions." Despite the media and sports bodies' repeated claims that the athletes testing positive constitute deviant individuals acting alone, Bette convincingly argues that doping practices in elite sports are the results of a "constellation of actors," which set the structural conditions making doping possible and fostering its spread (see also Bette and Schimank 2000).

Going beyond that, our analysis suggests that doping has long been considered a legitimate practice within the Italian elite sports world, long after the adoption of the first anti-doping provisions by the IOC and a few international sports federations in the 1960s. In other words, our analysis indicates that doping prohibition in sports rules and its criminalization in Italy have not always coincided with its delegitimation. Similar conclusions seem also plausible for other countries, in which doping

[15] See http://www.unire.gov.it/index.php/ita/Assi.

has not even been fully criminalized (T.M.C. Asser Instituut 2010; see also Chap. 1). In this and other respects, we see interesting and multiple parallels with insider trading, that is, the trading of a corporation's stock or other securities (e.g., bonds or stock options) by individuals with potential access to nonpublic information about the company. We briefly discuss each of these parallels, dealing last with the lack of synchrony between prohibition/criminalization and delegitimation processes and partially generalizing from Italy's experience to the rest of the world.

Both doping and insider trading are still not regulated uniformly by most countries in the world, even if there is a clear trend toward growing government controls and prohibition. The United States enacted restrictions of insider trading as early as 1934, but "insider trading in the rest of the world markets, with few exceptions, went virtually unregulated prior to the 1980s" (Newkirk 1998), and despite the recent adoption of insider trading bans in most countries, considerable differences remain in the scope of the provisions and the sentences foreseen (The Economist 2011d). Similarly, despite the adoption of the World Anti-Doping Code, some scholars still see considerable differences in the implementation of the WADA and UNESCO rules by the anti-doping panels of the national sports federations and courts (see Hendrickx 2008; Henne 2009). The differences are further exacerbated by the fact that key violations in the Code, such as doping use and trafficking, have no parallel in the criminal codes of many countries (Federal Ministry of the Interior 2009; T.M.C. Asser Instituut 2010: 23; see Chap. 1).

In addition to differences in legislation, there are also differences in enforcement. In the case of insider trading, countries still differ considerably in the degree with which they are ready to enforce their prohibitions, with the United States being perceived to be much tougher than the rest (Coffee 2007; The Economist 2011d). As we have seen in the previous pages, neither the Italian Athletic Federation FIDAL nor its international counterpart IAAF showed under Nebiolo's presidency great commitment in enforcing anti-doping rules. According to Hoberman (2012), the IOC showed very little interest in effectively pursuing doping almost until the end of the IOC presidency of Juan Antonio Samaranch (1980–2001). FIFA's more recent abysmal testing record (Hoberman 2012; see Chap. 1) and repeated corruption scandals (Kistner 2012) suggest that not even the major and richest sports federations are yet seriously committed to controlling doping. National sports federations and other sports governing bodies are likely to differ even more substantially from each other in financial means, the will of their higher ranking officials, and political support in implementing IOC and WADA rules. As mentioned in Chap. 1 (see Hoberman 2012; Rössner 2011: 420), governments also vary significantly in their determination and, if developing countries are included, in the means to implement the legislation against doping-related offenses they may have on the books.

Other similarities between doping in elite sports and insider trading involve the controversial nature of the two offenses, the arguments brought forward by policymakers, and the lack of scholarly consensus about the benefits of their regulation. Despite the regulatory efforts in both fields, both the offenses (and sports rule violations) of doping and insider trading remain inherently ambiguous. Even in the

United States, many forms of trading by corporate insiders remain legal, if this trading is done in a way that does not take advantage of nonpublic information. Likewise, the use of the same substance by the same athlete can be considered or not considered a case of doping depending on whether or not the athlete has a therapeutic use exemption. More generally, there is a thin and arbitrary line between legal and illegal performance-enhancing products, and Italy's Supreme Court has recently defended the argument of Turin Prosecutor Guariniello that the offenses of doping and sporting fraud may also entail the administration of legal drugs not included in the official prohibited list, if these are used off label, i.e., for purposes different than those officially foreseen, for example, to enhance performance (di Cassazione and Sezione Seconda Penale 2007). In the case of doping, the ambiguity is further enhanced by the fact that sports rules often do not have clear corresponding provisions in government law books.

The main argument in favor of regulating insider trading is fairness, the idea, as former SEC Chairman Levitt once put it, that "'the proverbial little guy' on Main Street should have the same fair chance as the big guys" (quoted in Newkirk 1998). A similar argument has also been used in the field of anti-doping, even if it is compounded with the protection of athletes' health and, more recently, with the partially overlapping idea of the "spirit of sport" (see Chap. 1). And as in the case of doping (e.g., Kayser et al. 2007), from the 1960s onwards scholars have repeatedly contested the benefits of regulating insider trading (e.g., Manne 1966; Carlton and Fischel 1982–1983).

Most crucially, both doping and insider trading have long been considered legitimate activities within their respective communities, and policy-makers' efforts to prohibit/criminalize them have not automatically changed these perceptions. As Clarke (1990: 162) noted in a study about financial crime in the City of London,

> it would have perplexed leading members of these institutions up to the end of the 1950s to be told that they were doing anything reprehensible in acting upon such information. It was precisely because of the access to such information that one was part of the City, and one was part of the City in the clear expectation of making a considerable amount of money.

Even in the United States, the enforcement of insider trading regulation has not always been consistent, and despite a few prominent trials involving Ivan Boesky and Michael Milken (Stewart 1992), among others, in the 1980s, insider trading has probably remained a frequent practice for hedge funds and other corporations seeking to maximize their earnings on the US securities markets, as suggested by several recent prominent trials in the USA (see The Economist 2011b, 2012 and Packer 2011).

Sports success, rather than financial profit, has always been the main motivation for doping in the organized sports world, but the state-doping programs in the former East Germany (Berendonk 1992; Franke 1995; Spitzer 1998) and the repeated scandals in a number of developed Western countries suggest that sports authorities and federation officials in other countries in addition to Italy long regarded doping a de facto legitimate practice or, even if they increasingly had "doubts" about its formal legitimacy, still supported or tolerated it in the pursuit of the higher goal of sports success. For a long time, sports officials were probably even convinced—or at least justified ex post their actions with the idea—of operating for a higher national interest, an excuse that was never available to insider traders. In West Germany, for example, a series of parliamentary hearings and the detailed historical reconstruction of Singler and Treutlein (2010: 202–239) document the attempts of the National Olympic Committee (NOK), the German Sport Federation (DSB), leading sports physicians, and several politicians in the mid-1970s to question and even weaken the IOC's prohibition of steroids; to minimize or deny the harms associated with their use; and, in some cases, even to legalize their administration to elite athletes by physicians. The overall aim of these maneuvers was to secure the "equality of chances" of West German athletes versus their East German counterparts, who were very effectively being doped by East German officials (see also Hoberman 2011b).

Doping scandals involving high-level sports federation officials have taken place even in the low-corruption Scandinavian countries, as the 2001 Lahti scandal shows. A few days before the start of the 2001 Nordic World Championships in Lahti, Finland, the team physician of the Finnish national ski team mistakenly left his bag containing plasma expander, bloody needles, and intravenous tubes at a petrol station. A scandal burst when six Finnish skiers tested positive for plasma expander a few days afterwards, and the bag was linked to the team physicians and positive tests. Most probably, the athletes had taken EPO and then used plasma expanders to lower their hematocrit levels before the races. A Doping Enquiry Taskforce (2001: 3) set up by the Finnish Ministry of Education to investigate the scandal concluded: "What made the Lahti doping cases serious was not only the large number of perpetrators, six, but also that doping had taken place under the auspices of Finnish Ski Federation coaching." In 2008, Kari-Pekka Kyrö, the former coach of the Finnish national team and the only person sentenced for the 2001 scandal, finally admitted that "in the 1990s there was a pharmacological program in the Finnish Ski Federation" and that Finnish skiers systematically took EPO, GH, and plasma expander (Hahn and Häyrinen 2008).

The scandal affecting the Austrian Ski Federation that burst at the 2006 Turin Olympic Games also suggests that doping has continued to be tolerated at the highest levels even in the current century. As seen in the introduction, this federation hired and protected the trainer Walter Mayer, even after he had been suspended by the IOC; allowed the doping of many of its biathlon and cross-country athletes under Mayer's supervision; and set up two hematological "laboratories" to check the athletes' blood values at their training location in Austria and at their premises at the Olympic Village in Turin. After these events became public thanks to the intervention of Italy's law enforcement agencies, the IOC Disciplinary Commission concluded that the whole Austrian Olympic Committee had

> breached its obligations under the Olympic Charter, the IOC Code of Ethics and applicable anti-doping regulations … 1. through its responsibility for the conduct of the Austrian Ski Federation, as well as for the anti-doping rule violations committed by its athletes and support staff at the Torino Olympic Games …; 2. by failing to prevent Mr. Mayer from participating in the Torino Olympic Games in breach of the IOC's decision against Mr. Mayer after the "Blood Bag Affair"… ; and 3. by failing to implement appropriate organisational

changes in an attempt to prevent a repeat of the problems experienced in 2002 (International Olympic Committee 2007).

Reflecting on the evolution of insider trading regulation, Nelken (2007: 758) presents this and other white-collar crimes as "index[es] of social change," stressing that social perceptions and legislation are often not synchronized with each other. When he examines the Enron scandal, Nelken makes a few considerations that are also fully applicable to doping in elite sports: "some relevant misbehavior was legally criminal but not widely stigmatized socially, other misconduct was socially disapproved of, but not technically criminal and the line between these was a changing one" (ibid.: 763). In the case of doping in elite sports, this mismatch is further exacerbated by the fact that sports rules are often distinct from government legislation and differ from the latter in their legitimacy and enforcement.

On a more positive note, the parallel between doping and insider trading also suggests that the enactment of government and sports law prohibitions has an impact on the perceived legitimacy of these activities, particularly if the introduction of new sports rules and criminal prohibitions is followed up by their consequent implementation. Both the corporate officials who might be tempted to trade on the basis of insider information and the athletes and their suppliers and protectors within the elite sports worlds are white-collar criminals–wrongdoers par excellence and are therefore sensible to deterrent measures, as they have a lot to lose.

The progressive delegitimation of doping can be clearly seen in the evolution of Italian sports body and federation officials' attitudes and practices described in the previous pages. Whereas in the 1980s high-level sports officials and university centers directly paid by CONI engaged quite openly in the administration of doping products with the open complicity of CONI and at least a few Italian sports federations, sports bodies have become much more cautious since the early 1990s and have set up anti-doping programs, even if, as in the case of corporate insiders, their increased compliance may be largely dictated by a rational assessment of the increased risk rather than the interiorization of the relevant government provisions.

We have no Italian data to support changes in the attitudes and behaviors of elite athletes. However, two independent studies focusing on elite cycling in France, Switzerland, and Belgium (Brissonneau et al. 2009) and in Australia (Hardie et al. 2010) have come to the conclusion that the attitudes and behaviors of at least the interviewed elite riders had changed considerably since the 1998 Festina affair, the resulting increase in anti-doping controls and progressive delegitimation of doping. As a former Australian elite rider admitted in an interview:

> A: Well, I think one of the things that's changed the most with the peloton at the moment is the fact that, back in the old days, everyone would talk about doping,
> and everyone would talk about what they're on and how much they're having, and
> this guy's was on this, and this guy's taken that and all this sort of thing and just
> completely open forum about doping basically. And it's got to the stage now, where if someone gets caught using something, there's guys in the bunch, and everyone just - they're on the outer, they're the ones getting the piss taken out of them, they're the ones that are not get.. that are getting fucked over in the crosswinds, and they're the ones that are getting slowly outed from the sport because socially they're not, they're not one of us anymore. They're the ones ruining the sport.

> Q: So, who "we" are has changed?
> A: Yes, so as a group we're all changing and trying to push out the cheaters, you know what I mean? That's one of the biggest things that's changed, and one of the … the things that's moving sport into a cleaner area (Hardie et al. 2010:10; see also Brissonneau et al. 2009).

As we will see in Chap. 8, some cautiously optimistic lessons for policy-making can be drawn from the parallel between doping and insider trading.

5.2 What is the Role of Underworld and Organized Crime in the Market?

In recent years a number of high-level international sports officials have emphasized the growing presence of the underworld in the market for doping products.[16] WADA Director General Howman has repeatedly denounced "the ever-increasing advance of the underworld into sport," adding that "the underworld was making a lot of money from trafficking and distributing prohibited substances … and that the same people who were making a lot of money out of the trafficking of prohibited substances were also making money out of illegal betting and general corruption around the fringes of sport" (World Anti-Doping Agency 2010d). Likewise, the IOC President Rogge has repeatedly warned of the danger posed by organized crime, albeit with particular reference to match fixing: "These are mafia links and mafia people and they bet at the same time while manipulating the result of a match" (e.g., Schlink 2011). In stressing the advance of the underworld, these officials presumably also refer to the well-publicized operations against the trade in steroids carried out by the US DEA and a few other law enforcement agencies (for the USA, see Fainaru-Wada and Lance 2006; Dohrmann and Llosa 2006; U.S. Drug Enforcement Administration 2007; for Europe, see Bundeskriminalamt 2011). We consider here the extent to which this analysis is applicable to the Italian case and, more generally, the role of organized crime in the market for doping products in Italy.

5.2.1 The Role of Italian Mafia Organizations

In the questionnaire that feeds the NAS Investigations Database, the NAS officers can note if the investigation they are reporting should be considered a case of "organized crime (common or mafia-type)." None of the 71 supply-related NAS investigations were listed as mafia-type organized crime. Twenty investigations were characterized as "common organized crime"; however, from the explanations and the descriptions provided, the respondents seem to mean "common crime" in at

[16] Several quotes are reported in Hoberman (2012: 2–3).

least ten cases rather than "common organized crime"—the expression "common crime" being much more current in the Italian language than "common organized crime.[17]

The analysis of the criminal proceedings and the expert interviews confirm the very limited involvement of Southern Italian mafia groups, such as Sicilian Cosa Nostra, the Calabrian 'Ndrangheta, and the Neapolitan camorra, in the production and distribution of doping products. Among the suppliers considered so far, there is only a specific type that can be traced back to Southern Italian mafia-type organized crime groups: the robbers attacking trucks containing medical drugs, who are often associated with Neapolitan camorra groups (Int-NAS-9 and -26). According to media sources, camorra groups also commissioned the theft of 80,000 EPO ampoules in 2000 in Malta, which were then distributed on the Neapolitan market (Fazzo and Mensurati 2002a).

More indirectly, health care professionals located in the Campania region and stealing from hospitals and pharmaceutical company storehouses seem to be advantaged vis-à-vis their counterparts in other Italian regions because they immediately find a stock of receivers, some of whom are associated with camorra groups and some work independently. The existence of "professional" underworld figures used to deal with many illegal and semi-illegal products, of which doping substances are only a small subset, has made Naples, according to Tau, "the capital" of Italy's market for doping products:

> A day a rider of another team, a guy I knew well, told me: "Why don't you go to Naples to buy it, there, it is very cheap." At that time I used to pay 4,000 EPO units 250,000 lire (approximately, 125 €), in Naples they sold me 10,000 units for 110,000 lire (55 €). There are at least 2,000 characters like Marzano [a policeman who had turned out to being a supplier of doping substances] in Naples, it is an extraordinary market. Everything gets out from the hospitals. I did at least 30 trips to Naples and I started knowing the people of the [doping] circles (Fazzo and Mensurati 2002b).

Members of some camorra groups also play an important role in the fixing of horse races, which seems to be particularly common in the area of Naples. As we have seen earlier, the fix can be achieved through the administration of drugs to horses—not only to enhance their performance but also to let them run more slowly than usually (Corbo 2004). This case can be read as a confirmation of Howman's earlier statement that the same underworld people who trade in doping substances also undermine the integrity of sports through illegal betting.

A few gym and fitness centers located in Calabria and selling steroids and other doping substances to their patrons are also suspected of being the property of persons linked, or perhaps even affiliated, with Calabrian 'Ndrangheta groups (Int-Pro-7). There is no clear-cut evidence, though. In any case, 'Ndrangheta's suspected involvement in those gyms does not seem to entail any special features in the doping practices within the gyms.

---

[17] A telling detail is the fact than even four investigations exclusively concerning the demand of doping, each of them involving only a single rider, were classified as "common organized crime."

It is worrying that the largest sales of gonadorelin were located in the region of Calabria and in the provinces of Salerno in Campania and Caltanissetta and Palermo in Sicily, in addition to the Novara and Ferrara provinces (see Table 2.16). As is well known, the three above-mentioned regions host many organized crime groups associated with the 'Ndrangheta camorra and Cosa Nostra, respectively. However, as no investigation has so far focused on gonadorelin diversion, we do not know if the exorbitant sales of this hormone only reflect the generous prescriptions and sales of complacent physicians and pharmacists or if, instead, they hint at an involvement of local organized crime groups in gonadorelin distribution.

Aside from these few cases, there is no evidence of traditional mafia organized crime in the market for doping products—despite the economic and political power that mafia groups enjoy in the South of the country (e.g., Paoli 2003b). As reported in the database, the five investigations carried out in Sicily and one conducted in Calabria do not show any involvement of the local mafia groups.

Neither camorra groups nor the overwhelming majority of the suppliers of doping products identified so far in Italian investigations are active as importers of doping products. Unlike the suspects targeted in the largest above-mentioned foreign investigations, the Italian suppliers do not yet appear, as a rule, sell abroad. The only exception here is represented by a few doctors servicing elite athletes, who indeed have an international clientele and, in one case at least, even occasionally operate abroad (Pasqualetto 2011; MacMichael 2011a).

5.2.2 Are the Enterprises and Networks of Suppliers a Form of Organized Crime?

NAS officers' uncertainty in characterizing the suppliers of doping products as common organized crime at least partially reflects the common understanding of organized crime in Italy. Unlike their counterparts in other countries, most Italian policy-makers, law enforcement officers, and the public still understand organized crime as a set of stable and large-scale criminal organizations, which are by and large exemplified by Southern Italian mafia organizations and particularly the Sicilian Cosa Nostra (Paoli and Fijnaut 2004). However, this "Italian" understanding of organized crime is no longer "mainstream" at the international level.

Whereas reference to large-scale organizations allegedly threatening world security is often made in policy documents,[18] the official definitions of organized crime are loose and vague. The UN Convention against Transnational Organized Crime of 2000, for example, has clearly adopted a lowest common denominator definition

[18] At the end of the UN World Ministerial Conference on Organized Transnational Crime, which took place in Naples in 1994, for example, its participants declared themselves "deeply concerned about the dramatic growth of organized crime over the past decade and about its global reach, which constitute a threat to the internal security and stability of sovereign States" (United Nations General Assembly 1994: 2).

with no strict criteria in terms of number of members and group structure. Article 2, paragraph (a) of the Convention states: "'Organized criminal group' shall mean a structured group of three or more persons, existing for a period of time and acting in concert with the aim of committing one or more serious crimes or offenses established in accordance with this Convention, in order to obtain, directly or indirectly, a financial or other material benefit" (United Nations General Assembly 2000: 25). Serious crime is defined by paragraph (b) of the same article as any offense punishable by a maximum deprivation of liberty of at least 4 years (ibid.). This means that the incisive investigative methods and other legislative and institutional changes foreseen by the Convention can be also applied to cliques, gangs, and networks that are very far removed from the stereotypes of organized crime dominating the media and political discourse (see Paoli 2008).[19] In the academic debate, no reference is made to minimum sentence, and organized crime is nowadays simply equated with illegal enterprises or even networks of loose partnerships and individuals trading in illicit products (e.g., van Duyne 1997; Bouchard and Morselli 2013).

From the academic perspective, the illicit enterprises set up by some suppliers of doping products, and even many looser partnerships developed by others even within legitimate institutional contexts, can be regarded as a form of organized crime. In a country like Italy in which the illegal trade in doping products is punished with imprisonment from 2 to 6 years (see Chap. 7), these enterprises would have no difficulty meeting all the requirements of the definition of organized crime contained in the UN Convention. What is crucial to stress, though, is the fact that these "organized crime" enterprises are not the expression of an outside, threatening underworld but are largely made up of white-collar crime offenders and are, to a considerable extent, internal to the world of sports.

5.2.3 Opening Up the Perspective: From Italy to the Rest for the World

This study has focused solely on the Italian market for doping products and we have collected only limited empirical evidence to assess what happens in other parts of the world. Nevertheless, some evidence from Italian investigations seems to confirm the involvement of organized crime groups in the foreign production of doping substances outside Italian borders. The main supplier of raw materials for the South African suspect running a transnational distribution ring of steroids and GH was a lab run by a Moldavian organized crime group (Int-NAS-9)—whatever the expression organized crime groups exactly means. Foreign investigations also show that criminal groups organize the transcontinental trade in doping products, as in the Operation Cyber Chase (U.S. Drug Enforcement Administration 2005), which

[19] As discussed in Paoli and Fijnaut (2004), European Union executive bodies also pursued an analogous "double-track" approach.

documented the production of steroids and other controlled substances in India—on the basis of raw materials produced in many other countries, including some European ones—and the marketing of these substances in the USA and elsewhere via Internet. The theft of 4,650,000 EPO ampoules in Nicosia, Cyprus, in 1999 also seems to presuppose the existence of a large organization, capable to receiving such an enormous quantity of drug (Donati 2007: 16). Media reports also show that criminal organizations, predominantly located in Asia but also active in Europe, engage in match rigging (Hill 2008). Just like the camorra, some of these groups appear to be simultaneously involved in illegal betting and the supply of doping products, thus presenting a formidable challenge to the integrity of sports.

Italian investigations, however, also indicate that many, if not most, foreign producers and wholesale distributors are not members of an elusive underworld but are former pharmaceutical employees, such as the above-mentioned Southern African suspect, or even belong to pharmaceutical companies operating on the fringe of legality in countries with lax or no regulations. As Howman himself (World Anti-Doping Agency 2010d) acknowledges, there is considerable overlap between the market for doping products and that for diverted or counterfeited pharmaceutical products. This overlap is also shown by some recent investigations of foreign law enforcement agencies. For example, the main defendant of US DEA's Operation "Gear Grinder," suspected of having produced more than 70 % of the illegal anabolic steroids seized in 2005 in the United States, was a pharmaceutical executive and trained veterinarian (Dohrmann and Llosa 2006).

Evidence from international scandals and foreign investigations also confirm the involvement of many people belonging to the world of sports in the supply of doping products. To mention just an example, at least two sports physicians of the respected University of Freiburg in Germany doped for over a decade until 2007 riders of Germany's largest and most successful cycling team—initially called Team Telekom and later T-Mobile—in their quality of team physicians. Among the athletes treated there were the two Tour de France winners, Bjarne Riis and Jan Ulrich (Dopingkommission 2009).

Of course, it may well be that members of veritable long-standing and powerful criminal organizations play an important role in the production and distribution of doping substances in Asia and elsewhere, as international sports and law enforcement officials report. International sports officials' emphasis on organized crime might also be justified from a policy-making perspective with the need to attract national governments' and the world public's attention on the problem of doping and to gain the momentum needed to bring about useful legislative reforms. However, by doing so, international sports officials should not fall into the trap of abdicating the sports world's responsibility for the problem of doping, presenting it as a problem largely caused by powerful, threatening forces outside the sports world.

If they speak of mafia, they should admit that there is a lot of *omertà* and conspiracy in the elite sports world, which are not the product of powerful mafia organizations' assaults but are, instead, the result of dynamics internal to the organized sports world. "The doping system is organized along mafia-like lines," stressed

WADA founding President Dick Pound, and rightly so (Großekathöfer and Gilbert 2008). True, the market for doping products generates much less violence than mafia organizations; however, it also produces considerable harms to the physical and psychological integrity of the final users. Moreover, the organized sports world's toleration of doping imposes an extremely high psychological pressure on all its participants to ensure compliance and prevent whistleblowers. The few athletes and team personnel who admit doping practices are ruthlessly marginalized, as it happened in Italy with rider Simeoni. For example, Jörg Jaschke, an Austrian rider who admitted doping and denounced the Freiburg University sports medicine physicians who had helped him dope after the 2007 Team Telekom-T-Mobile scandal and Operacion Puerto, was long harassed and marginalized from professional cycling. For several years Jaschke was unable to find a new team, until he decided to retire from professional cycling (taz 2011). This experience lead him to conclude that, at least in one respect, the organized sports word might behave even worse than mafia organizations: "The Mafia protects its people. In cycling, however, those who fall out of line even once are ruthlessly put down" (Kistner 2007).[20]

In other words, sports body officials should not repeat the mistake often made in the field of organized crime control of presenting the crime in question as an "alien" or "outside" threat. In the 1950s and 1960s, for example, many US politicians and policy-makers went as far as to state that US organized crime consisted almost exclusively of a nationwide, centralized criminal organization dominating the most profitable illegal markets and composed of migrants of Italian origin—initially called Mafia (U.S. Senate 1951) and, later on, La Cosa Nostra (Senate and Judiciary Committee 1957). This official view was dubbed as "alien conspiracy theory" by its critics (e.g., Smith 1975; Moore 1974). The latter rightly pointed out that there was a thriving domestic demand for the goods and services allegedly provided by the Mafia and that these goods and services were provided by a plurality of domestic actors.

More recently and in a more sophisticated way, EU policy-makers also presented organized crime as a threat that came predominantly "from the outside." In the 2003 European Security Strategy, the European Council (2003) considered organized crime as one of the key threats to Europe, alongside terrorism and regional conflicts, presenting Europe as "a prime target for organized crime." These pictures of an

[20] In the case of match rigging, veritable criminal organizations may play a more relevant role than in the market for doping products. International sports officials are to be praised for their efforts to draw the attention of governments, law enforcement agencies, and public opinion to this worrying phenomenon. In the case of match rigging, too, the IOC and key international sport federations should realize that their own inability to solve internal corruption problems and implement a rigorous integrity policy significantly enhances criminal organizations' chances of rigging matches and competitions. A recent book on the International Football Federation (FIFA) written by a leading German expert (Kistner 2012) is by no chance entitled "FIFA-Mafia." This title is well justified: to give just an example, between 1989 and 2001, FIFA Marketing Agency, ISL, paid bribes for at least 142 million Swiss francs to high-level sports officials from the IOC, several Olympic Committees, and above all FIFA itself. The former and honorary FIFA President Joao Havelange and his son-in-law were reported receiving at least 21 million Swiss francs with the knowledge of the current FIFA President Joseph Blatter, who was then secretary general (Weinreich 2012).

alien threat might have been necessary from a policy-making perspective to rally national politicians' and public support for legislation considerably enhancing law enforcement agencies' investigative powers and for institutional reforms overcoming previous police fragmentation. However, they do not reflect an accurate assessment of the organized crime situation in much of Europe and are not useful as a basis for concrete control efforts.[21] In Europe too, many organized crime activities thrive on the EU citizens' demand, and many EU citizens also actively participate in these organized crime activities. Indeed, some EU nations have become veritable powerhouses in key illegal markets—one just has to recall the role of the Netherlands in production and distribution of illegal drugs.

In the case of doping, we are even further away from the reality of an alien threat: even if underworld members may increasingly engage in the production and wholesale distribution of doping substances in Asia and elsewhere, most exchanges at the retail level as well as considerable fractions of the different distribution chains linking producers to final users are embedded in legitimate social relationships. As will become apparent in the final chapter, the white-collar crime nature of many doping violations—particularly within elite sports—means that alternative regulatory measures beyond the current focus on athletes' testing can and should effectively complement enhanced criminal repression. That is why, rather than emphasizing the underworld's role, we fully agree with another assessment of Howman's (2011a: 13):

> We must realize that, in most cases, it is not athletes acting alone who defeat everything for which they should stand. They are assisted, counselled, sometimes tricked and occasionally forced into the downward spiral of cheating. Coaches, trainers, medical doctors, scientists, sports administrators—even some misguided parents—all of whom ought to know better, make a mockery of their responsibilities and trivialize the years of training and dedication of the trusting athletes whom they betray. One of our missions at WADA is to make sure that it is not only the athletes who are sanctioned for doping offenses. Athletes are, of course, the instruments in which the doping occurs, but often they are less to blame than the coaches, doctors, lawyers, agents, trainers and others around them.

[21] For an overview of the many far-reaching legislative and institutional reforms introduced to enhance the fight against organized crime in Europe, see Fijnaut and Paoli (2004) and Fijnaut (2013).

Chapter 6
Revenues and Profits

Abstract In the sixth chapter of the book, we analyze the data available to estimate the financial dimensions of the Italian market for doping products, including the revenues and profits of different types of suppliers of doping products. As expected, this objective has been the most challenging of the whole project. As is well known in the literature on illegal markets, it is always very difficult to estimate the size of a market that is at least partially illegal (e.g., Reuter and Greenfield, World Economics 2(4):159–173, 2001). We hence have no ambition to provide a definitive estimate; rather, we make a first attempt to assess the retail revenues and hence financial dimensions of the market.

We proceed in three steps, the first two referring to the market in its entirety and the last focusing on the revenues and profits of different suppliers. First, we estimate the potential market value of the substances seized by NAS and other law enforcement agencies in Italy. Second, we assess the total retail expenditures—or the total financial size of the market—for doping substances, using the consumption estimates developed in Chap. 2. Third, we analyze the rather sketchy data collected concerning the revenues and profits of a few illegal suppliers of doping products in Italy. A preliminary condition for the first two steps is the determination of the prices of doping substances—and this is what we begin with.

Our main findings are that, with few exceptions, doping products are relatively cheap, certainly cheaper than illegal drugs, if they are bought at regular pharmacy prices or on the Internet. Therefore, the revenues generated by retail exchanges are also relatively modest, representing only a fraction of the revenues raised on the market for cocaine. We acknowledge, however, that our underlying consumption estimates severely underestimate the consumption of some of the most expensive substances and hence the related revenues.

L. Paoli and A. Donati, *The Sports Doping Market: Understanding Supply and Demand, and the Challenges of Their Control*, DOI 10.1007/978-1-4614-8241-3_6,

In this chapter we analyze the data available with a view to fulfill the fifth objective of our study: namely, to estimate the financial dimensions of the doping market, including the revenues and profits of different types of suppliers of doping products. As expected, this objective has been the most challenging of the whole project. As is well known in the literature on illegal markets, it is always very difficult to estimate the size of a market that is at least partially illegal (e.g., Reuter and Greenfield 2001). We hence have no ambition to provide a definitive answer to the research questions implicit in the fifth objective; rather, we make a first attempt to assess the retail revenues and hence financial dimensions of the market.

We proceed in three steps, the first two referring to the market in its entirety and the last focusing on the revenues and profits of different suppliers. First, we estimate the potential market value of the substances seized by NAS and other law enforcement agencies in Italy. Second, we assess the total retail expenditures—or the total financial size of the market—for doping substances, using the consumption estimates developed in Chap. 2. Third, we analyze the rather sketchy data collected concerning the revenues and profits of a few illegal suppliers of doping products in Italy. A preliminary condition for the first two steps is the determination of the prices of doping substances—and this is what we begin with.

Our main findings are that, with few exceptions, doping products are relatively cheap, certainly cheaper than illegal drugs, if they are bought at regular pharmacy prices or on the Internet. Therefore, the revenues generated by retail exchanges are also relatively modest, representing only a fraction of the revenues raised on the market for cocaine. We acknowledge, however, that our underlying consumption estimates severely underestimate the consumption of some of the most expensive substances and hence the related revenues.

6.1 The Retail Price of Doping Substances

As many doping substances consist of regular drugs, they have a legal market price. Moreover, as drugs in Italy are highly regulated, most of them are sold in pharmacies and have an official price, which is the same throughout the country. For all the substances recorded in the NAS Investigations Database, the first step has been to check on the Web sites of the Agenzia Italiana del Farmaco[1] and Pagine Sanitarie[2] if they were legally sold in Italy and, in that case, what their official price was. For the substances that have no therapeutic purpose or are not officially traded in Italy (3.4 % of the substances seized by NAS), we instead collected the prices on a few Internet Web sites.[3]

[1] See http://farmaco.agenziafarmaco.it/index.php.

[2] See http://www.paginesanitarie.com.

[3] Above all, we checked the following Web sites: http://www.mesomorphosis.com/; http://www.eurobolic.info/; and http://it.steroidset.com/. An important caveat is that Web sites offering doping products are online one day and disappear the next (see also Swedish National Institute of Public Health 2010: 15).

Whereas the existence of official prices represents a major difference vis-à-vis traditional illegal markets, the semi-illegal nature of the doping market implies that there is no certainty about the price paid by the final users. In most cases, in fact, the latter do not buy doping products at the official pharmacy prices. They may pay much more than the official price, if the substance is diverted from the storehouse of a drug manufacturer, distributor, health care center, or pharmacy or is sold by a pharmacist-cum-illegal supplier. Investigations show that some users, particularly those belonging to the elite market segment, are willing to pay a premium to be sure of the quality of the substances they take.

Other users, however, may pay much less than the pharmacy price, if they directly buy on the Internet a doping substance that is either counterfeited or produced in countries with lenient regulations or lax enforcement. For example, Deca Durabolin (nandrolone decanoate), a well-known anabolic steroid, is sold legally in Italy in an ampoule containing 25 mg/1 mL for 12.40 € (and as a prefilled injection at a slightly higher price).[4] On the Internet, however, it is sufficient to pay 10.20 € to buy a four times larger package of the same product (2 mL ampoule—100 mg/mL), produced by a Greek company called Norma.[5] Whereas the company seems to be legitimate,[6] the officers interviewed (Int-NAS-9 and -26) indicate that they have recently seized many Norma products that were of very bad quality, sometimes containing no active ingredient at all.

There is no guarantee, though, that Web sites always offer cheaper prices. A cartridge of 16 IU of Genotropin, for example, costs, according to Agenzia del Farmaco (as we duly noted in the NAS Investigations Database),[7] 232.24 € in a pharmacy in Italy. On a Web site,[8] the same package of Genotropin is sold for 159 € and on another for 299 €.[9]

A further complication is due to the fact that even if a substance is bought cheaply on the Internet, its final retail price may be substantially higher if the substance changes hands several times before reaching the final consumers. In face-to-face transactions, especially in the world of fitness, the final price paid by a user also often reflects his or her own doping experience, shrewdness, and financial means. As in the market for illegal drugs, retailers often adjust the prices of their doping products, and therefore their markup, to their users. According to a NAS officer, for example, a retailer's markup on an ephedrine ampoule may vary between 3 and 30 € (Int-NAS-5).

While we are aware of all these caveats, we have had no easy way to remedy the situation. It is beyond the purpose of the present study to make a systematic comparison between the official pharmacy prices of the drugs with potential doping

[4] See http://farmaco.agenziafarmaco.it/index.php?SEARCH=yes&S_DESCR_SPECIALITA=Deca+Durabolin&S_SOSTANZA=&S_DITTA=&SSN=&DSNOTA_AIFA=&GRUPPO_RICETTA=

[5] See http://www.steroid4u.eu/compra-iniettare-steroidi/deca-durabolin-norma?language=It. Accessed April 20, 2012.

[6] See http://www.normahellas.gr/uk/index.asp.

[7] See http://farmaco.agenziafarmaco.it/index.php?SCHEDA_CONF=yes.

[8] See http://www.steroid4u.eu/compra-umani-ormoni/genotropin-16-somatotropin?language=It.

[9] See http://www.eurobolic.com/index.php?main_page=product_info&products_id=342&language=de; accessed on April 19, 2012.

effects and the prices of the same substances sold on the Internet. Moreover, even if we had done this, we would still not know which price was finally paid by most users. To assess the financial dimensions of the market, we have simply used official prices for the substances legally available in Italy and the Internet prices found on an Internet Web site for the substances not available in the country. In other words, we have assumed that all users of doping substances available in Italy would buy them at the official market price, whereas the users of substances not available in Italy would buy them directly from an Internet Web site.

As already mentioned in Chap. 2, we did not have enough information to determine the active ingredients contained in about 10 % of the packages of doping substances seized by NAS branch offices between 1999 and 2009 and reported in the Database. Therefore, we could not establish the packages' price. To include these packages in the calculation of the doses seized, we have assumed that they would contain the average active ingredients of the packages of the same product (or classes of products). In the same way, here, rather than adding up the prices of the packages identified in detail, we have preferred to calculate the average price of a doping dose for each class of substances. This method has two advantages. First, it allows us to include all the substances reported in the NAS Investigations Database in the estimate of the financial dimensions of the market. Second, this average price can also be applied to the drugs seized by other law enforcement agencies and by NAS, which were not reported in the database.

Table 6.1 shows the average price of the doping doses of the different classes of substances, calculated on the basis of the assumptions just explained. Two things immediately catch the eye. First, the doping doses of most doping substances are very cheap. A dose of anabolic steroids, the class of substance most consumed by far, costs on average 1.12 €. Second, peptide hormones, growth factors, and related substances are much more expensive than all the other substances. In fact, the average price of a dose of such substances is 9.49 € but there are huge differences between the prices of the different substances included in such a category. In fact, whereas a dose of GH and other growth factors (1 IU or 0.0333 mg) cost on average 13.90 €, the official price of a dose of insulin (10 IU) is only 0.03 €. With average price per dose of about 3 €, EPO and most other related substances are in between: a dose of EPO (200 IU or 1 μg) costs 3.09 €, a dose of chorionic gonadotrophin (1,000 IU), for example, costs 3.27 €.

Only one doping substance, GH, has prices comparable to those of the most expensive illegal drugs and another one, gonadorelin, even exceeds them. In fact, whereas a dose of GH costs 13.90 €, a dose of heroin costs in 2010, the last year for which the data are available, 10.49 €; a dose of cocaine 17.29 €; and a pill of ecstasy 16.65 € (see Table 6.2).[10] With a price per dose exceeding 48 €, only gonadorelin is

[10] The Dipartimento Politiche Antidroga (2012b: 191) provides prices per street gram for heroin, cocaine, marijuana, and hashish. To make the comparison, we have hypothesized—based on the small literature about Italian local drug markets (e.g., Arlacchi and Lewis 1990; Paoli 2000)—that one can make four doses out of a gram of heroin or cocaine. The standard street dose of heroin and cocaine, in fact, is called *quartino*, i.e., quarter, even though it often contains less than 0.25 g. In the case of marijuana and hashish, we have calculated the price of a dose of cannabis by assuming that you can make three joints out of a gram.

Table 6.1 Active ingredients and average price of the doping doses of the different classes of substances seized by NAS between 1999 and 2009, as reported in the Database on NAS Investigations in euro (€)

Type of substance	Active ingredients of one dose	Average price/dose
Anabolic agents (including testosterone)	10 mg	1.12
Peptide hormones, growth factors, and related substances,[a] of which:	Variable	4.76
EPO and other similar hormones	200 IU or 1 µg	3.09
GH and other similar hormones	1 IU or 0.333 mg	13.90
Related substances[b], of which	Variable	2.50
Chorionic gonadotrophin	1,000 IU	3.27
Gonadorelin	1.2 mg	48.05
ACTH and other corticotrophins	0.25 mg	3.70
Insulin	10 IU	0.03
Beta-2 agonists	2 µg	0.20
Hormones and metabolic modulators	10 mg	1.26
Diuretics and other masking agents	25 mg	0.40
Stimulants	25 mg	0.60
Narcotics	50 mg	1.28
Glucocorticosteroids	25 mg	0.49
Beta-blockers	5 mg	0.26

Source: Our calculations on the basis of the Database on NAS Investigations

Notes: [a]4.76 € constitutes the weighted average price of the substances included in the category of peptide hormones, growth factors, and related substances based on the number of substances and types of packages seized by NAS, as reported in the NAS Investigations Database

[b]2.50 € constitutes the weighted average price of all the related substances belonging to the broader category of peptide hormones, growth factors, and related substances based on the number of substances and types of packages seized by NAS, as reported in the NAS Investigations Database

Table 6.2 Retail prices of the principal illegal drugs in Italy in euro (€)—2010

	Minimum price of a gram/pill	Maximum price of a gram/pill	Average price of a gram/pill	Average price of a dose
Hashish	8.9	13.5	11.2	3.73
Marijuana	7.7	9.4	8.55	2.85
Heroin	35.5	48.4	41.95	10.49
Cocaine	57.9	80.4	69.15	17.29
Ecstasy	14.8	18.5	16.65	16.65

Source: Our calculations on the basis of the data of the Dipartimento Politiche Antidroga (2012b : 191)

more expensive than all illegal hard drugs. The price per dose of EPO and most other related substances are similar to those of a hashish joint and are slightly more expensive than a marijuana joint. However, EPO cannot be bought as a single "micro" dose of 200 IU selected here as a unit; the minimum ampoule contains 1,000 IU and costs 16.54 €. All other doping substances are cheaper than even marijuana or hashish.

In making the comparison between the prices of illegal drugs and doping substances, it is also important to remember that a dose of an illegal drug gives a tangible satisfaction to its users whereas this is not true for all types of doping substances. A dose of stimulants, diuretics and other masking agents, beta-blockers, hormones stimulating the natural production of testosterone, or local anesthetics serves its purposes immediately. The two classes of substances mostly frequently seized and most likely to be also used—anabolic steroids and, with the exception of gonadorelin, all other peptide hormones, growth factors, and related substances—need to be taken for lengthy periods of time (the so-called cycles), sometimes several times a day, before they produce the desired effects.[11] For steroids, a cycle usually lasts 6–12 weeks. Then a break of 6–12 weeks follows before a new cycle is begun (see also Parkinson and Evans 2006; Swedish National Institute of Public Health 2010: 44). As a rule, two or more steroids are combined during a cycle (Parkinson and Evans 2006). An EPO treatment, for example, can last from a minimum of 2 to a maximum of 4 weeks, with weekly dosages oscillating between a minimum of 3,000 IU to a maximum of 6,000 IU. Hence, whereas the price of a single dose of doping substances is relatively cheap, a treatment with EPO or GH, lasting several weeks, can be quite expensive. A low-end 2-week EPO treatment of 3,000 IU per week costs about (3,000 IU/200 IU = 15 × 2 × 3.09 € =) 92.6 €.[12] A high-end 4-week treatment of 6,000 IU per week costs about (6,000 IU/200 IU = 30 × 4 × 3.09 €=) 370.3 €. While most elite athletes from resistance disciplines just undergo more than one or two treatments ahead of important competitions, a few elite riders may repeat such treatments up to six times per year, thus spending between 555.5 and 2,221.9 €, depending on the dosages and length of treatment. Despite the lower doses taken, a treatment with GH can easily be more expensive. According to wiretaps reported in NAS investigations and the advice found on specialized Italian Web sites,[13] Italian body-builders appear to use 10–15 IU of GH per week and thus would spend between 139 and 209 €, if they buy GH at the pharmacy price. The length of the treatment varies between 6 and 20 weeks, reflecting the users' financial means, body-building goals, and lack of awareness of the harms associated with GH use, and thus can cost between (13.90 € × 10 IU × 6 weeks =) 834 € and (13.90 € × 15 IU × 20 weeks =) 4,170 €. In contrast, a steroid cure, even if it lasts several weeks, remains cheap. A 3-week intake of three doses per day would cost about (3 doses × 21 days × 1.12 € =) 70 €.

[11] Reporting data from an Internet survey of 500 US users, Parkinson and Evans (2006) concluded that cycles had become longer in the 2000s than in the previous decade.

[12] We have reached this figure by multiplying the number of doses (3,000 IU × 2 weeks/200 IU) by the price per dose (9.491 €).

[13] For example, http://www.massimospattini.it/ORMONEDELLACRESCITAEBODYBUILDING.htm. Accessed June 19, 2012.

6.2 The Potential Market Value of the Substances Seized

To estimate the potential market value of the substances seized in Italy, we consider first the data available about the substances seized by NAS and other law enforcement agencies. Despite the CVD's existence, these data have never been systematically recorded by a central agency, let alone made comparable. In Chap. 2 we already presented the data relative to the seizures listed in the NAS Investigations Database. There, we concluded that in the period 1999–2009 NAS seized 7,176,780 packages of doping substances corresponding to 1,042 kg of active ingredients[14] and to 88 million doses of doping products. In this section, we estimate the active ingredients contained in substances seized by other law enforcement agencies during the period 1999–2011 and, in such a way, calculate the doses these substances represented on the basis of the parameters set in Chap. 2. Next, we do the same with the NAS seizures during 1999–2011 that were not, for whatever reason, included in the database or that were carried out after 2009 and add up all the different seizure data. Lastly, we multiply these doses of the different classes of substances seized with their average price.

6.2.1 The Doping Substances Seized by Law Enforcement Agencies Other than NAS

NAS is not the only law enforcement agency carrying out seizures of doping substances in Italy. The Agenzia delle Dogane (i.e., customs) and the Guardia di Finanza (i.e., tax police) often seize packages of doping substances when they cross Italy's borders. The latter force as well as the Polizia di Stato (i.e., Italy's regular police) conduct seizures in the rest of Italian territory. In one case, the Milan Municipal Police also made a very large seizure. The analysis of the law enforcement agencies' Web sites and of the doping-related news of the three main Italian news agencies—*Ansa*, *Agi*, and *Adnkronos*—allowed us to identify 65 seizures carried out by these forces between 1999 through the end of 2011.

The quality of these data was generally much lower than that of the data included in the NAS Investigations Database. While the Agenzia delle Dogane provides precise data,[15] the Guardia di Finanza[16] and Polizia di Stato[17] give less detail, from time to time merely referring to the collective number of packages of different categories seized.

---

[14] This sum does not include the active ingredients of peptide hormones, growth factors, and related substances, because they are not comparable to each other and to the other doping substances.

[15] See http://www1.agenziadogane.it/ed/motore_ricerca/?XML=/Agenzia_Dogane/_C=eJyLz2HILGGIL8tjcExPzavKTIx3yU9PzEtliC9kSMxLTMrPyayqSswryWSIz8gscSvNyWEwNGAAAPwEEjY_/_s=0&param_query=anabolizzanti.

[16] See http://www.gdf.gov.it/ricerca/ricerca.asp?testoRicerca=anabolizzanti&ok=ok.

[17] See http://poliziadistato.it/search/sh/.

Table 6.3 Substances seized by Italian law enforcement agencies other than NAS in 1999–2011

Type of substance	Pills, ampoules, and other packages seized	Active ingredients seized (mg)	No. of doping doses	% of total doses
Anabolic agents	493,713	83,048,870	8,304,887	83.34
Stimulants	55,404	28,568,750	1,142,750	11.47
Diuretics and other masking agents	355	55,750	2,230	0.02
Peptide hormones, growth factors, and related substances	34,752	Not comparable	514,850	5.17
Total	584,224	111,673,370	9,964,717	100.00

Source: Our calculations on the basis of the data retrieved on the Web sites of the Agenzia delle Dogane, Guardia di Finanza, Polizia di Stato, and Milan Municipal Police

To make these data comparable with those included in the NAS Investigations Database, we applied the conversion rates between different packages of the same classes of substances (e.g., 5.08 times more active ingredients contained in an ampoule than in a pill of anabolic steroids and 3.00 times in the case of corticosteroids) emerging from the NAS Investigations Database, when we had no exact information on the active ingredients contained in the packages seized by the law enforcement agencies other than NAS. In the few cases (6 out of 65) in which we also had no specific information about the classes of substances seized, we hypothesized that the share of the substance classes identified in the NAS Investigations Database could also be applied to the substances seized by the other law enforcement forces.

On the basis of these assumptions, we tentatively conclude that the other law enforcement forces seized a total of 584,224 packages of doping products between January 1999 and the end of 2011, corresponding to about 111.5 kg of active ingredients and to about ten million doping doses (see Table 6.3). The substances seized belong to only four categories of doping substances listed by WADA, i.e., anabolic agents, stimulants, peptide hormones, growth factors, and related substances and diuretics. These four categories also account for the bulk of the substances listed in the NAS Investigations Database. The comparison of the last column of Table 6.3 with the last column of Table 2.2, in fact, indicates that the share of the substance classes is roughly the same for the seizures carried out by NAS and by other law enforcement agencies. With 83.2 % and 83.3 %, respectively, anabolic steroids constitute in both cases the overwhelming category. Steroids are followed by stimulants, which account for 13.0 % of the substances reported in the NAS Investigations Database and 11.5 % of the substances seized by other law enforcement agencies. The latter have only seized, in percent values, more peptide hormones, growth factors, and related substances than NAS (5.2 % vis-à-vis 1.8 %). This higher value, however, is due only to one large seizure of EPO and GH (with active ingredients corresponding to over 10,000 ampoules!) carried out by the Guardia di Finanza in July 2009 (Capodacqua 2009).

Table 6.4 Substances seized by NAS and other Carabinieri units in 1999–2011, not reported in the Database on NAS Investigations

Type of substance	Pills, ampoules, and other packages seized	Active ingredients seized (mg)	No. of doping doses	% of total doses
Anabolic agents	395,713	62,466,970	6,246,697	86.90
Stimulants	44,404	12,958,750	518,350	7.20
Diuretics and other masking agents	354	4,425	177	0.01
Peptide hormones, growth factors, and related substances	12,250	Not comparable	423,450	5.89
Total	452,721	75,430,145	7,188,674	100.00

Source: Our calculations on the basis of the data retrieved from the newsflashes of Ansa, Agi, and Adnkronos

6.2.2 *The Total Amount of Doping Substances Seized in Italy and Their Potential Market Value*

The analysis of the doping-related news of the three main Italian news agencies also allowed us to identify an additional 44 seizures of doping products carried out by NAS and other Carabinieri units, with which NAS branch offices sometimes cooperate (see Chap. 7): 11 of them had taken place before the end of 2009 but were not included in the NAS Investigations Database. The rest had taken place from early 2010 to the end of 2011. As the data about these seizures were retrieved from the media, the same restrictions to data quality discussed earlier also apply here.

As shown in Table 6.4, we conclude that NAS and other units of the Carabinieri additionally seized 452,721 pills, ampoules, or other packages of doping substances, corresponding to about 75 kg of active ingredients and to 7.1 million doping doses in the period 1999–2011, in addition to the data reported in the NAS Investigations Database. These data show an even larger preponderance of steroids, which account for 87 % of all the doses seized.

By adding the doses of doping substances seized by NAS and other law enforcement agencies, we come to the conclusion that in the period 1999–2011 approximately 105 million doses have been seized in Italy, corresponding to 8.1 million doses on a yearly average (see Table 6.5). This figure is quite approximate, given the uncertainties on the substances and the active ingredients seized but it is the most comprehensive that we could develop. With 84.7 %, anabolic steroids account for the main share of the substances seized, followed by stimulants (12.7 %) and peptide hormones, growth factors, and related substances (2.4 %) All other classes of substances represent only marginal shares of the total. It is worthwhile noting that the yearly average underestimates the amount of products seized in recent years. However, we could not exclude the early seizures because the data in the NAS Investigations Database are reported by operation and many of these spanned over two or more calendar years.

Table 6.5 Doping doses seized in Italy in the period 1999–2011

Type of substance	Doses seized by NAS and other Carabinieri (CC) units: In database	Out of database	Total NAS/CC	Doses seized by other agencies	Total	%
Anabolic agents	74,547,623	6,246,697	80,794,320	8,304,887	89,099,207	84.68
Peptide hormones, growth factors, and related substances	1,604,608	423,450	2,028,058	514,850	2,542,908	2.42
Beta-2 agonists	4,890	0	4,890	0	4,890	0.00
Hormones and metabolic modulators	35,561	0	35,561	0	35,561	0.03
Diuretics and other masking agents	13,339	177	13,516	2,230	15,746	0.01
Stimulants	11,655,167	518,350	12,173,517	1,142,750	13,316,267	12.66
Narcotics	135	0	135	0	135	0.00
Glucocorticosteroids	181,965	0	181,965	0	181,965	0.17
Beta-blockers	11	0	11	0	11	0.00
Total	88,043,565	7,188,674	95,232,239	9,964,717	105,196,956	100.00
Yearly average	8,003,960[a]		7,325,557	766,517	8,092,073	

Source: Our calculations on the basis of the data presented earlier

[a]1999–2009

Table 6.6 Doping doses seized in Italy in the period 1999–2011 and their potential market value in euro (€)

Type of substance	Total doses seized	%	Average price	Potential value	%
Anabolic agents	89,099,207	84.68	1.12	99,612,913	75.56
Peptide hormones, growth factors, and related substances	2,542,908	2.42	9.49	24,132,196	18.30
Beta-2 agonists	4,890	0	0,20	978	0.00
Hormones and metabolic modulators	35,561	0.03	1.26	44,700	0.04
Diuretics and other masking agents	15,746	0.01	0.40	6,298	0.00
Stimulants	13,316,267	12.66	0.60	7,963,128	6.04
Narcotics	135	0.00	1.28	173	0.00
Glucocorticosteroids	181,965	0.17	0.49	89,163	0.06
Beta-blockers	11	0.00	0.28	3	0.00
Total	105,196,956	100.00		131,849,552	100.00
Yearly average	8,092,073			10,142,273	

Source: Our calculations on the basis of the data presented earlier

By multiplying the number of doses seized with the average price, we come to the conclusion that the drugs seized in Italy over the period 1999–2011 had a potential market value of 132 million euro—on average slightly more than 10.1 million euro per year (see Table 6.6). Given the much higher prices of most peptide hormones and related substances (on average 9.49 € per dose), the share of peptide hormones, growth factors, and related substances, in terms of potential market value, is six times higher than their share in terms of the number of doses seized (18.3 % vis-à-vis 2.4 %). As a result of this shift, the share of steroids is reduced from 84.7 to 75.6 %. This means, however, that steroids still account for over three-fourths of the substances seized in Italy, even in terms of the potential market value. Due to their low price, the share of stimulants also declines from 12.7 to 6.0 %. All other classes of doping substances remain irrelevant.

6.3 A Preliminary Estimate of the Financial Size of the Market

By combining our estimates of the average prices of the doses of the different doping products with our estimate of the quantities consumed in Italy (see Table 2.15), we can tentatively conclude that about 425 million euro are spent each year in Italy on doping products, excluding cannabis and cocaine (see Table 6.7). According to our calculations, steroids are worth 245 million euro; peptide hormones, growth factors, and related substances 113 million euro; and stimulants 31 million euro, followed by the other classes of substances at a great distance.

Steroids account for about more than half of the total retail expenditures (57.6 %), almost as much as their share of the quantities consumed (58.9 %; see Table 2.15).

Table 6.7 Estimated doping substance retail expenditures in euro (€)

Substances	Total dosesper class	Percent of total	Total expenditures	Percent of total
Anabolic agents	218,827,251	58.9	244,648,867	57.6
Peptide hormones, growth factors, and related substances	23,723,941	6.4	113,114,670	26.6
EPO and other similar hormones	7,675,907	2.1	23,488,275	5.5
GH and other similar hormones	3,767,419	1.0	52,291,775	12.3
Chorionic gonadotrophin	12,280,615	3.3	37,334,620	8.8
Beta-2 agonists	13,141,515	3.5	2,615,162	0.6
Hormones and metabolic modulators	132,968	0.0	167,140	0.0
Diuretics and other masking agents	32,446,708	8.7	12,881,343	3.0
Stimulants	51,775,905	13.9	30,961,991	7.3
Narcotics	7,000,000	1.9	8,974,000	2.1
Glucocorticosteroids	21,662,306	5.8	10,679,517	2.5
Beta-blockers	2,608,696	0.7	717,391	0.2
Total doses/expenditures	371,319,290	100.0	424,927,221	100.0

Source: Our calculations on the basis presented in the Database on NAS Investigations and the consumption profiles presented in Appendix B

Due to their relatively low prices (0.60 € per dose), stimulants' share of the retail expenditures (7.3 %) is lower than their share (13.9 %) of the quantities consumed. Diuretics and other masking agents and glucocorticosteroids also account for a much smaller share (3.0 % and 2.5 %, respectively) of the expenditures than their share of the quantities consumed (8.7 % and 5.8 %, respectively). In contrast, peptide hormones, growth factors, and related substances represent a much larger share of the expenditures (26.6 %) than their share of the quantities consumed (6.4 %) due to their high price.

At 425 million euro, the market for doping products generates substantially lower revenues than the market for illegal drugs. In a back-of-the-envelope calculation, we have in fact estimated the revenues of the Italian heroin market, which entails a comparable number of users, between a minimum of 2,419 million euro and a maximum of 5,292 million euro.[18] The Italian market for cocaine generates at

[18] According to the UNODC (2010: 41), about 18 metric tons of heroin at 70 % purity are consumed yearly in Italy each year. According to the data published by the Dipartimento Politiche Antidroga (2012a, b: 414), brown heroin, the type of heroin by far most widespread in Italy, has an average purity of 22 %. If this figure is accepted, we can hypothesize that 57.6 t of heroin at 22 % purity (18 t×3.2) are yearly consumed in Italy. However, the Dipartimento Politiche Antidroga does not distinguish purity data by different market levels. From previous studies (e.g., Paoli 2000) and expert interviews we know that retail heroin purity rarely exceeds 10 %. This means that the 18 t at 70 % that according to UNODC are yearly consumed in Italy need to be multiplied not by 3.2, but by 7, reaching a total of 126 t. As each gram costs 42 € in 2010, we can estimate the revenues generated by heroin retail purchases in Italy between a minimum of 2,419 million euro (at 22 % purity) and a maximum of 5,292 million euro (at 10 % purity).

Table 6.8 Doses of doping products consumed by an average athlete, an average body-builder, a super elite rider, and a super elite weightlifter and related expenditures in euro (€)

	Average athlete		Average body-builder		Super elite rider		Super elite weightlifter	
Substances	Doses	Exp.	Doses	Exp.	Doses	Exp.	Doses	Exp.
Anabolic agents	302	338	2,526	2,824	800	894	1,600	1,789
Peptide hormones, growth factors, and related substances[a]	133	1,263	55	520	280	2,657	360	3,417
Beta-2 agonists	88	17	0	0	240	48	200	40
Diuretics and other masking agents	216	86	1	0	0	0	1,200	476
Stimulants	165	99	394	235	400	239	300	179
Narcotics	47	60	0	0	160	205	240	307
Glucocorticosteroids	141	69	8	4	320	158	240	118
Beta-blockers	17	5	0	0	0	0	0	0
Total doses and expenditures	1,108	1,936	2,985	3,586	2,200	4,202	4,140	6,327

Source: Our calculations on the basis presented in the Database on NAS Investigations and the consumption profiles presented in Appendix B

Note: Totals may not match sums because of rounding

[a]We exclude GH and gonadorelin for athletes, as they were never detected in CVD's samples

least 3,685 million euro of revenues.[19] It is important to stress, though, that by excluding the consumption of GH and gonadorelin, we seriously underestimate the revenues generated by the market for doping products, as the two above-mentioned substances are by far the most expensive.

On the basis of the consumption profiles presented in Appendix B, we can also estimate how much the different classes of users on average spend yearly to buy doping substances (see Table 6.8). On average, athletes appear to spend about 1,936 € on a yearly basis, whereas body-builders spend about 3,586 €. This difference is partially due to the fact that we do not estimate GH and gonadorelin consumption in the case of athletes, as they were never detected in CVD's tests. As we have seen in the previous pages, GH and gonadorelin are the most expensive doping substances. More generally, our estimates reflect the biases of CVD's testing and, in particular, underestimate the share of other peptide hormones and related substances that are difficult to detect in urine samples but are more expensive than other doping

[19]To estimate the revenues generated by the retail cocaine market, we have multiplied the estimate of cocaine users (353,000, based on a 2010 past-year prevalence rate of 0.9 %; see Dipartmento Politiche Antidroga, 2011: 8) with the average amount consumed by each user, i.e., 30.2 g of pure cocaine, according to UNODC (2010: 71), thus reaching a 10.7 t figure (10,660,600 g). Although Italian law enforcement agencies do not collect purity data at different market levels, we know from previous studies (e.g., Paoli 2000) and expert interviews that retail cocaine purity hardly ever exceeds 20 % and is probably even lower. This means that the 10.7 t have to be multiplied by five and thus amount to 53.3 t (or 53,303,000 g) of cocaine at 20 % purity. As we know that a gram of street-level cocaine costs 69.15 € in 2010 (Dipartimento Politiche Antidroga 2012b: 191), we can estimate the revenues generated by cocaine retail purchases in 3,685,902,450 €.

substances. To an unknown extent, however, athletes' lower expenditures also reflect the fact that body-builders consume doping substances on a more regular basis and in larger amounts than athletes.

Within the group of athletes, consumption patterns, and therefore also expenditures, vary significantly depending on the discipline and the level at which the athletes compete. Excluding GH, we estimate that a super elite rider (row no. 9 the consumption profiles listed in Appendix B) spends 4,202 € for doping substances, twice as much as an average athlete. Reflecting the much heavier consumption patterns and the above-mentioned caveats, we hypothesize that a super elite weight-lifter (row no. 10) would invest more than three times as much (6,327 €) in the purchase of doping substances. It is worthwhile stressing that the amount effectively spent by users may vary considerably depending on whether they purchase cheaper, probably counterfeited, products on the Internet or if they are ready to contact suppliers they trust and pay a higher-than-average price to increase their chances of obtaining a high-quality product.

As we have already done in Chap. 2, we emphasize that the consumption profiles on which these estimates are based have only limited external validation. Therefore, the figures here presented should not be understood as exact estimates of the revenues generated by the Italian market for doping substances or of the amounts spent by different categories of users. They are, instead, merely indicative of their rough order of magnitude.

Our estimates are also partial because they do not include the market for doping methods, for which we have no means to estimate purchase patterns and expenditures. Delivered almost exclusively to super elite athletes, doping methods can be very expensive. Athletes resorting to them need thus to expect a much higher budget than those who merely use doping substances. Recently, doping methods have begun again to be en vogue among super elite riders, as a result of the tests that are now able to detect EPO in blood samples and of the introduction of the biological passport—two changes making the use of EPO riskier (see Chap. 2). In recent years, thus, super elite riders tend to use on average less EPO and only in micro-dosages and to resort more frequently to analogous transfusions, which are not detectable. This trend is also reflected in our estimate of the sums spent by a super elite rider in the purchase of doping substances (4,202 €). This sum would have been considerably higher a few years ago: Tau, the elite rider-turned-witness, reported that, as of 2002, many of his colleagues would have invested "at least 10,000 €" per year in doping substances (Fazzo and Mensurati 2002b; Tau's estimate, however, also included GH and gonadorelin expenses, which we exclude from our calculations).

It is also important to recall that doping substances represent only an item in the expenses list of the doping athletes, particularly super elite athletes, and/or their teams. In fact, the doping athletes or their entourage also need to pay frequent medical checkups, frequent urine and blood analyses, large amounts of dietary supplements, as well as the therapies necessary to treat the frequent pathologies associated with the excessive use of doping substances and methods. In addition, super elite riders frequently buy centrifuges and other equipment to monitor their own blood and heart frequency at night and a special freezing suitcase to preserve their own blood (Int-NAS-12, -13, and -15).

6.4 Illegal Suppliers' Revenues and Profits

According to several international policy-makers and law enforcement officers, the production and distribution of doping substances and specifically steroids guarantee very high profit margins, usually higher than those that can be made with illegal drug trafficking. For example, Andreas Holzer, a high-level Austrian police officer specialized in anti-doping, stressed in an interview that "the average production of a steroid package costs 0.50 € and will be sold for 35–40 € to the next distribution level" and that "the trade in doping products is much more lucrative [than the trade in illegal drugs]" (Gilbert 2010). The German Central Office for Customs Investigation Service regards the profits to be earned with the production of doping substances to be "comparable to the trade in illegal drugs" (Zollkriminalamt 2012). Accordingly, it costs about 750 € to import 400 g of the active ingredient of an anabolic steroid from China, an additional 85 € are needed to buy ampoules, and the 400 ampoules can earn about 10,000 €—a sum ten times higher than the original investment. Our data are only partial; however, they suggest lower profit margins for most suppliers of doping products active in Italy.

6.4.1 Producers' Revenues and Profits

As only a single illegal lab has been seized in Italy, we have no direct data to back the above-mentioned estimates of the average profit margin of the producers of doping substances. What we know is that the employee running that lab, D.B., did not earn much. According to the NAS officer who conducted that investigation (Int-NAS-9), D.B. received a 2,000 € monthly base salary from his foreign boss in addition to another 2,000–3,000 € representing a percentage of his sales. Most likely, D.B.'s boss, the South African producer running the network of illegal labs in different European countries, had much higher earnings, as probably did the Slovenian couple who ran for several years a big Internet distribution network and were finally arrested in December 2011 in Austria (Int-NAS-15). In neither case, however, do we have data to back these plausible assumptions. On the basis of the analysis carried out in Chaps. 3 and 4, it seems plausible to assume that there are not many suppliers involved in large-scale production in Italy and therefore not many people making a lot of money with this activity.

The other case close to production for which we have data about the suppliers' earnings concerns the improper sale of Genotropin (or GH) on the part of a Sandoz Italy commercial director and two sales representatives. The personal gains of the three main suspects were modest. The sales representative who was principally connecting Sandoz Italy to the physician generously prescribing GH to doping athletes and bodybuilders was wiretapped rejoicing at the prospect of a 5,000 € bonus (Tribunale di Rimini 2011). In addition to the immediate financial gain, the two pharmaceutical representatives probably hoped to be compensated for their "special" efforts with a faster promotion. Still, they risked their professional careers and clean criminal records for a very small sum of money, probably not realizing fully the illegal nature of their actions.

As the Sandoz Italy case well illustrates, the main gain of a doping transaction may not accrue to individuals but to the businesses and institutions the individuals represent. We have no exact data on how much money Sandoz Italy earned out of the improper sale of Genotropin. However, the revenues generated by the unlawful prescriptions of the Rimini doctor were very small in comparison with the company's overall revenues, even if we focus only on Sandoz Italy's revenues. (The assessment might have been different if the practices of the Sandoz commercial director and two sales representatives had been replicated in other parts of Italy, but there is no evidence that this was the case.)

The revenues are also likely to be corporate, if the substances are produced by a legitimate producer and then diverted to some more or less dubious channels to ultimately reach athletes or other users of doping products. Once again, we have no data to back up this supposition, not least because this diversion often takes place before the substances enter Italian territory and hence the sphere of competence of the Italian anti-doping investigators.

6.4.2 *Traders' Revenues and Profits*

What we know is that large-scale traffickers and specifically the importers (were able to) generate considerable, but not sensational, revenues. The large-scale 2000 investigation of the Bologna Branch Office detailed many of the purchases and sales of doping products made by P.B. during the period from January 1999 to March 2000. In that period, P.B. was reported to have bought doping substances for almost 286 million lire and to have raised revenues of almost 432 million lire (corresponding to 148,000 € and 223,000 €, respectively; see Table 6.9). The data for the months September 1999 through January 2000 were considered most realistic, as the NAS officers had by then achieved a better grasp of P.B.'s numerous commercial partners and were constantly monitoring him. In their expert report for the Bologna Prosecutor's Office, Donati and Magrì used these 5-month figures to estimate P.B.'s average monthly expenditures and revenues. By multiplying these figures by 11 months,[20] they concluded that P.B. had yearly expenditures of about 516 million lire (267,000 €) and revenues of 783 million lire (404,000 €). As shown in Table 6.9, the difference between revenues and expenditures amounted to 267 million lire (approximately 138,000 € or 34 % of the revenues). Donati and Magrì did not, however, regard this percentage as P.B.'s profit, despite the fact that this value would have already been much lower than the profit margins typical of illegal drug markets (e.g., Reuter 2013). Rather, on the basis of an analysis of the monthly transactions and other evidence, they concluded that a larger share of the expenditures had gone undocumented than that of the revenues and P.B.'s profit margin was around

---

[20] This choice is due to the fact that most commercial activities, including the sale of doping products, slow down considerably in Italy during the months of August.

Table 6.9 Doping substance expenditures and revenues made by P.B. during the period January 1999–March 2000 and ascertained by the Bologna NAS Branch Office—in lire

Month	Expenditures	Revenues	Difference
January 1999	8,169,000		−8,169,000
February 1999		665,000	665,000
March 1999	3,052,000	205,000	−2,847,000
April 1999	2,426,000	205,000	−2,221,000
May 1999	0	205,000	205,000
June 1999	10,775,000	11,979,000	1,204,000
July 1999	7,430,000	7,909,100	479,100
August 1999	1,350,000	7,349,000	5,999,000
September 1999	64,295,000	75,571,200	11,276,200
October 1999	43,752,000	71,495,500	27,743,500
November 1999	29,045,000	62,894,000	33,849,000
December 1999	38,683,000	49,007,000	10,324,000
January 2000	58,836,000	96,837,000	38,001,000
February 2000	17,975,000	34,382,000	16,407,000
March 2000	0	13,213,000	13,213,000
Total	285,788,000	431,916,800	146,128,800
Average Sept. 1999–Jan 2000*	46,922,200	71,160,940	24,238,740
Yearly expenditures/revenues	516,144,200	782,770,340	266,626,140

Source: Our calculations based on Donati and Magrì 2001

*The monthly averages were multiplied by 11 months, because most regular commercial activities, including the sale of doping products, slow down considerably in Italy during the month of August

20–25 %. Taking the transactions that were not documented into account, Donati and Magrì assessed P.B.'s real yearly revenues at about one billion lire (approximately 515,000 €).

On the basis of sketchier data, Donati and Magrì also estimated that another two large-scale suppliers, L.S. and V.G.F., might have raised in those same years at least twice as much revenue, that is, two billion lire (approximately one million euro) each. In the 2011 investigation of the Ancona Branch Office, V.G.F. was thought to generate at least 90,000–100,000 € monthly, which he then invested in cars, villas, and commercial properties (Int-NAS-10). Considering that V.G.F. has for decades been considered one of the largest illegal suppliers of doping substances, these are respectable sums but, as they refer to gross revenues, are not exorbitant, reflecting the low prices of the substances traded.

According to UN data UNODCCP 2001: 213), a kilogram of cocaine cost US$47,250 or about 70 million Italian lire (35,817 €) at the wholesale level in 2000. This means that it would have been sufficient to sell less than 30 kg of cocaine in order to generate revenues of two billion lire (roughly one million euro) in that year—and at the turn of the century several criminal organizations, some of them belonging to Southern Italian mafia groups, were able to import tons of cocaine even in single shipments. In the early 1990s, for example, a coalition of seven 'Ndrangheta groups succeeded in importing at least 11 t of cocaine in eight different shipments. The last shipment—5,490 k—was seized in March

1994 on the outskirts of Turin (Tribunale di Torino, 1994) and counted for several years as the world's largest cocaine seizure ever made outside of production areas.[21] At the above-mentioned wholesale price, this lot alone would have been worth 197 million euro, generating more than a billion retail revenues once the drug is cut for the final users.

At today's cocaine prices, which are slightly higher, the same sum of one million euro—the sum approximately earned by V.G.F. until his arrest in 2012—could be generated by the sale of 23 kg. In fact, according to the UNODC,[22] a kilogram of cocaine at the wholesale market level cost in Italy in 2009 US$57,153 or 43,280 €. For heroin, which is cheaper than cocaine (in 2009 a kilogram cost US$35,649 or 26,993 €), the same revenue of one million euro corresponds to the sale of 37 kg.

The very fact that V.G.F.'s revenues had remained nominally stable between 2000 and 2011—and hence had declined in real terms—could be a consequence of several investigations targeting him, which might have forced him to scale down his illegal business. The decline in revenues, however, can also suggest that whatever market power V.G.F., L.S., and P.B. might have had at the end of the 1990s has dissipated by now. In fact, as argued in Chap. 4, the opening up of Internet sales offers such a multiplicity of supply channels to customers that it is no longer possible for any single seller to set the prices and therefore earn large profits, except for products of restricted use and consumed only by elite athletes.

Further down the distribution chain, we have only sketchy data on the revenues raised by some middle-level suppliers. For example, the Guardia di Finanza agent and his jobless cousin who were based in Trieste and were focused on by the investigation "Triamin" of the Udine Branch Office sent 48,000 € to their partner, the Naples Polizia agent, via post transfers in 6 months. This sum was also meant to cover the costs incurred by the Naples agent to buy the products, which are not known. Exceeding the agent's yearly gross income, it nonetheless indicates that the trade in doping products can produce interesting side income for those involved in it (NAS Udine 2009b). The revenues raised by another mid-sized trafficker in Bologna were comparable. In the period between January 2002 and June 2003, D.P. received 145,000 € for the anabolic steroids he sold by post to customers outside the Bologna area in addition to what he earned by the distribution of drugs locally via face-to-face contacts (Tribunale di Ravenna 2004: 126).

The same considerations made earlier can be applied here. These middle-level suppliers belonging to the category of gym were able to earn considerable sums of money, which they could have never acquired with their legitimate professions. However, the revenues remain much lower than those of an illegal drug trafficker working at a comparable level. Whereas we do not have data for Italy, Kilmer and Reuter (2009) estimate that a single, 100 % pure, kilogram of heroin is sold at the

[21] Large-scale importers of illegal drugs were not only members of mafia groups. In the late 1990s, a former bank manager, P.C., was responsible for several 400–700 kg cocaine shipments and later sold the cocaine to a plurality of wholesale traffickers, including members of Southern Italian mafia groups, who resided in several parts of the country (Tribunale di Milano 1998).

[22] The prices of illegal drugs are published online as an appendix of the annual World Drug Report. See http://www.unodc.org/unodc/en/data-and-analysis/WDR-2011.html.

middle-wholesale level for US$66,000 in the UK and earns US$239,000 once it is cut and sold to the final users.

Notwithstanding the lack of precise figures, the NAS interviewees (e.g., Int-NAS-10, -15, -16, -26) agree that retailers and other low-level figures—such as body-building instructors, pharmacists, or nurses diverting drugs from hospital pharmacies—gain an—usually modest—extra income in addition to their legal salary with the sale of doping products. Body-builders, in particular, often use the money earned with this trade to finance their own consumption habits.

There are also a few people in Italy, however, who are able to make a lot of money with doping products. These are, above all, the physicians "treating" super elite athletes and a large clientele of anonymous clients with doping methods and other performance-enhancing products. Michele Ferrari earned until 2011 at least several million euro yearly (Int-Pro-3; Int-NAS-10): Armstrong alone transferred more than a million dollars in payments to the bank account of a Swiss company controlled by Michele Ferrari (US Anti-Doping Agency 2012c: 2). According to Tau, "some sports directors have [also] become rich with doping. Out of an average of 20 riders per team, at least 10 'dope' and each of them spends at least 10,000 €. You can work out the totals quickly" (Fazzo and Mensurati 2002b). The suppliers of elite athletes not only deal mostly with the most expensive products such as transfusions, GH, and EPO but can also obtain a premium for the alleged high quality of their products. According to a 2009 investigation by the Guardia di Finanza, the former technical commissioner of the Serbian national team bought a disposable ampoule of CERA (an EPO derivative) in Serbia for 150 € and sold it in Italy for 700 € (Capodacqua 2009).

As a result of the focus on the domestic market—in Chaps. 2, 3, and 4 we have detailed no exports except for the transit of steroid packages bound for the US soldiers in Iraq—the scale of the Italian suppliers' activities seems to be smaller than that of their illegal businesses targeted by some recent foreign investigations. A few examples will illustrate this point. The Philadelphia-based Internet organization disrupted by the US DEA in 2005 with the Operation "Cyber Chase" was allegedly able to distribute approximately 2.5 million dosage units of doping products per month (US Drug Enforcement Administration 2005). Three Mexican companies targeted by the 2006 Operation "Gear Grinder" had allegedly produced more than 70 % of the $56 million worth of illegal anabolic steroids seized annually in the United States (Dohrmann and Llosa 2006). More recently, even the German and Austrian police and customs were able to confiscate a stock of five million units of steroids, stimulants, and hormones in a single seizure (Bundeskriminalamt 2011; Smolka 2012, personal communication). In contrast, Italian law enforcement agencies seize on average eight million doses per year and the main Italian suppliers are thought to earn no more than a few million euro per year.[23]

---

[23] In making the comparison, though, it is important to recall that we do not know how the US DEA calculated the 2.5 million dosage units mentioned in the text and what the packages seized by the German and Austrian police forces effectively contained.

6.4.3 Legal or Illegal Revenues?

Reflecting the semi-illegal nature of the market for doping products, not all the revenues raised are illegal. The suppliers belonging to the category of gym and the body-builders buy the doping products on the illegal market—and therefore their revenues are also fully "black"—by which we mean that they are not declared to the tax authority—just like in a completely illegal market. Hospital employees usually steal doping products or recipes from hospital storehouses or pharmacies, and their profits are therefore always black.

The revenues raised by other illegal doping suppliers—in particular the three other types belonging to the category of health care and their respective wholesalers—are not always black, even when they arise from a criminal offense. This represents a further distinctive element of the market for doping products vis-à-vis completely illegal markets such as drugs. The Sandoz Italy commercial director and two sales representatives, for example, did not produce any black market revenue with the sale of GH. As seen earlier, their personal financial gain consisted in the premiums they received from their own company, whereas their company raised its legal sales of GH—albeit with illegal means.

Likewise, most colluding physicians and pharmacists usually earn regular money, which they do not hide—at least not completely—from the tax authorities (tax evasion is a frequent "sport" among Italy's independent freelancers (a category, that includes physicians, lawyers, and notaries and other high-level practitioners with their own firm or consulting room) but that's really another story; see Petrini 2012). Therefore, as in the case of the pharmaceutical company employees, the earnings physicians draw from their illegal doping activities remain rather close to the legal market prices. For example, the physician B.H.E. received a mere 4,000 € honorarium from Sandoz for his "marketing" of GH, and although the sentence is less clear on this issue, he issued regular invoices to his patients (Tribunale di Rimini 2011). Only physicians who have been banned from working with certain subsets of athletes, such as Michele Ferrari and Carlo Santuccione, need to find subterfuges to hide their profits, if they continue to provide doping advice and services. Ferrari, for example, collected his fees through a Swiss public limited company (U.S. Anti-Doping Agency 2012c: 7).

Chapter 7
Anti-doping Law Enforcement: Legislation, Actors, Outcomes, and the Challenges Ahead

Abstract The previous chapters have documented the numerous and high-level criminal investigations carried out in Italy on the production and trafficking of doping products. As mentioned in the introduction, these investigations have been made possible by three elements. The first consists of the Anti-Doping Act 376 of 2000 and specifically the wide-ranging offense of doping that the act established. The latter two elements are of institutional, rather than legal, nature: the existence of NAS, a law enforcement agency specialized in public health issues, and the autonomy of public prosecutors. In the seventh chapter of the book, we review the criminal law provisions of Italy's anti-doping legislation and describe the key institutions active in Italy in the fight against doping. In doing so, we also note the overall poor performance of the Italian judicial system, which partially results from the very autonomy of prosecutors and courts but is also the consequence of a plurality of other factors. We then present some statistical data about the outcomes of Italy's anti-doping criminal law actions (e.g., reports, arrests, convictions) and finally identify five main sets of challenges such actions face in addition to the fundamental one represented by the inefficiency of the overall judicial system. While four challenges are domestic, the fifth one results from the ineffective international police and justice cooperation.

The previous chapters have documented the numerous and high-level criminal investigations carried out in Italy on the production and trafficking of doping products. As mentioned in the introduction, these investigations have been made possible by three elements. The first consists of the Anti-Doping Act 376 of 2000 and specifically the wide-ranging offense of doping that the act established. The latter two elements are of institutional, rather than legal, nature: the existence of NAS, a law enforcement agency specialized in public health issues, and the autonomy of public prosecutors. In this chapter, we review the criminal law provisions of Italy's anti-doping legislation and describe the key institutions active in Italy in the fight against doping. In doing so, we also note the overall poor performance of the Italian judicial system, which partially results from the very autonomy of prosecutors and courts but is also the consequence of a plurality of other factors. We then present

L. Paoli and A. Donati, *The Sports Doping Market: Understanding Supply and Demand, and the Challenges of Their Control*, DOI 10.1007/978-1-4614-8241-3_7,

some statistical data about the outcomes of Italy's anti-doping criminal law actions (e.g., reports, arrests, convictions) and finally identify five main sets of challenges such actions face in addition to the fundamental one represented by the inefficiency of the overall judicial system. While four challenges are domestic, the fifth one results from the ineffective international police and justice cooperation.

7.1 The Criminal Law Provisions of Italian Anti-doping Legislation

Italy has a strong tradition of legislation in the anti-doping field: in fact, it has enacted no fewer than six anti-doping acts since 1950.[1] It is beyond the scope of the present study to analyze in detail the evolution of the entire spectrum of anti-doping legislation. We focus here exclusively on the criminal law provisions of the early anti-doping bills, Act 375/2000, and other relevant offenses foreseen by the Italian Criminal Code (CP).

7.1.1 The Early Provisions

The first bill that dealt with the topic of doping was Act 426 of 1942 that established CONI. This made CONI responsible for "the organization and enhancement of national sport and its orientation toward the athletes' improvement with particular consideration for the physical and moral improvement." The original version of Act 426/1942 also explicitly stated that performance-enhancing drugs or substances were not compatible with the core principles of sports fairness, correctness, and integrity, but it did not foresee any specific sanction (Dipani 2004: par. 2.1).

Doping was defined for the first time as a punishable offense by Act 1099 on "Health safeguards in sports activities" of October 26, 1971. In that bill, doping was established as a misdemeanor, not a felony. The athletes taking part in competitions and making use of performance-enhancing substances that may be harmful to their health (to be defined subsequently in a Ministry of Health Decree) were punished with a fine between 50,000 and 500,000 lire (article 3, section 1). A higher fine between 100,000 lire and one million lire[2] was foreseen for those who administered such substances to the athletes (article 3, section 2); the fine was to be tripled if the

---

[1] To this extensive domestic legislation should be added Italy's ratification of the Council of Europe and UNESCO Anti-Doping Conventions in 1996 and 2007, respectively, with Acts 522/1995 and 230/2007.

[2] At the official conversion rate established in 1999, these figures would correspond to 52 and 51,646 €. However, given the devaluation, this conversion underestimates the significance of the fines in the early 1970s.

substances were administered by sports officials or trainers or to minors (article 3, section 3).

Act 1099/1971 has been subjected to several criticisms from legal scholars. These condemned the bill's exclusive focus on sports competition, its failure to prohibit the consumption and administration of doping products during the training phase, and the fact that the bill foresaw no sanction for other possible suppliers, such as physicians and pharmacists (Dipani 2004, par. 2.1; Arioli and Bellini 2005: 4ff.; Centamore 2011: 11).

De facto, the law never went into effect. A month after its entry into force in March 1972, many public health responsibilities of the national Health Ministry, including those foreseen by Act 1099/1971, were decentralized to regional bodies, and these did not have the means to enforce the bill. Moreover, the Ministry of Health published only in 1975 the list of prohibited substances foreseen by the act and never updated it afterwards (Dipani 2004: par. 2.1).

In 1981 Act 689/1981 depenalized the offenses of doping foreseen by Act 1099/1971 and most other misdemeanors, for which only a fine was foreseen. In terms of sanctions, matters did not change significantly: the criminal fine foreseen by Act 1099/1971 was replaced with an administrative sanction, which was also a fine (Dipani 2004: par.2.1).[3] However, criminal procedural instruments were no longer available for the investigations.

Article 1 of Act 401/1989 ("Measures in the games and illegal betting sector to safeguard fair procedures in competitive sports") introduced the crime of "sporting fraud" into Italian criminal law. This offense is committed by "whoever offers or promises money or other advantages to the participant in a sports competition organized by CONI, UNIRE, or other sports bodies recognized by the Italian State and by the associations belonging to them, in order to achieve a result different from that resulting from a correct and fair competition, or commits other fraudulent acts aimed to the same purpose" (article 1, section 1). In such cases the defendant is to be punished with a prison sentence between a month and a year, and a fine ranging between 258 and 1,032 € (article 1, section 1). The second section of the same article goes on, stating, "the same sanction is to be imposed also on a competition participant who accepts money or other utility or advantage offered to him or receives a promise of any of these."

The bill was prompted by the first match-rigging scandals in football and the difficulties of applying the general offense of fraud foreseen by article 640 CP to them (Tribunale di Bologna 2004: 10–11). Over time, this bill was also used to sanction crimes related to doping, albeit in a partially controversial manner. Several Prosecutor's Offices charged suppliers of doping products with the offense of sporting fraud, and the first-degree courts subsequently convicted them, with their verdicts being upheld by higher courts up to the Corte di Cassazione. The first-degree sentence of Dr. Ferrari for the offense of sporting fraud was confirmed by the

[3] As early as 1985, the Ministry of Health classified all transfusions that are not carried out for the serious therapeutic reasons as blood doping, thus outlawing them.

Bologna Court of Appeals (Corte d'Appello di Bologna, 2006), which however had to apply the statute of limitations. Likewise, in 2007, the Corte di Cassazione (2007) found Giraudo and Agricola, the manager and chief sports physician of the Juventus football team, guilty of the offense of sporting fraud, although it too had to apply the statute of limitations.

With the verdict of January 25, 1996, however, the Corte di Cassazione established that the offense of sporting fraud could not be imposed on athletes who had merely taken doping products, despite the contrary verdicts of lower courts (Dipani 2004: par. 5.2; Centamore 2011: 14–16). One of our respondents, a senior officer working at NAS Headquarters, recalls the difficulties of carrying out the first anti-doping criminal investigations in the 1990s (Int-NAS-26). NAS officers initially referred to Act 1099/1971 but then could not use it to press criminal charges, because the offense foreseen by this act had been depenalized. Therefore, NAS had no choice but to use the offense of sporting fraud, hypothesizing that the doping athletes necessarily also wanted to manipulate the competition outcomes. Even before the final verdict of the Corte di Cassazione, many such proceedings did not end with a conviction, because it was very difficult to prove a causal link between the intake of doping substances and the manipulated performance.

If the doping agent is included among the psychoactive substances indicated in the tables prepared by the Ministry of Health, it is possible to apply Act 162 of June 26, 1990, and the Presidential Decree (DPR) 309 of October 9, 1990 ("Consolidated text of laws governing the control of narcotics and psychotropic substances, prevention, cure, and rehabilitation of the related states of drug dependency"), which foresee sanctions at the administrative and criminal level. Specifically, this bill can be applied to all doping cases involving the three illegal drugs—cannabis, cocaine, and heroin—that are also on the WADA Prohibited List. Since 2010, it can also be applied to nandrolone. In fact, the Ministry of Health added in that year this steroid to the list of psychoactive substances to be controlled under the DPR 309/1990 and later amendments, therefore sharply reducing the possibility of its legitimate consumption (Ministero della Salute 2010b).

Legislative Decree 539/1992 as well, implementing EEC Directive 92/26, concerning the classification for the provision of drugs for human use, set out criminal and administrative sanctions for those who provide prohibited drugs to athletes (Italy 2002: 15). However, these sanctions and the entire legislative decree, except for a single article, have been abolished by article 158 of the more recent Legislative Decree 219 of April 24, 2006.

Other provisions, which sometimes have been resorted to in NAS investigations but are not discussed in the literature, are included in the Presidential Decree (DPR) 43/1973 ("Consolidated text of the legal provisions concerning customs") and the Legislative Decree 178/1991 ("Implementation of European Commission's Directives concerning medicinal products for human use"). The alter decree has been repealed and substituted by Legislative Decree 219/2006, which implemented more recent European Commission directives on similar topics (see below).

7.1.2 Act 376 of December 2000

The problem of doping was fully addressed anew in December 2000 with an ad hoc bill—Act 376, "Discipline for the health protection of sports activities and the fight against doping."[4] This still constitutes the backbone of Italy's current anti-doping legislation and is considered "some of the most severe anti-doping legislation worldwide" (Centamore 2011: 18). It constituted a reaction to the scandals involving the Rome Anti-Doping Laboratory and Prof. Conconi's biochemical institute at the Ferrara University as well as the deficiencies and collusion shown by CONI in both cases.[5] Therefore, Act 376/2000 primarily addresses elite athletes. With the first investigations on doping in gyms and fitness centers just starting, the Italian lawmakers were not yet aware of the increasing spread of the consumption of doping products among body-builders and recreational athletes.

For the present purpose, the most relevant part of this bill is article 9, which reintroduces criminal provisions on doping into the Italian legal system. Given the bill's relevance, we start however with a general overview of all the nine substantive articles (the tenth merely concerns the bill's financing). Article 1 begins with a statement of principle: "sports activity is directed to the promotion of individual and collective health and must be inspired by the respect of ethical principles and educational values mentioned" in the 1989 Anti-Doping Convention of the Council of Europe. "Sports activity ... cannot be practiced with the aid of techniques, methodology, or substances of any nature that may endanger the psycho-physical integrity of the athletes."

The second section of this article defines doping:

> Doping consists of the administration or intake of drugs and biologically or pharmacologically active substances and the adoption or undergoing of medical practices not justified by pathological conditions and capable of modifying the psycho-physical or biological conditions of the body in order to alter the athletes' competitive performance.

The third section of this article states that the same practices, if meant to modify the results of anti-doping tests, also constitute doping. The fourth section authorizes the intake of prohibited substances or medical practices if they are justified by the athlete's pathological conditions. It is worthwhile stressing that the definition of sports competitions used in this article is broader than that of Act 401/1989, which prohibits sporting fraud only in the competitions organized by CONI, UNIRE, or other sports bodies recognized by the Italian State and by the associations belonging to them (Centamore 2011: 24–25).

---

[4] The text of the bill can be read online in Italian at http://www.camera.it/parlam/leggi/00376l.htm and in English at http://www.coni.it/fileadmin/_temp_/coni/pdf/legge376_2000_in_inglese.pdf.

[5] In Finland too, the scandal at the 2001 Lahti Nordic World Championships led the Doping Enquiry Taskforce set by the Ministry of Education to support a bill including doping offenses in the Criminal Code. "According to these amendments," the Taskforce wrote, "the administration of doping substances determined in the Criminal Code would be subject to public prosecution. This would primarily criminalise doping by coaches and physicians" (Doping Enquiry Taskforce 2001: 4).

Article 2 foresees that the drugs, pharmacologically or biologically active substances, and the methods are to be divided in classes established with a Decree by the Ministry of Health in agreement with the Ministry of Cultural Goods and Activities (which is responsible for sports in Italy) upon CVD's proposal. A crucial clause is that the classes of doping drugs, substances, and methods have to be established "also in respect of the provisions of the Strasbourg [i.e., Council of Europe] Convention .... and the indications of the IOC and other international sports ruling bodies." In fact, the first decrees establishing the list of doping substances and methods were not issued until October and December 2003 (Centamore 2011: 40), and in the meantime, contrary to the opinion of some scholars and some courts, Act 376/2000 could only be applied because of the reference to the lists of the Council of Europe Convention, the IOC, and WADA, as finally established by the Corte di Cassazione with a verdict of November 29, 2005 (ibid: 40–46).

Article 3 establishes CVD's functions and composition, which we will consider in the following section. Article 4 entrusts the tasks of carrying out anti-doping controls and a research program about doping substances and methods to one or more laboratories accredited by the IOC and other international sports bodies. Article 5 foresees the involvement of the regions in the prevention of doping and protection of public health in sports activities.

Article 6 has a crucial relevance because it obliges all sports bodies "to adapt their rules" to the bill's provisions, foreseeing sanctions, and disciplinary procedures for the athletes who are involved in doping practices or refuse to undergo controls.

Article 7 establishes an obligation for the producers, importers, and distributors of prohibited substances to send annually the data relative to the "quantities produced, imported and distributed and sold to the pharmacies, hospitals, and other authorized structures" for any single drug. Although this article would be essential to assess the absolute size of the legal segment of the market for each doping product and thus begin estimating the relative size of the illegal segment vis-à-vis the legal segment, it has not been enforced yet (Int-Oth-2; see also Evaluation Team 2002: 36).

Article 8 requires the Ministry of Health to submit an annual report to the Parliament about the implementation of the act.

Finally, article 9, the last substantive one, reintroduces criminal provisions on doping. The article begins with a classical subsidiarity clause: "if the behavior does not constitute a more serious offense." The seriousness of the offense can be measured on the basis of the sanctions foreseen for the offense of doping, imprisonment from 3 months to 3 years and a fine from 2,580 to 51,645 € (Dipani 2004: cap. 2, s 2.2).

The article further establishes two distinct types of offenses: doping and the trade in doping products, foreseeing two variants for the former. Its first section attributes the offense of doping to

> whosoever procures for others, administers, assumes or at any rate encourages the use of drugs or pharmacologically or biologically active substances included in the classes foreseen by article 2, section 1, which are not justified by pathological conditions and are designed to modify the psychophysical or biological conditions of the human organism in order to improve athletes' competitive performance or are directed to modify the controls on the use of such drugs or substances.

The second section foresees the same sanctions for "whosoever adopts or undergoes medical practices," such as blood doping, for the same aims stated in the first section. Both sections foresee some forms of conduct that are typical of athletes and others that are carried out by external persons—i.e., the suppliers, more specifically athletes' support personnel. The latter set of activities is very broad, as it ranges from the procurement to the prescription or the administration as well as aiding and abetting, but it is also uncontroversial. More controversially, the act also foresees the punishment of the athlete, but only if there is a specific criminal intent: i.e., if the athletes used doping products in order to modify the athlete's competitive performance or the results of the anti-doping controls. If instead the athlete is unaware of the administration of doping substances or products, he or she remains a victim.

Several scholars have criticized the criminalization of self-doping, arguing that this prohibition is not justified by the public good that the bill aims above all to protect, i.e., public health (Ferrara 2004: 122)—especially now that the consumption and possession of illegal drugs for personal use in Italy have been decriminalized (Traversi 2001: 105). Other scholars, as well as prosecutors and law enforcement agencies, justify the criminalization of self-doping with the reference to the respect of ethical principles and educational values contained in article 1 and hence the lawmakers' will to protect also the public good of the fairness and integrity of sports (Arioli and Bellini 2005: 73–74; Guariniello 2011, Int-NAS-26). In defense of the criminalization of athletes' doping, supporters of the current provisions stress, as Turin Prosecutor Guariniello does, "the offenses punishable under the 2000 law are fraudulent"—that is, as already mentioned, there has to be a specific criminal intent.[6] Guariniello further adds that the Italian criminal legislation offers more guarantees to the suspected athletes than the anti-doping sports rules.

According to Marzella (2004 quoted in Centamore 2011) and Centamore (2011), the criminalization of self-doping should have been better justified with the protection of the fairness and correctness of sports, referring not only to the ethical principles of sports but also to economic function of elite sports. Specifically, Centamore (2011: 30) argues,

> Self-doping is a fraudulent activity, that, next to the violation of the ethical values of sports also possesses an important financial competent. From this perspective, the protection of the 'clean' sports could justify the fight against doping with criminal law means, even though, given the financial aspect, its justification would lie more in the protection of patrimony and competition than in the protection of health.

International policy-makers were long skeptical of the criminalization of athletes' self-doping (see Evaluation Team 2002: 40; Vinton 2005). More recently, however, both prominent policy-makers, such as Pound (Großekathöfer and Gilbert 2008), and a number of scholars (e.g., Rössner 2009, 2011) have expressed no principal objections to the criminalization of elite athletes' self-doping.

---

[6] For the analysis of anti-doping legislation and policy, Prosecutor Guariniello has allowed us to openly identify him with his statements made as interviewee.

Regardless of scholars' and policy-makers' doubts, Italian public opinion generally welcomed the criminalization of doping in 2000 (e.g., Audisio 2000) as a sign of a renewed political will to control this problem, after the many scandals that had plagued Italy's sports world at the end of the 1990s. Since 2002 amendments of this controversial element of Italy's anti-doping law have been repeatedly discussed in the media; however so far no concrete steps have been taken (Centamore 2011: 54–55; int-Oth-1 and -2). Whatever the judgment on this issue, it is clear that the Italian lawmakers made two omissions in drafting the act's text: they forgot to criminalize the possession and purchase of doping substances as such (Arioli and Bellini 2005: 75) as well as the athlete's refusal to undergo a control (Evaluation Team 2002: 40). According to the already mentioned senior NAS officer (Int-NAS-26), a further weakness derives from the legal interpretation of the word "athlete" in article 9, section 1. The Italian jurisprudence as well as the Italian people understand this word as referring to the sportspeople who are enrolled in a national sports federation, associated discipline, or Ente di promozione sportiva. Therefore, athletes taking part in competitions without being enrolled in one of these associations cannot be charged with the doping offenses established by article 9, section 1.[7]

The seventh section of article 9 establishes the offense of trade in doping products. This states:

> Whoever trades with drugs or pharmacologically or biologically active ingredients belonging to the classes referred to by article 2, section 1, through channels different from the public or hospital pharmacies, public dispensaries, and other structures that directly detain drugs meant to be used on patients, is punished with imprisonment from 2 to 6 years and with a fine from €5,164 to €77,468.

This rule is intended to tackle illegal suppliers of doping products that operate outside the official distribution channels and because of the profit-making purposes that necessarily accompany a trading activity, it punishes the described types of conduct more severely than those listed in the first section of the same article. It is interesting to recall that this second offense was only introduced into the bill during the parliamentary debate at the suggestion of a few prosecutors, above all Pierguido Soprani from the Ferrara Prosecutor's Office and Giovanni Spinosa from Bologna, who were then coordinating the first seminal investigations on doping. With its verdict of February 20, 2003, the Corte di Cassazione established that a commercial activity such as that referred to in article 9, section 7, requires "continuity … and at least some elementary organization" (quoted in Arioli and Bellini 2005: 69). Unlike the basic doping offense, this second offense does not require a specific criminal intent. In order to be punished, the types of conduct foreseen by the seventh section do not need to be aimed at modifying an athlete's competitive performance.

[7] Although the Italian legislation was often criticized for being too extreme, its Swedish counterpart goes even further. In fact, the Swedish Doping Act prohibits all handling of doping substances, including possession and consumption, and punishes these behaviors with fines or sentences of imprisonment up to a maximum of 4 years (6 months in the case of consumption offenses) (Swedish National Institute of Public Health 2010: 10–11). Hungary also introduced in 1999 criminal sanctions for the use, possession, and trafficking of doping substances but in 2000 the Constitutional Court cancelled this amendment on the grounds that criminal law should be used only as last resort (Federal Ministry of the Interior 2009: 18–19).

Finally the third section of article 9 foresees some aggravating circumstances, with an increase of the punishment up to a third,

(a) If a health harm derives from the offense.
(b) If the offense is committed against a minor.
(c) If the offense is committed by a CONI component or an employee of a national sports federation, or a society, associations, or Ente recognized by CONI.

Additional sanctions are also foreseen for those who practice a health profession and those listed under c of the third section. If sentenced, the former are temporarily suspended from their professions, and the second are permanently banned from the top management of the respective sports bodies.

Given the different sanctions foreseen by article 9, sections 1, 2, and 7, the interception of telephone calls and other communications is allowed only in the case of section 7, i.e., in case of the suspected trade in doping products. According to the already mentioned senior NAS officer (Int-NAS-26), this is a further weakness of Act 376/2000. In fact, to tackle properly the problem of doping in sports, it would occasionally be necessary to wiretap athletes and their entourage, even if the latter do not fully engage in the "trade" of doping products, as established in article 9, section 7. For the same reasons, only suspects of the latter offense can be arrested by the judicial police without an initial authorization of the Judge for Preliminary Investigations. Even in these cases, however, the arrest needs to be confirmed within a maximum period of 48 h by a judge. Searches and seizures are authorized for both types of offenses. In the case of a suspected violation of the article 9, section 1, the law enforcement agencies are also authorized to carry out personal inspections including, if necessary, taking a blood sample from suspects (Centamore 2011: 50–54).

According to the general principles stated in articles 157 and 158 CP, the statute of limitation period is set at 5 years for all the offenses in article 9. The limitation period runs from the moment of the commission of the offense or, in case of a continuous offense, from the moment the offense was interrupted (Centamore 2011: 38).

All the NAS officers and prosecutor officers interviewed are unanimous in stressing the relevance of Act 376/2000 and specifically article 9 in their efforts to control the use, and especially the production and distribution, of doping products through criminal law. As we have seen in Chaps. 3 and 4, some important investigations were carried out even before the enactment of Act 376/2000 but all our respondents insisted that the criminal provisions of article 9 have hugely enhanced their possibility of interventions.

This assessment was confirmed, with four exceptions, by the heads of the 38 NAS branch offices who filled in a questionnaire on their anti-doping activities distributed by the NAS Headquarters. However, the four respondents who did not think that the Act 376/2000 has enhanced anti-doing investigations belong to NAS Branch Offices (Aosta, Bari, Caserta, and Viterbo) that have not been particularly active in this field. All other respondents praise Act 376/2000 for introducing criminal law sanctions for doping offenses, which have simplified the interpretation of suspects' behavior, and for enabling wiretappings in anti-doping investigations. Twenty-nine out of thirty-eight respondents also state that Act 376/2000 has helped raise the awareness and interest for the problem of doping among prosecutors and judges, who now realize that anti-doping investigations have a solid legal basis and the same prospects of a successful judicial outcome as investigations in other fields.

7.1.3 *The Applicable Offenses Foreseen by the Criminal Code*

Several offenses established by the Italian Criminal Code (CP) are also considered in the literature applicable to what we call in this report the trade in doping products. Indeed, as we will see in the following pages, some of these other offenses—along with several others—have also been concretely applied in anti-doping investigations.

The most relevant one is the offense of "administration of drugs in a dangerous way for public health" (article 445 CP)—the offense charged against Prof. Conconi by the Ferrara Prosecutor's Office. Article 445 CP states: "Whoever, trading, also without license, in medical substances, administers them in type, quality and quantity not corresponding to the medical orders or different from those declared or agreed upon, is punished with imprisonment from 6 months to 2 years and with a fine from €103 to €1,032." According to Marchese (2010) and (Centamore (2011: 17), the applicability of this offense to contemporary cases of doping is restricted by the fact that it presupposes a fraudulent administration—whereas doping in most cases involves fully consenting athletes. An experienced NAS officer (e.g., Int-NAS-26) also stresses that this article covers only some, by no means all, forms of supply of doping products: for example, given the article's focus on the administration of doping products, the law enforcement agencies could not charge with this offense a pharmacist who was merely selling, but not administering—as article 445 CP requires—a doping substance.

In other cases, the offense established by article 348 CP, "Illegal exercise of a profession," can also be applicable: "Whoever illegally exercises a profession for which a special state authorization is required, is punished with imprisonment up to 6 months or with a fine between €105 and €516."

Other articles of the Italian Criminal Code have also been deemed to be applicable in the scholarly literature, especially the different forms of injury (article 582 CP and following) and fraud (article 648 CP; Centamore 2011: 6–9). As we will see below, they find only limited application.

7.2 Public and Criminal Law Institutions Involved in Anti-doping

Act 376/2000 makes CVD the body principally responsible for coordinating Italy's anti-doping policy, except for the latter's criminal law provisions. As we have seen in the previous chapters, NAS carries out the bulk of anti-doping criminal investigations in Italy. In their anti-doping responsibilities, CVD and NAS interact with several other public bodies, being supported, but also occasionally constrained, by the latter.

7.2.1 Commission for the Vigilance and Control on Doping and the Protection of Health in Sports Activities (CVD) and the Other Public Law Bodies

Originally established as a body recognized by the Italian State in 1942, CONI has been since then the body principally responsible for the organization and regulation of the sports world in Italy. The Law Decree of No. 242 of July 23, 1999 ("Reorganization of the National Italian Olympic Committee"), redesigned CONI's goals, organization, and even position in the sports world and explicitly recognized its public law nature (for more details, see Nicolella 2008). As Nicolella (2008) maintains, with the reform "CONI consolidates its double position as a public body supervising the whole Italian sporting organization and as an Olympic Committee recognized by the IOC. Two different spheres of tasks and functions thus continue to be united in CONI, deriving from the fact that CONI is part of both the Italian state order and the international sports order." In particular, article 2 of that legislative decree made CONI "responsible, within the sports jurisdiction, for the adoption of measures preventing and suppressing the use of substances that alter the natural physical performance of athletes in sports activities."[8] CONI has been in charge of anti-doping testing of elite athletes since they were introduced by the IOC.

CVD has a much shorter history. In fact, as already mentioned, it was founded by article 3 of Act 376/2000. According to both the Italian Government (Italy 2002: 18) and the Council of Europe Evaluation Team (2002: 31), this decision manifests the Italian Government's direct assumption of responsibility in prevention and control of doping. It also "seems to indicate that the government doubts the ability of the sports movement to solve the doping problem, a distrust unquestionably related to the most recent cases uncovered in Italy and at international level" (ibid: 31).

The second section of article 3 establishes in detail CVD's composition and the expertise and background of its 20 members; it has partially been amended by article 3 of Act 183/2010. Accordingly, the CVD is composed of

- Five members appointed by the Minister of Health, one of whom is the President.
- Five members appointed by the Undersecretary responsible for sports at the Prime Minister's Office, one of whom is the Vice-President.
- Three members of the Conference of the Presidents of Italy's Regions and the autonomous Provinces of Trento and Bolzano.
- A member appointed by CONI.

---

[8] http://www.camera.it/parlam/leggi/deleghe/testi/99242dl.htm.

- A member appointed by the Higher Health Council.
- An officer of the Comando Carabinieri Tutela per la Salute [i.e., NAS] appointed by the Commander (Ministero della Salute 2012).

CVD's powers, as listed in article 3, section 1, of the Act 376/2000, are very broad: CVD

(a) Sets the classes mentioned in article 2, section 1, and revises them, according to the modalities foreseen by article 2, section 3.
(b) Determines, also in conformity with the IOC and other competent bodies and institutions' indications, the cases, criteria, and control methodologies of anti-doping controls and singles out the competitions and sports activities for which health controls are carried out by the laboratories referred to in article 4, section 1, considering the characteristics of the competitions and sports activities themselves.
(c) Carries out anti-doping and health promotion controls, through the laboratories referred to in article 4, also using physicians specialized in sports medicine; develops research programs on drugs, substances, and medical practices that can be used for doping purposes in sports activities.
(d) Singles out the collaboration forms concerning anti-doping controls with the National Health Service.
(e) Keeps operative contacts with the European Union and the international bodies, guaranteeing the participation in programs of anti-doping interventions.
(f) Can promote information campaigns for the protection of health in sports activities and the prevention of doping, in particular in all state and non-state schools of every type and rank, in collaboration with the public administration, the National Italian Olympic Committees, the national sports federations, the affiliated disciplines, and the private and public Enti di promozione sportiva, also using the activities of physicians specialized in sports medicine.

CVD's main activity has so far been the organization of anti-doping tests for recreational athletes, in addition to the update of Italy's prohibited list, which is largely dictated by WADA. Since 2003 CVD has progressively improved its performance and since 2008 has recorded an average 3.8 % positive rate, with an astonishing 4.8 % of positive tests in 2010 (see Table 2.6).[9] CVD's 2010 performance was largely due to the fact that Dr. Bellotti, who was then a CVD member, became responsible for planning and organizing the anti-doping tests. In particular, in contrast with the previous practices, Bellotti stopped planning in advance a calendar of anti-doping tests for the whole sporting season but instead selected the competitions for tests not only on the basis of his extensive knowledge of athletes' habits but also on the basis of the results of the immediately preceding tests and of the indications provided by NAS from its investigations. This collaboration is exemplary of what

[9] CVD's performance is even more astonishing than it first appears. In fact, CVD reports positive tests, whereas WADA's accredited laboratories merely report "adverse analytical findings." From the latter, the positive athletes who have a therapeutic use exemption are ultimately excluded, thus further reducing the 1 % average (see, e.g., WADA 2011a).

can be achieved through information sharing between anti-doping and law enforcement agencies. Moreover, Bellotti instructed the CVD representatives in charge of carrying out the tests not to reveal the final ranks of the athletes selected for testing until the end of the competitions in order to prevent any leakage from the competition organizers to the athletes (Int-Oth-2).

However, showing the lack of commitment of Italian politicians in anti-doping, the fourth Berlusconi cabinet (2008–2011) did not reappoint Bellotti in early 2011 at the end of the CVD's mandate, and the members of the following CVD, who were partially involved in conflicts of interest (see Chap. 5), did not show the same competence in pursuing positive athletes. It is a telling detail, for example, that CVD did not test any weightlifters in 2011, although weightlifting is a discipline with a well-known affinity to doping, and carried out very few tests during April and May, 2 months with a full competition calendar—choices that explain the lower positive rate (3.1 %) recorded in 2011 (Ministero della Salute and Istituto Superiore di Sanità 2012: 2–5; see Chap. 2).

Even in the field of testing, CVD does not yet exercise the full powers assigned to it by the law. As already mentioned in Chap. 2, an agreement signed in October 2007 by the then Minister of Health and the Minister of Youth Policies and Sports of the second Prodi cabinet (2006–2008) and the CONI President formalized an unofficial division of labor that had taken shape since CVD's establishment in 2000. Despite the fact that article 3, section 1, clause c of the Act 376/2000 clearly states that CVD "carries out anti-doping and health promotion controls, through the laboratories referred to in article 4" without reserving any role for CONI, the latter has continued to carry out anti-doping controls of elite athletes, focusing almost exclusively, as described in Chap. 2, on the high-end segment, i.e., the approximately 10,000 "super elite" athletes participating or likely to participate in international competitions. In the cited agreement, the three parties "agreed … to regard the national and international competitive sports activities as the prevalent object of CONI's anti-doping activities." At the same time, the agreement restricted CVD's competencies to recreational athletes. The parties also "agree[d] to consider the non-competitive activities and the competitive activities having no national relevance as the prevalent object of the anti-doping activities of the Commission" (Ministero della Salute 2007).

Despite the vague wording chosen, the agreement implies that CONI would—de facto exclusively—carry out anti-doping tests of super elite athletes, while CVD would test those whom we labeled in Chap. 2 "recreational athletes," that is, athletes taking part in "competitive activities having no national relevance"[10]—a division of labor that was aggressively defended by CONI when CVD tried to expand its sphere of action (Int-Oth-2). It is hard not to see the merits of the opinion of some observers, including Bellotti (2009) and several respondents (Int-NAS, 25 and 26; Int-Pro-1, 2, and 3; and Int-Oth-2), according to which the 2007 agreement overrules Act 376/2000. Against this background, the agreement appears to be a ploy to protect

[10] We presented the number and results of the anti-doping tests carried out by CVD and CONI in Chap. 2.

the elite segment of Italian sports from independent and effective anti-doping tests. As the 2007 agreement was signed by two ministers of the Prodi cabinet, we can also conclude that the latter too, not just right-wing politicians and cabinets, have protected the not-always-legitimate interests of CONI and the organized sports world.

As a result of the informal division of labor since 2000 and the 2007 agreement, CVD has very limited contacts with international anti-doping bodies, although CVD is entrusted with the maintenance of "operative contacts with the European Union and the international bodies" by article 3, section 1, clause e of Italy's anti-doping act. In fact, CONI, not CVD, has been identified by WADA as the Italian National Anti-Doping Organization (NADO). Reflecting Italians' limited awareness of conflicts of interests (see The Economist 2011c), this choice has few parallels among the 34 advanced nations belonging to the Organization for Economic Co-operation and Development (OECD). Only in Iceland, in fact, is the National Olympic Committee (NOC) at the same time the NADO. In all other OECD countries, a separate anti-doping agency has been established, even though in a number of cases the separation is not complete and many, if not most, NADOs seem to be at least partially dependent on NOCs' funding in order to carry out their activities (see T.M.C. Asser Instituut 2010).

The anomalous division of labor between CVD and CONI can also be questioned in light of the considerable differences in the number of positive tests obtained by the two bodies and their respective communication policies. As mentioned in Chap. 2, CONI had obtained a miserable average of 0.63 % in the years 2002–2007 and has published no data since then (see Table 2.5). By contrast, CVD publishes its reports yearly and since 2008 has had a six times higher positive rate than CONI's average rate. A further consequence of this division of labor between CVD and CONI is that anti-doping controls seem to neglect a large share of elite athletes. In fact, if CONI focuses on the 10,000 super elite athletes, and the CVD tests "recreational athletes," the consequence seems to be that most athletes competing in national competitions but not good enough to take part in international competitions are hardly ever targeted by anti-doping tests. More detailed information on CONI's anti-doping tests would be necessary to wipe this worrying hypothesis.

As foreseen by article 4 of the Act No. 376/200, the samples taken during anti-doping controls are materially analyzed by the Anti-Doping Laboratory in Rome, the only one in Italy accredited by the IOC. As noted by the Council of Europe Evaluation Team (2002: 20), "the most significant aspect provided for by article 4 of the Law is that the Anti-doping Laboratories be subjected to supervision by the Istituto Superiore di Sanità [Higher Institute of Health], the scientific body of the government which works alongside the Ministry of Health, and that any form of supervision on the part of the sports Organisation[s] be removed." CONI, however, is still responsible for the funding of the laboratory. This is, in fact, formally owned by the Italian Federation of Sports Medicine (FIMS), which however "does not have the necessary funds to run the laboratory" (ibid.: 37). The FIMS' ownership of the laboratory is thus described as "debatable" by the Council of Europe Evaluation Team, which is also critical of "th[e] separation of funding and supervisory bodies" (ibid.: 37).

According to one of our respondents (Int-Oth-2) and Donati himself, who served as CVD member from 2008 to 2010, each doping test costs approximately 500 €, including the laboratory equipment amortization costs and the personnel costs. We have no recent Italian data to validate these estimates. In 2002, however, CONI provided some figures about its own and the national sports federations' expenses to the Council of Europe Evaluation Team, which then carried out an assessment of Italian anti-doping legislation. CONI reported yearly 5,448,620 € in expenses for the entries "samples," "laboratory in Rome," and "laboratories abroad" for the years 1998 and 2000 for a total of 22,195 tests (Italy 2002: 18 and 23–27; see also Comitato Olimpico Nazionale Italiano 2012). A simple division suggests that a test costs 245 €, excluding personnel costs. The latter, in fact, are an independent category in the summary table of the Italian Government's report, referring to all of the about 50 CONI employees, so it is not possible to estimate which share of these costs should be attributed to anti-doping controls. However, there are no doubts that the latter are time-consuming: according to the same report, anti-doping controls rely on "the availability of almost 900 doctors trained in the correct [anti-doping] procedures" and "thirty per cent of the financial resources ... provided for under the Anti-doping Law are designated for the work of the accredited Laboratories" (Italy 2002: 20). In light of these data and statements, the above-mentioned estimate of 500 € cost per anti-doping test, including the laboratory equipment amortization costs and the personnel costs, seems plausible.[11]

According to the data reported to WADA, in 2010 the Rome Anti-Doping Laboratory conducted 10,128 tests (World Anti-Doping Agency 2011a). These tests presumably include CONI's tests in addition to the 1,115 ordered in that year by CVD (Ministero della Salute 2011b; see Table 2.6). Hypothesizing that each test costs 500 €, this means that over five million euro were invested in anti-doping controls in 2010 alone, which is in line with the sums reported by the Italian Government in 2002 to the Council of Europe Evaluation Team. For 2010, the Italian Anti-Doping Laboratory reported 137 adverse analytical findings, in which it presumably includes the 52 positive results achieved by CVD. This means that on average each of the adverse analytical findings, which, unlike CVD's positive results, still include athletes with therapeutic use exemptions, costs on average almost 37,000 €.

Both CVD and CONI have so far routinely reported the athletes who tested positive in anti-doping controls to the Rome Prosecutor's Office. According to several respondents (Int-NAS-16 and -26 and Int-Oth-2), the latter office dismisses many, if not most, of these proceedings, without even transmitting them to the appropriate Prosecutor's Offices. Therefore, CVD is planning to change this procedure and start

[11] Prof. Wilhelm Schänzer (2012, personal communication), head of the Cologne Anti-Doping Laboratory, provided data about the costs of anti-doping analyses, which confirm the plausibility of our estimate. According to Prof. Schänzer, the Cologne Anti-Doping Laboratory charges 150–180 € for the analysis of urine samples for the 200–300 substances prohibited in and out of competition. Another 150 € is invoiced for each urine EPO test, 100 € for each blood test for GH, and 40 € for the tests related to the biological passport. Schänzer added that there are also sampling, testing, and transport costs, but he could provide no exact data on them, as the German NADO is responsible for them.

filing reports of positive tests directly, with the help of NAS officers, to the Prosecutor's Offices that have territorial jurisdiction for the offense. CVD and CONI also routinely report positive tests to the Anti-Doping Prosecutor's Office of CONI, which is responsible for initiating disciplinary proceedings against the athletes who tested positive.

Visiting Italy in 2002, when the 2000 anti-doping act was beginning to be implemented and the division of labor between CONI and CVD was being shaped, the Council of Europe Evaluation Team (2002: 34) already noted "an obvious risk of overlapping responsibilities [between CONI and CVD] and a probable diminution in the overall deterrent effect for the same number of controls." As noted in Chap. 2, the team also stressed that too few out-of-competition tests were carried out by CONI. The Council of Europe team's other conclusions are worth being quoted at length:

> The federations' involvement in the present model seems too great to guarantee an independent system and maximum deterrence. … The evaluation team believes that unannounced out-of-competition controls should be increased bearing in mind the comments on how to make them effective. The evaluation team also voices its apprehensions concerning domestic co-ordination of the various anti-doping measures owing to the complexity of the system arising from the new legislation and above all the large number of stakeholders. The information contained in Italy's national report is insufficient to answer this concern. It seems that a single independent joint body comprising representatives from both the sports movement and the public authorities might be an effective solution and one which would have the merit of approaching international standards. The evaluation team believes that the setting-up of such a body to carry out controls would avoid unnecessary duplication and produce a more effective and deterrent system for the same financial outlay. In the view of the evaluation team there is no guarantee that the present CONI commission will be independent (Evaluation Team 2002: 34–35).

In other words, the Council of Europe team called, as we also do, for the centralization of anti-doping testing and other policy tasks in CVD, which is the only body that can guarantee the necessary independence vis-à-vis the organized sports world.

7.2.2 *Carabinieri Command for Health Protection (NAS)*

Comando Carabinieri per la Tutela della Salute, better known as NAS (the acronym of the original name, Nuclei Anti-Sofisticazioni e Sanità, i.e., Anti-adulteration and Health Units), is a unit specialized in health issues that makes up a separate section ("comando") of the Arma dei Carabinieri, one of Italy's two military police forces.

NAS was established in 1962 to deal primarily with the problem of food adulteration, which then began to raise social alarm. Initially, they consisted of a senior Carabinieri officer seconded to the Ministry of Health and 40 officers in six cities (Milan, Padua, Bologna, Rome, Naples, and Palermo; see Carabinieri 2012). Since the early 1960s, this specialized police unit has progressively expanded and now employs about 1,100 staff members. About 80–100 officers work at the NAS Headquarters in Rome. This includes the Operations and Analysis Departments in addition to the central administration, training, and logistics offices (Int-NAS-25).

The remaining personnel are active in one of the 38 individual NAS branch offices, which enjoy a high degree of operational independence and are distributed throughout the territory of Italy. The 38 branch offices form three main groups—North, Center, and South—whose coordinators, three senior NAS officers, are located in Milan, Rome, and Naples, respectively (NAS 2012). The large majority of NAS personnel are low-level officers. Out of 1,000 officers, only 30–35 of them are senior officers (Int-NAS-25 and -26; Ministero della Difesa 2009).

Formally renamed Carabinieri Command for Health Protection in 2005, NAS often cooperates closely with the provincial Carabinieri Commands and receives support from the latter whenever needed, for example, when they need extra manpower to carry out simultaneous searches. However, the NAS still work under the direct authority of the Ministry of Health. Their personnel comes from the Carabinieri ranks—and as such has the qualification of "officer of the judiciary police" with the resulting power to conduct a criminal investigation—but additionally takes part in specialization courses at the Ministry of Health. Thanks to such training, NAS officers also obtain the qualification and authority of "health inspector": this means that they can access—at all times—all the places where the food for human use is produced, administered, stored, or sold (see Ministero della Difesa 2009).

Throughout the years, NAS has expanded its authority and currently has four main areas of work: health (including all types of legal drugs), food, workplace safety, and doping (see Ministero dell'Interno 2006). Doping and health matters have increasingly become important priorities in the last few years. The rising problem of counterfeited drugs represents the interface between the latter two areas.

In the double capacity as officers of the judiciary police and health inspectors, NAS officers carry out both criminal investigations as well as administrative controls on the above-mentioned four topics in a variety of institutions, ranging from all the companies engaged in the food production and distribution sectors to hospitals and other health care centers, and from physicians' practices and pharmacies to nursing homes and drug manufacturers and distributors. Many of these administrative controls are increasingly dictated by EU directives and soft law.[12] NAS officers are occasionally confronted with the contradictions of this double role as officers of the judiciary police and health inspectors. As officers of the judiciary police, they are subordinated to the prosecutor who formally coordinates—de facto most often delegates them—a specific criminal investigation. As health inspectors, they have the primary aim of protecting citizens' health and, to fulfill such an aim, they may need, for example, to publish a warning about the danger of a specific product. Through the Ministry of Health, NAS are, in fact, part of the EU-wide Rapid Alert System for Food and Feed, which was established in 2002 by the Council of the European Union to allow food and feed control authorities to exchange information about serious health risks and control measures in a quick and effective way

[12] Soft law is the term applied to EU measures, such as guidelines, declarations, and opinions, which, in contrast to directives, regulations, and decisions, are not binding on those to whom they are addressed.

(NAS 2012).[13] In a few cases, such warnings have displeased the prosecutors coordinating the related criminal investigations. The latter tend to regret the breach of investigative secrecy not fully realizing that NAS has no choice, as EU law is higher ranked than criminal law.

NAS' first investigations on doping began almost casually in the late 1980s, when evidence of doping practices emerged in the course of investigations dealing with the theft of drugs from hospitals or other health centers or medical frauds, for example, on the basis of false prescriptions. They then slowly gained steam in some of the NAS branch offices and especially in Bologna (see Istituto Superiore di Sanità 2009). As seen in Chaps. 3, 4, and 5, the latter office already took a vanguard role in this field in the 1990s, carrying out several large-scale and/or high-level investigations, such as the investigations in the year 2000 into the trade of steroids and other doping substances in 128 gyms in several Italian regions and the two investigations concerning Prof. Conconi and Dr. Ferrari. According to an experienced officer (Int-NAS-10), the vanguard role played by the Bologna Branch Office is due to a combination of three factors: (1) its very skilled leadership, which established the branch office's excellent reputation with the local prosecutors; (2) the branch office heads' active promotion of anti-doping investigations; and (3) the presence of suppliers of doping products in Bologna and surroundings, who had a regional and even national relevance and therefore made prominent investigations possible. Whatever the reasons for the vanguard role, there is no doubt that the Bologna Branch Office has been a training ground for many NAS officers who have been responsible for some of the most penetrating anti-doping criminal investigations not only in Bologna itself but also at other branch offices, such as those in Brescia, Florence, and Padua.

A questionnaire sent from the NAS Headquarters and filled in by all 38 NAS branch offices indicates that their involvement in anti-doping investigations has remained uneven—and that anti-doping still constitutes a relatively minor task for NAS. In fact, out of about 1,000 persons working in the 38 branch offices, only 14 % of them are involved in anti-doping investigations—with percentages ranging from a minimum of 5 % to a maximum of 30 %. Only three branch offices indicate that a full-time equivalent officer is assigned to anti-doping activities, followed by another three where an officer works 70 or 80 % of his or her time on anti-doping issues. In total, we estimate that 47 full-time equivalents work yearly on anti-doping investigations, corresponding to 4.3 % of the NAS' overall personnel. It is hence clear that, despite their occasional media relevance, anti-doping investigations remain only one of the many activities carried out by NAS.

As the gross salary costs of a NAS officer is about 30,000 € per year, we estimate that the direct personnel costs of NAS anti-doping investigations are approximately 1,410,000 €. Even if we account for overhead at NAS Headquarters and working costs, NAS anti-doping action accounts for about a third of the 5,450,000 € invested yearly in testing by CONI and CVD.

---

[13] See http://ec.europa.eu/food/food/rapidalert/rasff_legal_basis_en.htm.

Table 7.1 Sport disciplines/contexts involved in NAS investigations as reported in the Database on NAS Investigations—1999–2010

Sports type	No.
Body-building	43
Body-building and gym sector	6
Gym sector	3
Body-building and cycling	1
Body-building, triathlon, and cycling	1
Body-building and gym sector, cycling, and boxing	1
Gym sector and combat sports	1
Gym sector and cycling	1
Gym sector and tennis	1
Cycling	9
Cycling, triathlon and swimming, rowing, skating, and tennis	1
Cycling and track and field	1
Riding	2
Total	71

Source: Our calculations on the basis of the Database on NAS Investigations

According to the information collected with the questionnaire, NAS investigations led to the reporting of 3,794 suspects and to the arrest of 446 for doping-related charges in the 11 years from 2000 to 2011. As in the case of personnel, the output of anti-doping investigations is not equally distributed among the 38 branch offices. Within the same time frame, NAS carried out 7,083 searches and conducted 823,878 h of wiretapping, with the same uneven distribution observed for the reports.

Our Database on NAS Investigations indicates that NAS anti-doping investigations have so far largely focused on the body-building and gym sector. In fact, out of a total of 71 investigations reported in the database, 43 exclusively concern body-building, six body-building and gyms, and three gyms alone. The only other sport repeatedly targeted by NAS in its investigations appears to be cycling (see Table 7.1). However, the database does not provide an exhaustive picture of NAS investigations even during the period 1999–2010 and does not include some early key investigations not related to body-building, such as those concerning Prof. Conconi, Dr. Ferrari, and the Bologna pharmacist, P.L., who all served athletes (and in the case of the Bologna pharmacy also trainers and team physicians) of different sports disciplines.

Over the years, NAS Headquarters have developed an increasingly close collaboration with CVD. The presence of a NAS officer in the CVD membership was not foreseen by Act 376/2000, but the cooperation was later formalized by Act 183/2010, which provided a NAS representative to be a member of CVD, and this cooperation has intensified recently. Since 2011, NAS officers often accompany incognito the CVD emissaries who are in charge of anti-doping tests. In their capacity as health officers, NAS personnel have the right to attend such tests. In their capacity as judicial police officers, they have the duty to report a suspected offense, such as a positive test or the omission of a test, to the local prosecutor's office.

Table 7.2 Doping doses seized in Italy by NAS, Carabinieri, and other police forces in the period 1999–2011

	NAS and other Carabinieri units	Other police forces	Total
Total doses	95,247,978	9,964,717	105,212,695
Percent	90.5 %	9.5 %	100.00 %

Source: Our calculations on the basis provided by the NAS Headquarters (2012) and retrieved from the Web sites of the Agenzia delle Dogane, Guardia di Finanza, Polizia di Stato, and Milan Municipal Police and from the newsflashes of Ansa, Agi, and Adnkronos

The close cooperation between CVD and NAS is also exemplified by the organization of a specialized anti-doping training course for 138 NAS officers, which was funded by CVD. The course participants obtained the title of "anti-doping investigative inspector" (Ministero della Salute 2010c). Another training course is planned for the fall of 2012 (Int-Oth-2).

7.2.3 Other Police Agencies

As already mentioned in the previous chapters, NAS is not the only law enforcement agency carrying out anti-doping investigations in Italy. The field is, in fact, quite crowded. In addition to the Carabinieri, of which the NAS is part, there is another general police agency, the Polizia di Stato, next to the Guardia di Finanza, Italy's tax and financial police, and the Agenzia delle Dogane, i.e., customs. In particular, the latter agency often intercepts packages containing doping substances when they enter or exit Italian territory; however it rarely pursues further the related investigations itself but rather passes them on to another police force. The Guardia di Finanza is also present at the border but, along with the Italian police, also conducts investigations throughout Italy.

As shown in Table 7.2, seizures by the Polizia di Stato, Guardia di Finanza, and Agenzia delle Dogane account for less than 10 % of the doping substances confiscated in Italy between 1999 and 2011. NAS, by contrast, carries out the overwhelming majority of seizures (90.5 %). However, it is worth noting that the data about the seizures of other police forces are of lower quality than the NAS data, and we therefore might underestimate the contribution of other police forces.

In the field of anti-doping as in other fields, there is little cooperation, and more rivalry, among Italian police forces, so there is hardly any exchange of data. NAS officers (Int-NAS-25 and -26), in particular, regret that the Agenzia delle Dogane do not automatically transfer to NAS all the cases initiated with the seizure of a package of doping substances at an entry or an exit point. The Agenzia delle Dogane instead often forwards such cases to the Guardia di Finanza, with which it has a close relationship because the latter is also present at the border. The NAS Headquarters have, however, recently intensified their cooperation with the Agenzia delle Dogane in the field of anti-doping and, more generally, in the fight against the trade in (counterfeited) pharmaceuticals.

7.2.4 Prosecutor's Offices and Courts: Independence …

Unless the suspects are minors, the prosecutors who can take charge of an anti-doping investigation are part of one of the 166 prosecutor's offices located at one of Italy's 166 local trial courts of first instance, the Tribunali ordinari (Ministero della Giustizia 2012).

Prosecutors are free to choose the agency to which they want to assign an investigation. In the field of anti-doping, all the seven prosecutors interviewed (Int-Pro-1-7) recognize—and, with a partial exception (see below), admit they are dependent upon—NAS' specialized competence. Unless another police unit conducts the initial seizure or reports a doping-related *notitia criminis* (i.e., the notice that a crime has been committed), Italian prosecutors tend to delegate anti-doping investigations to NAS, as both the prosecutors and NAS officers interviewed testify.[14] However, the prosecutors are under no obligation to do so and may also cooperate with another police agency if they want. Among the prosecutors interviewed, Dr. Guariniello is the only one who sometimes prefers to work, for very complex investigations, with the judicial police officers based in his prosecutor's office: the latter are generalist officers belonging to either the Polizia di Stato or the regular Carabinieri Commands, and Dr. Guariniello has established over the years a very close and trustful working relationship with them.

According to the Italian code of criminal procedure, the prosecutors have the exclusive power to initiate a criminal proceeding, have full responsibility for the related investigations, and give binding instructions to the police concerning what, whom, where, and how to investigate (Illuminati 2000: 113; 2005: 937–939; Davigo and Sisti 2012: 41–56). Despite the legal requirements, "in daily practice it is very unusual for the prosecutor to carry out directly all investigative acts" (Illuminati 2005: 939). Whereas prosecutors personally conduct all the investigative acts for major offenses (e.g., terrorism), in the case of lighter offenses they only provide general guidelines to the police and sometimes do "not give any instruction and … leave the police complete freedom of movement" (ibid.). Both the NAS officers and, with the exception of Dr. Guariniello, the prosecutors interviewed confirm the latter practices in the field of anti-doping. Even when the prosecutors provide general guidelines to NAS or other law enforcement officers, the latter enjoy a very high degree of autonomy in the daily management of the investigations. Police officers have the power to search and seizure only *in flagrante delicto* (in the act) or in other urgent situations; they need the authorization of a prosecutor in all other cases. In the case of wiretapping, the prosecutors themselves have to ask for authorization from the judge of preliminary investigations. The latter also issues arrest warrants at

[14] This thesis is based not only on the seven interviews with prosecutors carried out in the course of this project but also on Dr. Donati's extensive experience as a consultant for prosecutor's offices in anti-doping investigations, as well as his informal exchanges with the prosecutors and judges taking part in the first anti-doping training course organized jointly by CVD and the Higher Council of the Judiciary (known under the Italian acronym of CSM) in 2008.

the request of the prosecutor and reviews and authorizes the prosecutor's charges before the trial can start (Illuminati 2000: 113–114).

Among our interviewees, only Dr. Guariniello and his team insist on remaining fully in charge of criminal investigations in the field of anti-doping and other fields. Guariniello, for example, stated that he is very cautious in applying for wiretapping, because, when he decides to conduct wiretaps, he also listens to all of them himself. Another peculiarity of Dr. Guariniello's working method is the fact that he involves external consultants from the very beginning of an investigation, authorizing them also to take part in searches so that no piece of evidence may remain uncollected. The external consultants appointed by Guariniello also receive a copy of all the evidence collected and of the documents produced by the investigators and take part in the frequent meetings with the investigators and Guariniello's team of prosecutors. Dr. Guariniello's exceptional working method is, in fact, made possible by the organization of the Turin Prosecutor's Office. For the last few years this has been composed of seven "specialized groups," and Guariniello heads the group specialized in workplace safety and consumer protection, which is composed of 12 prosecutors (Procura della Repubblica presso il Tribunale di Torino, 2012).

Lacking such specialized teams, most other prosecutor's offices tend to delegate investigations to NAS or other police forces and to involve external consultants when they receive the final report of investigations in order to assess the evidence contained in such reports. This approach works fine with routine investigations, but in a specialized field such as that of anti-doping, where technical knowledge is often required, it occasionally leads to the inadvertent dismissal of important pieces of evidence, as the consultants do not contribute to the collection of evidence and are only called in after the investigation itself is finished.

As these different prosecutorial strategies indicate, most Italian prosecutors enjoy a high degree of autonomy in organizing their investigations and relationships with police forces as they deem appropriate within the broad parameters set by Italian procedural law. Aware of the abuses committed by the prosecutors controlled by the Minister of Justice during the fascist period, the drafters of the 1948 Italian Constitution rejected a nationwide hierarchical organization of prosecutors (Illuminati 2000: 111). Unlike its counterparts in other countries, the Italian Ministry of Justice has no authority to issue directives to the prosecutors to establish priorities or identify best practices; even the chiefs of the local prosecutor's offices and presidents of the local trial courts have only limited coordinating powers (Di Federico 2004; Fabri et al. 2003: 277–278; European Commission for the Efficiency of Justice of the Council of Europe 2007: 18). As Illuminati notes (2000: 111), "the power to prosecute is diffused and not centralised."

Each prosecutor's office and trial court also enjoys a high degree of managerial autonomy.[15] Prosecutor's offices' and trial courts' organization plans are subject only to the approval of the Consiglio Superiore della Magistratura (Italian Higher Council for the Judiciary, known by the Italian acronym of CSM) (European

[15] A little telling detail is that there seems to be not even a common nationwide template in which to write prosecutorial charges or court verdicts.

Commission for the Efficiency of Justice of the Council of Europe 2007: 18). This self-governing body of the judiciary was established by the 1948 Constitution, and two-thirds of its membership are composed of judges and prosecutors (collectively known in Italy as magistrates) elected by their colleagues.[16] At present it consists of 27 members.

CSM is also responsible for all decisions concerning judges and public prosecutors from recruitment to retirement (promotions, transfers, discipline, disability, etc.). The Ministry of Justice, by contrast, has only limited powers. The Italian Constitution explicitly assigns the Ministry of Justice two tasks: (a) the "organization and functioning of the services of the justice system" and (b) the prerogative of initiating disciplinary proceedings against magistrates. As in other countries in continental Europe, the Ministry of Justice is also responsible for preparing and running the budget of the entire judiciary and prison system and also recruits most of the nonjudicial personnel of the courts and prosecutor's offices (Di Federico 2004: 11).

According to Di Federico, director of the Research Institute on Judicial Systems at the National Research Council (CNR), "the role of the Italian Minister of Justice is much weaker than that of his colleagues in other countries of Western continental Europe" (ibid: 11), whereas the independence of Italian prosecutors and judges is particularly emphasized: "Among the civil law countries with a consolidated democratic system," Di Federico continues, "Italy is certainly the one where judicial independence has acquired the highest recognition both in terms of the amplitude of the law provisions formally intended for its protection and in terms of the way in which those provisions have been interpreted" (ibid.: 2). Pending since 2006 the establishment of an independent School of the Judiciary (Ministero della Giustizia 2012), CSM has been solely responsible for the initial education of the Italian magistrates (European Commission for the Efficiency of Justice of the Council of Europe 2007: 17ff.). Moreover, unlike other countries, Italian prosecutors and judges were until 2007 subject to only very limited evaluation. As Fabri et al. (2003: 63) note, formally, the career of judges "should be based on both merit and seniority, in practice, after several reforms that were passed in the 1960s and the 1970s, career advancement in status and salary are based only on seniority" (see also Davigo and Sisti 2012: 90–93). Only in 2006 were provisions introduced establishing a new system of evaluation of prosecutors' and judges' professionalism, capabilities, competences, and productivity (European Commission for the Efficiency of Justice of the Council of Europe 2007: 17).

In particular, Di Federico goes on, "Italy is the only democratic country where public prosecutors enjoy the same guarantees of independence as judges" (ibid.). Italian prosecutors have, in fact, the same background, career path, and salary of

[16] More specifically, the Constitution provides that two-thirds of the members must be magistrates and that one-third of the members be elected by Parliament among law professors and lawyers with 15 years of professional experience. It further provides that the CSM be presided over by the President of the Republic—de facto only a symbolic presidency—and include among its members the President of the Supreme Court of Cassation and the General Prosecutor of Cassation. The elected members of the judiciary are renewed *in toto* every 4 years.

judges.[17] After a competitive selection, young law graduates are hired to become either prosecutors or judges—which of these they become is decided on the basis of the vacancies at any particular moment in time and, in the course of their career, they may apply to be transferred from one court or prosecutor's office to another. Like judges, Italian prosecutors are totally independent of the Minister of Justice, whereas CSM is uniquely responsible for all the decisions concerning their careers. To give a term of comparison, French and German prosecutors are, instead, subordinated to the respective Ministries of Justice, and in France, where there is also a self-governing body for the judiciary, the section for prosecutors of the latter body has only advisory powers (Di Federico 2004: 12; Kilchling 2000).

This situation has both pros and cons. In a country in which politicians have been all too prone to exercise undue influence on prosecutorial and judicial decision-making,[18] prosecutors' and judges' independence is a crucial element in the effort to guarantee the impartiality of the judiciary and the equality of all citizens in front of the law. Judicial independence has also enabled penetrating criminal investigations against powerful politicians and state representatives in office not only in the field of anti-doping but also in the area of corruption and organized crime; these investigations have few parallels in other countries. One just has to recall the two trials against Giulio Andreotti, which began in the early 1990s. Andreotti has been one of Italy's most important politicians in the postwar period: he has been a member of parliament since 1948, prime minister seven times, and a government minister countless times. In 1993 he was accused of membership in a mafia-type criminal organization (Cosa Nostra) by the Palermo Prosecutor's Office and of having ordered the murder of a journalist by the Perugia Prosecutor's Office. After 8 years of trials, Andreotti was finally not convicted. However, the Palermo judges concluded that there was proof that Andreotti had supported Cosa Nostra until 1980 but had to apply the statute of limitations until that period (e.g., Tranfaglia 2001)—the frequent outcome, as we have seen, of many prominent trials in Italy.[19] More recently, Silvio Berlusconi, even when he was Italy's Prime Minister, was repeatedly charged with serious offenses above all by the Milan Prosecutor's Office. These repeated charges led to an impasse between two state powers that can hardly

---

[17] Italian prosecutors earn as much as judges of the same seniority, whereas in many countries that are members of the Council of Europe, they earn considerably less. See CEPEJ (2010).

[18] A blatant example of such pressure is represented by the ministerial inspections sent by the first Berlusconi cabinet to the Milan Prosecutor's Office in 1994 and 1995 in an attempt to sabotage the anti-corruption ongoing investigations ("Mani Pulite") of that office (Travaglio, n.d.). In most cases, though, such undue pressures take place more covertly and with the acquiescence of the magistrates.

As already mentioned, the Rome Prosecutor's Office was long known by the nickname of "porto delle nebbie," i.e., "the fog port," because many local prosecutors and judges had close links with politicians of the majority parties and did not press charges against them or their patrons. For the acquiescence of a large part of the judiciary to the dominant political class until the 1960s, see Di Lello (1994).

[19] See also Paoli (2003b) for a general overview of the relationship between mafia organizations and political power.

be imagined in any developed country: Berlusconi neither stepped down nor was he able to curb the prosecutors' autonomy.[20]

In a similar fashion, the charges raised against three presidents and the secretary general of the Italian National Olympic Committee hardly have any foreign parallel in the field of anti-doping (Procura della Repubblica presso il Tribunale di Ferrara 2000). Comparable charges against top sports officials were raised only against the leaders and a few executors of the state doping program in the German Democratic Republic (DDR)—but only after that political regime had collapsed and at the hand of West German prosecutors and judges (Berendonk 1992; Franke 1995; Spitzer 1998). We will probably never know if the high degrees of collusion and involvement in anti-doping activities revealed in the proceeding against Pescante and other CONI officials are uniquely Italian or instead similar practices occurred elsewhere but have never been brought to light by a judicial investigation (Procura della Repubblica presso il Tribunale di Ferrara 2000; Tribunale di Ferrara 2003). In other words, we will never know the extent of the discovery of such high-level collusion due to the fierce independence of the Italian prosecutors and the moral courage of a few of them, such as Dr. Pierguido Soprani who, based at the Ferrara Prosecutor's Office, led the case against Conconi and Pescante and the other CONI officials amid incredible difficulties. In the field of anti-doping, other very courageous and determined magistrates have been Dr. Giovanni Spinosa, who brought Michele Ferrari to trial and coordinated several early anti-doping investigations in Bologna, and Dr. Raffaele Guariniello, who ordered the searches at the CONI's anti-doping lab in 1998 and at the Turin Olympic Games in 2006 and successfully pressed charges against the chief manager and physician of Italy's most powerful football team, Juventus.[21]

---

[20] Berlusconi finally stepped down in November 2011, but he only did it under the pressure of the international markets worried about the euro crisis and Italian public debt, not because of the criminal charges he faced. As a matter of fact, Berlusconi was finally found convicted of tax fraud in July 2013. In several of his proceedings, the statute of limitations expired, the last being a bribery case that was thrown out by a court in Milan in February 2012 (Povoledo 2012). Berlusconi is currently on trial on charges of abuse of power and paying for sex with an underage nightclub dancer (Povoledo 2012).

[21] Dr. Guariniello's reputation is not only due to these anti-doping proceedings as he has been a pioneer in many white-collar crime investigations as well. For example, in early 2012 a court in Turin accepted Guariniello's request to sentence the former owner and director of Eternit Italy, the Italian subsidiary of a Swiss-Belgian industrial group, which had produced asbestos in a Piedmont city and other sites in Italy (and elsewhere). Guariniello demanded 20 years in jail for both men, for "causing a continuing disaster in health and environment" and for willfully neglecting safety regulations in the workplace. As Watermann (2012) writes, "he is to be admired for being the first public prosecutor in Europe, perhaps even in the world, to undertake such an important prosecution – and of such breath-taking scale."

Less than 1 year earlier, Guariniello's investigations had led to the first-degree sentencing of the chief executive of German steelmaker ThyssenKrupp's Italian unit, Herald Espenhahn, and five other managers. The court ruled they should be held responsible for a fire that had killed seven workers in 2007. Espenhahn was convicted of murder and sentenced to 16½ years in jail, the other five managers were convicted on manslaughter charges and received 10-year-plus sentences, and the company was fined one million euro ($1.45 million; e.g., Associated Press 2011).

The advantages of Italian prosecutors' independence are evident in the case of the planning of the raid at the 2001 Giro d'Italia by the Florence Branch Office and Prosecutor's Office. The NAS officer who then took charge of the raid visited a Florence prosecutor, showing him the many syringes and empty drug packages left by the riders and their support personnel in the hotels close to Florence during a Giro stage in Tuscany (Int-NAS-16). He, therefore, suggested that the prosecutor organize searches at the end of a subsequent stage to see what products the riders were effectively using. With the bag containing the retrieved material, the prosecutor immediately made a call to the Florence Chief Prosecutor and came back to the NAS officer after 10 min saying: "Yes, we'll do it" (Int-NAS-16). It is hardly imaginable, although we have no direct proof of it, that a raid at one of the largest national sports events would have been decided on in such a speedy and uncomplicated way elsewhere.

This episode, however, also shows a disadvantage of Italian prosecutors' independence, the lack of coordination. In fact, the effectiveness of the Florence NAS Branch Office's raid ended up being undermined by a contemporaneous raid among the Giro riders organized by the Padua Prosecutor's Office. In the small town of San Remo the presence of so many law enforcement officers during the Giro stage did not go unnoticed; noticing the arrival of the police officers, many riders and support personnel probably had the time to get rid of most of the prohibited substances and equipment they were carrying with them (Int-NAS-16; see also NAS Firenze 2002).

The Council of Europe team that evaluated Italian anti-doping legislation and policy in 2002 also noted the lack of a clear strategy in anti-doping criminal law interventions:

> Apart from describing general statutory provisions, Italy's national report does not clearly state Italy's strategy for controlling the import, movement, possession, distribution and sale of banned doping agents. The meetings of the evaluation team with police, judicial and customs representatives during the visit showed that action was being taken in this field and had produced practical results, but its organisation remains vague in the minds of the authors of the national report. Indeed, the positive results noted by some of the people to whom we spoke seemed due more to personal initiatives or random factors than to co-ordinated and systematic organization (Evaluation Team 2002: 35–36).

Given the lack of prioritization, coordination, and evaluation of prosecutorial action, criminal investigations in anti-doping and other fields end up depending to a considerable degree on the good will and dedication of the individual prosecutors, despite the fact that Italy formally subscribes to the so-called principle of legality: accordingly, prosecution is mandatory, unless there is a manifest lack of sufficient evidence to institute a proceeding (Illuminati 2000: 111). One example will suffice to clarify this point. Even though other Serie A and Serie B football clubs were repeatedly reported to be following Juventus' medical practices that were eventually considered to be doping and sporting fraud by Italy's Supreme Court (di Cassazione and Sezione Seconda Penale 2007; see also Chaps. 2 and 3), no other prosecutor has followed Guariniello's footsteps and launched an investigation on this topic. The arbitrariness is further increased by the fact that the initial reports of a police force or a citizen are supposed to be assigned by chance to prosecutors, and specifically to the one of them who is "on duty." These arrangements are particularly negative in the specialized and highly technical field of doping. In the interviews, several NAS officers and prosecutors interviewed noted that not all prosecutors are equally interested in anti-doping investigations and some of these are not even familiar with the specialized anti-doping legislation (see infra).

7.2.5 *Prosecutor's Offices and Courts: … and Poor Performance*

The "anarchy" of the Italian judicial system is an important element, by no means the exclusive one, to explain the very poor performance of the entire Italian judicial system. Other relevant factors are the personnel shortages, the disorganization of prosecutor's offices and trial courts, and, in criminal matters, the generous protections granted to defendants by Italian criminal procedural law.

As for the personnel shortages, it is enough to recall that in 2011 courts and prosecutor's offices lacked on average 15 % of their judicial personnel (Severino 2012). Equally serious was until a few years ago the lack of nonjudicial personnel, which, for example, averaged 11 % in 2002 (Ministero della Giustizia 2002: 19–27). Two pieces of information are also sufficient to illustrate the disorganization of prosecutor's offices and trial courts: computerization has proceeded slowly (Contini and Fabri 2006), albeit with some recent improvements (Severino 2012), and 2,000 judicial offices are currently spread out over 3,000 buildings, a fact that, according to the Minister of Justice herself, "the country can no longer afford" (ibid.).

The personnel shortages and poor organization of the prosecutorial offices also imply a heavy toll for anti-doping investigations. For example, the Mantua Prosecutor's Office formally charged the Mantua pharmacist and the riders and managers of the elite cycling team Lampre in April 2012 on the basis of an investigation started in November 2008. After NAS and the consultants concluded their reports in September 2010, the prosecutor in charge of the proceedings needed a year and a half just to formalize his charges and submit them to the judge for preliminary investigations due to the lack of administrative support and other tasks. Considering the fact that the statute of limitations period is set at 5 years for the offenses foreseen in article 9 of Act 376/2000 from the moment of the commission of the offense and three stages of trial foreseen by Italian procedural code, chances are high that no final conviction will be issued in the Mantua proceeding because the statute of limitations has expired.

The generous protections to defendants are a consequence of the introduction of a new code of criminal procedure in 1989. This reform was meant to introduce a fully fledged accusatorial system into a Continental legal system, but it came up against the reluctance of the judges and prosecutors working in the system to lose control of the trial. The result was, according to Nelken (2004: 13–14), that

> the new protections for the accused that characterise the adversarial system were simply added to the previous ones characteristic of the older inquisitorial type of system. The system now seeks to incorporate protections designed to foreground the forensic heat of the adversarial trial together with reliance on double checking by different judges in the three stages of trial that include the right to a full rehearing of the facts on appeal. Even relatively trivial criminal cases can need to be viewed by as many 30 people with legal training. Bureaucratic procedural requirements include complex notification rules for all parties to the trial that can be easily manipulated if the accused changes his address or lawyer regularly. What this means is that there is little incentive for lawyers to use any of the alternatives to trial. By holding out and exploiting all procedural rights there is a good chance that the case will be time- blocked before it runs its full course of all three trial stages (see also Davigo and Sisti 2012).

The code of criminal procedure also sets complicated rules to establish which judge has territorial jurisdiction to hear a case (articles 8 and 9).[22] On the basis of these rules, anti-doping proceedings, as much as other criminal proceedings, are often split in several tranches, each to be heard by a different court. In such a way, the overall picture reconstructed by police officers and prosecutor often gets lost, and courts have trouble understanding the larger context within which the conduct of "their" defendant took place. In particular, because of the frequent fractioning of anti-doping proceedings, it becomes very difficult to prove the existence of a criminal organization between defendants tried by different courts (Int-NAS-25 and -26).

According to the data reported by the Italian Minister of Justice Paola Severino (2012), as of June 2011 there were over nine million judicial proceedings waiting for trial. Whereas the number of criminal law proceedings waiting for trial is "only" 3.4 million and is thus considerably lower than the 5.5 million civil law proceedings, the consequences of this backlog are particularly dire. In fact, 28,000 people are being held in prisons while awaiting trial, amounting to 42 % of the whole prison population (ibid.). According to Severino, a civil law proceeding lasts on average 7 years and 3 months and a criminal law case 4 years and 9 months.[23] Writing in 2004, Di Federico (2004: 10) noted that a considerable number of criminal proceedings last more than 10 years, and 130,000 criminal proceedings had been thrown out of court in 1998 alone under the statute of limitations. Against this background, it becomes more understandable why defendants who can afford good lawyers—starting with former Prime Minister Berlusconi, who is Italy's richest man, but including also the physicians, pharmacists, and sports officials involved in anti-doping proceedings—can escape convictions by having their cases thrown out of court under the statute of limitations.

Among the nations of the European Union, Italy has always received, year after year, by far the highest number of monetary sanctions for the violations of article 6, section 1, of the European Convention on Human Rights, which requires that judicial proceedings be terminated in a reasonable time (ibid. and European Commission

---

[22] The code can be consulted online: http://www.altalex.com/index.php?idnot=2031.

[23] The Bank of Italy estimates that the inefficiency of the civil judicial system has a negative impact on the overall GDP corresponding to 1 % (quoted in Severino 2012).

for the Efficiency of Justice of the Council of Europe 2010). As late as 2008, the last year for which the data are available, Italy was condemned 54 times, a fact that, according to the European Commission for the Efficiency of Justice (European Commission for the Efficiency of Justice of the Council of Europe 2010: 141), "reveals that the structural difficulties of this state have not been solved so far." Reflecting on the poor performance of the Italian judicial system, the then Prosecutor General at the Naples Court of Appeals, De Tullio (2002: 14–15), noted that this situation generates "the certainty of impunity in criminal matters and the uselessness of judicial interventions in civil matters, which is what is hoped by offenders and debtors and feared by victims and creditors." Despite the touch of Southern Italian emphasis, it is hard to disagree.

7.3 Offenses, Suspects, Defendants, and Verdicts

In this section, we attempt to quantify Italy's criminal action against doping. We consider first the offenses reported and charged, the number of suspects and defendants, and outcomes of the anti-doping criminal proceedings initiated in Italy.

7.3.1 Offenses and Suspects Reported by NAS

As already mentioned, NAS reported 3,794 suspects to public prosecutors and arrested 446 persons for doping-related offenses in the period 2000–2011. Interestingly, the suspects were reported or arrested not only for the offense of doping, trade in doping products, or sporting fraud but also for many other offenses, few of which are associated in the scholarly literature with doping. Our Database on NAS Investigations does not always provide the number of suspects reported or arrested for each offense but shows how frequently the different offenses were referred to in the 80 investigations listed. After the offenses of doping and trade in doping products, which were resorted to in 58 investigations, the most frequently applied offense was "receiving" (article 648 CP), which was mentioned in 40 investigations, followed by the "administration of drugs in a dangerous way for public health" (article 445 CP) and the "illegal exercise of a profession" (article 348 CP), which were used in 32 and 31 cases, respectively (see Table 7.3). Reports were also done in 25 investigations for 2 successive legislative decrees implementing different European directives concerning medicinal products for human use (Legislative Decrees 178/1991 and 219/2006) and in 18 cases for the consolidated act on illegal drugs (DPR 309/1990 and successive amendments). More rarely, NAS investigators also proposed prosecutors to apply several other offenses.

Table 7.3 Offenses reported in the Database on NAS Investigations—2000–2009

		No.
Offenses foreseen by the Criminal Code		
Article 314 CP	Embezzlement	4
Article 322 CP	Instigation to corruption	1
Article 326 CP	Revelation of government secrets	1
Article 348 CP	Illegal exercise of a profession	31
Article 379 CP	Aiding and abetting	1
Article 416 CP	Criminal organization	18
Article 443 CP	Trade or administration of tainted drugs	13
Article 445 CP	Administration of drugs in a dangerous way to public health	32
Article 469 CP	Counterfeiting of stamps of public authentication or certificates	1
Article 476 CP	"Falsità materiale" (alteration or forgery of documents) committed by the civil servant in public acts	1
Article 477 CP	"Falsità materiale" (alteration or forgery of documents) committed by the civil servant in administrative certificates or authorizations	7
Article 483 CP	"Falsità ideologica" (making false statements) committed by a private person in a public act	2
Article 586 CP	Death or injury as a consequence of other crime	1
Article 624 CP	Theft	5
Article 640 CP	Fraud	11
Article 648 CP	Receiving	40
Offenses foreseen by special acts		
Article 9 of Act 376/2000	Doping	58
Article 9 of Act 401/1989	Sporting fraud	5
Article 73 DPR 309/1990	Illicit production, trafficking, and detention of narcotics or psychotropic substances	18
Article 282 and 295 of DPR 43/1973	Consolidated text of the legal provisions concerning customs ("Smuggling in the movement of goods across land borders and customs points" and "Aggravating circumstances of smuggling")	2
Article 6, 8 and 23 of Legislative Decree 178/1991	Implementation of European Commission's Directives concerning medicinal products for human use (later repealed by Legislative Decree 219/2006)	20
Article 6, 50 and 147 of Legislative Decree 219/2006	Implementation of European Commission Directive 2001/83/CE (and successive amendments) on the community code relating to medicinal products for human use and of Directive 2003/94/CE laying down the principles and guidelines of good manufacturing practice in respect of medicinal products for human use	5

Source: Database on NAS Investigations (2012)

7.3.2 Proceedings Initiated and Persons Charged

According to data calculated by the Italian Statistical office (Istat) for this report, 313 criminal proceedings were initiated by the prosecutor's offices, among others, for the offense of doping foreseen by Act 376/2000 between 2001 and 2009, 35 on average per year. Over the years, there has been a considerable increase in the number of proceedings: whereas only 14 proceedings were initiated on average in the period 2001–2005, this figure grows to 61 for the period 2006–2009 (see Table 7.4). Throughout the period, the same number of proceedings approximately involved charges under section 1 (generic doping offenses) and 7 (illegal trade in doping substances) of article 9 of the Act 376/2000: 150 versus 163. We do not know, however, the exact number of the offenses charged.

In total, 286 persons were charged for the offense of doping and/or less serious related offenses, on average 32 persons per year throughout the period 2001–2009 (see Table 7.4). By comparing the number of defendants for whom doping was the most serious offense charged[24] in the periods 2001–2005 and 2006–2009 we note the same increase in prosecutorial action noted for the proceedings: there were 16 such defendants on average per year in the first period and 51 in the second.

From 2006 onwards we also know the exact number of persons charged (whereas until then only the most serious offense was recorded for each defendant). In total 683 persons were charged for doping in the period 2006–2009, 253 for the generic offenses foreseen by the first section and 430 for the trade in doping products foreseen by the seventh. On average, during these 4 years, 171 people were charged, 63 for the first section and 108 for the seventh. This datum is interesting in two ways. First, it shows that quite a considerable number of people are charged for doping offenses on a yearly basis. Second and quite unexpectedly, more people were charged for the illegal trade in doping products than for the more frequent and less serious conduct prohibited by section 1 of article 9. This second finding is however less surprising than it seems at first. In fact, the offenses foreseen under the first section of article 9 focus on athletes and their support personnel and must be aimed at enhancing performance. In contrast, the offense of trade in doping products covers the entire spectrum of the market, including the transactions targeting body-builders and other noncompetitive users.

Between 1990 and 2009, 1,143 proceedings were initiated under article 1 of Act 401/1989 and 729 persons were charged in a proceeding in which the offense of sporting fraud was the most serious offense charged, on average 37 proceedings and 86 persons per year (see Table 7.5). As in the case of doping offenses, there has been an increase in prosecution in the period 2006–2009. In fact in those 4 years, we know that on average 91 proceedings were initiated and 86 people were charged, for

[24] Istat can also only provide data about the persons charged for the most serious offense in each proceeding until 2006. This means that all the defendants of that proceeding are associated with the most serious offense, even if they were not charged for it.

Table 7.4 Number of criminal proceedings including the offenses foreseen by article 9, section 1 or 7, Act 376/2000, number of persons charged for whom one of the offenses was the most serious offenses charged (A), and exact number of persons charged for each offense (B)—2001–2009

	Section 1			Section 7			Total		
	Proceedings	Persons charged (A)	Exact no. of persons charged (B)	Proceedings	Persons charged (A)	Exact no. of persons charged (B)	Proceedings	Persons charged (A)	Exact no. of persons charged (B)
2001	1	2		0	0		1	2	
2002	3	2		1	3		4	5	
2003	9	4		9	7		18	11	
2004	14	11		8	7		22	18	
2005	10	15		15	30		25	45	
2006	31	36	76	42	30	156	73	66	232
2007	19	7	40	34	28	116	53	35	156
2008	27	21	73	22	25	44	49	46	117
2009	36	23	64	32	35	114	68	58	178
Total 2001–2009	150	121	n.a.	163	165	n.a.	313	286	n.a.
Average 2001–2009	17	13	n.a.	18	18	n.a.	35	32	n.a.
Total 2001–2005	37	34	n.a.	33	47	n.a.	70	81	n.a.
Average 2001–2005	7	7	n.a.	7	9	n.a.	14	16	n.a.
Total 2006–2009	113	87	253	130	118	430	243	205	683
Average 2006–2009	28	22	63	33	30	108	61	51	171

Source: Istat (2012)

Table 7.5 Number of criminal proceedings including the offenses foreseen by Act 401/1989 and Articles 348 and 445 of the Italian Criminal Code, number of persons charged for whom one of the selected offenses was the most serious offense charged (A), and exact number of persons charged for each offense (B)—1990–2009

	Article 1 Act 401/1989			Article 348 CP			Article 445 CP		
	Proceedings	Persons charged (A)	Exact no. of persons charged (B)	Proceedings	Persons charged (A)	Exact no. of persons charged (B)	Proceedings	Persons charged (A)	Exact no. of persons charged (B)
1990	0	0	n.a.	181	200	n.a.	3	1	n.a.
1991	0	0	n.a.	293	345	n.a.	6	9	n.a.
1992	0	0	n.a.	396	496	n.a.	9	7	n.a.
1993	0	0	n.a.	402	499	n.a.	3	5	n.a.
1994	0	0	n.a.	537	643	n.a.	9	7	n.a.
1995	24	6	n.a.	633	716	n.a.	6	7	n.a.
1996	27	30	n.a.	498	579	n.a.	8	20	n.a.
1997	21	66	n.a.	651	706	n.a.	19	13	n.a.
1998	39	9	n.a.	588	674	n.a.	18	7	n.a.
1999	27	21	n.a.	596	747	n.a.	30	18	n.a.
2000	33	3	n.a.	440	537	n.a.	12	4	n.a.
2001	75	33	n.a.	645	657	n.a.	22	17	n.a.
2002	69	54	n.a.	577	626	n.a.	27	17	n.a.
2003	129	30	n.a.	650	722	n.a.	18	9	n.a.
2004	129	39	n.a.	673	748	n.a.	28	10	n.a.
2005	207	96	n.a.	703	810	n.a.	29	12	n.a.
2006	46	42	94	719	718	1,162	55	15	199
2007	82	83	148	925	889	1,320	32	18	82
2008	98	86	183	831	790	1,145	37	17	73
2009	137	131	236	942	936	1,469	28	9	36
Total 1990–2009	1,143	729	n.a.	11,880	13,038	n.a.	399	222	n.a.
Aver. 1990–2009	57	36	n.a.	594	652	n.a.	20	11	n.a.
Total 2001–2009	972	594	n.a.	6,665	6,896	n.a.	276	124	n.a.
Average 2001–2009	108	66	n.a.	741	766	n.a.	31	14	n.a.
Total 2006–2009	363	342	661	3,417	3,333	5,096	152	59	390
Average 2006–2009	91	86	165	854	833	1,274	38	15	98

Source: Istat (2012)

whom sporting fraud was the most serious offense. For the period 2006–2009 we also know the exact number of people charged with sporting fraud, namely, 661 corresponding to 165 each year. However, we do not know exactly how many of these proceedings and persons charged are related to doping, even if the previous analysis has shown that particularly before the passage of Act 376/2000 the offense of doping fraud was used to prosecute doping practices.

The same caveats apply to the data concerning the two articles of the criminal code most closely related to doping, "administration of drugs dangerous to public health" (article 445 CP) and "abusive exercise of a profession" (article 348 CP). In the period 2006–2009, 3,417 and 153 criminal proceedings included either the first offense or the second offense (854 and 38 on average per year, respectively) and 5,096 and 390 persons were charged (on a yearly basis 1,274 and 98, respectively). However, a large number of them—in the case of article 348 the overwhelming majority—are not related to doping, and the data provide no clues to differentiate the doping-related proceedings from those that are unrelated.

7.3.3 Court Verdicts

It is not exactly known how many convictions Italian courts have handed down for doping and related offenses. Istat records only final convictions and according to its data there was no final conviction for doping in the years 2007–2009. This outcome is not surprising considering the fact that few anti-doping proceedings were started before 2004 because of the uncertainties concerning the list of doping substances and methods (which was first published in late 2003; see Centamore 2011: 40) and that a criminal proceeding lasts on average 4 years and 9 months (Severino 2012). In other words, many of the anti-doping proceedings reviewed in Chaps. 3, 4, and 5 have not yet gone through all three levels of Italy's court system. Moreover, we know from other sources, including our interviewees (Int-Pro-1-7), that several courts have handed down several convictions and acquittals in the first instance even if we lack a full picture. In particular, the 30 respondents to Centamore's survey indicated that at least 30 convictions under article 9 of Act 376/2000 were issued in the period 2001–2007 in their judicial districts (17 in district of the Padua Prosecutor's Office, and 9 and 4 in the districts of the Florence and Milan Court of Appeals, respectively). Centamore's respondents also added that the trial ended with the acquittal of the defendants in at least four other cases (Centamore 2011: 57–58). Our interviewees (Int-NAS-16; Int-Pro-5) also indicated other nonfinal convictions for doping offenses, for example the 4-month suspended prison sentence and 4,000 € fine imposed on football player Fernando Couto in 2007 (AFP 2007), and the conviction of the masseur of the Mercatone cycling team who had been caught with doping substances during the 2001 Giro d'Italia raid in San Remo (Tribunale di San Remo 2005).

To our knowledge, the additional sanctions foreseen by the third section of article 9 have been applied only once, in the first-degree verdict of the Bologna Court against Michel Ferrari (Tribunale di Bologna 2004).

Table 7.6 Persons convicted with a final verdict for the offense of sporting fraud and related penalties[a]—2007–2009

	Fine	<1 month	2–3 years	5–10 years	>10 years	Total[b]
2007	6	2		2	4	18
2008	10	3		2	4	25
2009	1		1	2	2	7
Total	17	3	1	6	10	50

Source: Istat (2012)

[a]We report only the classes of penalties for which a verdict was listed

[b]The total number of persons convicted is higher than the sum of the individual penalties because not all verdicts specify a sentence for each separate offense

From Istat data, we know that in the period 2007–2009 Italian courts issued 50 final verdicts for sporting fraud (see Table 7.6). In particular, in 17 verdicts courts imposed only a fine and in three others, a prison sentence shorter than a month. There were also some heavy sentences, though, including five of imprisonment between 5 and 10 years and 10 of more than 10 years of imprisonment. We do not know, however, how many of these verdicts effectively concern doping as opposed to other cases of sporting fraud.

From both the interviews and the proceedings collected, we also know that at least 20 bargaining agreements (in lieu of conviction) were made over the past years for the offenses of doping or trade in doping products, including in the proceedings resulting from the 2001 raid at the Giro d'Italia and those known as "Oil for Drug," "Athena," and "Triamin" (Int-NAS-1, -2, -3, -9, -10, -13, -14, and -16; Tribunale di San Remo 2005; Procura della Repubblica presso il Tribunale di Bergamo 2009). Centamore's respondents also reported that the prosecutors and defendants had reached bargaining agreements in at least six proceedings involving the same offenses (six in districts of the Florence Court of Appeals and one in Padua district; see Centamore 2011: 57–58). A bargaining agreement (*patteggiamento*) is a form of diversion: it consists of an exchange between a reduced sentence and the defendant's waiver of the trial that is approved and issued by a judge. The sentence is to be reduced up to one-third of the applicable sentence, provided the latter does not exceed 5 years of imprisonment. *Patteggiamento* is similar to the US plea bargain but it differs from the latter in that the defendant in Italy is not required to plead guilty. Therefore, the court verdict that imposes the sentence agreed by the two parties is not a conviction, since the prosecutor does not prove the defendant's guilt during the trial and the judge, notwithstanding his or her supervision of the agreement, only summarily ascertains the offense (Illuminati 2000: 116–118; Davigo and Sisti 2012: 126–136).

The 30 respondents in Centamore's survey also indicate that at least 83 anti-doping proceedings (with charges based on article 9 of Act 376/2000) were suspended in the period 2001–2007 due to lack of sufficient evidence or the statute of limitations (Centamore 2011: 57–58). In the previous chapters, we also noted the devastating effects of the statute of limitations on several prominent and less prominent anti-doping proceedings. Some of them did not even end with a verdict, whereas in other cases convictions in the first instance were not confirmed by higher courts. For example, the Ferrara Court had to dismiss the proceeding against Prof. Conconi, despite "the seriousness and convergence of all the evidence" (Tribunale di Ferrara 2003: 46) because the limitation period had begun. The well-documented charges against three CONI Presidents for colluding with Prof. Conconi in distributing drugs in a dangerous way to public health (article 445 CP) did not even reach the court hearing (Procura della Repubblica presso il Tribunale di Ferrara 2000). In the case against Dr. Ferrari, the Bologna Court of Appeals did not confirm his conviction in the first instance for sporting fraud due to the limitation period, despite the existence of "an imposing series of circumstantial evidence" (di Bologna and Prima Sezione Penale. Sentenza in data 22 maggio 2006). For the same reasons, the Rome Court of Appeals annulled in 2011 the whole proceeding against I.I., fiancé and manager of the female body-builder who had died in Rome in 2004, after I.I. had received a 6-year prison sentence in the first instance for the abusive exercise of a profession and the administration of dangerous drugs (article 348 and 445 CP; La Gazzetta di Modena 2012).

On the basis of the more precise data provided by NAS and Istat, we can thus confirm the conclusions reached by Centamore in his evaluation of Italian anti-doping criminal legislation. On the one hand, the number of proceedings initiated is "relatively high." On the other hand, the majority of these proceedings "do not end with a verdict but are terminated for different reasons. Among them, in addition to the difficulty of collecting hard evidence, procedural impediments are presented, some of which are probably related to the beginning of the limitation period" (Centamore 2011: 61).

Although the Italian judicial system is hardly able to exercise its fundamental function of sanctioning illegal behaviors, our judgment is not entirely negative. As Giuseppe Maria Berruti (2011), a high-level Italian judge, notes, criminal prosecution has become "a means of social knowledge" and therefore exercises an important "sociological function" so much so that Berruti speaks of a "nemesis of the [Italian] criminal trial": "the trial hardly convicts or acquits [its defendants]. It does not have the time. Rather, it makes facts known even beyond their juridical relevance. It makes people discuss and reflect."

This positive, albeit residual, function of law enforcement is particularly evident in the case of doping. Even when they do not end in a final conviction, Italian anti-doping criminal investigations provide the necessary evidence for successful disciplinary proceedings under sports rules. This point is vividly shown by the statistics produced by Ulrich Haas (personal communication, 2012), based on the cases he has reviewed as judge at CAS. Accordingly, Italy is virtually the only country initiating proceedings against athletes' support personnel, with over 90 % of such cases. During an informal conversation, Haas made an important point: Italian law enforcement agencies are very good in collecting the evidence, as they can conduct criminal investigations on doping matters. They are very slow in processing the cases, so the statute of limitations runs out on many of them. From the perspective of sports arbitration, however, it is not relevant whether the Italian criminal proceedings end with a conviction or not. Rather it is important that sports federations and CAS receive information. From this point of view, Haas concluded, Italy is very effective.

As we will discuss in the final chapter, these observations further indicate the potential of close cooperation between law enforcement and anti-doping agencies.

7.4 The Challenges of Anti-doping Law Enforcement

We identify five main sets of difficulties faced by the current anti-doping law enforcement in Italy, in addition to the fundamental challenge deriving from the inefficiency of the Italian judicial system, which we have discussed in detail in the previous pages. The first challenge set concerns the Act 376/2000 and related legislation; the second set results from prosecutors' and judges' insufficient knowledge of the problem of doping and anti-doping legislation; the third is due to the limited cooperation with sports authorities; the fourth concerns CVD's role in Italy's anti-doping policy; and the fifth relates to the problems of international police and judicial cooperation. In dealing with first four domestic challenges, we first summarize the opinion of our respondents and then present our own position and make recommendations to Italian policy-makers. For the final challenge, we discuss the difficulties faced by Italian law enforcement agencies and prosecutors but wait to discuss our recommendations until the final chapter, when we consider the general lessons to be learned from this case study.

7.4.1 The Shortcomings of Act 376/2000

As mentioned earlier, specialized prosecutors and law enforcement officers are unanimous in assessing very positively Act 376/2000 and emphasizing that it has significantly enhanced anti-doping investigations in Italy. They thus only criticize—or better suggest how to improve—some specific aspects of the act. A few NAS officers and prosecutors (Int-NAS-26; Int-Pro-4 and -5) criticize the link that article 9, section 7, of Act 376/2000 makes between the trade in doping substances and the unauthorized trade in legitimate drugs for human use. The latter is, in fact, a mere administrative infraction, and linking article 9, section 7, of Act 376/2000 with it often weakens the criminal prosecution of doping practices, particularly in the eyes of prosecutors and judges who are not experienced in the field of anti-doping (Int-NAS-26). The above-mentioned NAS officer and other respondents (e.g., Int-NAS-10, -25, and -26) also regret that Act 376/2000 does not allow the use of undercover agents. They also consider a serious deficiency of the act that it does not allow wiretapping of athletes and their support personnel suspected of anti-doping practices under article 9, section 1, of Act 376/2000. (The act does allow wiretapping for crimes covered by article 9, section 7.) These respondents emphasize that on some occasions wiretapping constitutes the only means to cast light on the illegal practices in the sports world. Along the same lines, the NAS officers and many of the prosecutors interviewed (Int-Pro-2-6) plea for the full equivalence of the illegal trade in doping products with the trafficking of illegal drugs, including the establishment of a specific offense of criminal organization for the purpose of trading in doping products as it already exists for drug trafficking (article 74 DPR 309/1990). The proponents of such change anticipate that, on the basis of the new provision, judges would more frequently authorize wiretapping in anti-doping proceedings than they do now (Int-Pro-3).

The most controversial part of Act 376/2000 is the criminalization of athletes for their use of doping products. Whereas there is no consensus among scholars and policy-makers, most Italian law enforcement officers and prosecutors specialized in anti-doping have no problems with it. As a matter of fact, a few NAS officers and prosecutors (Int-NAS-9; Int-Pro-5) believe that the Italian law does not go far enough. Specifically, they regret that article 9, section 1, of Act 376/2000 does not also allow the criminal prosecution of recreational athletes using doping substances or methods. In fact, in the Italian jurisprudence only athletes enrolled with a sports federation, associated discipline, or Ente di promozione sportiva are considered to be addressed by article 9, section 1, of Act 376/2000 (Int-NAS-9; Int-Pro-5). These and other experts (e.g., Dipani 2004) also regret that the Act 376/2000 provides no incentives to athletes—in terms of a sanctioning benefit or a prosecution waiver—to collaborate with judicial authorities.

While we share the latter criticism, we have an intermediate position concerning the criminalization of doping athletes. On the one hand, we recognize an individual right to self-harm, all the more so that this right has long been recognized by the Italian antidrug legislation, which foresees only administrative sanctions for the possession of illegal drugs for personal use. The longer evolution of illegal drug policies also demonstrates the many harms that result from the criminalization of illegal drug use (e.g., Paoli et al. 2009; Stevens 2011). On the other hand, athletes using doping products do not only harm themselves but also cheat and manipulate the results of sports competitions—a conduct that justifies the criminalization of doping athletes. We would thus be in favor of repealing the criminalization of athletes using doping products only if the offense of sporting fraud would be reformulated (in Italy or introduced in other countries) in such a way that the doping athletes could be charged and sentenced for sporting fraud instead of doping. (Along similar lines, Rössner (2009, 2011) has called for the introduction of the offense of sporting fraud through doping in Germany. Rössner also wrote a bill containing such an offence, which the Bavarian Minister of Justice Beate Merk presented to the German Second Chamber in 2007 without finding a supporting majority.)

A related technical problem in Act 376/2000, which is pointed out in the literature but not mentioned by our interviewees, is also its failure to criminalize the mere possession of doping products (e.g., Arioli and Bellini 2005: 75). As a result of this lapse of the Italian lawmakers, the Turin Court could not convict two athletes of the Austrian Olympic cross-country ski team who had been involved in the Turin Olympic Games scandal (Tribunale di Torino 2012c).

In our view, another weakness of Act 376/2000, which no interviewee mentioned, derives from its focus on doping in elite sports. The criminal provisions of Act 376/2000 were not inspired by the awareness of the spread of doping practices in recreational sports, did not anticipate the mass distribution of doping substances via the Internet, and therefore do not explicitly criminalize the import of these substances from abroad or address the law enforcement officers' difficulties in securing proof from abroad to back charges in Italy (Int-NAS-26; see also infra).

7.4.2 *Prosecutors' and Judges' Insufficient Knowledge of Doping and Anti-doping*

As both NAS officers and the prosecutors themselves testify, single prosecutors and judges differ significantly in their awareness of the problem of doping and in their familiarity with the anti-doping legislation. Answering a specific question of the questionnaire sent by the NAS Headquarters, 9 out of 38 branch offices declared that even the introduction of Act 376/2000 had not stimulated a growing interest of the judiciary in the topic of doping. During the interviews, a few NAS officers recalled that they had reported doping-related offenses to the prosecutors with jurisdiction without ever receiving any feedback (Int-NAS-8, -9, -17, and -18). A few years back, the Council of Europe Evaluation Team (2002: 36) also observed that "[police] co-operation with the judiciary seems quite difficult to achieve in certain cases."

More generally, NAS officers stress that there are considerable differences between prosecutor's offices and individual prosecutors in terms of their interest in anti-doping investigations and that it is crucial to identify an interested and competent prosecutor to work with for the success of an investigation (e.g., Int-NAS-10, -16, -25, and -26). Even five out of the seven prosecutors interviewed (Int-Pro-1, -2, -3, -4, and -5) confirm that many of their colleagues and judges have difficulties understanding the dynamics and harmfulness of the distribution, administration, or consumption of doping products. For example, whereas they all understand the simplest cases of doping, such as the use of stimulants before a competition to enhance performance, many prosecutors and judges have troubles recognizing a hormone-based treatment during training as a doping offense under article 9, section 1, of Act 376/2000, as the hormone treatment only boosts an athlete's performance indirectly and cumulatively (Int-Pro-3). One of our interviewees, a chief prosecutor, recalls that he once had to secure the coordination of an anti-doping investigation that a younger colleague was terminating without realizing its relevance and potential (Int-Pro-4).

Prosecutors and judges have themselves expressed the need to receive training on anti-doping; to start fulfilling this demand, CVD and CSM jointly organized in 2008 a specialized training course of both groups. All together, 64 magistrates attended the course—and all of them appreciated it (Int-Pro-2 and -6 and personal communication to Donati, who was one of the course lecturers). A new course was planned for December 2012 (Ministero della Salute 2010c).

Fully aware of the technical knowledge necessary to master complicated proceedings on doping or health issues, Dr. Guariniello from the Turin Prosecutor's Office has repeatedly suggested the establishment of nationwide prosecutor's offices specialized in health matters and work-related injuries, modeled after the existing

Direzione Nazionale Antimafia, a body in charge of coordinating anti-mafia investigations throughout Italy (e.g., La Repubblica 2011). Guariniello's ideas are not uncontroversial among his colleagues (e.g., Int-Pro-5). Answering a specific question about the idea of establishing sections specialized in anti-doping investigations in Centamore's survey, none of the seven respondents supported the proposal. Most of them argued that there are not sufficient anti-doping proceedings to justify such a step (Centamore 2011: 55–60). Dr. Guariniello himself realizes that the establishment of specialized sections is feasible only in the larger prosecutor's offices as there is no room for specialization in the smaller ones. That is why he suggests the idea of establishing a national specialized prosecutor's office on health issues.

We support Dr. Guariniello's proposal, which goes in the same direction of specialized prosecutor's offices established in other countries or territories, such as Austria and, in Germany, the states Bavaria (Gräber 2011) and Baden-Württemberg (Justizministerium Baden-Württemberg 2012). As long as such a specialized prosecutor's office is not established, the training of police officers, prosecutors, and judges remains the main venue to raise the awareness of the problem of doping and spread some detailed knowledge about the criminal law instruments available.

Under the current system, prosecutors and judges are largely dependent on NAS officers and/or external consultants for specialized knowledge. NAS themselves may need to resort to consultants given the wide array of doping substances and methods, and the need to reconstruct the effects pursued by the users, the side effects, the therapeutic and doping dosages of each product, and different combinations of products in a criminal proceeding. The task of these consultants is to make sure that evidence is collected in a systematic and incontrovertible way so that it can withstand the challenges of the defense lawyers. In prominent trials, the latter also appoint consultants with the main task of questioning the solidity of the evidence collected by the police and prosecutor.

Selecting competent and independent consultants is not an easy matter. Even if they are university professors, those who are knowledgeable about doping products mostly have close contacts with the sports world and therefore know athletes, physicians, team managers, or sports federation officials who might be interested directly or indirectly in the proceeding. A further difficulty arises from the fact that in important proceedings, defense lawyers can afford to pay much higher fees to consultants than the prosecutor's offices or courts can. As a result of this gap, defense consultants are often considerably more experienced than those of the prosecution. In more than one case, consultants initially working for the prosecutor's offices or courts were later hired by defense lawyers, thus sharing an insider's knowledge of the prosecution strategies with the latter (Int-Pro-1, -3, -4).

As mentioned earlier, consultants' expertise has not yet been fully exploited in many anti-doping proceedings in Italy. Perhaps due to limited funds, many prosecutors tend to engage consultants only for specific aspects and at the end of the investigations carried out by the police, thus losing much precious input that the consultants might have given in earlier phases (Int-Pro-1). As Guariniello has suggested, we believe that it is crucial to engage trusted and competent consultants from the early phases of anti-doping investigations and, in Chap. 8, we suggest that

NADO officials could take over such role, if some basic conditions, which are not yet fulfilled in Italy, concerning the NADOs' independence, integrity, and mission are met.

7.4.3 The Limited Cooperation between Sports Bodies and Law Enforcement Agencies

Even leaving aside the cases of sports bodies' open protection of doping in elite sports discussed in Chap. 5, several NAS officers (e.g., Int-NAS-9, -25, -26) and prosecutors (e.g., Int-Pro-1 and -3) still lament the persistent lack of collaboration on the part of some sports federation and other sports body officials.

The cooperation between sports bodies and CONI, on the one hand, and police and prosecutor's offices, on the other, seems to have improved slightly in more recent years. As already mentioned, CVD and CONI automatically report all cases of athletes testing positive to the Rome Prosecutor's Offices. In Centamore's survey, the representatives of six prosecutor's offices indicated that they had initiated some recent anti-doping proceedings on the basis of reports by the sports federations (Centamore 2011: 59). Despite these positive examples, Centamore concludes that "the limited reporting of all concerned parties is regarded as one of the major reasons for the difficulties in the prosecution. This is above all to be explained with the fact that the cooperation between federations and the government agencies is not trouble-free" (ibid.: 61).

Both NAS officers and prosecutors are very interested in a closer cooperation with sports federations and CONI, rightly pointing out that both parties could draw advantages from it (e.g., Int-NAS-1, -9, -10, -16, -25, and -26; Int-Pro-1 and -6). On the one hand, sports bodies are much quicker in dealing with anti-doping proceedings, and the latter's sanctions are usually more certain and effective: a 2-year ban from competitions imposed after a few months can "hurt" an elite athlete much more than a 2-year suspended prison sentence imposed 5 or 6 years after the fact. On the other hand, Italian police and prosecutors have much more effective means to collect evidence which can be also used in sports anti-doping proceedings. We obviously share these views.

7.4.4 CVD's Deficient Coordination of Italy's Anti-doping Policy

As we have seen earlier, since 2008 CVD has progressively established a close pattern of cooperation with NAS, with a high representative of the latter being a formal CVD member (Int-NAS-26). According to several observers (Int-Oth-1 and -2), this cooperation has been crucial to improve CVD's testing strategies, leading to an increase of positive results (see Table 2.6). It is less praiseworthy, though, that since its establishment in 2001, CVD has not yet sought contact with other police forces, in particular with customs, which carry out numerous seizures of doping substances at the borders. The present study, for example, constitutes the first attempt to monitor anti-doping criminal action in Italy and its outcomes. CVD has never required Italy's police forces to submit data about the seizures of doping products nor requested the Italian Ministry of Justice or Istat data about the number of indictments and verdicts filed for doping-related offenses (Int-Oth-1).

In our opinion, CVD should become responsible for the monitoring of anti-doping criminal action against doping, regularly inviting all parties to take part in meetings to exchange data and views about successes and impediments. The potential value added of a closer cooperation between CVD and law enforcement agencies is also demonstrated by the case of Alex Schwazer, Olympic 50 km race walk champion at the Peking Olympics, who tested positive for EPO in an anti-doping test conducted by WADA shortly before the 2012 London Olympic. In fact, the idea to submit Schwazer to a pre-Olympic test came from an ongoing criminal investigation coordinated by the Padua Prosecutor's Office.

As already mentioned, CVD's coordination role is further hampered by the 2007 agreement between the then Minister of Health, Minister of Youth and Sports Activities, and CONI President, which granted CONI de facto exclusive authority in testing Italy's elite athletes (see Ministero della Salute 2007). We thus propose to repeal that 2007 agreement and to go back to the provisions of Act 376/2000. Such a step would have at least three different benefits. First, unlike in the present situation, no sets of elite athletes would be neglected. Second, CVD could decide on a yearly basis what portions of the anti-doping test budget would be devoted to the different classes of athletes. Third, the anti-doping tests of all athletes could profit from, and provide input to, criminal anti-doping investigations, strengthening the pattern of cooperation with NAS initiated when Dr. Bellotti and Dr. Pacifici took charge of anti-doping testing.

An institution can never be better than its members. To improve CVD's action and, more generally, anti-doping policies in Italy, it is therefore crucial to appoint as CVD members competent and independent experts who are committed to the control of doping practices and to the minimization of the resulting public health problems; at the same time these experts must be untainted by even the suspicion of a conflict of interest.

7.4.5 The Challenges of International Police and Judicial Cooperation

In addition to the domestic challenges, Italian criminal law action against doping is hampered by the serious difficulties in international police and judicial cooperation. These difficulties result, first of all, from the fact that few other countries in Europe and elsewhere recognize doping as a criminal offense and, if they do so, they only recognize the illegal trade in doping products, but not an athlete's use of performance-enhancing products, as a criminal offense (for a review of the legislation in other countries, T.M.C. Asser Instituut. 2010 and Houlihan and García 2012). Italian prosecutors (Int-Pro-1–7) and NAS officers (Int-NAS-1, -2, -9–11, -16, and -25–26) recall that they often receive negative replies, or no reply at all, from foreign prosecutor's offices, when they send rogatory letters to request the latter's cooperation in an anti-doping investigation. As Dr. Guariniello (2011) noted in a 2011 symposium,

> Th[e] discrepancy [in legislation] leads to highly negative effects. We need only consider that doping often constitutes a phenomenon with deep and widespread international ramifications. It is therefore easy to understand that, during most prosecutions for the crime of doping, it has been necessary to carry out actions in other countries for the success of the investigation and we have therefore sent formal written requests to foreign legal authorities for communication and notification purposes and also for the purposes of evidence-gathering. The outcome of these requests has unfortunately often been disappointing, even in Europe: in some cases the response was inadequate; in others it was late (even years late); in other cases, no response was received at all.

Some prosecutors (Int-Pro-1, -3, -4) have thus even stopped filing rogatory letters or do so only very rarely, to avoid wasting time. In particular, NAS officers (Int-NAS-9 and -11) report that it is very difficult to persuade a foreign judicial authority to shut down a Web site selling steroids and other doping products to Italian customers. Even in the few cases in which the Web site is closed, it reappears after a few days with a new IP address in another country.

Next to the problem resulting from the heterogeneity of national criminal legislation on doping matters, complicated and slow bureaucratic mechanisms further hamper the cooperation between prosecutors in anti-doping and other criminal matters. When a prosecutor wants to request evidence or an investigative act from a foreign counterpart, he (or she) has to submit his (or her) rogatory letter to the Ministry of Justice, which then translates the letter and sends it to its counterpart in the selected country; the latter ministry finally forwards it to the prosecutor's office with jurisdiction. The answers, if sent at all, also go through the same lengthy procedure. According to our Italian interviewees (Int-Pro-1–7 and Int-NAS-1, -2, -9–11, -16, and -25–26), Eurojust, an agency of the European Union set up in 2002 to intensify and facilitate cooperation among the prosecutors of the 27 EU Member States, has only marginally improved the situation. Whereas the Eurojust national members may facilitate the initial contact, the requesting prosecutor still has to write a normal rogatory letter, which follows the usual procedures.

The NAS officers with more international experience (Int-NAS-11, -16, and -26) are more positive about their cooperation with colleagues in other countries: over the years, trusted personal relationships have developed, which are often based on the recognition of Italian NAS officers' lengthy experience in anti-doping criminal investigations. As much as possible, these police officers help each other, and since 2009 Interpol's anti-doping section has become a useful reference and connecting point between police officers from different countries involved in anti-doping investigations. However, despite the informal ties, police officers are required to go through the official rogatory channels controlled by prosecutors, when they need evidence for a trial.

In addition to difficulties of the international police and justice cooperation, Guariniello (2011) criticizes the lack of information exchanges on the doping-related case law in different countries:

> The newspapers often give an account of criminal investigations brought in this or that country. But it is then virtually impossible to find out the outcome of the proceedings instigated as a result of those investigations. In such cases it would instead be very useful to exchange procedures and, in particular, verdicts handed down in the field of doping by judges around the world.

In the following chapter, we suggest that, among other things, setting up such an international database could become a new task for WADA.

Chapter 8
Synthesis of Findings and Lessons for Policy-Making

Abstract In the eighth and final chapter of this book, we synthesize the main findings of our seminal study on the market for doping products in Italy and draw policy lessons for the future development of international anti-doping policy. The general aim of the study has been to analyze the production and distribution of doping products and to understand how anti-doping criminal provisions and their enforcement can contribute to the control of doping within and outside the sports worlds. In other words, given WADA and other policy-makers' growing dissatisfaction with the traditional anti-doping athlete-focused approach, we have considered the extent to which law enforcement action and intelligence sharing between law enforcement agencies and national anti-doping organizations can become—in the words of WADA President John Fahey—as "the future of anti-doping" (UK Antidoping, 2011).

In the first part, we present the main findings of the study, by organizing them into eight topics: doping products and their harms; our estimates of the numbers of users and the size of the market; the suppliers' main characteristics and types; the distribution chains and market relationships; the role played by organized sports world and organized crime in the supply of doping products; our estimates of the revenues of the overall market for doping products as well as the revenues and profits of the suppliers; the legislation and the institutional actors underpinning Italy's anti-doping policy; and the latter's outcomes and related challenges.

In the second part, we consider the extent to which our findings on Italy can be generalized to other countries by comparing them with the international literature on doping. Drawing on the findings of the present study, the international literature as well as the research on illegal drug policy and crime control, we also propose lessons for the world's anti-doping policy-making. Our main conclusion is that criminal law enforcement has an unexploited, crucial (though limited), potential role in anti-doping. Therefore, we recommend that all countries should pass appropriate legislation on the basis of a standardized model so as to facilitate international police and judicial cooperation (and in the meanwhile exploit the equivalent offenses

L. Paoli and A. Donati, *The Sports Doping Market: Understanding Supply and Demand, and the Challenges of Their Control*, DOI 10.1007/978-1-4614-8241-3_8,

that already exist in most countries), provide their law enforcement agencies with the technical, institutional, and financial resources necessary to effectively investigate the problem of doping, foster the cooperation between these agencies and anti-doping organizations, and remain aware of the limits and harms of criminal law enforcement.

The present study draws its main motivation from the growing dissatisfaction of WADA and numerous international and national policy-makers with the traditional anti-doping approach. Whereas the latter has focused on athletes' testing and is increasingly perceived to be ineffective, law enforcement action and intelligence sharing between law enforcement agencies and national anti-doping organizations are now being presented—in the words of WADA President John Fahey—as "the future of anti-doping" (UK Antidoping, 2011).

In this study, we have examined Italy's anti-doping criminal law experience with the general aim of analyzing the production and distribution of doping products and understanding how anti-doping criminal provisions and their enforcement can contribute to the control of doping within and outside the sports world. Since the late 1990s, in fact, Italy has played a pioneering role in the criminal law control of doping, and numerous investigations have shed light in Italy on different facets of the problem of doping and specifically of the supply of doping products. By analyzing an extensive sample of these primary sources and interviewing over 30 police officers and prosecutors who have been in charge of them, we have mapped the distribution system of doping products from producers to final users in Italy and built a typology of suppliers, identifying their motivations, modus operandi, and mutual relationships and assessing their revenues and profits. On the basis of the same and other secondary sources, we have also evaluated the legislative bases, actors, and outcomes of Italy's anti-doping criminal law action, identifying a series of challenges that this action faces. To provide necessary context for assessing the supply of doping products, we have also estimated the size and financial dimensions of the Italian market for doping products—to our knowledge our study constitutes the first attempt to estimate these aspects of a national market for doping products.

Conceptually, our starting assumption has been to consider doping in terms of a market, and specifically as a semi-illegal market, at least from the point of view of criminal law. Contrary to what happens in the market for traditional illegal drugs, such as heroin and cocaine, the legal status of most doping products varies contextually. A drug may begin its "life" as a legal product at one end of the supply chain and conclude its "life" as an illegal product at the other. In particular, the effective legal status of a supply-side activity varies along the distribution chain and, for the same activity, from country to country. Even within each country, differences depend on the products exchanged, the final uses of the products, the applicable offenses, and the good faith of some suppliers.

What are the main findings of our case study and, above all, which generic conclusions and lessons can be drawn from Italy's anti-doping criminal law experience for the "future of anti-doping"?

8.1 Findings on Italy's Market for Doping Products and Anti-doping Policy

We summarize below the main findings of our study, organizing them into eight topics: doping products and their harms; our estimates of the numbers of users and the size of the market; the suppliers' main characteristics and types; the distribution chains and market relationships; the role played by organized sports world and organized crime in the supply of doping products; our estimates of the revenues of the overall market for doping products as well as the revenues and profits of the suppliers; the legislation and the institutional actors underpinning Italy's anti-doping policy; and the latter's outcomes and related challenges.

8.1.1 Doping Products and Their Harms

The Italian market encompasses the full range of the doping substances and methods (i.e., collectively referred to as products) that the IOC, since the late 1960s, and WADA, since 2001, have prohibited in sports. The availability of the substances is proven by the seizures carried out by NAS (the current official denomination is Carabinieri Command for Health Protection). This is a separate unit ("comando"), specialized in health issues, of the Arma dei Carabinieri, one of Italy's two military police forces. During the 11-year period 1999–2009, NAS seized over seven million packages of doping substances, and we estimate these quantities correspond to over 1,000 kg of active ingredients and to 88 million doping doses of these substances.[1] With 83 % of the doses, anabolic agents constitute the lion's share of the doping substances seized by NAS. The 88 million figure does not include cannabis and cocaine, which fall outside NAS' competences, even though they are on IOC and WADA's prohibited list. Anti-doping investigations also indicate the frequent administration of doping methods and particularly of autologous and heterologous transfusions.

Additionally, Italy's anti-doping investigations corroborate the findings of the international scientific literature about the harmfulness of the use of doping products. In particular, several key investigations originated from the suspicious death of a young athlete or body-builder suspected of using steroids and other doping products, and at least one court ruling proved the causal connection between the abuse of steroids and the death of a female body-builder (e.g., NAS Firenze, 2005; NAS Padova, 2009). Anecdotal evidence suggests that further harms derive from the frequent, often unsupervised, mixing of different products, including illegal drugs and counterfeited doping substances, and the circumstances of use.

[1] For the units of measure adopted in calculating the doping doses of the different substances, see Chap. 2.

8.1.2 Demand

Despite the persistent international policy focus on doping among the few elite athletes taking part in national or international competitions, doping has become a veritable public health issue. If we consider all substances included in the WADA Prohibited List, we conservatively estimate 253,700 users of doping products in Italy. If we exclude cannabis and cocaine, we reach the lower estimate of 218,700 users. Even the lower figure of 218,700 users of doping products is comparable to the number of heroin misusers estimated in Italy (218,425 people based on a prevalence rate of 5.5 per thousand among residents aged 15–64; Dipartimento Politiche Antidroga, 2011: 78).[2] However, it is somewhat lower than the estimated number of cocaine users (353,000 people based on a 2010 past-year prevalence rate of 0.9 %) and dramatically lower than the estimated number of cannabis users (over two million users of cannabis based on a last-year prevalence rate of 5.2 %; ibid., 2011: 8).

In particular, we have identified and estimated two major components of the demand for doping products: athletes who constitute 73 % of the users (or 69 % if cannabis and cocaine are excluded) and body-builders who account for 27 % (or 31 % if cannabis and cocaine are excluded). These estimates are based on different data sources. For athletes, we have relied on the rates of positive results on the total tests carried out by Italy's Anti-Doping Commission (CVD)[3] among recreational athletes, defined as those who take part in subnational competitions. These rates are about three times higher than the rates on average reported by WADA-accredited Anti-Doping Laboratories (e.g., World Anti-Doping Agency 2011a)[4] and five to six times higher than the latest rates published by the Italian National Olympic Committee (CONI) with reference to its own anti-doping tests (Comitato Olimpico Nazionale Italiano 2012). In fact, CVD's rates averaged 3.8 % in the last 2 years for which the data are available, 2010 and 2011. We have applied these rates to the Italian Statistical Office's (Istat's) estimate of 4,690,000 athletes aged 15 or older (Istat, 2007: 3), reaching thus an estimate of 184,000 athletes using at least one of the doping substances prohibited by WADA. Excluding those testing positive for cannabis or cocaine, we come up with the lower figure of 150,000 doping athletes.

Whereas we have had no means to estimate separately the number of elite and recreational athletes, we have identified about 10,000 "super elite" athletes, i.e., those who participate or have very good chances of participating in international

---

[2] Our estimate of the number of users of doping products is more than twice as large as the estimated number of heroin users emerging from the last population survey (98,000 people based on a 2010 past-year prevalence rate of 0.25 %; see Dipartimento Politiche Antidroga, 2011: 8).

[3] The official Italian name is Commissione per la vigilanza ed il controllo sul doping e per la tutela della salute nelle attività sportive (Commission for the Vigilance and Control on Doping and the Protection of Health in Sports Activities), which is shortened in CVD.

[4] Moreover, CVD's data refer to positive results, whereas WADA (2011a: 1) merely reports "adverse analytical findings," from which the cases of users with a Therapeutic Use Exemption need to be subtracted.

competitions and are therefore most likely to be targeted by CONI's anti-doping tests. Even if they are most frequently tested—CONI carries out on average ten times more tests than CVD—the super elite constitute a tiny minority of the total number of athletes and even of those who use doping substances or products. Nonetheless, the super elite athletes who have tested positive for doping products, or have been suspected of taking such products but have never been caught, constitute powerful negative role models for the millions of recreational athletes, noncompetitive sportspersons, and physically inactive people. If they become coaches or officials of sporting organizations, super elite and elite athletes who used doping products during their sporting careers are likely to socialize future generations of promising athletes into accepting such illegal practices.

We emphasize that our estimate of the number of athletes using doping substances is very conservative, as it is based on the results of anti-doping tests of urine samples, which cannot detect many current doping products, such as growth hormone (GH) and gonadorelin. As these tests are taken immediately after competitions, we also underestimate the use of other doping substances consumed out of, rather than in, competition. We also have no means to estimate the number of athletes using doping methods as opposed to doping substances, but we suppose that there are not many athletes who exclusively use the former without the latter.

For body-builders, we base our estimate on a screening of a wide sample of Italy's gyms carried out in 2007 by the Ministries of Sports and Social Solidarity and the findings of many NAS investigations that have targeted gyms. On the basis of these data sets, we conclude that 16.25 % of all Italian gyms with body-building equipment have been involved in the distribution of doping substances and that one third of the potential body-builders attending them—about 68,700—use doping products on an occasional or habitual basis, primarily anabolic steroids alone or in combinations with other doping substances (such as stimulants and GH).

We have had no means to estimate the consumption of doping substances among the remaining noncompetitive sportspersons and physically inactive people. Despite the lack of clear evidence, we hypothesize that the consumption of doping products among noncompetitive sportspeople and those who do not engage in any sport has grown in recent years, as a result of the general medicalization of society and the growing emphasis on performance (e.g., Ehrenberg, 1991; Gasparini, 2004; Hoberman, 2005).

In a preliminary attempt to scope the quantities consumed, we have developed average consumption profiles of 100 hypothetical users of doping substances (excluding cannabis and cocaine), drawing from the extensive experience of a member of the research team (Donati) as coach of several Italian national teams, CONI and CVD official, and consultant to over 15 anti-doping criminal investigations. We have had our consumption profiles validated by two Italian experts, Dr. Bellotti and Dr. Pacifici, a former and current member of CVD (respectively) with responsibility for anti-doping testing. The body-builders' consumption profiles are also consistent with the dosages described in the international literature (e.g., Parkinson and Evans, 2006). With these exceptions, our consumption profiles lack external validation: we thus present them as a work in progress, hoping to obtain feedback and suggestions for improving them from other experts worldwide.

On the basis of the 100 profiles, we estimate that on a yearly basis over 371 million doping doses are consumed annually in Italy. Among them, steroids represent the lion's share with 59 % of the market, followed by stimulants with 14 %. Our calculations also show that body-builders account for a very large share of the market (55 %), even if they represent only 31 % of the users. Body-builders, in fact, consume steroids and other doping products continuously throughout the year, and some of them take very large dosages, whereas athletes are usually more selective in their choices of doping products and, depending on the products, take them only during training, for a few weeks or months, or just before a competition. Despite their imprecision, these calculations confirm the earlier statement that doping is above all a public health problem and not just a problem of elite sports.

8.1.3 Suppliers

At the risk of some oversimplification, the illegal suppliers of doping products we have singled out from the investigations carried out by NAS and other police forces are mostly male, Italian citizens and, with few exceptions, rarely have criminal records. With the exception of hijackers who steal doping substances from trucks and a few others, most suppliers of doping products also have a legitimate professional position. On the basis of the latter criterion, we have identified ten main types of illegal suppliers of doping products in Italy and grouped them in five main categories, providing detailed examples in Chap. 3 for each type. The first category, "gym," consists of the two types of illegal suppliers who are most heavily represented in the investigations considered: gym managers or owners and body-building instructors, on the one hand, and managers or owners of dietary supplement shops, on the other hand. The second category, "health care," consists of four types: pharmacists, physicians, hospital employees, and employees or sale representatives of pharmaceutical and para-pharmaceutical companies (including not only manufacturers but also distributors). Two other types, staff members of sports teams and federations compose the third category, which we refer to as the "organized sports world." The fourth category refers to the world of horseracing and includes breeders, veterinarians, and drivers. The fifth category, which we term "use," consists of athletes, body-builders, and their close relatives. (We stretch here the definition of "occupation" to include sporting and body-building activities.) Finally, we include an "other" category for those suppliers who cannot be distinguished on the basis of a specific profession or occupation.

Unlike drug traffickers or dealers, not all suppliers of doping products are driven by profit. Nonfinancial motives—usually sports success—play a larger part for suppliers belonging to the organized sports world and for suppliers who are athletes.

8.1.4 Distribution Chains and Market Relationships

To clarify the (often variable) market position of the different types of suppliers, we have identified the sources and distribution levels of the different doping products, distinguishing between doping substances and methods, on the one hand, and among different doping substances, on the other. In the case of doping methods, we conclude that there is hardly a distribution system as these methods are administered using legitimate and often banal medical instruments.

All doping substances, by contrast, entail a distribution system that has a changing number and type of suppliers depending on the substances and quantities traded and the degree of entrepreneurship of the final users. The legal status of the exchanges and transactions also varies. Some substances, above all steroids, are produced exclusively for doping purposes in pharmacies or in illegal labs, in Italy or abroad. A large, but not precisely known, share of the doping substances sold in Italy appear to have been produced by legitimate drug manufacturers located in Italy or abroad and to have been diverted at some stage from the legal distribution chain. As Italian anti-doping investigations prove, the diversion can take place at different levels of the distribution chain. Employees or managers of the Italian or foreign drug manufacturers or their distributors may decide to divert some of the legal production to the illegal market. Drugs may also be stolen from storehouses or trucks of drug distributors or from hospitals or, more rarely, pharmacies by personnel of these institutions or by external thieves in Italy and abroad. Italian and foreign pharmacists may also purposively divert doping products, but they may also be unaware of the non-therapeutic purposes for which some of their customers buy drugs and sell the latter drugs either on the basis of a prescription written by a corrupt physician or of a false or stolen prescription. In some foreign countries, pharmacists may be allowed by the domestic laws to sell drugs, whose sale and use are instead restricted in Italy.

Given the multiplicity of doping products available and the fact that, within each class, several products are functionally equivalent, users can obtain their products of choice from a variety of retailers representing the final link of alternative distribution chains. Doping products' availability has been tremendously increased by the spread of Web sites selling steroids and other doping products on the Internet, so much so that users can nowadays bypass the whole domestic distribution chain and comfortably order doping products on the Internet and have them delivered by mail at home.

Unlike illegal drug traffickers or dealers, the majority of the suppliers of doping products can hide their illegal transactions and their relationships with their "doping partners"—their own suppliers, collaborators, and customers or patients—behind the legitimate roles they play in their businesses, organizations, or professions. The embeddedness of doping-related supply-side activities in legitimate professions, roles, and institutional settings often makes unnecessary the development of separate illegal enterprises to run these activities. The very embeddedness of doping supply-side activities in legitimate professions, roles, and institutions is suggestive of white-collar crime and the related and partially overlapping concepts of occupational, corporate, and organizational crime.

Some illegal suppliers, though, have trouble finding a professional cover to hide the production, import (i.e., smuggling), and wholesale distribution of illegally manufactured doping products. At the higher levels of the market and especially for steroids, illegal enterprises sometimes develop that are similar to those operating in illegal drug markets. Like the latter, the former at least in Italy tend to remain small and incorporate illegal relationships and transactions into blood or family relationships to reduce their vulnerability to law enforcement efforts (e.g., Reuter, 1983; 1985; Moore, 1974: 15–31).

Reflecting the white-collar background of most suppliers, the suppliers of doping products in Italy are rarely reported to use violence, except for the truck hijackers. Except for a single, not well-organized attempt, the anti-doping investigations and our respondents also provide no evidence of suppliers of doping products bribing or attempting to bribe public officials. Even if they do not resort to violence or bribes, some suppliers of doping products cheat their "customers"—probably to a larger extent than their counterparts in illegal markets. Particularly in elite sports, different types of suppliers—e.g., physicians, pharmacists, coaches, and sports federation officials—abuse their positions of authority and the athletes' and the latter's parents' trust by prescribing, selling, or administering the athletes doping products and convincing them of the necessity and harmlessness of doping products.

8.1.5 The Role of National Sports Bodies and of Organized Crime

The most startling peculiarity of Italy's market for doping products is the protection that officials and staff members of sports authorities, such as CONI and key sports federations, have repeatedly provided to the market servicing elite athletes—in addition to serving as outright suppliers of doping products in a small number of well-documented cases. As scandals and criminal proceedings indicate, the representatives of national sports bodies, including some very high-ranking officials, exercised their roles as "protectors" quite openly until the late 1990s. Since then, no cases of overt high-level complicity have come to the fore, but the national sports bodies' apparent lack of interest in a thorough fight against doping still emerges from several criminal proceedings and outright policy choices.

On the contrary, the analysis of the criminal proceedings and the expert interviews indicate a very limited involvement of Southern Italian mafia groups in the production and distribution of doping products. Among the suppliers considered so far, there is only a specific type that can be traced back to Southern Italian mafia-type organized crime groups: the hijackers stealing doping substances from trucks, who are often associated with Neapolitan camorra groups. Members of some camorra groups also play an important role in the fixing of horse races, which is often achieved by doping the horses. These practices thus confirm WADA's worried analyses that the same underworld people who trade in doping substances also undermine the integrity of sports through illegal betting (e.g., World Anti-Doping Agency 2010d).

The illicit enterprises set up by some suppliers of doping products and the looser partnerships developed by others even within legitimate institutional contexts meet all the requirements of the definitions of organized crime set forward at the international level, above all by the 2000 UN Convention against Transnational Organized Crime. Regardless of the labels chosen, one should not forget the fact that, with the exception of a limited number of underworld characters, most suppliers of doping products have a legitimate professional background, with a non-negligible share of them belonging to the organized sports world. Hence, even if underworld members may increasingly engage in the production and wholesale distribution of doping substances in Asia and elsewhere, the booming supply of doping products in developed countries is far from being an alien conspiracy threatening the immaculate world of sports from the outside.

8.1.6 Revenues and Profits

Judging on the basis of their legal market prices, the doping doses of most doping products are cheaper than those of illegal hard drugs, such as heroin and cocaine. There are only two exceptions: GH, an 1 IU of which costs slightly more than a retail dose (0.25 g) of heroin (10.49 €) and slightly less than a dose (again 0.25 g) of cocaine (17.29 €, see Dipartimento Politiche Antidroga, 2012b: 191); and gonadorelin, whose price per dose (48 €) even exceeds that of heroin and cocaine. The price per dose of EPO (3.09 € per 200 IU) and most other related substances are similar to those of a hashish joint (3.73 €) and are slightly more expensive than a marijuana joint (2.85 €). All other doping substances are cheaper than even marijuana or hashish. For example, a 10 mg dose of steroids costs 1.12 €.

We stress, however, some important caveats in our analysis. Most users do not buy doping products at the official pharmacy prices. They may pay much more than the official price, if the substance is diverted from the storehouse of a drug manufacturer, distributor, health care center, or pharmacy or is sold by a pharmacist-cum-illegal-supplier, hoping to obtain an original, high-quality product. Other users, however, may pay much less than the pharmacy price, if they directly buy on the Internet a doping substance that is either counterfeited or produced in countries with lenient regulations or lax enforcement.

Using the official pharmacy prices and, for the few substances not officially traded in Italy, their Internet prices, we estimate the potential market value of the doping substances seized in Italy by all law enforcement agencies during the period 1999–2011 is 132 million euro.

Using the same price information and the earlier estimates of the quantities consumed, we estimate the yearly revenues generated by the Italian market for doping products at about 537 million euro. Steroids account for about 245 million euro or 46 % of the total revenues, thus less than their share of the quantities consumed

(58.9 %) due to steroids' relatively low prices. For the opposite reasons, peptide hormones, growth factors, and related substances represent a much higher share of the total revenues (41.9 % or 225 million euro) than their share of the quantities consumed (6.4 %) due to their high price.

We stress that our estimates are very conservative, as we do not estimate athletes' consumption of the two most expensive doping substances, GH and gonadorelin, as they were never detected in CVD's tests. More generally, our estimates reflect the biases and limits of CVD's testing and, in particular, underestimate the share of other peptide hormones and related substances that are difficult to detect in urine samples but are more expensive than other doping substances. Despite these caveats, the revenues generated by the market for doping products probably remain considerably smaller than the revenues of the illegal drug market. To have a comparison, we estimate the retail revenues of the Italian heroin market, which has a similar number of users, between a minimum of 2,419 million euro and a maximum of 5,292 million euro.

8.1.7 Anti-doping Law Enforcement: Legislation and Actors

All law enforcement officers and experts interviewed agree that the introduction of wide-ranging anti-doping criminal provisions with Act 376/2000 boosted criminal investigations on doping. We should not lose sight, however, of the fact that NAS and prosecutor's offices conducted several penetrating investigations even before the adoption of this act, resorting to suitable provisions in the Italian Criminal Code and to the offense of sporting fraud, which was introduced with Act 401/1989.

Act 376/2000 establishes three distinct types of doping offenses. The first two concern both athletes and their support personnel for procuring, administering, assuming, or even encouraging the use of doping substances or methods, with the aim of improving an athlete's competitive performance or to modify the results of an anti-doping test (article 9, sections 1 and 2). The third offense is the most innovative, as it tackles suppliers who trade in doping substances outside the official distribution channels (article 9, section 7). Imprisonment from 3 months to 3 years and a fine from 2,580 to 51,645 € are the sanctions foreseen for the first two offenses; imprisonment from 2 to 6 years and a fine from 5,164 to 77,468 € are foreseen for the third offense. Given the differences in sanctions, interception of telephone calls and other communications is allowed only for the third offense.

Act 376/2000 cleverly foresees three aggravating circumstances, in particular, if the offender is "a CONI component or employee of a national sports federation" and also provides additional sanctions for them and those practicing a health profession.

Act 376/2000 can also be praised for setting up a 20-member national Anti-Doping Commission, CVD, even before the establishment of a NADO was requested by WADA. CVD is entrusted by Act 376/2000 with the development and update of Italy's own prohibited list, the organization of anti-doping controls, and the maintenance of operative contacts with the European Union and the international bodies. However, CVD's role has been obscured by CONI, which has managed to remain in charge of anti-doping tests of elite athletes in Italy and to be recognized as Italy's NADO by WADA—despite the fact that CVD's testing effectiveness is much higher than CONI's. Although CVD has developed in recent years close collaboration with NAS, a representative of which is a CVD member, it has not played a major role in the criminal action against doping. Intelligence sharing between CVD and NAS has only begun in 2008.

Not surprisingly, two other institutions have played pivotal roles in the anti-doping law enforcement in Italy: NAS and prosecutor's offices. NAS consists of 38 centers composing a separate unit of the Carabinieri, which is composed of about 1,100 members and operates under the direct authority of the Ministry of Health.

Anti-doping constitutes only one of the NAS' tasks. According to a survey among the 38 NAS directors, only 14 % of the local personnel are involved in anti-doping investigations, amounting to 14 full-time equivalents per year. Notwithstanding the limited human resources invested in anti-doping investigations, in 11 years from 2000 to 2011, NAS investigations led to the report of 3,794 suspects and to the arrest of 446 persons for doping-related charges. Over the years, NAS has also been responsible for about 90 % of the seizures of doping products carried out in Italy. However, NAS has no exclusive competence in this field, and Italy's other police forces have also been active.

We estimate the direct personnel costs of NAS anti-doping investigations in about 1,410,000 € yearly. Even if we account for overhead at NAS Headquarters and working costs, NAS anti-doping action accounts for about a third of the 5,450,000 € invested yearly in testing.

Italy's penetrating criminal investigations against state representatives in office in the field of anti-doping (as well as of corruption and organized crime) would have most likely not been possible, if Italy's prosecutors had not been fully independent of the executive branch of government. The extreme independence of prosecutors, however, entails not only advantages but also some serious disadvantages, such as the lack of prioritization, coordination, and evaluation of prosecutorial action. Despite Italy's adherence to the principle of legality, criminal investigations in anti-doping and other fields end up depending to a considerable degree on the good will and dedication of the individual prosecutors. This is particularly dire in a technical and specialized field such as that of doping, where not all prosecutors are equally aware of the problem and familiar with the special legislation.

8.1.8 Anti-doping Law Enforcement: Outcomes and Challenges

Together with personnel shortages, the disorganization of prosecutor's offices and courthouses and, in criminal matters, the generous protections granted to defendants by Italian criminal procedural law, prosecutors' (and judges') independence contribute to the very poor performance of the entire Italian judicial system. This problem also manifests itself in the field of anti-doping.

According to data calculated by the Italian Statistical office (Istat) for this study, 313 criminal proceedings were initiated by the prosecutor's offices for the offense of doping foreseen by Act 376/2000 (sometimes in combination with other crimes) between 2001 and 2009, 35 on average per year. For the period 2006–2009, we also know that a total of 683 persons were charged for doping. (We also have data on other offenses applied, but we do not know how many of these cases effectively concern doping.) Even though we lack exact estimates, the number of final verdicts on the basis of Act 376/2000 appears to be much more limited. We identify three main explicative factors to explain this imbalance. First, not many anti-doping criminal proceedings were started before 2004 because CVD published its prohibited list only at the end of 2003 and, as a result, many anti-doping proceedings are still ongoing (in Italy there are three stages of trial, and a criminal proceeding lasts on average 4 years and 9 months; Severino, 2012). Second, many trials end up with a bargaining agreement, which is formally not a conviction and is not recorded by Istat in relation to doping. Third and most seriously, the statute of limitations expires on many proceedings before a final sentence is issued. Taking advantage of the inefficiency of the Italian judicial system and the generous protection granted by Italian procedural code, many defendants—in particular, those who can afford good defense lawyers—are able to avoid a conviction in such a way.

Even when they do not end with a criminal conviction, Italian criminal investigations often lead to sport disciplinary proceedings, not only against athletes but also against the latter's support personnel.

In addition to the inefficiency of the overall judicial system, we have identified five challenges that hamper anti-doping criminal action in Italy. Four of them are domestic: (1) minor legislative issues concerning Act 376/2000 and related provisions; (2) prosecutors' and judges' insufficient knowledge of the problem of doping and anti-doping legislation; (3) law enforcement agencies' limited cooperation with sports authorities; and (4) CVD's deficient coordination of Italy's anti-doping policy. The fifth challenge stems from the difficulties of an effective international police and justice cooperation. In particular, these difficulties result from both the heterogeneity of national criminal legislation on doping matters and the complicated and slow bureaucratic mechanisms regulating exchanges between prosecutors of different countries in anti-doping and other criminal matters.

8.2 Generic Conclusions and Lessons for Policy-Making

In this section, we consider the extent to which our findings on Italy can be generalized to other countries by comparing them with the international literature on doping (both academic and grey; see Chap. 1). Drawing on the findings of the present study, the international literature, as well as the research on illegal drug policy and crime control, we also propose lessons for the world's anti-doping policy-making.

8.2.1 Doping Products and Their Demand

- The super elite athletes targeted by CONI, the IOC, and WADA represent a tiny minority of total users of doping products or even the total number of athletes using such products. From a public health perspective it hardly makes sense to focus predominantly on super elite athletes, and it would be advisable to broaden the policy focus to include recreational athletes and noncompetitive sportspeople.

Whereas Italian top elite athletes number only about 10,000, we estimate that there are 185,000 athletes and 69,000 body-builders using doping in products in Italy for a total of 254,000 users. Even if the top elite athletes would all take illegal performance-enhancing drugs—an assumption that is obviously unrealistic—they would represent only 3.9 % of the total number of users of doping products. It is also important to recall that the figure of 254,000 underestimates the total demand, as it reflects the positive rates of official anti-doping tests and does not account for use among noncompetitive sportspersons other than body-builders and physically inactive people. With a more encompassing estimate of the demand for doping products, the share of top elite athletes among users would be even more marginal. Despite the lack of precise data, the share of elite athletes out of the total population of recreational and elite athletes and the total number of users of doping products is not likely to be much different in other countries.

- Doping substances are used for many different purposes, not just to enhance performance and produce a range of effects, including some short-term effects perceived as positive by the users and short-term and long-term adverse effects. These effects are not yet well understood in the literature and more research is needed to anticipate and treat them. On the basis of solid research results, WADA could also better defend its choices of prohibiting certain substances or methods.

As our study and the international literature indicate (e.g., Parkinson and Evans, 2006; Kanayama et al. 2008), performance enhancement is not the exclusive or main goal of many users of doping products. Most of the heaviest users, i.e., body-builders, use doping substances for image-enhancing, rather than for performance-enhancing, purposes. The international literature also shows that doping products are used for additional purposes, e.g., in the case of steroids, to enhance aggressiveness or courage and the feeling of omnipotence (for a review of the literature, see Swedish National institute of Public Health, 2010: 56–57). Users also occasionally use some of the substances on the WADA's Prohibited List for their psychoactive effects. These are documented in several doping substances—for example, stimulants—even leaving aside cannabis, cocaine, and opiates.

Not only positive but also negative effects are associated with the regular intake of doping products. As shown by a growing body of literature and indirectly confirmed by the present study, the use of steroids produces multiple and serious adverse consequences. The harmful effects associated with other substances have been studied less systematically, but the available evidence suggests that some of them might be at least as harmful as steroids. More research is needed to ascertain the short- and long-term effects of all doping substances. More research is also necessary to understand the effects of polypharmacy, which are as yet little understood in the literature. The few existing studies (for a review, see Dodge and Hoagland, 2011) show that the severity of the undesired effects depends on a variety of factors, from the type and combination of products taken, the dose and duration of administration, as well as the gender of the person taking them.

Even less is known about the effects of counterfeited products. Worryingly, a study in the Netherlands (de Hon and van Kleij, 2005) has shown that at least 50–60 % of the products illegally obtained do not contain what is declared on the label. Hence, its authors appropriately conclude that "as long as there are no quantitative data available on the health damage that occurs as a result of doping use, a well-balanced decision on the possible introduction of alternative approaches cannot be made" (ibid.: 7).

- Given the similarities and partial overlap between doping substances and legal and illegal psychoactive drugs (such as alcohol, tobacco, heroin, cocaine, and other illegal drugs), doping-focused demand-side interventions could and should profit from the best practices developed to prevent and reduce the demand for legal and illegal psychoactive drugs and the harms associated with their consumption.

Even leaving aside cannabis, cocaine, and opiates, several substances on the WADA's Prohibited List, such as stimulants and steroids, produce psychoactive effects. Just like the most dangerous illegal drugs, these doping substances also have the potential to produce physical and/or psychological dependence in a significant share of their users (e.g., Kanayama and Pope, 2012). Given these similarities and partial overlap, we are convinced that anti-doping control and prevention efforts could profit from the best practices developed in the field of alcohol, tobacco, and illegal drugs to prevent and reduce their demand and harms.

Sweden has gone as far as to pursue an integrated approach to deal with all legal and illegal psychoactive substances, including doping. In 2010, in fact, the Swedish government approved the bill "A Cohesive Strategy for Alcohol, Narcotic Drugs, Doping and Tobacco (ANDT) Policy" "to facilitate state management of public support in the ANDT sphere, to improve coordination and cooperation and to develop a cohesive view of the common factors underlying the origins of the problems and their solutions" (Ministry of Health and Social Affairs, Sweden 2010). While this integrated approach has not yet been evaluated, it seems promising. At the very least in the field of prevention, anti-doping interventions could profit from the best practices already developed in the prevention of illegal drug and alcohol misuse. In some cases, anti-doping interventions could also easily be integrated with drug and alcohol prevention initiatives: in all three fields, in fact, the most effective universal prevention interventions are those that enhance life-skills rather than the more traditional information campaigns in schools (European Monitoring Centre on Drugs and Drug Addiction 2011: 27–28; Singler and Treutlein, 2001; Singler, 2011).

- Many users of doping products seem to be not sufficiently aware of the adverse effects deriving from their consumption patterns. It is thus necessary to provide reliable, evidence-based information about the harms associated with doping products particularly through targeted campaigns directed at potential and current users and, more generally, to develop a harm reduction approach in sports.

Despite the lack of empirical studies on the issue, Italian criminal investigations have repeatedly shown that most users rely almost exclusively on word of mouth or Internet forums to decide which products and in which dosages they should take (see Chap. 4). The situation does not appear to be fundamentally different in other countries. There too, users and prospective users gather a large amount of information from friends and are overconfident in the information they have received from their friends and via the Internet (e.g., De Hon and van Kleij 2005; Larance et al., 2008). According to the Swedish National Institute of Public Health (2010: 67), "the degree to which information on these discussion forums are based on science varies and the full panorama of effects are rarely conveyed. A large part of the knowledge conveyed via the websites above is detailed and based on personal experience, assumptions and rumours."[5]

In Italy and elsewhere, only a small minority of the users, primarily elite athletes, has access to the advice of complacent physicians or pharmacists (see Chap. 3). However, given the subordination of these physicians and pharmacists' professional ethics to the goals of sports success or personal or institutional profit, even their advice is no guarantee of protection from the adverse effects of doping products (see also Waddington, 2011).

In Italy, no government agency or sports body has ever systematically informed current and potential users of doping products of the harms associated with these products. Only two anti-doping hot-lines have been established, one by CVD and the other more recently and more successfully by the Health Sanitary System of the Modena Province (Int-Other-1 and 2). Other countries, particularly in Northern Europe, have been more active, going beyond the anti-doping phone and Internet hot-lines, which have been set up in a number of countries (e.g., Denmark, Sweden, The Netherlands; see Anti Doping Denmark et al. 2012: 75, 78, 81). In 2012, the Dutch Ministry of Health, Welfare and Sport, for example, specifically established a specific Web site—www.internetpillen.nl—providing information about the risks of fake/counterfeit pills, which are often supplied via the Internet (Anti Doping Denmark et al. 2012: 95). Additionally, the Dutch and Danish anti-doping authorities and the county of Stockholm recently launched multimedia information campaigns targeting young men working out in fitness centers. A peculiarity of the Dutch campaign was the emphasis on harm reduction. The Danish and Swedish campaigns also aimed at informing and training fitness instructors (including those in training) and the owners of fitness centers. Anti Doping Denmark, for example,

[5] See also the 2012 comparative report "Strategy for Stopping Steroids" produced by the anti-doping agencies of five EU countries (Denmark, Sweden, The Netherlands, Poland, and Cyprus) under the aegis of Anti Doping Denmark (2012: 78).

also produced a fitness handbook with advice and guidelines on anti-doping for fitness personnel (ibid.: 73–87). In turn, the Polish and Cypriot anti-doping authorities launched information campaigns targeting recreational and elite athletes (ibid.: 88–91).

Building on these seminal experiences, other domestic and supranational anti-doping bodies could also consider setting up Web sites and media campaigns providing objective information and advice to current and potential users of doping products, their relatives, and other stakeholders. As in Denmark and in Sweden, they should also consider involving gyms and fitness centers in anti-doping prevention to make sure that the prevention and information campaigns reach many users. If they decide to do so, they are probably likely to find interested partners. The European Health and Fitness Association (2012), the leading umbrella organization representing the entire gym and fitness sector in Europe, issued a press release in early 2012 "to demand co-operation with anti-doping authorities." The EHFA also established an Anti-Doping Charter which states the following:

> The European health and fitness sector is committed to improving the health of European citizens and as such it is fundamentally opposed to the use of doping and other performance-enhancing substances that harm health. EHFA and its members commit to do their utmost to eradicate doping practices and will cooperate with the EU Commission, doping agencies, authorities and governments in studying and implementing the most effective policies, campaigns and measures to combat doping. The sector commits to educate and inform its employees and customers, and to provide information and guidance for operators to have in place effective anti-doping measures (ibid.)

Sports authorities and governments should also deal with what Coakley and Pipe (2009: 218) call "the deep hypocrisy involved in elite power and performance sports." That is, they should start critical discussions on the use of currently accepted performance-enhancing strategies, such as injecting painkilling drugs, hydration strategies, playing with pins in broken bones and with high-tech casts to hold broken bones together during competitions. The Italian Supreme Court officially labeled as doping the off-label misuse of legitimate drugs when it reviewed the verdict of the Turin courts against the manager and chief physician of the Juventus football club (Corte Suprema di Cassazione 2007). Those proceedings, as well as research in other countries (e.g., Waddington, 2011), indicate that abuse of legitimate drugs and other accepted performance-enhancing strategies are common. Rightly, Coakley and Pipe (2009: 219) argue that they foster a sports culture in which the use of doping products is defined as logical and courageous.

To deal with these contradictions, which undermine the rationale of anti-doping provisions, a harm reduction approach is necessary, in which the emphasis is no longer placed exclusively on the goals, i.e., the medals to be won, but also on the means to reach these goals and the possible harms associated with them. As suggested by Coakley and Pipe (2009: 218–219), specific measures implementing such a harm reduction approach would include allowing athletes to play only if they have been certified as "well" (not simply "able to compete") by two independent physicians, establishing health and injury education programs for young athletes and establishing rules clearly indicating that certain risks to health are undesirable and even unnecessary.

- Heavy users, to be found especially among body-builders and the athletes of specific disciplines, such as weightlifters, disproportionately suffer more harms than other users. It is therefore sensible to develop control and treatment programs specifically focusing on them.

Italian criminal investigations and our own consumption profiles confirm what is known from the international literature: namely, that body-builders and some categories of athletes, such as weightlifters and throwers, have tended since at least the 1980s to consume doping products in larger dosages and more frequently than other users (see Chap. 2). The international literature also indicates that these users are likely to suffer the most harms (e.g., Kanayama et al. 2003, 2008; Singler and Treutlein, 2010: 186–197).

As far as controls in fitness centers are concerned, Denmark has probably gone the furthest of all other European countries. In fact, on the basis of the 2005 Act on Promotion of Doping-Free Sport, the Danish anti-doping agency has the authority to enter into anti-doping agreements with fitness centers and other private or public institutions that offer sports and related activities, ensuring that these centers and institutions undertake doping controls and impose sanctions in accordance with the guidelines that apply to Danish sports federations, i.e., in accordance with the WADA Code. In June 2010, 50 % of all commercial fitness centers had a doping control agreement with Anti Doping Denmark (Anti Doping Denmark et al. 2012: 56). Since July 2008, Danish fitness centers are obliged to display clear signs indicating whether they have entered into a collaboration agreement with Anti Doping Denmark, and the police can impose sanctions on any centers that fail to comply with the rules (ibid.: 38–39). On the basis of the cooperative agreements, Anti Doping Denmark has authority to carry out tests in fitness centers. Confirming the seriousness of the problem, this testing activity has shown that approximately one out of five of the fitness visitors tested had used prohibited substances, primarily steroids, a percentage that has remained constant over the past 5 years (ibid.: 56).[6] A positive doping test results in 2 years' suspension from the center.

The Danish approach remains controversial. For different reasons, none of the other countries that participated in the Strategy for Stopping Steroids project (Sweden, the Netherlands, Poland and Cyprus) has introduced doping tests in fitness centers, despite the fact that the project included "anti-doping organisations and countries that are among the leaders in anti-doping work in the fitness sector" (ibid.: 7).

Whether or not anti-doping controls in gyms and fitness centers are established, it is clear that the athletes and body-builders who began using steroids and other drugs in large quantities in the 1980s are now entering middle age and are likely to suffer from the long-term psychiatric and medical consequences of this form of substance abuse (Kanayama et al. 2008). It is therefore necessary to develop

---

[6] It must be stressed that the selection process is not random: test personnel chooses the fitness center visitors to be tested who are most likely to have used drugs. The proportion of positive cases is therefore not representative of the total number of centers visitors (Anti Doping et al. 2012: 56).

treatment programs specifically targeting this class of substance abusers. In the Netherlands efforts have been made since the 1990s to offer specialized treatment to the users of doping products and an Anabolics Clinic was set up in 2010 (Anti Doping Denmark et al. 2012: 115–116). Likewise, in Sweden, two public hospitals offer specialized treatment for steroid abuse. Their experience suggests that both the (former) users and the normal physicians treating them often fail to recognize that specific complaints are linked to (past) steroid use (ibid.: 121–123). "With a lack of a holistic approach, various side-effects are most often treated rather than the whole" (Swedish National Institute of Public Health, 2010: 76). However, the methods and experience that do exist are as yet sparsely documented, and the research on effective treatment methods is still very limited (ibid.).

Our study has also shown that several athletes, such as those treated by Faraggiana, were doped directly by physicians of Italian national sports federations and therefore under the indirect responsibility of the Italian National Olympic Committee (CONI), which is a public body (see Chap. 3). Among them, Pietro Pujia went as far as to sue the Italian Weightlifting Federation and CONI in 1989 for having obliged him to take steroids since he was 13 years old, including before the 1988 Seoul Olympic Games. Pujia's aim was to obtain compensation for his back problems. Although we do not know the final outcome of that trial, we are convinced that the Italian Government—and by extension all governments in a similar situation—have the moral duty to provide adequate treatment to athletes who doped and were doped in the name of a misconceived national pride.

In Germany a special bill was passed in 2002 to provide financial support to the "doping victims" of the former German Democratic Republic (GDR). On the basis of that bill, more than 300 athletes received compensation (Müller-Platz et al. 2006: 20). Even if no systematic state doping program was ever established in Italy and other Western countries as in the GDR, Western national sports federations and Olympic Committees, and indirectly, the national governments that profited from doped athletes' international victories, are under the moral obligation to support the aging athletes who are now suffering the long-term consequences of their past-doping practices.

8.2.2 Supply

- A semi-illegal market for doping products is likely to have developed in all countries in which there is a widespread demand for such products. There is a need to know more about the extent, organization, and dynamics of semi-illegal markets for doping products in other countries.

As seen in the introduction, the academic and grey literature and the numerous scandals periodically involving elite athletes demonstrate that there is a demand for doping products among elite and recreational athletes and noncompetitive sportspeople in other countries as well. It is enough to recall that some tens of millions of individuals are estimated worldwide to have used steroids alone, reflecting an average lifetime prevalence of steroid use of at least 3 % in young men (Kanayama et al., 2009). Although the prevalence of other substances is less well researched, it is probable that the users of these substances also add up to a few million users worldwide.

You do not have to be trained in economics to suppose that if there is a demand, there is also a supply. For a considerable share of the users in numerous countries, it may still be possible to obtain these substances through legal channels. In a 2006 survey of fitness center visitors in Germany, for example, almost half of the users of anabolic steroids reported that they were able to obtain the drugs from physicians by prescription or directly from pharmacies without prescription (Striegel et al., 2006). In most countries, though, next to legal channels, illegal distribution channels are bound to have developed—not unlikely those brought to light by Italian criminal investigations.

The exact configuration of the different national markets for doping products obviously needs to be ascertained through empirical studies. It may well be that not all types of suppliers singled out in our case study of Italy are active in other countries (e.g., hijackers stealing medical drugs from trucks). In Italy as well as in other countries, the share of doping substances illegally produced versus diverted also needs to be assessed more precisely than we could do in the present study.

The role of national sports bodies in the supply of doping products also needs to be examined empirically in each national context. It could well be that, given Italy's high levels of general corruption (Transparency International, 2011), the complicity and tolerance long shown by Italian sports bodies have no exact parallel elsewhere. Given the foreign cases discussed in Chap. 5, however, other national sports bodies, governments and observers, should not be too quick in downplaying the wheeling and dealing of Italian sports body officials as uniquely Italian.

Notwithstanding the need to know more about the specifics of each individual (sub)-national market, it seems safe to hypothesize that a semi-illegal supply of doping products—that is, a supply consisting of both legal and illegal distribution channels—has also developed in the overwhelming majority of developed countries where doping products are consumed. Even in countries where the production and distribution of doping substances do not constitute a separate offense, the suppliers and in particular the importers of these substances are likely at the very least to violate provisions regulating the distribution and import of pharmaceutical drugs. As we have seen in Chap. 7, some of the offenses reported by NAS in their anti-doping investigations refer to Italian acts implementing EU directives concerning customs or medicinal products for human use (e.g., European Commission Directive 2001/83/CE and Directive 2003/94/CE). These directives are bound to have been implemented also in other EU countries.

- Users of doping products can obtain them through a multiplicity of channels linked to different distribution chains, among which the Internet has become increasingly relevant. Given the large variety of products, their widespread availability, and the lessons to be drawn from the "war on drugs," supply-side interventions in the field of doping must be given realistic objectives, drawing from the realization that no doping-free world is possible.

The previous analysis has demonstrated ad abundantiam that Italian users of doping products often have multiple sources available for products of the same class. In Italy as elsewhere the product availability has been greatly enhanced by the Internet. As of April 2012, for example, a Google search for "buy steroid" delivered 13,700,000 hits, up from four million hits in 2000 and five million hits in 2010–2011 (see also U.S. Government Accounting Office 2005).[7] Vis-à-vis illegal drugs, the availability of doping products is further increased by the fact that many doping substances have functional equivalents: for example, if a specific brand of steroids is temporarily unavailable, users can easily find plenty of alternatives available on the market, original and counterfeited.

Most academics and a growing number of policy-makers agree that it is not possible to eliminate or even reduce consistently the availability of illegal drugs through supply-oriented policy interventions, which usually mean criminal prosecution, interdiction of the drugs at the border and, in producing countries, eradication (and alternative development). It is enough to recall that despite the $1 trillion (Mendoza, 2010) spent by the US government on the war on drugs, the prices of the two major hard drugs, heroin and cocaine, have declined consistently from the 1980s onwards, suggesting an increase in their availability (Reuters 2012). Even if local reductions in opium or coca production are possible, the illegal drug industry is like a balloon: when it is "squeezed" or curbed in one location, it tends to "bulge" or re-emerge in another location (Paoli et al. 2009; see also, Dorn, 1992; Friesendorf, 2007; Nadelmann, 1989; and Seccombe, 1995). These views, long held by critical scholars and observers, are finally also becoming accepted among politicians and policy-makers. Made up of many former heads of state and government, the Global Commission on Drug Policy (2011: 2) declared in 2011 the war on drugs a failure: "Vast expenditures on criminalization and repressive measures directed at producers, traffickers and consumers of illegal drugs have clearly failed to effectively curtail supply and consumption." Serving heads of state in Latin America, most vocally the President of Guatemala, Otto Perez Molina, have made these views their own, calling for alternatives to prohibition (Haddow, 2012). While the Obama administration still resists fundamental changes to US drug polices, even the current U.S. drug czar, Gil Kerlikowske (2012) conceded that an approach based "on 'War on Drugs' law enforcement centric mentality … is not humane, effective, or grounded in evidence."

Whereas the "war on drugs" expression and mentality is increasingly questioned in the field of drug policy, a growing number of national and international policy-makers have recently advocated a "war on doping": among them, UCI President Pat McQuaid (*Winnipeg Free Press*, 2006, MacMichael 2011b), UNESCO Director General Koichiro Matsuura (UNESCO, 2007) and the European Commission

---

[7] The earlier figures were stated by Holz, an Interpol officer specialized in anti-doping issues at a WADA Foundation Board Meeting in November 2010 (World Anti-Doping Agency 2010e).

(2006). Although it is not always clear what is meant with this expression, we believe that it carries a lot of baggage and should be avoided. The war on doping can hardly be given the same goal as the war on drugs, i.e., the elimination of doping substance production (United Nations General Assembly Special Session 1997), because most doping substances are, unlike heroin or cocaine, regular, sometimes life-saving, medical drugs. Their complete elimination is thus not even desirable.

Even if it were, it would not be possible. Given the characteristics of the market for doping products, criminal prosecution and interdiction alone are even less likely to be successful in reducing significantly the availability of doping products than they have been in the case of illegal drugs. Many doping substances and all the equipment necessary for doping methods are produced legitimately and only later diverted and/or misused for doping purposes. Even when the substances are produced illegally, the production often takes places in kitchen labs that almost anybody with some basic chemical knowledge can set up and run. Equally hopeless are the chances of eliminating the (illegal) trade. Even in Sweden, a nation seeking to achieve a "society free from illegal drugs and doping" (e.g., Ministry of Health and Social Affairs, Sweden 2010: 3), customs is able to check only 0.1 % of the around 250,000 packages arriving daily at Sweden's main international airport (Swedish National Institute of Public Health, 2010: 64). The US General Accounting Office (U.S. Government Accounting Office 2005: 7) also admitted that "the sheer volume of mail [arriving daily at the US international airports], along with the steps illegal steroid suppliers use to disguise their product and the labor intensive nature of the inspection process itself, present formidable challenges to CPB [U.S. Customs and Border Patrol Agency] in its efforts to interdict the entry of anabolic steroids into the United States."

These considerations do not mean, however, that all supply-side interventions are useless. They do mean, as even IOC President Rogge concedes, that "we cannot win the war on doping" (*AFP*, 2002). Given the IOC's record in anti-doping (see Chap. 1), some observers might fear that Rogge's argument is just an excuse to justify the IOC and WADA's meager testing results, but the same point is also made by academic scholars, such as Bette (2011: 165): "we must first of all realize that the complete elimination of the doping problem is not in sight" (see also Jacobs and Samuels, 1994–1995).

Admitting the limits of current policies does not also mean advocating the legalization of doping, however. Unless we are prepared to allow even minors to use all doping substances and methods in the most dangerous possible dosages and combinations, no full legalization of doping products or illegal drugs is possible (see Courtwright, 2001). And if a market is highly regulated, as the market for doping products would inevitably be if it were legalized, incentives unavoidably develop to bypass restrictive regulations (for example, to protect minors) and trade in these products illegally. Moreover, as Wiesing (2011) has convincingly argued, legalization would not reduce restrictions on athletes' freedom, because sports authorities would still need to make sure that athletes take only the permitted and not the prohibited, more dangerous, products. At the same time, athletes would be forced to take additional avoidable health risks, as they would take ever larger doses, or more dangerous types, of doping products in order to remain competitive, and the sports world would definitively lose its role model function.

Drawing on these realizations, national governments, international sports authorities, and organizations should be committed to adopting a mix of policy interventions: in this mix, standard supply-side interventions, such as criminal prosecution and interdiction, are necessary to signal society's disapproval of certain behaviors, to identify and punish suppliers (effectively deterring those with a white-collar background), and to promote the development of a market that causes the least possible harm to users, the organized sports world, other stakeholders, and society in general. In drug policy, for example, a multipronged or integral policy approach is now being pursued within the EU, in which law enforcement is one of its components along with prevention, treatment, harm reduction, and reintegration (European Monitoring Centre on Drugs and Drug Addiction 2011).

In anti-doping and other fields, policy-makers should not lose sight of the fact that all interventions and particularly criminal prosecution not only have expected benefits but are also likely to cause unintended harms; they should not forget that the ultimate aim of policy must be to minimize the overall harm deriving from the problem itself and the policy interventions (McCord, 2003; Greenfield and Paoli, 2012). Going back to the founder of criminology, Cesare Beccaria, for example, criminological research shows that the celerity and certainty of punishment, not its severity, are most effective in fostering deterrence—in this respect it is obvious that Italy scores abysmally—whereas the severity of punishment causes the most harm (Wright, 2010). And as the expected benefits of policy interventions do not always materialize and the unintended harms are hard to predict in advance, the interventions should also be thoroughly evaluated after the first few years of implementation and then on a regular basis afterwards.[8]

- The embeddedness of exchanges of doping products in legitimate relationships and the white-collar background of many suppliers and elite athletes constitute opportunities for controlling doping that have not yet been sufficiently exploited.

[8] While looking for the right mix of policy interventions, policy-makers tackling the problem of doping might draw useful lessons from the history of the international drug control regime. Whereas recent history forcefully demonstrates the difficulty of reducing the demand for illegal drugs through supply-side interventions, the policy and market developments in the 1920s and 1930s indicate that these interventions heavily impact the types and modus operandi of the suppliers, wiping out the least harmful and most deterrable suppliers and thus inadvertently provoking harm. In those two decades, in fact, the League of Nations was quite effective in using the power of adverse publicity and managed to convince all the large pharmaceutical companies to reduce diversion and cut heroin production drastically. Coupled with the criminal law restrictions enforced by national governments, the League's successful interventions transformed the market. In the early 1920s, the illicit trade in narcotics depended to a large extent on diverting legally manufactured drugs. Underworld members were typically located at the bottom of the drug-manufacturing and marketing system. In combination with manufacturers and numerous middlemen and retail outlets, they diverted a portion of the product to non-medical consumers. By the beginning of World War II, however, professional criminals were almost alone at the beginning of the process, owning clandestine factories around the world and resorting to extensive violence and corruption to promote and defend their business (e.g., Meyer and Parssinen, 1998; Paoli et al. 2009).

As argued in Chaps. 3 and 4, many, if not most, suppliers of doping products in Italy have legitimate professions and occupations and meet the most stringent legalistic requirements of the definition of white-collar crime (e.g., Tappan, 1947; Gobert and Punch, 2003). The same is certainly true for many elite athletes. The few existing studies touching on the supply of doping products in other countries also confirm the embeddedness of doping exchanges in legitimate relationships (e.g., Laure and Binsinger, 2005; Striegel et al., 2006; Brissonneau, 2007; Fincoeur, 2009 ; see Chap. 1). Even in countries with no specific criminal offense of doping, many suppliers of doping products and elite athletes can thus be regarded as white-collar criminals, if the term "white-collar crime" is understood in a broad way to encompass not only criminal offenses but also violations of regulatory laws and sports rules, as is often done in the white-collar crime debate (e.g., Nelken, 2007). As white-collar criminals, both the suppliers of doping products and elite athletes are more vulnerable to the deterrent effects of criminal prosecution than ordinary offenders, because they have much more to lose than the latter—as the parallel between doping and insider trading suggests (see Chap. 4).

Among white-collar crime scholars and policy-makers there has been a long-standing opposition between those favoring a deterrence approach and those promoting compliance approaches, between punishment and persuasion (e.g., Hawkins, 1984; Pearce and Tombs, 1990). On the basis of his research into the success and failure of regulation in different industries and businesses, Braithwaite has fruitfully suggested to go beyond this opposition. In his view, interventions aimed at securing businesses' compliance need to be combined and reinforced with other sanctioning interventions aimed at deterrence. This mix is known as "responsive regulation" and can best be achieved through an "enforcement pyramid" (Ayres and Braithwaite, 1992: 35). As Braithwaite (2011: 475) notes, "the paradox of responsive regulation is that by having a capability to escalate to tough enforcement, most regulation can be about collaborative capacity building." At the bottom of the pyramid, attempts are initially made to coax compliance by persuasion. Moving up the enforcement pyramid, increasingly severe interventions are used when dialogue or more modest sanctions fail. In the case of a recalcitrant company, for example, a regulator might escalate from persuasion to a warning, to civil sanctions, to criminal sanctions, and up to the temporary suspension or permanent revocation of a license to operate.

With a few adaptations, Braithwaite's enforcement pyramid could be easily extended to the control of doping in sports. Consisting of education and prevention, the lowest levels of the pyramid are already present in a large number of countries, at least in law books and policy documents (these are what we earlier called the first and second pillars of anti-doping policies; see Chap. 1). The higher levels of the pyramid, i.e., a range of increasingly more punitive approaches and sanctions, by and large still need to be developed. The first step, which has already been taken in Italy but not in many other countries, would be to introduce criminal offenses and sanctions specifically targeting suppliers of doping products. Criminal sanctions should by no means be limited to fines or imprisonment. Appropriately, the Italian anti-doping criminal legislation foresees additional sanctions for health practitioners, and for CONI and sports body officials, even though, to our knowledge, an additional sanction has been applied only once (Tribunale di Bologna, 2004; see Chap. 7).

In addition or in parallel to criminal sanctions, national and international sports authorities could also impose punitive sanctions to target sports federations and teams providing doping products to their athletes or encouraging or tolerating their athletes' doping practices. The current World Anti-Doping Code (World Anti-Doping Agency 2009c) is very vague in this respect and sets no specific sanction against sports bodies or other institutions of the organized sports world, except for teams involved in a team sport.[9] However, sports (and criminal) sanctions against sporting bodies have the potential to be at least as, if not more effective than, criminal sanctions against individuals. The founding president of WADA, Dick Pound (2011b), for example, suggested that the IOC should ban a national team or even an entire country from participating in Olympic Games, if a sports federation or the entire national Olympic Committee did not prove to be making serious efforts in controlling doping. Either the IOC, the national Olympic Committee, NADO or government could impose what Braithwaite calls "corporate capital punishment," i.e., the permanent revocation of a sporting body's license to operate.

Such suggestions are in line with the sociologists' insight that doping in elite sports is far more than the behavior of deviant individuals and results from the interaction of different actors, who form a "constellation" which includes the organized sports world, the public, the mass media, and economic and political actors (Bette and Schimank, 2000; Waddington, 2000; Bette, 2008; see Chap. 1). The corollary of such analyses is that doping in professional sports can only be reduced through "constellation management," as opposed to relying only on repressive or preventive intervention focusing on individual athletes (Bette 2011: 169–170). Along similar lines, to curb the supply of doping products to noncompetitive sportspeople, the most punitive sanctions could consist of suspending or revoking the operating license of a gym or fitness center whose managers or employees have been repeatedly involved in the supply of doping products.

We emphasize that governments have more leverage in securing anti-doping compliance in elite sports than they do in industries, simply because most national sports federations, with the exception of the football federations and a few others, depend on government funding. As Bette (2011: 169–170) also points out, "a lot could be achieved with money that you either make available to sports organizations or withdraw in case of observed deviance or lack of cooperation." Bette also clearly states the rationale for such an approach (ibid.): "subsidizing the organized elite sports can only be legitimate for policy-makers because the sports world has given itself its own rules and behavioral codex, which do not violate existing

[9] Article 11, §2 merely establishes that "if more than two members of a team in a Team Sport are found to have committed an anti-doping rule violation during an Event Period, the ruling body of the Event shall impose an appropriate sanction on the team (e.g., loss of points, Disqualification from a Competition or Event, or other sanction) in addition to any Consequences imposed upon the individual Athletes committing the anti-doping rule violation." Article 12 adds that "nothing in the Code precludes any Signatory or government accepting the Code from enforcing its own rules for the purpose of imposing sanctions on another sporting body over which the Signatory or government has authority."

government laws." Through their funding, government bodies could easily create incentives for serious anti-doping interventions, for example, by making the allocation of funding dependent on the implementation of specific anti-doping interventions and demanding the reimbursement of funding if these interventions are not implemented. Investigating the doping scandal at the 2001 Lahti (Finland) Nordic World Championships (see Chap. 6), the Doping Enquiry Taskforce (2001: 3) set up by the Finnish Ministry of Education argued that "A federation is always responsible for its own activities," and proposed that the ministry "refrain from paying one million FIM of the 4.52 million granted to the Ski Federation for 2001 because of the failure to comply with the conditions for government aid. In addition, future aid should be dependent on the anti-doping action of the Federation in the coming years." The Ministry of Education enforced the Taskforce's suggestions. Appropriately, the IOC Disciplinary Commission imposed a US$1 million fine on the Austrian Olympic Committee after the 2006 doping scandal at the Turin Olympic Games (International Olympic Committee 2007).

In other words, effective supply-side interventions, including but going beyond criminal prosecution, are possible. These interventions can reduce both the trade and use of doping products, especially in the organized sports world, but they presuppose a political will that many governments and sports ruling bodies (see below) have yet to show consistently.

- The organized sports world has not always been committed and is, despite the best intentions of WADA's leadership, unable to detect and prosecute suppliers of doping products. Therefore, national governments need to intervene directly, through a system of incentives and sanctions, to make sure that the suppliers of doping products are tackled by both cases under sports rules and criminal law proceedings.

Our analysis demonstrates that top-level officers of CONI and key sports federations have long tolerated and even fostered doping practices of elite athletes in Italy. The foreign cases briefly discussed in Chap. 5 show that this tolerance and complicity are not uniquely Italian phenomena. Even if there is no clear evidence that other national sports ruling bodies have openly fostered doping practices, the impression is that many of them are not yet seriously committed to the detection and prosecution of suppliers of doping products (see also Chap. 1). As in the case of insider trading (see Chap. 4), doping behavior and the supply of doping products have long been considered de facto legitimate activities even after the introduction of the first generalized prohibitions in the 1960. In a 2011 hearing of the German Federal Parliament Sports Commission, Dr. Katja Mühlbauer, the head of the first German prosecutor's office specialized in anti-doping, assessed as follows the German sports federations' cooperation in anti-doping:

> I will answer first the question concerning the federations' reporting [of doping suspicions]. There has been no reporting by federations. In two and half years we have received no reports. … All in all, we have found a rather hostile attitude from the sports federations. In the beginning we looked for contacts, but our efforts were more or less directly rejected. The prosecutor's office was not welcome there (Sportausschuss des Deutschen Bundestages 2011: 36; see also Singler, 2011).

As Coakley and Pipe (2009: 218) put it, "it is not possible to effectively control the use of performance-enhancing substances when federations and teams encourage general overconformity to the norms of the sports ethic." Our analysis of the IOC's long-standing support of Prof. Conconi also indicates that international sports authorities have long lacked commitment to anti-doping (see Chap. 5). As shown in Chap. 1, other scholars and observers confirm our findings.

Even if they are determined, national and international sports ruling bodies often do not have the means to detect and prosecute suppliers. To quote Pound (2011b) again:

> In the case of doping, there are many measures which sport organizations have no legal power to take or adopt. They cannot enter premises to seize evidence. They cannot tap or intercept phone and other messages which might be evidence of corruption. They cannot compel the giving of evidence under oath. They cannot seize funds. They cannot require the licensing of organizations or individuals beyond the scope of their own jurisdiction. They cannot demand access to information in the possession of public officials. They cannot demand or obtain banking records or records of transfer of funds. These measures are, uniquely, in the hands of public authorities.

Although three of the eight doping violations included in the World Anti-Doping Code also address suppliers, WADA (2013d) itself admits that the current control regime has "focus[ed] squarely on athletes." Whereas WADA's establishment in 1999 marks so far the highest point of governments' intervention in anti-doping, the moment might have come to realize that even WADA, despite the best intentions of WADA's leadership, cannot tackle the supply of doping products and that they have to take even more direct responsibility for this task.

In doing so, governments should be driven not only by the pursuit of effectiveness in doping control but also by the pursuit of fairness. Francesca Delon, one of the few athletes who found the courage to report her trainer to the CONI Anti-Doping Prosecutor's Office for advising her and other athletes to take steroids and other doping substances, rightly noted the following:

> I told only the truth to the judge. I did it because whenever there is a case of doping, people say: It is the athlete's fault, and the athlete is found guilty, is punished. And rightly so. However, I ask myself: And those behind the scenes, when do they pay? Because those who advise and propose [the use of doping products] are at least as guilty as the athlete who agrees to take them. It is right to share the burden, as the trainer is very important for a boy or girl [playing sports], has an enormous power of persuasion (Zambardino, 1993a).

Driven by the simultaneous pursuit of effectiveness and fairness, governments should also make sure that the few athletes who have the courage to become whistleblowers are protected from the revenge of their trainers, employers, and colleagues and are able to continue pursuing their sporting careers.

8.2.3 Policy

- Anti-doping law enforcement is more effective than testing in documenting sports rule violations by athletes' support personnel, revealing the mechanisms and actors involved in the supply of doping products and deterring at least some of the latter. Criminal investigations can also provide the necessary evidence to build the cases for sports rule proceedings against athletes and their support personnel. However, they presuppose an integrated approach with no a priori distinction between the use of doping products in elite sports and other contexts.

By comparing NAS and testing costs and estimating that the former are about a third of the latter, we have shown that criminal investigations, even if they are substantial and continuous such as in Italy, are much cheaper than testing. The difference in costs has also been emphasized by high-level WADA officers. In a 2011 speech, WADA President Fahey noted that law enforcement action and intelligence sharing between law enforcement agencies and national anti-doping organizations constitute not only the future of anti-doping but are "far less expensive than taking blood and urine and going to laboratories" (e.g., UK Antidoping, 2011).

Law enforcement action is not only cheaper but also more effective. As Turin prosecutor Guariniello (2011) notes, "In Turin, during the 2006 Winter Olympics, it took one night of raids to collect items that a thousand tests carried out by a renowned laboratory on urine and blood samples had failed to bring to light." Referring to the same event, Prof. Arne Ljungqvist (2010), WADA Vice President and the head of the IOC Medical Commission, echoes Guariniello: "if there had not been the Italian law, the case would have never been detected, as all athletes tested negative. You can draw your own lessons from it."

The few other national law enforcement agencies that have been granted jurisdiction in the field of anti-doping also report positive experiences, with a rapid increase in the number of investigations, suspects, and substances seized (for Denmark, see Anti Doping Denmark et al. 2012: 100–101; for Australia, Australian Sports Anti-Doping Authority 2012; for Austria, Holzer's intervention in Sportausschuss des Deutschen Bundestages 2011: 14–16; for Germany, Gräber, 2011 and Mühlbauer's intervention in Sportausschuss des Deutschen Bundestages 2011: 16–18).

Some NADOs also highly praise the cooperation with law enforcement agencies. In its 2010–2011 Annual Report, for example, the Australian Anti-Doping Agency (ASADA) wrote the following:

> Good relationships between ASADA and relevant government and non-government agencies are critical to eliminating doping in sport. One of our vital partnerships is with the Australian Customs and Border Protection Service (Customs), the agency responsible for seizing importations of prohibited substances entering Australia. During the year, we continually received assistance from Customs while also working collaboratively on a number of individual investigations. In 2010–2011 we analysed 2,968 referrals of performance and image-enhancing drugs (Australian Sports Anti-Doping Authority 2012: 51).

The disproportionate number of cases involving athletes' support personnel that originated from Italian investigations and have been dealt by CAS (Haas, personal communication, 2012; see Chap. 7) further indicates the potential of intelligence and evidence sharing between anti-doping and law enforcement agencies. Criminal proceedings are slow and, especially in Italy, may not even end up with a conviction. However, law enforcement agencies have investigative methods, such as searches and wiretapping, that are not available to sports ruling bodies. The difference law enforcement methods can make is well illustrated by USADA's recent action against Armstrong. An ongoing investigation on Dr. Michele Ferrari carried out by NAS and coordinated by the Padua Prosecutor's Office provided decisive documental evidence to corroborate the incriminating statements of Armstrong's former team colleagues and other riders (U.S. Anti-Doping Agency 2012c: 58, 60, 82–86, 99).

Despite their more limited powers, sports bodies and NADOs have something to offer too: they can rapidly impose sanctions, such as a competition ban, that are much more effective against elite athletes and their teams than the prospect of having to pay a fine or even serving time in prison 2 or 3 years after the start of an investigation. (As noted earlier, however, the World Anti-Doping Code does not yet foresee effective sanctions for sports organizations other than teams.) NADO officers, in particular, could also serve as experts in criminal proceedings, thus alleviating the crucial knowledge problems emphasized by numerous Italian prosecutors (see Chap. 7 and infra).

Even more fundamentally, NADOs can raise awareness for the problem of doping among law enforcement agencies. In 2010, for example, Danish customs (SKAT) decided to target doping substances in its control work, after having started collaborating closely with the local NADO; this led to a rapid increase in seizures. Building upon these initial experiences, in 2010 Danish customs decided to prioritize the trade in doping substances and set up an impressive nationwide campaign, which included the following measures.

- Further training of customs officers in doping-related matters.
- Further training of sniffer dogs to teach them to detect doping substances.
- Targeted control operations throughout Denmark at airports, ports, border crossings, and mail and courier centers.
- Increased collaboration with key individuals at mail and courier centers who can alert SKAT to suspicious consignments.
- Risk analyses and blocking of consignments in the customs clearance systems, profiling of individual persons connected with doping substances, chemicals, ampoules, and equipment and other items that can be used for illegal production of doping substances.
- Post-analysis of doping cases by SKAT.
- Creation of a relevant contact network with other authorities in Denmark and abroad, including customs authorities and the police.
- Preventive measures such as information campaigns, lectures, and creation of a page on SKAT's Web site for preventive information.
- Collaboration on projects involving white-collar crime on the Internet.
- Targeted PR (public relations) regarding anti-doping work.
- A focus on doping by police officers who investigate and deal with doping cases to enable prosecution of the parties involved (Anti Doping Denmark et al. 2012: 101).

This impressive program could serve as inspiration for any customs agency that intends to intensify its anti-doping activities. However, law enforcement action and intelligence sharing between law enforcement agencies and national anti-doping organizations presuppose that the latter and WADA are willing—and have the financial and personnel means—to go beyond their current focus on doping in elite sports and address instead the entire spectrum of misuse of doping products for performance- or image-enhancing purposes and the related channels of supply. In fact, law enforcement agencies cannot know in advance if a supplier is servicing elite or recreational athletes or noncompetitive sportspeople. Indeed, as the Italian experience shows, many suppliers, with the partial exception of those belonging to the organized sports world, are happy to make money by offering their drugs and services to different types of users.

- Criminal investigations are hampered by the lack of harmonized cross-national criminal legislation. Given the cross-national nature of many doping exchanges, comparable offenses and sanctions need to be introduced in order to prevent criminal investigations from stopping at the national borders.

As shown in Chap. 7, many law enforcement officers in Italy complain about the difficulties of international cooperation. On the one hand, they point to the complicated and slow bureaucratic mechanisms regulating exchanges between prosecutors of different countries—a general problem in police and judicial cooperation in criminal matters. On the other, the Italian police officers and prosecutors unanimously stress that the difficulties of international cooperation are further sharpened, in the case of anti-doping, by the lack of harmonized legislation.

The assessments of Italian law enforcement officers are echoed by those of their foreign counterparts. Asked to assess the availability of steroids over the Internet, the US General Accounting Office came to the following conclusion:

> There is a readily available supply of steroids worldwide, because in most countries, anabolic steroids can be sold legally without a prescription. Thus many foreign distributors do not violate the laws of their countries when they sell these substances to people in the United States. As a result, US law enforcement agencies have difficulty in obtaining assistance from their foreign counterparts in investigations of such distributors (U.S. Government Accounting Office 2005: 5).

Even Mathieu Holz (2012), the Interpol officer responsible for anti-doping, complained about "the lack of priority in many states and a not harmonized regulation in the field"—despite the fact that article 8 of the 2005 UNESCO Convention against Doping in Sport (2007) calls on State Parties to "adopt measures against trafficking to athletes" (see also Chap. 1).

In Chap. 1 we already discussed the large differences in anti-doping legislation, even within the EU. As long as these differences persist, it is evident that anti-doping international police and judicial cooperation cannot work effectively and that law enforcement action against the supply of doping products cannot reach its full potential. Therefore, we recommend that all countries pass appropriate legislation on the basis of a standardized model so as to facilitate international police and judicial cooperation. At the very least, pending such a harmonization process, domestic law enforcement officers should be informed about those offenses covered by other countries' special laws, which might at least partially correspond to similar domestic legislation.

- To be conducted effectively, criminal investigations require specialized knowledge on the part of the relevant police officers and prosecutors. Various measures can and should be taken to develop such specialized knowledge.

The previous chapters have forcefully shown the fundamental role played by NAS in Italy's anti-doping investigations. Chapter 7 has also indicated the key contribution that can be made by the experts appointed to serve as consultants in criminal proceedings but has also shown the difficulties of recruiting competent and unbiased ones. These difficulties could easily be alleviated, if NADO officers would serve as consultants. However, their involvement in criminal proceedings is advisable, only if the NADOs are completely independent on the organized sports world and are willing to abandon the exclusive focus on elite athletes—two conditions that are not yet fulfilled in Italy. The Italian experience also demonstrates that anti-doping training courses for police and customs officers, prosecutors, and judges can also be an effective means to increase the awareness for the problem of doping in the law enforcement and criminal justice community as well as the specialized knowledge necessary to carry out effective anti-doping criminal investigations.

These findings confirm a point aptly made by Turin prosecutor Guariniello (2011), namely, that "good legislation alone is not enough to combat doping." To make sure that the laws are enforced, Guariniello has proposed some operational guidelines based on his experience in the field:

- Specialization of magistrates (prosecutors, judges).
- Searches and wiretaps.
- Immediate appointment of expert witnesses with a view to their active participation in preliminary investigations.
- Presence of expert witness reports in the records (inspections, searches, summary information, analysis of telephone conversations, interviews).
- Establishment of an ongoing relationship with expert witnesses: regular joint meetings with expert witnesses in the various fields (medicine, chemistry, pharmacology) to request information and guidelines to help conduct investigations, to understand the evidence required, to guarantee consistency and the exchange of information, to speed up the filing of expert witness reports (and if necessary of interim reports).
- Participation of the Public Prosecutor of First Instance in the appeal.
- Exchange of investigation protocols and experiences acquired between prosecutors' offices.
- Ongoing relationship with Judicial Police bodies.
- Joint training opportunities for magistrates and inspectors (technical subjects, interpretation of rules, activities of the Judicial Police) (Guariniello, 2011).

Another option that has also been discussed in Chap. 7 and advocated by Guariniello is the establishment of prosecutor's offices specialized in doping or health-related offenses. Two such specialized offices have been recently established in two southern German states, namely, Bavaria and Baden-Württemberg in 2009 and 2011. The records of the older Bavarian prosecutor's office vividly demonstrates the veritable leaps forward in the criminal prosecution of doping that can be achieved when a specialized team is set up, even in the absence of legislative changes (Gräber, 2011).

8.2.4 General

- We still have insufficient knowledge about many key facts and trends related to doping. In order to develop and implement effective prevention and control policies, it is necessary to set up, under WADA's coordination, national and international monitoring systems of the demand and the supply of doping products and of the concrete outcomes of anti-doping policies.

Even in a country such as Italy, which has shown over the years an unusual awareness for the problems of doping, many important data about this problem still remain uncollected. For example, some NAS officers (Int-NAS-10 and 25) noted that they are occasionally informed of emergency admissions seemingly caused by the abuse of steroids or other products, but that there is no protocol making sure that all suspicious admissions are recorded and reported. Until the present study, no effort had been made to centralize and make comparable the data about the substances seized by Italy's police forces.

The Swedish government has recently fully recognized the need for a comprehensive monitoring system on doping. In fact, one of the key provisions contained in the 2012 Action Plan for Alcohol, Narcotics, Doping and Tobacco (ANDT) policy consists of the development of a functioning national monitoring system for the ANDT strategy (Government Offices of Sweden 2012).

Ideally, the new national and international monitoring systems should collect data on the following items:

- On the demand side:
  - The number of respondents in household, school, and gym surveys admitting the use of steroids and other doping products.
  - The types and quantities of doping products consumed.
  - The number of doping-related emergency admissions and deaths.
- On the supply side:
  - The amounts of doping substances seized on the basis of standardized units so that the amounts can be added and compared.
  - The share of counterfeited products out of those seized and sold.
  - The prices of the different products, distinguishing between prices of substances at the wholesale and retail level.
  - The share of the worldwide production of some key drugs, such as steroids, EPO, and GH being misused for doping purposes.
  - New products entering the market.

- Concerning anti-doping policies:
  - Doping-related criminal offenses and sanctions foreseen in different countries.
  - The number of criminal proceedings and their outcomes (reports, suspects, defendants, case law and sanctions).

Some of the above-mentioned demand-related data are already being collected in several countries, albeit not always in a consistent and comparable manner. A number of countries, particularly in Scandinavia but also elsewhere (e.g., the Netherlands and USA; see Anti Doping Denmark et al. 2012; Johnston et al., 2012), routinely survey high-school students and/or households about their use of steroids, as has also taken place in Italy with the Italian Drugs and Alcohol Population Survey in 2007 (see Chap. 2). Whereas the Italian government has never officially published its 2007 household survey data and has stopped collecting them in a more recent survey, other nations do publish these data in national reports, but the latter have never been centralized. Data about steroid use among 15–16-year-old adolescents have instead been collected in a standardized way in several waves since 1997 as part of the European School Survey on Alcohol and Other Drugs (ESPAD). In 2007, the study comprised 35 countries and more than 100,000 students (Hibell et al., 2009; see also Hibell et al., 1997, 2000). Given the concentration of doping use in gyms and fitness centers, it would also be advisable to organize periodic surveys among their patrons, as already happens in Sweden (Swedish National Institute of Public Health, 2010: 33). Ideally these surveys should be conducted on the basis of a standardized questionnaire to be used in different countries.

Very little information is as of yet available on other demand-side data. As discussed in the preceding pages, only a few studies have collected episodic data on the types and quantities of substances consumed and users' polypharmacy (e.g., Perry et al., 2005; Parkinson and Evans, 2006); they have, however, used different methodologies so that their results are not directly comparable. We are not aware of any country publishing data on doping-related emergency admissions and deaths.

As far as demand-related data are concerned, WADA or other bodies willing to set up such an international monitoring system could rely upon existing regional networks, such as ESPAD. These bodies could also take contact with the European Monitoring Centre on Drugs and Drug Addiction (EMCDDA), an EU agency that was set up in 1993 to provide the European Community (now EU) and its Member States with "factual, objective, reliable and comparable information at European level concerning drugs and drug addiction and their consequences" (European Monitoring Centre on Drugs and Drug Addiction 2012). Since then, the EMCDDA has dramatically improved the quantity and quality of the data available, particularly about the demand for illegal drugs, setting up a network of national Focal Points in the EU's 27 Member States and its associated countries (Norway and Turkey; see European Monitoring Centre on Drugs and Drug Addiction 2011). In the last few years, the EMCDDA has also been attempting to develop and collect indicators concerning drug supply. Alternatively, WADA and other bodies could also enhance the existing cooperation with the United Nations Office on Drugs and Crime (UNODC), which also collects data on illicit drug demand and supply from the states that are party to the three UN conventions which constitute the pillars of the international drug control regime (see United Nations Office on Drugs and Crime 2012).

Given the more limited scope, the data collected by the EMCDDA through its networks of Focal Points are of better quality than those collected by UNODC. If WADA could reach an agreement with the EMCDDA, it might be able to set up a monitoring system at least for the prevalence of steroids in the general or school populations, the number of doping-related deaths, and emergency admission in large parts of Europe or all over the world in a relatively timely and cost-effective manner. If these data already exist at the national level, the EMCCDA's national Focal Points would only have to add an item to their data collection protocols. If the data do not yet exist, the joint requests of WADA and EMCDDA might stimulate the collection of such items over time, setting up the positive dynamics that also enhanced the collection of drug-related data. A similar attempt, even if localized on a single continent, could become the cornerstone of a worldwide monitoring system. Countries like Australia and the USA that are already collecting data on the consumption of doping products would most likely be interested in contributing to it.

Aware of EMCDDA's difficulties in setting up indicators for drug supply trends, we anticipate greater hurdles in collecting comparable supply-side data than in collecting data on demand. As far as illegal drugs are concerned, in fact, law enforcement agencies have their own data collection and storing procedures, which are difficult to standardize because they usually reflect the requirements of different criminal justice systems. Nonetheless, WADA's eventual efforts to set up an international monitoring system of the supply of doping products might profit from the very novelty of the topic, as national data collection procedures might not be yet rigidly institutionalized as in the case of illegal drugs.

Data about the amounts of doping substances seized serve to monitor both the supply and policy outcomes. Given the multiplicity of products and different packaging available, crucial responsibility is to establish standardized units of measure, similar to the doping doses "invented" by NAS and Donati, to make sure that the seizure data from the individual countries can be compared and combined.

Whereas it is up to academic scholars to research the adverse effects of the different doping products, the national and international monitoring systems should collect data on the quality of the products seized and (if possible) sold, that is, the share of counterfeited products out of the total amount seized and sold. By collecting information on specialized Web sites, the national governments, NADOs, and/or WADA could also rather easily collect information on the prices of the different products. If these Internet data were complemented with data drawn from criminal investigations, those responsible for the monitoring systems could also distinguish between wholesale and retail prices. As happens in the field of illegal drugs (U.S. Drug Enforcement Administration 2012), sample purchases could be arranged at regular intervals to monitor the prices and quality of the substances bought.

The national governments, NADOs, and/or WADA could also develop early warning systems to monitor the new substances entering the market, as was done by

De Hon and Van Kleij (2005) for the Netherlands. These two researchers regularly accessed Internet forums to become aware of the new products being consumed. Internet searches, eventually supplemented by criminal investigations, could complement well the activities of the European Observatory for New Doping Substances established in 2011 at the German Sport University (2011) in Cologne, Germany. This observatory aims to obtain timely information about new drugs produced by the pharmaceutical industry that can be misused for doping purposes.

If it decides to establish an international early warning system, WADA could again profit from the EMCDDA's experience, which collects data on new psychoactive substances within EU jointly with Europol (European Monitoring Centre on Drugs and Drug Addiction 2012). EMCDDA not only warns its national Focal Points about the availability of new substances but also collects information on these substances through the Focal Points. In at least one case, EMCDDA has collected data on a psychoactive substance that is also used for doping purposes, GHB or γ-Hydroxybutyric acid (European Monitoring Centre on Drugs and Drug Addiction 2002).

Last but not least, national and international policy-makers are called on to collect data about the share of the worldwide production of some key drugs, such as steroids, EPO, and GH, being misused for doping purposes. For some drugs with limited therapeutic value, such as gonadorelin, estimating this share could be rather straightforward, once the global production figures become available. For other drugs with multiple therapeutic usages, it would be much more difficult to monitor the share of legitimately produced drugs that end up on the doping market. However, such estimates are crucial to negotiate a reduction of global drug production with pharmaceutical companies or at the very least to convince these companies to introduce more effective controls to cut down diversion.

We are not in a position to assess the extent to which, beyond Italy, national monitoring systems concerning anti-doping policies are already in place. The international monitoring system would have to be set up almost from scratch. However, the technical challenges are less daunting than for supply-side data; setting up an international monitoring system on anti-doping policies and their outcomes is primarily a question of political will. Houlihan and García (2012), for example, published a report on doping-related legislation and sanctions in 2012, which had been commissioned by UNESCO and WADA. Beyond legislation, WADA could start requesting, and publishing on its Web site, data about the number of doping-related suspects and proceedings as well as the outcomes of those proceedings from the states party to the UNESCO Convention on a voluntary basis and then formalize the requirements after a trial period. Alternatively, WADA could instruct its NADOs to collect such data. Through the NADOs, WADA could also obtain copies of the verdicts of doping-related criminal proceedings and publish them on its Web site, after deleting all personal identification data, as it already does for CAS decisions.

We are convinced that with time such a monitoring system would not only give a much better overview of the different facets of the doping problem and related policy responses worldwide and allow evidence-based evaluations of the policy effectiveness but could also reciprocally stimulate national policy-makers to emulate the best practices of other countries.

8.3 Concluding Remarks: WADA at a Crossroad

We are fully aware of the fact that many of the above-mentioned suggestions and lessons for policy-making fall outside the scope of WADA's current mandate. Nonetheless, we are convinced that WADA can play a crucial role in campaigning to implement them.

In our view, WADA, along with its funding bodies and sponsors, finds itself at a crossroad. Pursuant to its current mandate, WADA may continue to focus on elite sports, as it has done until now. If its mandate were to be expanded, however, WADA could attempt to tackle the problem of doping in all its aspects. Remaining focused on elite athletes' testing means neglecting the reality of the public health problem represented by the spread of doping product use among recreational athletes and noncompetitive sportspeople. In our view, a broader approach could also help better contain the problem of doping in sports. Our analysis of the Italian market for doping products has clearly shown that there is no clear-cut separation between elite and recreational sports. As argued in the previous pages, criminal prosecution and other supply-side interventions can deliver positive results but presuppose an integrated approach, with no a priori distinction between doping in sports and other contexts. In fact, the law enforcement agencies and other bodies eventually called on to implement such interventions cannot know in advance who the final customers of the suppliers they investigate are. To quote once more the Italian Prosecutor Guariniello (2011), "numerous investigations and verdicts have shed light on the criminality of the trade in performance-enhancing substances, even if the trader has no intention of altering the competitive performance of athletes. This situation is exemplified by the trade directed at users who do not take part in competitive activities even though they attend fitness clubs or take part in sporting activities."

To enable WADA to adopt a broader approach encompassing different aspects of the doping problem, national governments are called on not only to broaden WADA's mandate but also to provide it with sufficient resources to manage the new tasks and operate effectively. "The sport industry is estimated now to be an $800 billion a year business," WADA Director General Howman (2011a) notes. Referring to the yearly amounts worldwide invested in anti-doping, he goes on: "Spending $300 million to protect the integrity of such a business does not seem to be an awful amount of money. In fact, one could easily mount an argument that sport is not spending enough to defeat the biggest scourge it currently confronts."

Alas, since 1999 many national governments have not shown persistent commitment in supporting WADA's activities. Governments, for example, often fail to pay their promised contributions on time, sometimes not paying at all, or oppose even modest increases in WADA's budget (Sportausschuss des Deutschen Bundestages 2011: 12).[10] Since the IOC has a policy of only matching payments that governments

[10] In 2012, for example, WADA (2013b) invoiced national governments US$13,201,048 but received only US$10,613,946, thus US$2,596,102 less than expected. As the IOC pays only matching funds, WADA thus faced an unexpected loss of over $5 million dollars corresponding to about 20 % of its budget.

have already made to WADA, when governments fail to pay a certain amount, the IOC also refuses to pay the same amount; as a result, WADA loses twice the amount the governments have held back (World Anti-Doping Agency 2013b, c). In such a way, governments prevent WADA from fulfilling properly even its current mandate—for example, due to financial restrictions, not all samples are tested for EPO (Howman, 2011a).

To quote once again Pound (2011a):

> How committed are both governments and sports authorities to the fight against doping in sport, as measured by how much they are willing to support the activities of WADA? My experience is that the sports authorities in particular are unwilling to recognize the importance of and to support robust anti-doping programs. The Government members of WADA are consumed by finding ways to reduce their expenditures, rather than to increase them.
>
> We regularly encounter statistical manipulation by governments. When the absolute numbers are ridiculously low, given the challenges faced in the fight against doping in sport, people point to percentages, rather than numbers. An annual budget of US$25 million to cover 215 countries is miniscule. If we wish to increase a budget category from, say, $6 million to $12 million, the absolute amount of $6 million, divided by 2, to result in governments paying, collectively, $3 million, is minimal. But, instead, they resort to percentages, screaming that it represents a 100 % increase. This is particularly the case for governments, which, in my view, confuse, perhaps deliberately, effective programming and budget management. This put in play their real commitment to the fight against doping in sport.
>
> At the same time, all parties, both government and sport, are continually calling upon WADA to increase its activities, but they are unwilling to pay for such activities.
>
> Parties, particularly the sport side of the equation, are continually looking for ways to transfer their responsibility for anti-doping activities to someone else, whether WADA or governments.

If governments and sports ruling bodies do not show a more consistent engagement against doping, they should not be surprised if the outcomes of anti-doping policies are disappointing.

Appendix A

Suppliers

- Gender.
- Age at the time of investigation.
- Education at the time of investigation.
- Ethnicity/nationality/country of residence.
- Involvement in producing/trafficking doping products, including the level or stage of the market and role in producing/trafficking enterprises, if relevant.
- Background and possible role in elite or recreational sport (e.g., professional criminal, physician, team manager, professional or recreational sportsman, student).
- Criminal records.
- "Criminal career" (e.g., how did the offender start producing/trafficking doping products; was he/she involved in any other related or unrelated criminal activities?).
- Motivation (e.g., money, medals, prestige, other).

Enterprises and modus operandi (For each item, we are interested in both the current state of play and in trends or shifts over time.)

- Composition and stability of producing/trafficking enterprises (including number of "employees," duration of "employment" relationships, and duration of overall enterprise).
- Level or stage of market at which enterprises operate (wholesale, middle, retail).
- Doping products produced/trafficked.
- Production/trafficking throughput, consisting of scale (minimum, maximum, and average quantity of substances produced/trafficked) and frequency.
- Production/trafficking techniques (e.g., use of labs, techniques, smuggling, marketing and other sales techniques, dilution or "cutting," internet use).
- Production/trafficking sites (e.g., legitimate pharmaceutical businesses, homes, gyms, professional premises, schools and universities, internet, others).

L. Paoli and A. Donati, *The Sports Doping Market: Understanding Supply and Demand, and the Challenges of Their Control*, DOI 10.1007/978-1-4614-8241-3,

- Sources of financing for production and trafficking enterprises (e.g., reinvestment of doping revenues or revenues from other crimes, misappropriation of university/public funds, misuse of sport team funds, legitimate income, other).
- Sources of products (diversion vs. black market; domestic vs. foreign).
- Efforts to conceal doping business/degree of secrecy, including adaptive responses to law enforcement and judicial actions.
- Use or threat of use of violence.
- Use of corruption.
- Revenues, profits, shares of profits spent and saved, and location of spending and savings (do funds flow out of or remain in Italy?).

Products and markets (For each item, we are interested in both the current state of play and in trends or shifts over time.)

- Doping products, i.e., substances and methods, produced/trafficked.
- Market levels or stages for each product.
- Throughput of products at each market level or stage, accounting, if possible, for product dilution or "cutting."
- Costs of production/trafficking at each market level or stage.
- Prices of products at each market level or stage.
- Estimation of number of production/trafficking enterprises for each product and at each market level or stage.
- Relationships among enterprises (e.g., collaboration or competition).
- Degree of integration of market for each doping product with markets for other doping products and other legal and illegal drugs.
- Number of users of main doping products, distinguishing, if possible, between past and current users and between occasional and heavy users.
- Amounts used, distinguishing between occasional and heavy users.

Control efforts (For each item, we are interested in both the current state of play and in trends or shifts over time.)

- Number of anti-doping investigations, reports, and arrests per year and per regional unit of the NAS (Nuclei Antisofisticazioni e Sanità) of the Carabinieri.
- Number of anti-doping investigations, reports, and arrests per year by other police units or law enforcement authorities.
- Resulting convictions and sentences, including the nature of sentences (e.g., monetary fines, losses of titles, imprisonment).
- Personnel and other resources devoted to anti-doping per NAS unit.
- Relationships between NAS/anti-doping units and judicial authorities (What priority do prosecutors and judges give to anti-doping investigations? How have their attitudes changed over time? Do they appear to be adhering to a particular policy or are their actions more reflective of single personalities?).
- Relationships between NAS/anti-doping units and the Commissione per la Vigilanza ed il controllo sul Doping e per la tutela della salute nelle attività sportive (hereafter CVD).

- Number of criminal investigations arising from anti-doping tests of athletes.
- Relationships between NAS/anti-doping units and international police agencies.
- Number of anti-doping investigations in Italy that originate from, or involve some amount of international cooperation.
- Challenges that anti-doping law enforcement and judicial authorities face, especially with respect to supply control.

Appendix B

Preliminary Estimate of the Doses of Doping Substances Consumed in Italy and Their Value on the Basis of 100 Consumption Profiles

L. Paoli and A. Donati, *The Sports Doping Market: Understanding Supply and Demand, and the Challenges of Their Control*, DOI 10.1007/978-1-4614-8241-3,

Key data

Athletes (4.685.257)

Rate of positive cases in CVD's 2008–2011 tests (3,8%)

Estimate athlete users (150.000=68,6%)

Estimate body-builder users (68.700=31,4%)

Total number of estimated users 218.700

Doping doses consumed yearly by 100 ideal typical users of doping products

	Stimulants	*Diuretics*	*Gluco-corticoste-roids*	*Anabolic agents*	*Peptide hormones*	*Beta-blockers*	*Narcotics*	*Hormone modulators*	*Beta-2 agonists*	*Total*
Elite athletes										
Cyclist	400	–	320	800	280	–	160	–	240	2,200
Weightlifter	300	1,200	240	1,600	360	–	240	–	200	4,140
Rower	–	–	280	700	240	–	120	–	–	1,340
Recreational athletes										
Cyclist	240	–	200	600	260	–	–	–	200	1,500
Juniores cyclist	160	–	160	800	240	–	80	–	200	1,640
Sprinter cyclist	240	–	220	600	260	–	80	–	300	1,700
Long-distance cyclist	160	–	280	500	220	–	120	–	200	1,480
Long-distance cyclist	160	–	200	600	200	–	80	–	220	1,460
Long-distance cyclist	160	–	220	600	220	–	160	–	200	1,560
Long-distance cyclist	200	–	120	500	160	–	80	–	200	1,260
Long-distance cyclist	140	–	120	240	200	–	80	–	240	1,020
Long-distance cyclist	140	–	100	360	120	–	–	–	200	920
Sprinter cyclist	160	–	80	300	80	–	80	–	160	860
Sprinter cyclist	240	–	160	440	120	–	–	–	100	1,060
Track & field—roadrunner	80	–	80	140	160	–	–	–	–	460
Track & field—long-distance runner	80	–	80	140	120	–	–	–	–	420
Track & field—long-distance runner	80	–	60	140	120	–	–	–	–	400
Track & field—long-distance runner	80	–	40	200	120	–	–	–	–	440

	Stimulants	*Diuretics*	*Gluco-corticoste-roids*	*Anabolic agents*	*Peptide hormones*	*Beta-blockers*	*Narcotics*	*Hormone modulators*	*Beta-2 agonists*	*Total*
Track & field—long-distance runner	80	–	80	140	160	–	–	–	–	460
Track & field—long-distance runner	80	–	60	100	120	–	–	–	–	360
Track & field—sprinter	140	1,100	160	300	160	–	–	–	220	2,080
Track & field—thrower	200	1,600	240	500	160	–	–	–	300	3,000
Track & field—walker	80	–	80	200	120	–	–	–	–	480
Rower	80	–	140	360	120	–	40	–	160	900
Rower	80	–	160	300	120	–	–	–	–	660
Canoeist	160	–	120	300	160	–	40	–	160	940
Canoeist	80	–	180	300	140	–	–	–	160	860
Cross-country skier	120	–	140	160	140	–	–	–	–	560
Cross-country skier	80	–	100	80	160	–	–	–	–	420
Cross-country skier	120	–	140	160	160	–	–	–	–	580
Swimmer	120	–	120	400	120	–	–	–	200	960
Swimmer	80	–	80	320	160	–	–	–	200	840
Tri-athlete	120	–	240	320	120	–	40	–	–	840
Tri-athlete	200	–	180	240	160	–	–	–	–	780
Tennis player	120	–	160	400	160	–	–	–	240	1,080
Football player	140	–	180	440	160	–	40	–	300	1,260
Football player	200	–	180	400	160	–	40	–	240	1,220
Football player	140	–	220	320	180	–	80	–	200	1,140
Football player	200	–	140	300	120	–	40	–	240	1,040
Football player	200	–	180	220	140	–	80	–	120	940
Football player	220	–	80	240	120	–	40	–	120	820
Football player	160	–	220	240	180	–	40	–	120	960
Football player	160	–	60	120	160	–	40	–	120	660
Football player	200	–	160	240	160	–	60	–	200	1,020
Basket player	120	–	80	220	160	–	40	–	–	620
Basket player	160	–	80	160	160	–	160	–	–	720
Rugby player	200	–	280	280	160	–	160	–	80	1,160

(continued)

(continued)

	Stimulants	Diuretics	Gluco-corticoste-roids	Anabolic agents	Peptide hormones	Beta-blockers	Narcotics	Hormone modulators	Beta-2 agonists	Total
Rugby player	160	–	220	200	120	–	120	–	–	820
Downhill skier	180	–	120	200	120	–	–	–	–	620
Slalom skier	120	–	80	200	120	–	–	–	–	520
Long-distance skater	160	–	160	240	120	–	–	–	–	680
Long-distance skater	140	–	220	200	120	–	–	–	–	680
Long-distance wheelchair athlete	160	–	120	200	120	–	40	–	–	640
Martial arts player	240	1,400	120	300	120	–	160	–	–	2,340
Martial arts player	240	1,200	80	180	–	–	120	–	–	1,820
Martial arts player	340	1,400	160	300	120	–	120	–	–	2,440
Water polo player	400	–	220	180	–	–	–	–	–	800
Gymnast	180	800	180	180	–	–	40	–	–	1,380
Weightlifter	300	1,600	220	300	80	–	120	–	–	2,620
Weightlifter	400	2,000	160	280	–	–	120	–	–	2,960
Du-athlete	300	1,000	140	40	–	-	–	–	–	1,480
Pentathlete	240	–	100	140	–	–	–	–	–	480
Biathlete	–	–	100	120	–	–	–	–	–	220
Ice skater	240	–	–	140	120	–	–	–	–	500
Golf player	–	–	–	120	80	400	–	–	–	600
Other sports	320	600	–	140	80	800	–	–	–	1,940
Other sports	200	1,000	120	–	80	–	160	–	–	1,560
Other sports	–	–	–	40	–	–	–	–	–	40
Other sports	–	–	–	120	–	–	–	–	–	120
Total doses used by ideal typical athletes	*11,380*	*14,900*	*9,720*	*20,840*	*9,180*	*1,200*	*3,220*	–	*6,040*	*76,480*
%	*14.88*	*19.48*	*12.71*	*27.25*	*12.00*	*1.57*	*4.21*	–	*7.90*	*100.00*
Total doses used by 150,000 athletes	*24,739,130*	*32,391,304*	*21,130,435*	*45,304,348*	*19,956,522*	*2,608,696*	*7,000,000*	–	*13,130,435*	*166,260,870*

	Stimulants	Diuretics	Gluco-corticoste-roids	Anabolic agents	Peptide hormones	Beta-blockers	Narcotics	Hormone modulators	Beta-2 agonists	Total
Body-builders										
Body-builder	360	5	20	3,200	60	–	–	10	–	3,655
Body-builder	400	–	–	2,400	60	–	–	–	–	2,860
Body-builder	400	–	–	2,800	50	–	–	10	–	3,260
Body-builder	440	–	–	2,400	60	–	–	–	–	2,900
Body-builder	460	–	20	2,800	60	–	–	10	–	3,350
Body-builder	340	–	–	2,000	60	–	–	–	–	2,400
Body-builder	400	–	40	2,800	50	–	–	–	–	3,290
Body-builder	440	–	–	2,200	60	–	–	–	–	2,700
Body-builder	370	5	–	3,200	50	–	–	–	–	3,625
Body-builder	350	–	–	2,400	60	–	–	–	–	2,810
Body-builder	470	–	–	2,800	30	–	–	–	–	3,300
Body-builder	350	–	10	2,200	50	–	–	10	–	2,620
Body-builder	500	–	10	2,000	50	–	–	–	–	2,560
Body-builder	320	–	–	3,000	60	–	–	–	–	3,380
Body-builder	360	5	–	2,600	40	–	–	–	–	3,005
Body-builder	400	–	–	2,200	60	–	–	–	–	2,660
Body-builder	420	–	40	2,500	80	–	–	–	–	3,040
Body-builder	380	–	20	3,000	40	–	–	–	–	3,440
Body-builder	440	–	–	2,400	40	–	–	10	–	2,890
Body-builder	400	5	–	2,500	80	–	–	–	–	2,985
Body-builder	400	–	–	2,200	60	–	–	–	–	2,660
Body-builder	380	–	20	2,400	60	–	–	–	–	2,860
Body-builder	440	–	–	2,600	40	–	–	–	–	3,080
Body-builder	320	–	–	2,400	80	–	–	–	–	2,800
Body-builder	360	5	–	3,000	60	–	–	–	–	3,425
Body-builder	400	–	20	2,200	40	–	–	–	–	2,660
Body-builder	400	–	40	2,500	60	–	–	10	–	3,010
Body-builder	380	–	–	2,200	60	–	–	–	–	2,640

(continued)

(continued)

	Stimulants	Diuretics	Gluco-corticoste-roids	Anabolic agents	Peptide hormones	Beta-blockers	Narcotics	Hormone modulators	Beta-2 agonists	Total
Body-builder	380	–	–	2,600	40	–	–	–	–	3,020
Body-builder	400	–	–	2,000	40	–	–	–	–	2,440
Body-builder	340	–	–	2,800	60	–	–	–	5	3,205
Total doses used by ideal typical body-builders	*12,200*	*25*	*240*	*78,300*	*1,700*	–	–	*60*	*5*	*92,530*
%	*13.18*	*0.03*	*0.26*	*84.62*	*1.84*	–	–	*0.06*	*0.01*	*100.00*
Total doses used by 68,700 body-builders	*27,036,774*	*55,403*	*531,871*	*173,522,903*	*3,767,419*	–	–	*132,968*	*11,081*	*205,058,419*

Summary Calculations: estimated doses of doping substances consumed in Italy and their value, by type of users and classes of substances

	Stimulants	Diuretics	Gluco-corticoste-roids	Anabolic agents	Peptide hormones	Beta-blockers	Narcotics	Hormone modulators	Beta-2 agonists	Total
Doses used by athletes	24,739,130	32,391,304	21,130,435	45,304,348	19,956,522	2,608,696	7,000,000	–	13,130,435	166,260,870
Doses used by body-builders	27,036,774	55,403	531,871	173,522,903	3,767,419	–	–	132,968	11,081	205,058,419
Total doses	51,775,905	32,446,708	21,662,306	218,827,251	23,723,941	2,608,696	7,000,000	132,968	13,141,515	371,319,289
% doses	13.94	8.74	5.83	58.93	6.39	0.70	1.89	0.04	3.54	100.00
Price per dose in Euro	0.60	0.40	0.49	1.12	4.77	0.28	1.28	1.26	0.20	
Total value in Euro	30,961,991	12,881,343	10,679,517	244,648,867	113,114,670	717,391	8,974,000	167,140	2,615,162	424,760,081
% value of doses	7.29	3.03	2.51	57.60	26.63	0.17	2.11	0.04	0.62	100.00
Value in Euro of athletes' doses	14,794,000	12,859,348	10,417,304	50,650,261	95,151,787	717,391	8,974,000	–	2,612,957	196,177,047
Value in Euro of body-builders' doses	16,167,991	21,995	262,212	193,998,606	17,962,884	–	–	167,140	2,205	228,583,034
Athletes' average doses	164.93	215.94	140.87	302.03	133.04	17.39	46.67	–	87.54	1,108.41
Body-builders' average doses	393.55	0.81	7.74	2,525.81	54.84	–	–	1.94	0.16	2,984.84
Athletes' average expense in Euro	98.63	85.73	69.45	337.67	634.35	4.78	59.83	–	17.42	1,307.85
Body-builders' average expense in Euro	235.34	0.32	3.82	2,823.85	261.47	–	–	2.43	0.03	3,327.26

References

Adnkronos. (1998). *Commissione Grosso: Doping, 'Federcalcio Corresponsabile'*. Retrieved from http://www.adnkronos.com/Archivio/AdnAgenzia/1998/10/14/Sport/COMMISSIONE-GROSSO-DOPING-FEDERCALCIO-CORRESPONSABILE_172900.php

AFP. (2002). *IOC cannot win doping war, says Rogge*. Retrieved from http://archives.dawn.com/2002/01/01/spt14.htm

AFP. (2007). *Couto receives suspended prison sentence for doping*. Retrieved from http://www.soccerway.com/news/2007/April/02/couto-receives-suspended-prison-sentence-for-doping/

AFP. (2011, November 14). *WADA chief says more must be done in doping fight*. Retrieved from http://www.google.com/hostednews/afp/article/ALeqM5g9YYPqsDJbXuqeugjD3f7IL9q0FQ?docId=CNG.f8a1357252414e391fa429a67d8b9601.4a1

Akinde, M. (2006). Cycling's winter of discontent. The reason why. *Daily Peloton*. Retrieved from http://www.dailypeloton.com/displayarticle.asp?pk=10163

Anti Doping Denmark, Dopingautoriteit, STAD, Instytut Sportu and CyADA. (2012). *Strategy for stopping steroids*. Retrieved from http://www.antydoping.pl/upload/2012/strategy_for_stopping_steroids_report_web.pdf

Arioli, G., & Bellini, V. (2005). *Disposizioni penali in materia di doping*. Milan: Giuffré.

Arlacchi, P., & Lewis, R. (1990). *Imprenditorialità illecita e droga. Il mercato dell'eroina a Verona*. Il Mulino: Bologna.

Ashenden, M., Gough, C., Garnham, A., Gore, C., & Sharpe, K. (2011). Current markers of the Athlete Blood Passport do not flag microdose EPO doping. *European Journal of Applied Physiology, 111*(9), 2307–2314.

Associated Press. (2008, October 3). *Doping inquiry is halted*. Retrieved from http://query.nytimes.com/gst/fullpage.html?res=9F07EFDD113FF930A35753C1A96E9C8B63

Associated Press. (2011, April 15). *Italian reports: Thyssenkrupp executives convicted*. Retrieved from http://www.boston.com/business/articles/2011/04/15/italian_reports_thyssenkrupp_executives_convicted/

Associated Press. (2012, August 13). IOC chief lauds efforts to fight doping at London Games. *Boston Globe*. Retrieved from http://www.bostonglobe.com/sports/2012/08/12/olympic-notebook/6QBoz6j52wezZ0q09ryyCP/story.html

Audisio, E. (1986, March 1986). I sussurri dopo la droga. *La Repubblica, 18*. Retrieved from http://ricerca.repubblica.it/repubblica/archivio/repubblica/1986/03/20/sussurri-dopo-la-droga.html

Audisio, E. (1987a, October 29). A un anno da Seoul lo sprint azzurro e' di nuovo nel caos. *La Repubblica, 26*.

Audisio, E. (1987b, December 16). Hanno ucciso l'atletica. *La Repubblica, 49*. Retrieved from http://ricerca.repubblica.it/repubblica/archivio/repubblica/1987/12/16/hanno-ucciso-atletica.html

L. Paoli and A. Donati, *The Sports Doping Market: Understanding Supply and Demand, and the Challenges of Their Control*, DOI 10.1007/978-1-4614-8241-3,

Audisio, E. (1987c, December 24). Nebiolo fugge nel silenzio. *La Repubblica, 17*. Retrieved from http://ricerca.repubblica.it/repubblica/archivio/repubblica/1987/12/24/nebiolo-fugge-nel-silenzio.html

Audisio, E. (2000, November 18). Ora la legge apre una nuova era Abbiate la forza di applicarla. *La Repubblica, 58*. Retrieved from http://ricerca.repubblica.it/repubblica/archivio/repubblica/2000/11/18/ora-la-legge-apre-una-nuova-era.html

Audisio, E. (2007, May 9). Ho parlato, mi hanno distrutto ma adesso la svolta è matura. *La Repubblica, 58*. Retrieved from http://ricerca.repubblica.it/repubblica/archivio/repubblica/2007/05/09/ho-parlato-mi-hanno-distrutto-ma-adesso.html

Australian Senate Standing Committee on the Environment, Recreation and the Arts. (1989). *Drugs in Sport* (so-called Black Report). Canberra: Australian Government Publishing Service.

Australian Sports Anti-Doping Authority. (2012). 2010:11 Annual Report. Retrieved from http://www.asada.gov.au/publications/annual_reports/asada_annual_report_2010_11/downloads/ASADA_annual_report_2010_11.pdf

Ayres, I., & Braithwaite, J. (1992). *Responsive regulation: Transcending the deregulation debate*. New York: Oxford University Press.

Backhouse, S., McKenna, J., Robinson, S., & Atkin, A. (2007). *International literature review: Attitudes, behaviours, knowledge and education—Drugs in sport: Past, present and future*. Retrieved from http://www.wada-ama.org/rtecontent/document/Backhouse_et_al_Full_Report.pdf

Baker, J. S., Graham, M., & Davies, B. (2006). Gym users and abuse of prescription drugs. *Journal of the Royal Society of Medicine, 99*, 331–333.

Bannenberg, B., & Rössner, D. (2006). Straftat gegen den Wettbewerb. Plädoyer für den Einsatz des Strafrechts bei Dopingverstößen. In J. Weinreich (Ed.), *Korruption im Sport. Mafiöse Dribblings, Organisiertes Schweigen* (pp. 214–227). Leipzig: Forum.

Bassons, C. (2000). *Positif*. Paris: Stock.

BBC. (2009). *Boonen banned from Tour de France*. Retrieved from http://news.bbc.co.uk/sport2/hi/other_sports/cycling/8041462.stm

Beel, A., Maycock, B., & McClean, N. (1998). Current perspectives on anabolic steroids. *Drug and Alcohol Review, 17*, 87–103.

Bellotti, P. (1999). Perizia del dottor Pasquale Bellotti e del centro di ematologia dell'ospedale Careggi di Firenze.

Bellotti, P. (2009). Relazione al II Master Intensivo per Ispettore Investigativo Antidoping.

Berendonk, B. (1992). *Doping: von der Forschung zum Betrug*. Hamburg: Rowohlt.

Bergonzi, P., & Kindhauser, E. (2001). Die seltsamen Methoden des «Dottor Mito» *Die Weltwoche* (No. 38/2001). Retrieved from http://www.weltwoche.ch/ausgaben/2001-38/artikel-2001-38-die-seltsamen-me.html

Berruti, G. M. (2011, July 27). Perché i magistrati sono protagonisti. *La Repubblica, 28*. Retrieved from http://ricerca.repubblica.it/repubblica/archivio/repubblica/2011/07/27/perche-magistrati-sono-protagonisti.html

Berwick, A. (2011). *A European declaration of independence*. London. Retrieved from http://unitednations.ispnw.org/

Berwick, A. (2011). *A European declaration of independence*. London. Retrieved from http://unitednations.ispnw.org/archives/breivik-manifesto-2011.pdf

Bette, K. (2008). Doping im Leistungssport—zwischen individueller Schuld und kollektiver Verantwortung. *Deutsche Zeitschrift für Sportmedizin, 59*(1), 5–11.

Bette, K. (2011). *Sportsoziologische Aufklärung: Studien zum Sport der modernen Gesellschaft*. Bielefeld: transcript.

Bette, K., & Schimank, U. (2000). Doping als Konstellationsprodukt. Eine soziologische Analyse. In: M. Gamper, J. Mühlethaler, & F. Reidhaar (Eds.), *Doping. Spitzensport als gesellschaftliches problem* (pp. 91–112). Zürich: NZZ.

Bette, K., & Schimank, U. (2006). *Doping im Hochleistungssport. Anpassung durch Abweichung*. Suhrkamp: Frankfurt.

Blackshaw, I. (2012). *Winning the war on doping*. Retrieved from http://www.asser.nl/default.aspx?site_id=11&level1=13910&level2=13974&level3=&textid=35949

Blackshaw, I. *ISLJ Opinion: WADA should ban athletes who take recreational drugs*. Retrieved from http://www.asser.nl/default.aspx?site_id=11&level1=13910&level2=13974&level3=&textid=35961

Blumenthal, Z. (2010). The punishment of all athletes: The need for a new world-antidoping code in sports. *Journal of International Business & Law, 9*, 201–230.

Bolding, G., Sherr, L., & Elford, J. (2002). Use of anabolic steroids and associated health risks among gay men attending London gyms. *Addiction, 97*, 195–201.

Bouchard, M., & Morselli, C. (2013). Opportunistic structures of organized crime. In L. Paoli (Ed.), *Oxford handbook of organized crime*. New York: Oxford University Press.

Braithwaite, J. (1984). *Corporate crime in the pharmaceutical industry*. London: Routledge.

Braithwaite, J. (1985). White collar crime. *Annual Review of Sociology, 11*, 1–25.

Braithwaite, J. (1993). The transnational regulation of the pharmaceutical industry. *Annals of the American Society of Political Sciences, 535*, 12–30.

Braithwaite, J. (2011). Fasken lecture: The essence of responsive regulation. 44 U.B.C. L. Review: 475–520.

Braithwaite, V., & Braithwaite, J. (n.d.). *An evolving compliance model for tax enforcement*. Retrieved from http://vab.anu.edu.au/pubs/1/anevolvingcompliance.pdf

Brissonneau, C. (2007). Le dopage dans le cyclisme professionnel au milieu des années 1990: une reconstruction des valeurs sportives. *Déviance et Société, 2*, 129–148.

Brissonneau, C., Aubel, O., & Ohl, F. (2008). *L'épreuve du dopage. Sociologie du cyclisme professionnel*. Paris: Presses Universitaires De France.

Brissonneau, C., Defrance, J., Fincoeur, B., Lentillon-Kaestner, V., & Ohl, F. (2009). *Carrière sportive et socialisation secondaire en cyclisme sur route : Les cas de la Belgique, la France et la Suisse*. Lausanne: World Anti-Doping Agency.

Brown, G., & Abrahams, B. (2007, December 18). Santuccione banned for life (1st ed.). *Cycling News*. Retrieved from http://autobus.cyclingnews.com/news.php?id=news/2007/dec07/dec18news

Buckley, W. E., Yesalis, C. E., III, Friedl, K. E., Anderson, W. A., Streit, A. L., & Wright, J. E. (1988). Estimated prevalence of anabolic steroid use among male high school seniors. *Journal of the American Medical Association, 260*, 3441–3445.

Bundeskriminalamt. (2011). *Operation "Sladge-Hammer" und "International Pharmaceuticals"*. Retrieved from http://www.bmi.gv.at/cms/BK/presse/files/2_2_2011_Operation_Sladge_Hammer_und_intern_Pharmaceuticals.pdf

Camoni, L., Franco, M., Pugliese, L., Biondi, M., & Rezza, G. (1997). Gli steroidi anabolizzanti come sostanza d'abuso. *Bollettino Per Le Farmacodipendenze E L'alcoolismo, 20(4)*.

Capodacqua, E. (1989a, October 13). Obbligati a prendere steroidi. *La Repubblica, 38*. Retrieved from http://ricerca.repubblica.it/repubblica/archivio/repubblica/1989/10/13/obbligati-prendere-steroidi.html

Capodacqua, E. (1989b, October 12). Seul, fu anche doping italiano. *La Repubblica, 38*.

Capodacqua, E. (1993, November 4). I due Conconi. *La Repubblica, 25*. Retrieved from http://ricerca.repubblica.it/repubblica/archivio/repubblica/1993/11/04/due-conconi.html

Capodacqua, E. (1996a, October 26). 'Attenti, vi aspettano fate sparire tutto'. *La Repubblica, 42*. Retrieved from http://ricerca.repubblica.it/repubblica/archivio/repubblica/1996/10/26/attenti-vi-aspettano-fate-sparire-tutto.html

Capodacqua, E. (1996b, November 1). Tutti i veleni finiscono in Procura. *La Repubblica, 46*. Retrieved from http://ricerca.repubblica.it/repubblica/archivio/repubblica/1996/11/01/tutti-veleni-finiscono-in-procura.html

Capodacqua, E. (1997, March 15). *La Repubblica, 51*. Retrieved from http://ricerca.repubblica.it/repubblica/archivio/repubblica/1997/03/15/il-laboratorio-dei-misteri.html

Capodacqua, E. (2000a). Accuse choc da Ferrara: il Coni dietro al doping. *La Repubblica*. Retrieved from http://www.repubblica.it/online/sport/pantapro/con/con.html?ref=search

Capodacqua, E. (2000b, December 21). Doping, non c'è solo Pantani inchiesta sul ct Fusi e Tonkov. *La Repubblica, 57*. Retrieved from http://ricerca.repubblica.it/repubblica/archivio/repubblica/2000/12/21/doping-non-solo-pantani-inchiesta-sul.html

Capodacqua, E. (2001, February 13). Processo al dr. Ferrari E si riapre il caso gH. *La Repubblica, 54*. Retrieved from http://ricerca.repubblica.it/repubblica/archivio/repubblica/2001/02/13/processo-al-dr-ferrari-si-riapre-il.html

Capodacqua, E. (2002a, June 6). Brescia, inchiesta sul calcio il caso Guardiola nel mirino. *La Repubblica, 58*. Retrieved from http://ricerca.repubblica.it/repubblica/archivio/repubblica/2002/06/06/brescia-inchiesta-sul-calcio-il-caso-guardiola.html

Capodacqua, E. (2002b, April 27). Il medico dei ciclisti al farmacista Hai il Dhea? Voglio 30 scatole. *La Repubblica, 46*. Retrieved from http://ricerca.repubblica.it/repubblica/archivio/repubblica/2002/04/27/il-medico-dei-ciclisti-al-farmacista-hai.html

Capodacqua, E. (2003, November 20). Il file Dblab con i valori del sangue alterati. *La Repubblica, 60*. Retrieved from http://ricerca.repubblica.it/repubblica/archivio/repubblica/2003/11/20/il-file-dblab-con-valori-del-sangue.html

Capodacqua, E. (2009, November 20). Padova, inchiesta doping arrestato dirigente Serbia. *La Repubblica, 60*. Retrieved from http://www.repubblica.it/2009/07/sport/ciclismo/doping-ct-serbia/doping-ct-serbia/doping-ct-serbia.html

Carabinieri. (2012). *Comando Carabinieri per la tutela della salute*. Retrieved from http://www.carabinieri.it/Internet/Cittadino/Informazioni/Tutela/Salute/default.htm

Carlton, D. W., & Fischel, D. (1982–1983). The regulation of insider trading. *Stanford Law Review, 35*, 57.

Cascella, P. (2008, July 30). Anabolizzanti Marco Verzelli di nuovo in manette, *7 of the Bologna section*. Retrieved from http://ricerca.repubblica.it/repubblica/archivio/repubblica/2008/07/30/anabolizzanti-marco-verzelli-di-nuovo-in-manette.html

Casoni, I., Ricci, G., Ballarin, E., Borsetto, C., Grazzi, G., Guglielmini, C., et al. (1993). Hematological indices of erythropoietin administration in athletes. *International Journal of Sports Medicine, 14*(6), 307–311.

Centamore, R. (2011). Gutachten Italien. In M. Parzeller (Ed.), *Rechtsvergleich der strafrechtlichen Normen und der strafprozessualen Verfolgung des Dopings im Leistungs- und Spitzensport in Deutschland, Frankreich, Italien, Schweiz und Spanien*. Bonn: Bundesinstitut für Sportwissenschaft.

Chambliss, W. J. (1967, Summer). Types of deviance and the effectiveness of legal sanctions. *Wisconsin Law Review*, 703–719.

Chantal, Y., Soubranne, R., & Brunel, P. C. (2009). Exploring the social image of anabolic steroids users through motivation, sports personship orientations and aggression. *Scandinavian Journal of Medicine & Science in Sports, 19*(2), 228–234.

Chiusano, M. (1993, March 19). Test sul sangue a Lillehammer, con prudenza .... *La Repubblica, 30*. Retrieved from http://ricerca.repubblica.it/repubblica/archivio/repubblica/1993/03/19/test-sul-sangue-lillehammer-con-prudenza.html

Chiusano, M. (2000, October 15). Medaglie nella tempesta. *La Repubblica, 57*. Retrieved from http://ricerca.repubblica.it/repubblica/archivio/repubblica/2000/10/15/medaglie-nella-tempesta.html

Christiansen, A. V. (2005). The legacy of Festina. Patterns of drug use in European cycling since 1999. *Sport in History, 25*(3), 497–514.

Clarke, M. (1990). *Business crime: Its nature and control*. Oxford: Polity Press.

Clinard, M., & Quinney, R. (1973). *Criminal behavior systems: A typology* (2nd ed.). NewYork: Holt, Rinehart and Winston.

Cnn.com. (2006). *Rumsas receives suspended sentence*. Retrieved from http://edition.cnn.com/2006/SPORT/01/26/cycling.rumsas/

Coackley, J., & Pipe, E. (2009). *Sport in society: Issues and controversies*. Boston: McGraw Hill.

Coffee, J. C. (2007). Law and the market: The impact of enforcement. *Columbia Law and Economics Working Paper No. 304*. Retrieved from http://heinonline.org/HOL/Page?handle=hein.journals/pnlr156&div=15&g_sent=1&collection=journals

Comitato Olimpico Nazionale Italiano. (2008). *I numeri dello sport. Monitoraggio CONI_FSN-DSA*. Retrieved from http://www.coni.it/fileadmin/ops2008/Tavole_Nazionali_Sintetiche_FSN-DSA__2008.pdf

Comitato Olimpico Nazionale Italiano. (2012). *Dati statistici*. Retrieved from http://www.coni.it/index.php?dati_statistici.;http://www.coni.it/fileadmin/_temp_/coni/pdf/controlli_statistici_1987_2000.pdf

Comitato Olimpico Nazionale Italiano and Censis Servizi. (2008, November 1). *I Rapporto Sport & Società*. Retrieved from http://www.coni.it/fileadmin/ops2008/09/ReportSport_e_Societ_2008_01.pdf

Commissione per la vigilanza ed il controllo sul doping e per la tutela della salute nelle attività sportive. (2009, September 28–October 1). Quaderni didattici del Corso per Ispettori antidoping, Roma Istituto Superiore di Sanità.

Conconi, F., Casoni, I., Manfredini, F., Mazzoni, G., Grazzi, G., Guglielmini, C., et al. (1994). Est-il possible de déceler la prise d'érythropoiétine en sport? In P. Hemmersbach & K.I. Birkeland, (Eds.). Blood samples in doping control: Proceedings of the Second International Symposium on Drugs in Sports. Towards the use of blood samples in doping control (pp. 133–140). Oslo: Pensumtjeneste.

Conference of Parties to the International Convention against Doping in Sport. (2011, November 1). Implementation of Article 8 of the International Convention against Doping in Sport. Item 7.2 of the Provisional Agenda. ICDS/3CP/Inf.2. Retrieved from http://unesdoc.unesco.org/images/0021/002140/214045e.pdf

Conrad, P. (2007). *The medicalization of society: On the transformation of human conditions into medical disorders*. Baltimore: Johns Hopkins University Press.

Contini, F., & Fabri, M. (2006). Tecnologie e organizzazione giudiziaria in Italia e in Europa. *Sociologia del Diritto, 2*, 129–140.

Corbo, A. (2004, December 23). Delitti, bicarbonato e cocaina in vent' anni di business e sangue. *La Repubblica, 2 of the Naples section*. Retrieved from http://ricerca.repubblica.it/repubblica/archivio/repubblica/2004/12/23/delitti-bicarbonato-cocaina-in-vent-anni-di.html

Corte d'Appello di Bologna. 2006. Sentenza in data 22 maggio. N 2005/0831 R.G.

Corte Suprema di Cassazione. (2007). Sentenza sul ricorso proposto dalla Procura Generale presso la Corte d'Appello di Torino e dal difensore dell'imputato A.G. avverso la sentenza emessa dalla Corte d'Appello della stessa città in data 14 dicembre 1985. Sentenza n. Reg. Gen. N. 19255/06.

Court of Arbitration for Sport. (2008). *Arbitral Award delivered by the Court of Arbitration of Sport*. CAS 2008/A/1516 WADA v/CONI, FITET and Piacentini. Retrieved from http://www.wada-ama.org/rtecontent/document/CAS_2008_A_1516.pdf

Courtwright, D. T. (2001). *Forces of habit: Drugs and the making of the modern world*. Cambridge: Harvard University Press.

Crosetti, M. (2006). Cinquanta indagati diciotto gare sospette. *La Repubblica*. Retrieved from http://ricerca.repubblica.it/repubblica/archivio/repubblica/2006/05/11/cinquanta-indagati-diciotto-gare-sospette.html

Crowe, J. (2001). Dr. Robert Kerr; Center of Controversy over steroids for athletes: obituaries. *Los Angeles Times*. Retrieved from http://articles.latimes.com/2001/jan/05/local/me-8650

cyclingnews.com. (2000, November 4). Retrieved from http://autobus.cyclingnews.com/results/2000/nov00/nov4news.shtml

D'Hont, J. (2007). *Memoires van een wielerverzorger*. Leuven: Van Halewyck.

Davigo, P., & Sisti, L. (2012). *Processo all'italiana*. Roma: Laterza.

De Arcangelis, I. (2006, May 5). Doping per truccare corse di cavalla. *La Repubblica, 6 of the Naples section*. Retrieved from http://ricerca.repubblica.it/repubblica/archivio/repubblica/2006/05/05/doping-per-truccare-corse-di-cavalli.html

De Arcangelis, I. (2008, November 27). La farmatruffa del doping ricette fasulle: Sette arresti. *La Repubblica, 2 of the Napoli section*. Retrieved from http://ricerca.repubblica.it/repubblica/archivio/repubblica/2008/11/27/la-farmatruffa-del-doping-ricette-fasulle-sette.html

De Hon, O., & van Kleij, R. (2005). Kwaliteit van Illegale Dopingmiddelen. Capelle aan de IJssel: Nederlands Centrum voor Dopingsvraagstukken. Retrieved from http://www.dopingautoriteit.nl/media/files/documenten/Kwaliteit%20Illegale%20Dopingmiddelen.pdf

de Mondenard, J. (1984). *Drogues et dopages*. Paris: Chiron.

de Mondenard, J. (2004). *Dictionnaire de Dopage*. Paris: Masson.

de Mondenard, J. (2009). *La grande imposture*. Paris: Hugo&C.

De Paoli Vitali, E., Guglielmini, C., Casoni, I., Vedovato, M., Gilli, P., Farinelli, A., et al. (1988). Serum erythropoietin in cross-country skiers. *International Journal of Sports Medicine, 9*(2), 99–101.

De Tullio, R. (2002). Relazione del Procuratore Generale, Renato De Tullio, della Corte di Appello di Napoli per l'inaugurazione dell'anno giudiziario 2002.

Department for Culture, Media and Sport. (2009). Consultation on establishing a modernised UK anti-doping organisation. Retrieved from http://www.culture.gov.uk/images/consultations/NADO_consultation.pdf

Der Kurier. (2011, December 31). Doping-Dealer_Pärchen in Kärnten verhaftet.

Der Spiegel. (2003, March 23). Conconi-Prozess abgebrochen: Schwarzer Tag für Italiens Anti-Doping-Kampf. Retrieved from http://www.spiegel.de/sport/sonst/0,1518,242164,00.html

Di Federico, G. (2004). Independence and accountability of the judiciary in Italy. The experience of a former transitional country in a comparative perspective. Retrieved from http://siteresources.worldbank.org/INTECA/Resources/DiFedericopaper.pdf. In A. Sajò (Ed.), *Judicial integrity* (pp. 181–205). Leiden: Koninklijke Brill.

Di Federico, G. (Ed.). (2012). *Ordinamento giudiziario: uffici giudiziari, CSM e governo della magistratura*. Padova: CEDAM.

Di Lello, G. (1994). *Giudici*. Palermo: Sellerio.

DiePresse.com. (2012, January 1). *Millionengewinn mit Doping: Ehepaar in Kärnten verhaftet*. Retrieved from http://diepresse.com/home/sport/mehrsport/720535/Millionengewinn-mit-Doping_Ehepaar-in-Kaernten-verhaftet

Dipani, D. (2004). Aspetti penalistici del doping sportivo. Tesi di laurea. Retrieved from http://www.overlex.com/tesi_doping_indice.asp

Dipartimento Politiche Antidroga. (2010). Relazione annuale al Parlamento sull'uso di sostanze stupefacenti e sulle tossicodipendenze in Italia. Dati relativi all'anno 2009 e elaborazioni 2010. Retrieved from http://www.politicheantidroga.it/media/333133/relazione%202010.pdf

Dipartimento Politiche Antidroga. (2011). Relazione annuale al Parlamento sull'uso di sostanze stupefacenti e sulle tossicodipendenze in Italia. Dati relativi all'anno 2010 e elaborazioni 2011. Retrieved from http://www.politicheantidroga.it/progetti-e-ricerca/relazioni-al-parlamento/relazione-annuale-2011/presentazione.aspx

Dipartimento Politiche Antidroga. (2012a). Data concerning the prevalence of anabolic steroid use in Italy collected through the 2007 Italian Population Survey on Alcohol and other Drugs (IPSAD). Unpublished document.

Dipartimento Politiche Antidroga. (2012b). Relazione annuale al Parlamento sull'uso di sostanze stupefacenti e sulle tossicodipendenze in Italia. Dati relativi all'anno 2011 e elaborazioni 2012. Retrieved from http://www.politicheantidroga.it/progetti-e-ricerca/relazioni-al-parlamento/relazione-annuale-2012/presentazione.aspx

Dodge, T., & Hoagland, M. F. (2011). The use of anabolic androgenic steroids and polypharmacy: A review of the literature. *Drug and Alcohol Dependence, 114*(2–3), 100–109.

Dohrmann, G., & Llosa, L. F. (2006, April 24). Operation gear grinder shut down a flourishing drug business in a BALCO-scale investigation of major steroid trafficking. *Sports Illustrated*. Retrieved from http://sportsillustrated.cnn.com/vault/article/magazine/MAG1110809/index.htm

Donati, A. (1989). *Campioni senza valore*. Firenze: Ponte alle Grazie.

Donati, A. (2003). Anti-doping: The fraud behind the stage. *Ergogenics*. Retrieved from http://www.ergogenics.org/donati.html

Donati, A. (2005). *Relazione al Parlamento sullo stato delle tossicodipendenze: confronto dei risultati delle due ricerche IPSAD ed ESPAD*. Report prepared for the Comitato Scientifico del Ministero.

Donati, A. (2007). *World traffic in doping substances*. Retrieved from http://www.wada-ama.org/Documents/World_Anti-Doping_Program/Governments/WADA_Donati_Report_On_Trafficking_2007.pdf

Donati, A. (2012). *Lo sport del doping. Chi lo subisce, chi lo combatte*. Torino: Edizione Gruppo Abele.

Donati, A., & Magrì, L. (2001). Stima degli importi complessivi delle cessioni. Rapporto preparato per la Procura della Repubblica presso il Tribunale di Bologna.

Donati, A., Pesce, C., & Giampietro, M. (2011). *Prevenire il doping tra gli studenti*. Rome.

Doping Enquiry Taskforce. (2001, May 23). Report. Retrieved from http://www.minedu.fi/export/sites/default/OPM/Julkaisut/2001/liitteet/opm_57_doping_en.pdf?lang=fi

Dopingkommission. (2009). Abschlussbericht der Expertenkommission zur Aufklärung von Dopingvorwürfen gegenüber Ärtzen der Abteilung Sportmedizin des Universitätsklinikums Freiburg. Retrieved from http://www.uniklinik-freiburg.de/presse/live/abschlussbericht/Abschlussbericht.pdf

Dorn, N. (1992). Clarifying options on drug policy. In P. A. O'Hare, R. Newcombe, A. Matthews, E. C. Buning, & E. Drucker (Eds.), *The reduction of drug-related harm* (pp. 108–121). London: Routledge.

Dorn, N., Levi M., Artingstall D., & Howell J. (2009). Impacts of financial crimes and amenability to control by the FSA: Proposed framework for generating data in a comparative manner. *Social Sciences Research Network*. Retrieved from http://papers.ssrn.com/sol3/papers.cfm?abstract_id=1458366

Dorn, N., Levi, M., & King, L. (2005). *Literature review on upper level drug trafficking*. Home Office Online Report 22/05.

Dubin, C. L. (1990). *Commission of inquiry into the use of drugs and banned practices intended to increase athletic performance*. Ottawa: Canadian Government Publishing Centre.

Dunning, E. (1986). The dynamics of modern sport: Notes on the achievement-striving and the social significance of sport. In N. Elias & E. Dunning (Eds.), *Quest for excitement*. Oxford: Blackwell.

DuRant, R. H., Ashworth, C. S., Newman, C., & Rickert, V. I. (1994). Stability of the relationships between anabolic steroid use and multiple substance use among adolescents. *Journal of Adolescent Health: Official Publication of The Society for Adolescent Medicine, 15*(2), 111–116.

Ehrenberg, A. (1991). *Le culte de la performance*. Parijs: Calmann-Lévy.

Elkin, S. L., Brady, S., & Williams, I. P. (1997). Bodybuilders find it easy to obtain insulin to help them in training. *British Medical Journal, 314*(*7089*), 1280.

Eric, J. (1999). Chercheur du CIO et faiseur de champions. Conconi, roi de l'hémotransfusion, est soupçonné de dopage en Italie. *Liberation*. Retrieved from http://www.liberation.fr/sports/0101288625-chercheur-du-cio-et-faiseur-de-champions-conconi-roi-de-l-hemotransfusion-est-soupconne-de-dopage-en-italie

Escriva, J. (2001). Sport intensif et dopages entre normes et déviances. *Sociétés contemporaines, 44*, 129–147.

European Commission. (2006). Community support plan to combat doping in sport. Communication from the Commission to the Council, the European Parliament, the Economic and Social Committee and the Committee of the Regions: Community support plan to combat doping in sport. *COM(99)*, 643. Retrieved from http://europa.eu/legislation_summaries/education_training_youth/sport/l35003_en.htm

European Commission. (2007). *White Paper on Sport* (SEC (2007) 932). Retrieved from http://ec.europa.eu/sport/white-paper/doc/wp_on_ sport_en.pdf

European Commission. (2013). "Doping." Retrieved from http://ec.europa.eu/sport/what-we-do/doc29_en.htm

European Commission for the Efficiency of Justice of the Council of Europe. (2007). *Monitoring and Evaluation of Court System*. A Comparative Study Report prepared by the Research Team, Gar Yein Ng, Marco Velicogna and Cristina Dallara and discussed by the CEPEJ-GT-EVAL at their 8th meeting. Retrieved from http://www.coe.int/t/dghl/cooperation/cepej/series/Etudes6Suivi_en.pdf

European Commission for the Efficiency of Justice of the Council of Europe. (2010). *European Judicial Systems. Edition 2010 (data 2008): Efficiency and Quality of Justice*. Retrieved from http://book.coe.int/EN/ficheouvrage.php?PAGEID=36&lang=EN&produit_aliasid=2341

European Health and Fitness Association. (2012, March 5). European fitness sector demands co-operation with anti-doping authorities after research results are released. Press release. Brussels. Retrieved from http://www.ehfa.eu/uploads/media/EHFA_Press_Release_FAD_5_March_2012.pdf

European Monitoring Centre on Drugs and Drug Addiction. (2002). Report on the risk assessment of GHB in the framework of the joint action on new synthetic drugs. Luxembourg: Office for Official Publications of the European Communities. Retrieved from http://bookshop.europa.eu/is-bin/INTERSHOP.enfinity/WFS/EU-Bookshop-Site/en_GB/-/EUR/ViewPDFFile-OpenPDFFile;pgid=y8dIS7GUWMdSR0EAlMEUUsWb0000E-15-WQB;sid=56A6JK1836E6K-ER5ICkg89ZqsMkVqqv4XM=?FileName=TD3901045ENC_002.pdf&SKU=TD3901045ENC_PDF

European Monitoring Centre on Drugs and Drug Addiction. (2011). Annual Report 2011. The state of the drugs problem in Europe. Retrieved from http://www.emcdda.europa.eu/publications/annual-report/2011

European Monitoring Centre on Drugs and Drug Addiction. (2012). *Early warning system*. Retrieved from http://www.emcdda.europa.eu/themes/new-drugs/early-warning

European Union Council. (1997, August 15). Action plan to combat organized crime adopted by the Council on 28 April 1997. *Official Journal of the European Communities, C 251*, 1–16.

European Union Council. (1998, December 29). Joint Action of 21 December 1998 adopted by the Council on the basis of Article K.3 of the Treaty on European Union, on making it a criminal offence to participate in criminal organisation in the Member States of the European Union, *Official Journal of the European Communities, L 351*, 0001–0003.

European Union Council. (2003, December 12). *A secure Europe in a better world: European security strategy*. Retrieved from http://europa.eu/legislation_summaries/justice_freedom_security/fight_against_organised_crime/r00004_en.htm

Evaluation Team. (2002). Report of the Evaluation Team. In Council of Europe (Ed.), Italy: Compliance with commitments project—Respect by Italy of the anti-doping convention. Report by Italy and the evaluation team: 31–43. Ref. T-DO (2002) 36. Retrieved from http://www.coe.int/t/dg4/sport/commitments/antidoping/T-DO_2002_36_EN_eval_Report_Commit_Italy.pdf

Evans, N. A. (1997). Gym & Tonic: A profile of 100 male steroid users. *British Journal of Sports Medicine, 31*, 54–58.

Evans, N. A. (2004). Current concepts in anabolic-androgenic steroids. *The American Journal of Sports Medicine, 32*, 534–542.

Evans-Brown, M., McVeigh, J. Perkins,C. & Bellis. M. A. (2012). *Human Enhancement Drugs: The Emerging Challenges to Public Health*. Liverpool: Health Observatories in England.

Fabri, M., Carnevali, D., Contini, F., Dallara, C., & Sibilla, F. (2003). Quality and justice in Italy. In M. Fabri, P. M. Langbroek, & H. Pauliat (Eds.), *The administration of justice in Europe: Towards the development of quality standards*. Lo Scarabeo: Bologna.

Fainaru-Wada, M., & Lance, W. (2006). *Game of shadows: Barry Bonds, BALCO, and the steroids scandal that rocked professional sports*. New York: Gotham.

Fazzo, L., & Mensurati, M. (2002a, June 1). Doping, la rotta della camorra così si riforniscono atleti e cavalla. *La Repubblica, 48*. Retrieved from http://ricerca.repubblica.it/repubblica/archivio/repubblica/2002/06/01/doping-la-rotta-della-camorra-cosi-si.html

Fazzo, L., & Mensurati, M. (2002b, May 30). Un pentito contro Simoni Doping nel Giro che ha vinto. *La Repubblica, 53*. Retrieved from http://ricerca.repubblica.it/repubblica/archivio/repubblica/2002/05/30/un-pentito-contro-simoni-doping-nel-giro.html

Federal Ministry of the Interior. (2009). Survey among EU Member States on the criminal liability of athletes for the possession of doping agents. Results—German initiative—As of July 2008. Unpublished document.

Federazione Italiana Atletica Leggera. (2012). Tutela della salute: normative: Le norme che regolano l'accertamento dell'idoneità. I link alla documentazione antidoping nazionale ed internazionale, il contatto del telefono verde e antidoping. Retrieved from http://www.fidal.it/content/Tutela-della-salute-normativa/49875

Federazione Italiana Pesistica. (2012). *Cenni storici*. Retrieved from http://www.federpesistica.it/it/index.php?option=com_content&view=category&layout=blog&id=82&Itemid=459

Ferrara, S. D. (2004). *Doping antidoping*. Padova: Piccin.

Fijnaut, C. (2013). European Union organized crime control policies. In L. Paoli (Ed.), *Oxford handbook of organized crime*. New York: Oxford University Press.

Fijnaut, C., & De Ruyver, B. (2008). *Voor een gezamenlijke beheersing van de drugsgerelateerde criminaliteit in de Euregio Maas-Rijn*. Liège: Euregio Maas-Rijn.

Fijnaut, C., & Paoli, L. (Eds.). (2004). *Organised crime in Europe: Concepts, patterns and policies in the European Union and beyond*. Dordrecht: Springer.

Fincoeur, B. (2009). Lutte antidopage et cyclisme à deux vitesses: évolution du rapport au dopage chez les cyclistes belges depuis l'affaire Festina. *Revue internationale de criminologie et de police technique et scientifique, 3*(9), 207–220.

Fineschi, V., Riezzo, I., Centini, F., Silingardi, E., Licata, M., Beduschi, G., et al. (2007). Sudden cardiac death during anabolic steroid abuse: Morphologic and toxicologic findings in two fatal cases of bodybuilders. *International Journal of Legal Medicine, 121*(1), 48–53.

Fisher, I., & Macur, J. (2006, February 24). Olympics: Drug tests negative as Games near end. *The New York Times*. Retrieved from http://www.nytimes.com/2006/02/24/sports/24iht-olydrugs.html

Fmk. (2011). *Tough on doping, tough on the causes of doping—Francesco Conconi and the introduction of the H-test*. Retrieved from http://www.podiumcafe.com/2011/2/16/1997823/tough-on-doping-tough-on-the-causes-of-doping-francesco-conconi-and

Franke, W. W. (1995). Funktion und Instrumentalisierung des Sports in der DDR: Pharmakologische Manipulationen (Doping) und die Rolle der Wissenschaft. In Deutscher Bundestag (Ed.) *Bericht der Enquete-Kommission Aufarbeitung von Geschichte und Folgen der SED-Diktatur in Deutschland* (vol. III/2, pp. 905–1143).

Frezzi, T. (2011). Smantellato maxi traffico internazionale di anabolizzanti. Sessantenne anconetano in manette. *Fatto e Diritto*. Retrieved from http://www.fattodiritto.it/smantellato-maxi-traffico-internazionale-di-anabolizzanti-sessantenne-anconetano-in-manette/

Friesendorf, C. (2007). *U.S. foreign policy and the war on drugs: Displacing the cocaine and heroin industry*. London: Routledge.

Gamba, E. (2004, November 27). L' ombra doping su 4 anni di Juve. *La Repubblica, 14*. Retrieved from http://ricerca.repubblica.it/repubblica/archivio/repubblica/2004/11/27/ombra-doping-su-anni-di-juve.html

Gardiner, H. (2009, September 2). Pfizer pays $2.3 billion to settle marketing case. *The New York Times*. Retrieved from http://www.nytimes.com/2009/09/03/business/03health.html

Gasparini, W. (2004). Le corps performant par le dopage. Notes sociologiques. *Drogues, santé et société, 3*(1), 57–68.

Gaumont, P. (2005). *Prisonnier du dopage*. Paris: Grasset & Fasquelle.

Geis, G. (1992). White-collar crime: What is it? In K. Schlegel & D. Weisburg (Eds.), *White-collar crime reconsidered* (pp. 31–52). Boston: Northeastern University Press.

German Sport University Cologne. (2011, August 4). Erste Europäische Beobachtungsstelle für neue Dopingsubstanzen. Press Release no. PM1152. Retrieved from http://www.dshs-koeln.de/wps/portal/de/home/institutions/press/aktuelles/pressemeldungen/pm1152?WCM_PORTLET=PC_7_D5U2

Geyer, H. (2012). Personal communication.

Gilbert, C. (2010, December 6). Spiegel-Gespräch: Wie die Mafia. *Der Spiegel, 49*. Retrieved from http://www.spiegel.de/spiegel/print/d-75477023.html

Global Commission on Drug Policy. War on drugs. Report. Retrieved from http://www.globalcommissionondrugs.org/wp-content/themes/gcdp_v1/pdf/Global_Commission_Report_English.pdf

Gobert, J., & Punch, M. (2003). *Rethinking corporate crime*. London: Butterworths.

Government Offices of Sweden. (2012). Measures targeting children and young people and reduced cannabis abuse prioritised in the Government's ANDT policy 2012. Retrieved from http://www.sweden.gov.se/sb/d/15471

Gräber, K. (2011, September 12–14). Die bayerische Schwerpunktstaatsanwaltschaft Doping: Ein Erfahrungsbericht. Speech at the international symposium "Sportmedizin und Doping in Europa," Freiburg.

Graham, M. R., Davies, B., Grace, F. M., Kicman, A., & Baker, J. S. (2008). Anabolic steroid use: Patterns of use and detection of doping. *Sports Medicine, 38*(6), 505–525.

Graham, M. R., Ryan, P., Baker, J. S., Davies, B., Thomas, N., Cooper, S., et al. (2009). Counterfeiting in performance- and image-enhancing drugs. *Drug Testing and Analysis, 1*(3), 135–142.

Greenfield, V. A., & Paoli, L. (2012). If supply-oriented drug policy is broken, can "harm reduction" help fix it? *The International Journal on Drug Policy, 23*(1), 6–15.

Groleau, C. S. (2009). Weird science: A look at the World Anti-doping Agency's questionable testing methods and the need for change to protect international athletes. *Quinnipiac Health Law Journal, 13*, 85–116.

Großekathöfer, M., & Gilbert, C. (2008, December 1). Wir haben zu wenig Waffen. *Der Spiegel, 48*. Retrieved from http://www.spiegel.de/spiegel/print/d-62332847.html

Guariniello, R. (2011, September 12–14). Anti-doping investigations in Italy: Football and the 2006 Turin Olympic Games. Speech at the international symposium "Sportmedizin und Doping in Europa", Freiburg.

Haas, U. (2012). Personal communication.

Haddow, D. (2012, April 18). Did Cartagena mark the beginning of the end of the war on drugs? *The Guardian*. Retrieved from http://www.guardian.co.uk/commentisfree/2012/apr/18/cartagena-war-on-drugs

Hahn, T., & Häyrinen, R. (2008, June 25). Doping im finnischen Skisport. Die schmutzigen Neunziger. *Süddeutsche Zeitung*. Retrieved from http://www.sueddeutsche.de/sport/doping-im-finnischen-skisport-die-schmutzigen-neunziger-1.203060

Hahn, T., & Kistner, T. (2003). Doping-Affäre: Ski-Trainer Walter Mayer festgenommen. *Süddeutsche Zeitung*. Retrieved from http://www.sueddeutsche.de/sport/doping-affaere-ski-trainer-walter-mayer-festgenommen-1.395208

Haller, M. (1990). Illegal enterprise. A theoretical and historical interpretation. *Criminology, 28*(2), 207–235.

Hamilton, T., & Coyle, D. (2012). *The secret race: Inside the hidden world of the Tour de France: Doping, cover-ups, and winning at all costs*. London: Bantam Press.

Handelsman, D. J., & Gupta, L. (1997). Prevalence and risk factors for anabolic-androgenic steroid abuse in Australian high school students. *International Journal of Andrology, 20*, 159–164.

Hanstad, D. V., & Loland, S. (2009). Elite level athletes' duty to provide information on their whereabouts: Justifiable anti-doping work or an indefensible surveillance regime? *European Journal of Sport Sciences, 9*(1), 3–10.

Hanstad, D. V., Smith, A., & Waddington, I. (2008). The establishment of the World Anti-Doping Agency: A study of the management of organizational change and unplanned outcomes. *International Review for the Sociology of Sport, 43*, 227–249.

Hard, M. (2010). Caught in the net: Athlete's rights and the World Antidoping Agency. *Southern California Interdisciplinary Law Journal, 19*, 533–564.

Hardie, M., Shilbury, D., Ware, I., & Bozzi, C. (2010). I wish i was twenty one now—Beyond doping in the Australian Peloton. *Victoria: Deakin University faculty of Business and Law*. Retrieved from http://www.newcyclingpathway.com/wp-content/uploads/2010/09/21-NOW-FINAL-.pdf

Harris, G. (2009, September 2). Pfizer pays $2.3 billion to settle marketing case. *The New York Times*. Retrieved from http://www.nytimes.com/2009/09/03/business/03health.html

Harth, W., Seikowski, K., Hermes, B., & Gieler, U. (2008). New lifestyle drugs and somatoform disorders in dermatology. *Journal of the American Academy of Dermatology, 22*(2), 141–149.

Hartmann, P. (2003, November 21). Dottore Mabuse und die Nackte van Goya. Conconi-Prozess endet mit Freispruch. *Neuer Zürcher Zeitung*. Retrieved from http://www.nzz.ch/aktuell/startseite/newzzDN9U3129-12-1.333417

Hawkins, K. (1984). *Environment and enforcement: Regulation and the social definition of pollution*. Oxford: Clarendon Press.

Henderson, J. (2001, July 8). The 10 greatest cheats in sporting history. *The Observer*. Retrieved from http://observer.guardian.co.uk/toptens/story/0,,1079053,00.html

Hendrickx, F. (2008). *Doping the athlete in an age of presumed innocence: What if the lawyer wins the race? Lectures for the XXIst century* (pp. 181–205). Leuven: Leuven University Press.

Henne, K. E. (2009, December 31). The origins of the International Olympic Committee Medical Commission and its technocratic regime: An historiographic investigation of anti-doping regulation and enforcement in International Sport. Final Report. Retrieved from oc.rero.ch/lm.php ?url=1000,44,38,20100301152359-AF/2009_-_The_Origins_of_the_International_Olympic_Committee_Medical_Commission_-_HENNE_K.pdf

Hibell, B., Andersson, B., Ahlström, S., Balakireva, O., Bjarnason, T., Kokkevi, A., et al. (2000). *The 1999 ESPAD report: Alcohol and other drug use among students in 30 European countries*. Stockholm: Swedish Council for Information on Alcohol and Other Drugs.

Hibell, B., Andersson, B., Bjarnason, T., Kokkevi, A., Morgan, M., & Narusk, A. (1997). *The 1995 ESPAD report: Alcohol and other drug use among students in 26 European countries*. Stockholm: Swedish Council for Information on Alcohol and Other Drugs.

Hibell, B., Guttormsson, U., Ahlström, S., Balakireva, O., Bjarnason, T., Kokkevi, A., et al. (2009). *The 2007 ESPAD report: Substance use among students in 35 European countries*. Stockholm: Swedish Council for Information on Alcohol and Other Drugs.

Hildebrandt, T., Langenbucher, J., Carr, S., Sanjuan, P., & Park, S. (2006). Predicting intentions for long-term anabolic-androgenic steroid use among men: A covariance structure model. *Psychology of Addictive Behaviors, 20*(3), 234–240.

Hill, D. (2008). *The fix: Soccer and organized crime*. Toronto: McClelland & Stewart.

Hoberman, J. M. (2001). How drug testing fails. The politics of doping control. In W. Wilson & E. Derse (Eds.), *Doping in elite sport* (pp. 241–274). Champaign: Human Kinetics.

Hoberman, J. M. (2002). A pharmacy on wheels: Doping and community cohesion among professional cyclists following the Tour de France Scandal of 1998. In V. Møller & J. Nauright (Eds.), *The essence of sport* (pp. 107–127). Odense: UP of Southern Denmark.

Hoberman, J. M. (2005). *Testosterone dreams: Rejuvenation, aphrodisia, doping*. Los Angeles: University of California Press.

Hoberman, J. M. (2011a). "Athletes in handcuffs?" The criminalization of doping. In M. McNamee & V. Møller (Eds.), *Doping and anti-doping policy in sport: Ethical, legal and social perspectives* (pp. 99–110). London: Routledge.

Hoberman, J. M. (2011b). Il costo dei record. *Sds, Scuola dello sport, XXIX (86),* 3–9.

Hoberman, J. M. (2012). Doping, gambling, and the decline of the IOC-Mimeo.

Hoberman, J. M. (n.d.). Preliminary report: Lance Armstrong and the doping culture of the Tour de France. Mimeo.

Holz, M. (2012, March 19–20). *The Interpol involvement against the trafficking of doping substances*. Paper presented at the Sportsvision 2012, Copenhagen. Abstract retrieved http://www.sportvision2012.eu/files/EU2012_Web/Downloads/BA_Compiled_Final.pdf

Houlihan, B. (2001). *Sport, policy and politics: A comparative analysis*. London: Routledge.

Houlihan, B. (2002). *Dying to win: Doping in sport and the development of anti-doping policy*. Strasbourg: Council of Europe.

Houlihan, B., & García, B. (2012, August). *The use of legislation in relation to controlling the production, movement, importation, distribution and supply of performance-enhancing drugs in sport (PEDS)*. Retrieved from http://www.wada-ama.org/Documents/World_Anti-Doping_Program/WADP-Legal_Library/National_Legislation/UNESCO-Legislative-Research-Report-FINAL.pdf

Howman, D. (2011a, December 1). Current challenges and issues of anti-doping. Speech held at PCC Conference, New York. Retrieved from http://www.wada-ama.org/Documents/News_Center/Speeches_Presentations/2011/WADA_DHowman_PCC_Current_Challenges_and_Issues_for_Anti-Doping_2011_12_01.pdf

Howman, D. (2011b, March 16–17). World sports law report. Tackling doping in sport 2011. Twichenham Stadium. Retrieved from http://www.playthegame.org/knowledge-bank/articles/wada-warns-against-criminals-taking-control-in-sport-5125.html

Huestis, M. A., Mazzoni, I., & Rabin, O. (2011). Cannabis in sport—Anti-doping perspective. *Sports Medicine 41(11)*, 949–966.

Il Corriere della Sera. (2005). Doping al Tour, arrestato Dario Frigo. Retrieved from http://www.corriere.it/Primo_Piano/Sport/2005/07_Luglio/13/frigo.shtml

Il Corriere della Sera. (2009). Culturista uccide a coltellate la moglie. Retrieved from http://archiviostorico.corriere.it/2009/aprile/18/Culturista_uccide_coltellate_moglie_co_7_090418011.shtml

Il Fatto Quotidiano. (2011). L'Emilia Romagna travolta anche dallo scandalo doping. Retrieved from http://www.ilfattoquotidiano.it/2011/06/09/lemilia-romagna-travolta-anche-dallo-scandalo-doping/116833/

Il Giorno. (2011, October 11). Doping: arrestato Seccarecci, body builder. Retrieved from http://www.ilgiorno.it/milano/cronaca/2011/10/11/598315-doping.shtml

Il Nuovo ciclismo. (2007). L'allarme di Botrè (FMSI): 400.000 italiani assumono doping. Retrieved from http://ilnuovociclismo.forumfree.it/?t=21223457

Il Resto del Carlino. (2011, August 24). Preso il "capo dei capi" del traffico di doping. Retrieved from http://www.ilrestodelcarlino.it/pesaro/cronaca/2011/08/24/567854-doping_arrestato.shtml

Illuminati, G. (2000). Italy. In T. Vander Beken, & M. Kilchling (Eds.), *The role of the public prosecutor in the European criminal justice system* (pp. 111–124). Brussel: Koninklijke Vlaamse Academie van België voor Wetenschappen en Kunsten.

Illuminati, G. (2005). Italy. In P. Tak (Ed.), *Tasks and powers of the prosecution services in the EU member states* (Vol. 2, pp. 935–954). Nijmegen: Wolf.

International Olympic Committee. (2007). Summary of the IOC disciplinary commission recommendations regarding the National Olympic Committee of Austria (Österreichisches Olympisches Comité—*ÖOC*). Retrieved from http://www.olympic.org/Documents/Reports/EN/en_report_1183.pdf

International Olympic Committee. (2007). Torino 2006: Six Austrian athletes declared permanently ineligible. Press release. Retrieved from http://www.olympic.org/news?articleid=54762

Istat. (2007). La pratica sportiva in Italia: *Anno 2006*. Retrieved from http://www.coni.it/fileadmin/ops2008/Istat_sport_2006_Presentaz_070620.pdf

Istat. (2012). Data on doping-related criminal proceedings calculated for the present projects. Mimeo.

Istituto Superiore di Sanità. (2009). *Quaderni didattici del Corso per Ispettori antidoping*. Roma: Istituto Superiore di Sanità.

Italy. (2002). Report by Italy. In Council of Europe (Ed.), Compliance with Commitments Project—Respect by Italy of the Anti-Doping Convention, Italy. Report by Italy and the evaluation team. pp. 3–30. Ref. T-DO (2002) 36. Retrieved from http://www.coe.int/t/dg4/sport/commitments/antidoping/T-DO_2002_36_EN_eval_Report_Commit_Italy.pdf

Jacobs, J., & Samuels, B. (1994–1995). The drug testing project in international sports: Dilemmas in an expanding regulatory regime. *Hastings International & Company Law Review 18*, 557–589.

Johnston, L. D., O'Malley, P. M., Bachman, J. G., & Schulenberg, J. E. (2012). *Monitoring the Future national survey results on drug use, 1975-2011. Volume I: Secondary school students*. Ann Arbor: Institute for Social Research, The University of Michigan.

Jones, J., & Maloney, T. (2004). Pantani dead at 34. *Cyclingnews.com*. Retrieved from http://autobus.cyclingnews.com/news.php?id=news/2004/feb04/feb15news1

Josti, G. (1994, January 17). Moser: "non vedo l' ora di riprovarci." *Corriere della Sera, 34*. Retrieved from http://archiviostorico.corriere.it/1994/gennaio/17/Moser_non_vedo_ora_riprovarci_co_0_940117184.shtml

Justizministerium Baden-Württemberg. (2012, April 4). Schwerpunktstaatsanwaltschaft zur Verfolgung von Dopingstraftaten eingerichtet. Retrieved from http://www.justiz-bw.de/servlet/PB/menu/1275867/index.html?ROOT=1153239

Kanayama, G., Boynes, M., Hudson, J. I., Field, A. E., & Pope, H. G., Jr. (2007). Anabolic steroid abuse among teenage girls: An illusory problem? *Drug and Alcohol Dependence, 88*, 156–162.

Kanayama, G., Brower, K. J., Wood, R. I., Hudson, J. I., & Pope, H. G. (2009). Anabolic–androgenic steroid dependence: An emerging disorder. *Addiction, 104*, 1966–1978.
Kanayama, G., Gruber, A. J., Pope, H. G., Borowiecki, J. J., & Hudson, J. L. (2001). Over-the-counter drug use in gymnasiums: An underrecognized substance abuse problem? *Psychotherapy and Psychosomatics, 70*, 137–140.
Kanayama, G., Hudson, J. I., & Pope, H. G., Jr. (2008). Long-term psychiatric and medical consequences of anabolic-androgenic steroid abuse: A looming public health concern? *Drug and Alcohol Dependence, 98*, 1–12.
Kanayama, G., Hudson, J. I., & Pope, H. G. (2009). Features of men with anabolic androgenic steroid dependence: A comparison with nondependent AAS users and with AAS nonusers. *Drug and Alcohol Dependence, 102*, 130–137.
Kanayama, G., & Pope, H. G., Jr. (2012). Illicit use of androgens and other hormones: Recent advances. *Current Opinion in Endocrinology, Diabetes, and Obesity, 19*(3), 211–219.
Kanayama, G., Pope, H. G., Cohane, G., & Hudson, J. I. (2003). Risk factors for anabolic androgenic steroid use among weightlifters: A case-control study. *Drug and Alcohol Dependence, 71*(1), 77–86.
Kanayama, G., Pope, H. G., Jr., & Hudson, J. I. (2001). 'Body image' drugs: A growing psychosomatic problem. *Psychotherapy and Psychosomatics, 70*, 61–65.
Kashkin, K. B., & Kleber, H. D. (1989). Hooked on hormones? An anabolic steroid addiction hypothesis. *Journal of the American Medical Association, 262*(22), 3166–3170.
Katz, M. L., & Rosen, H. S. (1994). *Microeconomics* (2nd ed.). Burr Ridge, IL: Irwin.
Kayser, B., Mauron, A., & Miah, A. (2007). Current anti-doping policy: A critical appraisal. *BMC Medical Ethics, 8*, 2.
Keane, H. (2005). Diagnosing the male steroid user: Drug use, body image and disordered masculinity. *Health (London, England), 9*(2), 189–208.
Kerlikowske, R. G. (2012, May 21). Principles of modern drug policy. Statement of the Government of the United States of America World Federation Against Drugs 3rd World Forum. Retrieved from http://www.whitehouse.gov/ondcp/news-releases-remarks/principles-of-modern-drug-policy-directors-remarks-at-the-world-federation-against-drugs
Kilchling, M. (2000). In Tom Vander Beken & Michael Kilchling (Eds.), *Deutschland: The role of the public prosecutor in the European criminal justice system* (pp. 73–94) Brussel: Koninklijke Vlaamse Academie van België voor Wetenschappen en Kunsten.
Kilmer, B. & Reuter, P. (2009, November/December). Prime numbers: Doped. *Foreign Policy*, 34–35. Retrieved from http://www.foreignpolicy.com/articles/2009/10/19/prime_numbers_doped
Kindlundh, D. P., Isacson, D. G., Berglund, L., & Nyberg, F. (1998). Doping among high school students in Uppsala, Sweden: A presentation of the attitudes, distribution, side effects, and extent of use. *Scandinavian Journal of Social Medicine, 26*, 71–74.
Kistner, T. (2007, July 1). Jaksches Weg zum Geständnis Sicherheit für den Kronzeugen. *Süddeutsche Zeitung*. Retrieved from http://www.sueddeutsche.de/sport/jaksches-weg-zum-gestaendnis-sicherheit-fuer-den-kronzeugen-1.867286
Kistner, T. (2012). *FIFA-Mafia: Die schmutzigen Geschäfte mit dem Weltfußball*. Munich: Droemer Knaur.
Kläber, M. (2010). *Doping im Fitness-Studio. Die Sucht nach dem perfekten Körper*. Bielefeld: transcript.
Koert, A. W. A., & van Kleij, R. (1998). *Handel in doping: Een verkennend onderzoek naar de handel in dopinggeduide middelen in Nederland*. Nieuwegein: Arko.
Kokkevi, A., Fotiou, A., Chileva, A., Nociar, A., & Miller, P. (2008). Daily exercise and anabolic steroids use in adolescents: A cross-national European study. *Substance Use & Misuse, 43*, 2053–2065.
Korkia, P., & Stimson, G. V. (1997). Indications of prevalence, practice and effects of anabolic steroid use in Great Britain. *International Journal of Sports Medicine, 18*, 557–562.
Kornbeck, J. (2009, October 23–24). Europäische Harmonisierung der Dopingbekämpfung? Paper presented at "Dopingbekämpfung im Sport als gesamteuropäische Aufgabe," Europäische Akademie Otzenhausen.

Kraska, P., Bussard, C., & Brent, J. (2010). Trafficking in bodily perfection: Examining the late-modern steroid marketplace and its criminalization. *Justice Quarterly, 27*(2), 159–185.

Krejza, M. (2009, May 13–15). *Criminalisation of trade in doping substances*. Speech held at the Eu Conference on Anti-Doping, Athens. Retrieved from http://ec.europa.eu/sport/library/documents/c2/michal_krejza_speech.pdf

La Gazzetta di Modena. (2012). Gli anabolizzanti, la morte della sua donna e un iter giudiziario lungo otto anni. Retrieved from http://gazzettadimodena.gelocal.it/cronaca/2012/01/13/news/gli-anabolizzanti-la-morte-della-sua-donna-e-un-iter-giudiziario-lungo-otto-anni-1.3062695

La Repubblica. (1987, August 30). Doping Tordelli accusa la Fidal, *45*. Retrieved from http://ricerca.repubblica.it/repubblica/archivio/repubblica/1987/08/30/doping-tordelli-accusa-la-fidal.html

La Repubblica. (1997, April 9). Per il caso Di-Terlizzi richiesta nuova perizia, *50*. Retrieved from http://ricerca.repubblica.it/repubblica/archivio/repubblica/1997/04/09/per-il-caso-di-terlizzi-richiesta-nuova.html

La Repubblica. (1999, April 25). Moser ai Nas è vero, ho fatto emotrasfusione, *48*. Retrieved from http://ricerca.repubblica.it/repubblica/archivio/repubblica/1999/04/25/moser-ai-nas-vero-ho-fatto-emotrasfusione.html

La Repubblica. (2000, October 27). E il Coni smantella la sua Commissione, *12*. Retrieved from http://ricerca.repubblica.it/repubblica/archivio/repubblica/2000/10/27/il-coni-smantella-la-sua-commissione.html

La Repubblica. (2001, April 5). Il giudice: Guandalini cedette farmaci dopanti, *4 of Bologna section*. Retrieved from http://ricerca.repubblica.it/repubblica/archivio/repubblica/2001/04/05/il-giudice-guandalini-cedette-farmaci-dopanti.html

La Repubblica. (2002, March 21). Il lungo elenco del nandrolone, *54*. Retrieved from http://ricerca.repubblica.it/repubblica/archivio/repubblica/2002/03/21/il-lungo-elenco-del-nandrolone.html

La Repubblica. (2004a, January 22). Al macello gli animali malati, *4 of the Palermo section*. Retrieved from http://ricerca.repubblica.it/repubblica/archivio/repubblica/2004/01/22/al-macello-gli-animali-malati.pa_013al.html

La Repubblica. (2004b, October 12). Dagli anabolizzanti all' infarto muore ex star del baseball Usa, *59*. Retrieved from http://ricerca.repubblica.it/repubblica/archivio/repubblica/2004/10/12/dagli-anabolizzanti-all-infarto-muore-ex-star.html

La Repubblica. (2005, August 4). 'Gillet sapeva di doparsi'. *4 of the Bari section*. Retrieved from http://ricerca.repubblica.it/repubblica/archivio/repubblica/2005/08/04/gillet-sapeva-di-doparsi.html

La Repubblica. (2008). Corse truccate, cavalli dopati—Nuova tegola sull'ippica italiana. Retrieved from http://www.repubblica.it/2008/12/sezioni/sport/ippica-indagine/ippica-indagine/ippica-indagine.html?ref=search

La Repubblica. (2010). Rapinavano Tir in tutta Italia, sette arresti. Retrieved from http://napoli.repubblica.it/cronaca/2010/02/23/news/rapinavano_tir_in_tutta_italia_sette_arresti-2621979/index.html?ref=search

La Repubblica. (2011, April 17). La vittoria più importante del pm d' assalto Ma il mio pool rischia lo smantellamento, *10*. Retrieved from http://ricerca.repubblica.it/repubblica/archivio/repubblica/2011/04/17/la-vittoria-piu-importante-del-pm.html

Labre, M. P. (2002). Adolescent boys and the muscular male body ideal. *Journal of Adolescent Health, 300*(4), 233–242.

Lager, G., & Ljungqvist, A. (2011). *Doping's Nemesis—Arne Ljungqvist*. Cheltenham: Sports Books.

Lambert, M. I., Titlestad, S. D., & Schwellnus, M. P. (1998). Prevalence of androgenic-anabolic steroid use in adolescents in two regions of South Africa. *South African Medical Journal, 88*, 876–880.

Lane, S. (2012). WADA to consider change of status for Cannabis. *The Age*. Retrieved from http://www.theage.com.au/sport/wada-to-consider-change-of-status-for-cannabis-20120502-1xzg9.html

Larance, B., Degenhardt, L., Copeland, J., & Dillon, P. (2008). Injecting risk behaviour and related harm among men who use performance- and image-enhancing drugs. *Drug and Alcohol Review, 27*(6), 679–686.

Laub, J. H., & Sampson, R. J. (2003). *Shared beginnings, divergent lives: Delinquent boys at age 70*. Cambridge: Harvard University Press.

Laure, P., & Binsinger, C. (2005). Adolescent athletes and the demand and supply of drugs to improve their performance. *Journal of Sports Science and Medicine, 4*, 272–277.

Leland, H. E. (2002). Insider trading: Should it be prohibited? *Journal of Political Economy, 100*(4), 859–887.

Leone, L. (2010a, June 30). Rapporto finale di valutazione del progetto sperimentale "Palestra Sicura" Regione Emilia Romagna. Draft.

Leone, L. (2010b, February 2). Valutazione progetto palestra sicura: prima rilevazione regione Emilia Romagna. Presentation made at the Direzione Generale Sanità e Politiche Sociali Regione Emilia-Romagna, Bologna.

Littman, J. (2012). *Bodybuilding and the olympics—An ongoing controversy*. Retrieved from http://www.empowernetwork.com/ladyjean/blog/bodybuilding-and-the-olympics-an-ongoing-controversy/?id=ladyjean

Ljungqvist, A. (2009). Opening Address at the UNESCO "Conference of Parties to the International Convention against Doping in Sport", Mimeo.

Ljungqvist, A. (2010). Der Anti-Doping-Kampf als Aufgabe des IOC. In W. Blumenthal (Ed.), *Der Kampf gegen Doping: Die gesellschaftliche Verantwortung von Sport und Politik auf Nationaler und internationaler Ebene* (pp. 19–36). *Sankt Augustin/Berlin: Konrad-Adenauer-Stiftung e. V.* Retrieved from http://www.kas.de/wf/doc/kas_20651-544-1-30.pdf?100929165220

Longman, J. (1998, February 12). IOC ban on Marijuana now subject to debate. *The New York Times*. Retrieved from http://www.nytimes.com/specials/olympics/nagano/sno/021298oly-marijuana.html

Longman, J. (1998, December 26). Unbelievable performances: A special report. Widening drug use compromises faith in sports. *The New York Times*. Retrieved from http://www.nytimes.com/1998/12/26/sports/unbelievable-performances-special-report-widening-drug-use-compromises-faith.html?src=pm

Lucidi, F., Grano, C., Leone, L., Lombardo, C., & Pesce, C. (2004). Determinants of the intention to use doping substances: An empirical contribution in a sample of Italian adolescents. *International Journal of Sport Psychology, 35*, 133–148.

Lüdke, S., Sauer, M., Paul, M., & Schänzer, W. (2007). The Cologne import information system: A tool to highlight long term trends in the Black Market for drugs and doping substances. In W. Schänzer, H. Geyer, A. Gotzmann, & U. Mareck (Eds.), *Recent advances in doping analysis* (pp. 441–444). Köln: Sportverlag Strauß.

Lundby, C., Robach, P., & Saltin, B. (2011). The evolving science of detection of 'blood doping'. *British Journal of Pharmacology, 165*, 1306–1315.

Lundby, C., Robach, P., & Saltin, B. (2012). Are the anti blood doping efforts effective?—Present and future. *British Journal of Pharmacology*. doi:10.1111/j.1476-5381.2011.01822.x1.

Lyttman, J. (2010). *Bodybuilding and the olympics: An ongoing controversy*. Retrieved from http://buildmusclemassnow.com/bodybuilding-and-the-olympics-an-ongoing-controversy/

MacAloon, J. (2001). Doping and moral authority: Sports organizations today. In W. Wilson & E. Derse (Eds.), *Doping in elite sport* (pp. 205–224). Champaign, IL: Human Kinetics.

MacMichael, S. (2011a). Italian press says Armstrong secretly paid Ferrari via Swiss company. *Road.cc*. Retrieved from http://road.cc/content/news/44348-italian-press-says-armstrong-secretly-paid-ferrari-swiss-company

MacMichael, S. (2011b). UCI President Pat McQuaid insists cycling is winning the war against the dopers. *Road.cc*. Retrieved from http://road.cc/content/news/44660-uci-president-pat-mcquaid-insists-cycling-winning-war-against-dopers

Macur, J. (2006, February 19). 2006 Olympic winter games: Drug testing; Looking for doping evidence, Italian Police Raid Austrians. *The New York Times*. Retrieved from http://select.nytimes.com/gst/abstract.html?res=F40714FF3A5A0C7A8DDDAB0894D

Maillo, L. (2008). Anaphylactic shock with multiorgan failure in a cyclist after intravenous administration of Actovegin. *Annals of Internal Medicine., 148*(5), 407.

Manne, H. (1966). *Insider trading and the stock market*. New York: The Free Press.

Marchese, T. (2010). *Il doping nell'ordinamento generale e in quello sportivo*. Bari: Cacucci.

Marino, G. (2011, May 23). I farmaci della camorra. *La Repubblica, 24*. Retrieved from http://ricerca.repubblica.it/repubblica/archivio/repubblica/2001/05/23/farmaci-della-camorra.html

Mayer, W. (2010). . *und plötzlich war ich ein Verbrecher—Die Machenschaften der Funktionäre im Leistungssport und die große Frage, ob dieser denn nicht pervers ist*. Wien: Egoth.

McCabe, S. E., Brower, K. J., West, B. T., Nelson, T. F., & Wechsler, H. (2007). Trends in non-medical use of anabolic steroids by U.S. college students: Results from four national surveys. *Drug and Alcohol Dependence, 90*, 243–251.

McCord, J. (2003). Cures that harm: Unanticipated outcomes of crime prevention programs. *The Annals of the American Academy of Political and Social Science, 587*, 16–30.

McGrath, M. (2008, July 21). Concerns over Olympic drug test. *BBC News*. Retrieved from http://news.bbc.co.uk/2/hi/science/nature/7516484.stm

Mcgrath, M. (2008, July 15). "Concerns over Olympic drug test." *BBC*. Retrieved from http://news.bbc.co.uk/2/hi/7516484.stm

McNamee, M., & Møller, V. (Eds.). (2011). *Doping and anti-doping policy in sport: Ethical, legal and social perspectives*. London: Routledge.

McQuaid, P. (2011, September 12–14). Implementing the anti-doping policy of the union cycliste internationale. Presentation made at the international symposium sports medicine and doping in Europe, Freiburg.

Melia, P., Pipe, A., & Greenberg, L. (1996). The use of anabolic-androgenic steroids by Canadian students. *Clinical Journal of Sport Medicine, 6*, 9–14.

Mendoza, M. (2010). US war on drugs has met none of its goals: AP impact. *Huffington Post*. Retrieved from http://www.huffingtonpost.com/2010/05/13/us-war-on-drugs-has-met-n_n_575351.html

Mercy, M. (2004, December 9). "Geen alternatief voor doping." *De Standaard*. Retrieved from http://www.standaard.be/artikel/detail.aspx?artikelid=G78ASA03

Meyer, K., & Parssinen, T. (1998). *Webs of smoke: Smugglers, warlords, spies and the history of the International Drug Trade*. Lanham: Rowman and Littlefield.

Millar, D. (2012). *Racing through the dark: The fall and rise of David Millar*. Phoenix: Orion.

Ministero del Lavoro, della Salute e delle Politiche Sociali. (2009). Reporting system doping—antidoping. Anno 2008. Allegato II Relazione al Parlamento sullo stato di attuazione della legge 14 dicembre 2000, n. 376. Retrieved from http://www.salute.gov.it/imgs/C_17_pubblicazioni_1192_ulterioriallegati_ulterioreallegato_1_alleg.pdf

Ministero dell'Interno. (2006). Decreto 28 aprile 2006: Riassetto dei comparti di specialità delle forze di polizia. Retrieved from http://www.interno.it/mininterno/export/sites/default/it/sezioni/servizi/legislazione/polizia/legislazione_769.html

Ministero della Difesa. (2009, May 5). Decreto del 26 febbraio 2008: Riordino del Comando carabinieri per la tutela della salute. *Gazzetta Ufficiale, 102*. Retrieved from http://lexambiente.it/polizia-giudiziaria/213/5122-Polizia%20Giudiziaria.%20Carabinieri%20NAS.html

Ministero della Giustizia. (2002). Relazione del Ministero sull'amministrazione della giustizia per l'inaugurazione dell'anno giudiziario 2002. Retrieved from http://giustizia.it/studierapporti/ag2002/ag2002MG_ndx.htm

Ministero della Giustizia. (2012). *Giustizia map*. Retrieved from http://www.giustizia.it/giustizia/it/mg_4.wp?facetNode_1=3_2&selectedNode=3_2_4

Ministero della Salute. (2007, October 16). Atto di intesa per la lotta al doping tra il Ministro della Salute, il Ministro delle Politiche Giovanili ed Attività Sportive ed il Presidente del CONI. Retrieved from http://www.salute.gov.it/imgs/C_17_pubblicazioni_704_allegato.pdf

Ministero della Salute. (2010a). Dati sull'attività di controllo antidoping: Anno 2009. Allegato II della Relazione al Parlamento. Retrieved from http://www.salute.gov.it/antiDoping/archivioDocumentiDoping.jsp?lingua=italiano&menu=documentazione

Ministero della Salute. (2010b). Decreto 11 giugno 2010: Aggiornamento e completamento delle Tabelle contenenti l'indicazione delle sostanze stupefacenti e psicotrope relative a composizioni medicinali, di cui al Decreto del Presidente della Repubblica 9 ottobre 1990, n, 309, e successive modificazioni ed integrazioni con l'inserimento dello steroide anabolizzante nandrolone. *Gazzetta Ufficiale*, serie generale n. 145 of June 24, 2010. Retrieved from http://www.normativasanitaria.it/jsp/dettaglio.jsp?id=34277

Ministero della Salute. (2010c). Relazione al Parlamento sullo stato di attuazione della legge 14 dicembre 2000, n. 376 nonché sull'attività svolta dalla Commissione per la vigilanza ed il controllo sul *doping* e per la tutela della salute nelle attività sportive—Anno 2009. Retrieved from http://www.salute.gov.it/antiDoping/archivioDocumentiDoping.jsp?lingua=italiano&id=1449

Ministero della Salute. (2011a). Dati sul consumo di farmaci e prodotti salutistici (non vietati per doping) da parte degli atleti controllati—Anno 2010. Allegato III della Relazione al Parlamento. Retrieved from http://www.salute.gov.it/imgs/C_17_pubblicazioni_1614_ulterioriallegati_ulterioreallegato_2_alleg.pdf

Ministero della Salute. (2011b). Dati sull'attività di controllo antidoping—Anno 2010. Allegato II della Relazione al Parlamento. Retrieved from http://www.salute.gov.it/antiDoping/archivioDocumentiDoping.jsp?lingua=italiano&menu=documentazione

Ministero della Salute. (2012). Commissione nazionale. Retrieved from http://www.salute.gov.it/antiDoping/paginainternaDoping.jsp?menu=commissione&lang=italiano&id=131

Ministero della Salute and Istituto Superiore di Sanità. (2012). Reporting system doping antidoping 2011. Retrieved from http://www.salute.gov.it/imgs/C_17_pubblicazioni_1732_allegato.pdf

Ministero della Solidarietà Sociale. (2006). Relazione annuale al parlamento sull'uso di sostanze stupefacenti e sulle tossicodipendenze in Italia—2005. Retrieved from http://www.politicheantidroga.it/media/187573/relazionealparlamento2005.1189084817.pdf

Ministero dello Sport e Ministero della Solidarietà Sociale. (2008). Censimento delle palestre esistenti nelle Regioni Apulia, Emilia Romagna, Latium, Trentino Alto Adige and Veneto. Roma, mimeo.

Ministry of Health and Social Affairs, Sweden. (2010). A cohesive strategy for alcohol, narcotic drugs, doping and tobacco (ANDT) policy—A summarised version of Government Bill 2010/11:47. Retrieved from http://www.sweden.gov.se/content/1/c6/18/03/81/d054fbfb.pdf

Mitchell, G. J. (2007, December 13). *Report to the Commissioner of Baseball of an independent investigation into the illegal use of steroids and other performance enhancing substances by players in major league baseball.* Retrieved from http://graphics8.nytimes.com/packages/pdf/sports/mitchell_report_20071213.pdf

Mitten, M. J. (2009). Legal issues arising out of blood testing for human growth hormone. *Drug Testing and Analysis, 1*, 434–436.

Møller, V. (2008). *The doping devil.* Copenhagen: Books on Demand.

Moore, W. H. (1974). *The Kefauver committee and the politics of crime, 1950–1962.* Columbia: University of Missouri Press.

Mørbekerg, J. (2011, September 12–14). Nordic winter sports, biological passport, and the legal challenges. Presentation made at the international symposium sports medicine and doping in Europe, Freiburg.

Moresco, G. (2005, May 20). Plebiscito per Petrucci ma col pasticcio Di Centa. *La Repubblica, 56.* Retrieved from http://ricerca.repubblica.it/repubblica/archivio/repubblica/2005/05/20/plebiscito-per-petrucci-ma-col-pasticcio-di.html

Moresco, G. (2005b, April 11). Rosati e Santilli tornano i soliti noti dell' antidoping. *La Repubblica, 51.* Retrieved from http://ricerca.repubblica.it/repubblica/archivio/repubblica/2005/04/11/rosati-santilli-tornano-soliti-noti-dell-antidoping.html

Müller, R. (2010). History of doping and doping control. In Detlef Thieme & Peter Hemmersbach (Eds.), *Doping in sports: Handbook of experimental pharmacology* (vol. 195). Berlin: Springer. Retrieved from http://www.anabolicsteroidcalculator.com/resources/articles/ebooks/doping/chapter1.pdf

Müller, E., Melioli, G., & Minuto, F. (2002). Perizia per conto della Procura della Repubblica presso il Tribunale di Torino sul caso GH.

Müller-Platz, C., Boos, C., & Klaus Müller, R. (2006). *Doping beim Freizeit- und Breitensport.* Berlin: Robert-Koch-Institut. Retrieved from http://www.drogenbeauftragte.de/fileadmin/dateien-dba/DrogenundSucht/Medikamente/Bilder/Downloads/Doping_beim_Freizeit-_und_Breitensport_060901_Drogenbeauftragte.pdf

Nadelmann, E. A. (1989). Drug prohibition in the United States: Costs, consequences, and alternatives. *Science, 245*, 939–947.

NAS. (2011). Comando Carabinieri per la tutela della salute. Reparto Analisi. Definizione delle dosi delle sostanze dopanti. Mimeo.

NAS. (2012). Comando Carabinieri per la tutela della salute. Reparto Analisi. Cenni storici. Retrieved from http://www.carabinieri.it/Internet/Cittadino/Informazioni/Tutela/Salute/

NAS Bologna. (2000, June 21). Comando Carabinieri per la tutela della salute. Nucleo Antisofisticazioni e Sanità di Bologna. Procedimento penale a carico di S. M. + altri. Atti relativi all'indagine delegata sul commercio clandestino di sostanze ormonali e a effetto anabolizzante destinate al doping umano. Informativa conclusiva. Rif. Proc. Pen. n. 1701/99-21 RGNR.

NAS Brescia. (2011). Comando Carabinieri per la tutela della salute. Nucleo Antisofisticazioni e Sanità di Brescia. Informativa finale sull'esito delle indagini effettuatenei confronti di G.N. + altri.

NAS Firenze. (2002). Comando Carabinieri per la tutela della salute. Nucleo Antisofisticazioni e Sanità di Firenze. Informativa finale sull'esito delle indagini effettuate: Operazione Quadrifoglio.

NAS Firenze. (2005). Indagine oil for drug. Informativa conclusiva sull'esito delle indagini.

NAS Napoli. (2003). Comando Carabinieri per la tutela della salute. Nucleo Antisofisticazioni e Sanità di Napoli. *Comunicazione notizia di reato (ex art. 347 CPP)* alla Procura della Repubblica presso il Tribunale di Santa Maria Capua Vetere. Procedimento penale n. 10493/2002 RGNR.

NAS Padova. (2009, November 3). Comando Carabinieri per la tutela della salute. Nucleo Antisofisticazioni e Sanità di Padova. Operazione "Flebo": Utilizzo di sostanze dopanti nel ciclismo e nel rugby. Relazione al 2° Master Investigativo Antidoping. Rome.

NAS Treviso. (2009, November 3). Carabinieri per la tutela della salute Nucleo Antisofisticazioni e Sanità di Treviso. Indagine "Muscoli e Fiale". Relazione al 2° Master Investigativo Antidoping. Rome.

NAS Udine. (2009a). Carabinieri per la tutela della salute Nucleo Antisofisticazioni e Sanità di Udine. California. Relazione al 2° Master Investigativo Antidoping, Rome.

NAS Udine. (2009b). Carabinieri per la tutela della salute Nucleo Antisofisticazioni e Sanità di Udine. Triamin. Relazione al 2° Master Investigativo Antidoping, Rome.

Nelken, D. (2004). Using the concept of legal culture. *Australian Journal of Legal Philosophy, 29*, 1–26.

Nelken, D. (2007). White collar crime. In M. Maguire, R. Morgan, & R. Reiner (Eds.), *The Oxford handbook of criminology* (4th ed., pp. 733–770). Oxford: Oxford University Press.

Neuer Zürcher Zeitung. (2000, November 3). *EPO für alle: Conconi soll sich EPO gespritzt haben—Ende der Befragungen in Lille*. Retrieved from http://www.limmatsharks.com/presse/nzz001103.html

Neuer Zürcher Zeitung. (2004). *Ein belastender Freispruch Conconis*. Retrieved from http://www.nzz.ch/aktuell/startseite/newzzDRRCIMIZ-12-1.226964

Newkirk, T. C. (1998). *Speech by SEC staff: Insider trading—A U.S. perspective*. Retrieved from http://www.sec.gov/news/speech/speecharchive/1998/spch221.htm#FOOTNOTE_52

Nicolella, G. (2008). *L'ordinamento sportivo e le organizzazioni collettive: il CONI*. Retrieved from http://www.altalex.com/index.php?idnot=42496

Nilsson, S., Biagi, A., Marklund, B., & Fridlund, B. (2001). The prevalence of the use of androgenic anabolic steroids by adolescents in a county of Sweden. *European Journal of Public Health, 11*, 195–197.

Numa, M. (2010). Anabolizzanti, poliziotti in manette: Il traffico passava dalle loro mani: 21 agenti denunciati in tutta Italia. *La Stampa*. Retrieved from http://www3.lastampa.it/torino/sezioni/cronaca/articolo/lstp/280202/

Oldersma, F., Snippe, J., & Bieleman, B. (2002). *Doping en handel: Onderzoek naar aard en omvang van dopinghandel en ontwikkeling van indicatoren*. Groningen/Rotterdam: Bureau Intraval.

Pacifici, R., & Donati, A. (2011). Consulenza tecnica nel procedimento penale 5876/08 Procura della Repubblica presso il Tribunale di Mantova, Mimeo.

Packer, G. (2011, June 27). A dirty business: New York City's top prosecutor takes on Wall Street crime. *The New Yorker*. Retrieved from http://www.newyorker.com/reporting/2011/06/27/110627fa_fact_packer#ixzz1r6YB8jN7

Pallesen, S., Josendal, O., Johnsen, B. H., Larsen, S., & Molde, H. (2006). Anabolic steroid use in high school students. *Substance Use & Misuse, 41*, 1705–1717.

Paoli, L. (2000). *Pilot project to describe and analyse local drug markets—First Phase Final Report: Illegal drug markets in Frankfurt and Milan*. Lisbon: EMCDDA.

Paoli, L. (2002a). Flexible hierarchies and dynamic disorder: The drug distribution system in Frankfurt and Milan. *Drugs: Education, Prevention and Policy, 9*(2), 143–151.

Paoli, L. (2002b). The paradoxes of organized crime. *Crime, Law and Social Change, 37*(1), 51–97.

Paoli, L. (2003a). Die unsichtbare Hand des Marktes: Illegaler Drogenhandel in Deutschland, Italien und Russland. *Kölner Zeitschrift für Soziologie und Sozialpsychologie, 43*(Sonderheft), 356–383.

Paoli, L. (2003b). *Mafia brotherhoods: Organized crime, Italian style*. New York: Oxford University Press.

Paoli, L. (2008). Organized crime: New label, new phenomenon or policy expedient? *International Annals of Criminology, 46*(1/2), 37–60.

Paoli, L. (2012). Doping and anti-doping: Neglected issues in criminology. *European Journal of Crime, Criminal Law and Criminal Justice, 20*(3), 231–238.

Paoli, L. (2013). *Oxford handbook of organized crime*. New York: Oxford University Press.

Paoli, L., & Fijnaut, C. (2004). Introduction to Part I: The history of the concept. In C. Fijnaut & L. Paoli (Eds.), *Organised crime in Europe: Concepts, patterns and policies in the European Union and beyond* (pp. 21–46). Dordrecht: Springer.

Paoli, L., Greenfield, V. A., & Reuter, P. (2009). *The world heroin market: Can supply be cut?* New York: Oxford University Press.

Paoli, L., & Reuter, P. (2008). Drug trafficking and ethnic minorities in Western Europe. *European Journal of Criminology, 5*, 13–37.

Paoli, L., & Singler, A. (Eds.). (2013). *Sportsmedizin und Doping in Europa*. Bonn: Bisp.

Parkinson, A. B., & Evans, N. A. (2006). Anabolic androgenic steroids: A survey of 500 users. *Medicine and Science in Sports and Exercise, 38*(4), 644–651.

Pärssinen, M., Kujala, U., Vartiainen, E., Sarna, S., & Seppälä, T. (2000). Increased premature mortality of competitive powerlifters suspected to have used anabolic agents. *International Journal of Sports Medicine, 21*(3), 225–227.

Parzeller, M. (Ed.). (2011). *Rechtsvergleich der strafrechtlichen Normen und der strafprozessualen Verfolgung des Dopings im Leistungs- und Spitzensport in Deutschland, Frankreich, Italien, Schweiz und Spanien*. Bonn: Bundesinstitut für Sportwissenschaft.

Parzeller, M., Prittwitz, C., Bratzke, H., Caldarelli, M., Centamore, R., Lapetra Costa, M., et al. (2009/2010). Rechtsvergleich der strafrechtlichen Normen und der strafprozessualen Verfolgung des Dopings im Leistungs- und Spitzensport in Deutschland, Italien, Frankreich, Schweiz und Spanien. *BISP-Jahrbuch Foschungsförderung, 2009/10*, 315–326.

Pasqualetto, A. (2011). Ricchi con i super atleti dopati» Sotto accusa le banche svizzere. *Corriere della Sera*. Retrieved from http://archiviostorico.corriere.it/2011/settembre/21/Ricchi_con_super_atleti_dopati_co_9_110921008.shtml

Pearce, F., & Tombs, S. (1990). Ideology, hegemony, and empiricism. Compliance theories of regulation. *British Journal of Criminology, 30*(4), 423–443.

Pearsall, J. (Ed.). (1998). *The new Oxford dictionary of English*. New York: Oxford University Press.

Pearson, G., & Hobbs, D. (2001). *Middle market drug distribution*. London: Home Office Research, Development and Statistics Directorate.

Perry, P. J., Andersen, K. H., & Yates, W. R. (1990). Illicit anabolic steroid use in athletes: A case series analysis. *The American Journal of Sports Medicine, 18*, 422–428.

Perry, P. J., Kutscher, E. C., Lund, B. C., Yates, W. R., Holman, T. L., & Demers, L. (2003). Measures of aggression and mood changes in male weightlifters with and without androgenic anabolic steroid use. *Journal of Forensic Science, 48*, 646–651.

Perry, P. J., Lund, B. C., Deninger, M. J., Kutscher, E. C., & Schneider, J. (2005). Anabolic steroid use in weightlifters and bodybuilders: An internet survey of drug utilization. *Clinical Journal of Sport Medicine, 15*(5), 326–330.

Peters, C., Schulz, T., & Michna, H. (Eds.). (2002). *Biomedical side effects of doping*. Project for the European Union. Cologne: Sport und Buch Strauss.

Peterson, A. (2010). But she doesn't run like a girl ..: The ethic of fair play and the flexibility of the binary conception of sex. *Tulane Journal of International and Comparative Law, 19*, 315–330.

Petersson, A., Garle, M., Granath, F., & Thiblin, I. (2006). Morbidity and mortality in patients testing positively for the presence of anabolic androgenic steroids in connection with receiving medical care. A controlled retrospective cohort study. *Drug and Alcohol Dependence, 81*(3), 215–220.

Petrini, R. (2012, May 12). *2012: già sottratti 190 milioni così evadono i professionisti*. Retrieved from http://www.repubblica.it/economia/2012/05/11/news/dossier_fisco-34892200/?ref=HREC1-4

Petróczi, A., Mazanov, J., Nepus, T., Backhouse, S. H., & Naughton, D. P. (2008). Comfort in big numbers: Does over-estimation of doping prevalence in others indicate self-involvement? *Journal of Occupational Medicine and Toxicology, 3*, 19.

Pontani, A. (1996, May 11). Un totoministri anche per il CONI. *La Repubblica, 42*. Retrieved from http://ricerca.repubblica.it/repubblica/archivio/repubblica/1996/05/11/un-totoministri-anche-per-il-coni.html

Pope, H. G., & Brower, K. J. (2009). Anabolic–androgenic steroid related disorders. In B. Sadock & V. Sadock (Eds.), *Comprehensive textbook of psychiatry* (9th ed., pp. 1419–1431). Philadelphia, PA: Lippincott Williams & Wilkins.

Pope, H. G., & Katz, D. L. (1994). Psychiatric and medical effects of anabolic-androgenic steroid use: A controlled study of 160 athletes. *Archives of General Psychiatry, 51*(5), 375–382.

Pope, H. G., Olivardia, R., Gruber, A. J., & Borowiecki, J. (1999). Evolving ideals of male body image as seen through action toys. *International Journal of Eating Disorders, 26*, 65–72.

Pope, H. G., Phillips, K. A., & Olivardia, R. (2000). *The Adonis complex: The secret crisis of male body obsession*. New York: Free Press.

Pound, R. W. (2011a, September 12–14). WADA—A success story? Presentation made at the Freiburg Symposium sports medicine and doping, Freiburg.

Pound, R. W. (2011b, October 3–6). Responses to corruption in sport. Speech at Play the Game, Cologne.

Povoledo, E. (2012, February 25). Italian court throws out case against Berlusconi. *The New York Times*. Retrieved from http://www.nytimes.com/2012/02/26/world/europe/bribery-case-against-berlusconi-is-thrown-out.html?_r=1

PR Newswire. (2004). *Lance Armstrong response to Dr. Michele Ferrari Italian Court decision*. Retrieved from http://www.prnewswire.co.uk/cgi/news/release?id=131301

Preble, E., & Casey, J. J. (1969). Taking care of business, the heroin user's life on the street. *International Journal of the Addiction, 4*, 1–24.

Pressi, L. (1996). Deposizione presso i carabinieri del NAS di Firenze, nell'ambito dell'indagine giudiziaria della Procura della Repubblica presso il Tribunale di Arezzo, poi trasmessa per competenza presso la Procura della Repubblica presso il Tribunale di Firenze.

Procura della Repubblica presso il Tribunale CEPdi Torino. (2012). *I Magistrati_I gruppi specializzati*. Retrieved from http://www.procura.torino.it/mag_gruppi.aspx

Procura della Repubblica presso il Tribunale di Bergamo. (2009). Richiesta di applicazione di misure cautelari nei confronti di P. + altri. Procedimento 8992/01 RGNR.

Procura della Repubblica presso il Tribunale di Bolzano. (2002). Richiesta di applicazione di misure cautelari nei confronti di P.M. + 5. R.G.N.R. 503/02.

Procura della Repubblica presso il Tribunale di Ferrara. (2000). Richiesta di archiviazione parziale. Procedimento penale control Pescante Mario + 13 altri. N. 893/99/21 R.G. notizie di reato/Mod. 21.

Punch, M. (1996). *Dirty business: Exploring corporate misconduct: Analysis and cases*. London: Sage.

Quaglio, G., Fornasiero, A., Mezzelani, P., Moreschini, S., Lugoboni, F., & Lechi, A. (2009). Anabolic steroids: Dependence and complications of chronic use. *International Emergency Medicine, 4*(4), 289–296.

Quotidiano.net. (2001). *Doping: rinvio a giudizio per 18 persone nel mondo del ciclismo*. Retrieved from http://qn.quotidiano.net/2001/05/02/2111814-Doping-rinvio-a-giudizio-per-18-persone-nel-mondo-del-ciclismo.shtml

Read, B. (2010). WADA ignore calls for change, confirming cannabis will remain a banned substance in sport. *The Australian*. Retrieved from www.foxsports.com.au/other-sports/wada-ignore-calls-for-change-confirming-cannabis-will-remain-a-banned-substance-in-sport/story-e6frf56c-122594351485

Rechtskommission des Sports gegen Doping. (2005). *Abschlussbericht zu möglichen gesetzlichen Initiativen für eine konsequente Verhinderung, Verfolgung und Ahndung des Dopings im Sport*. Frankfurt: Deutscher Olympischer Sportsbund. Retrieved from http://www.dosb.de/fileadmin/fm-dosb/downloads/dosb/endfassung_abschlussbericht.pdf

Reiss, A. J., Jr., & Tonry, M. (1993). Organizational crime. In A. J. Reiss & M. Tonry (Eds.), *Crime and justice—The law: Crime in complex organizations* (Vol. 18, pp. 1–10). Chicago: University of Chicago Press.

Reuter, P. (1983). *Disorganized crime: The economics of the visible hand*. Cambridge, MA: MIT Press.

Reuter, P. (1985). *The organization of illegal markets: An economic analysis*. Washington, DC: National Institute of Justice.

Reuter, P. (2013). Drug trafficking. In L. Paoli (Ed.), *Handbook of organized crime*. New York: Oxford University Press.

Reuter, P., & Greenfield, V. (2001). Measuring global drug markets; How good are the numbers and why should we care about them. *World Economics, 2*(4), 159–173.

Reuter, P., & Haaga, J. (1989). *The organization of high-level drug markets: An exploratory study*. Santa Monica, CA: RAND.

Reuters. (2007, April 2). *Pfizer to pay $35 mln in Genotropin settlements*. Retrieved from http://www.reuters.com/article/2007/04/02/idUSWNAS544720070402

Reuters. (2007). *Pfizer to pay $35 mln in Genotropin settlements*. Retrieved from http://www.reuters.com/article/2007/04/02/idUSWNAS544720070402

Reuters. (2012). *Olympics-Athletics-Schwazer tested positive for EPO*. Retrieved from http://www.reuters.com/article/2012/08/07/olympics-dope-ita-schwazer-idUSL4E8J74MR20120807

Riis, B. (2012). *Riis*. Kingston upon Thames: Vision Sports.

Rössner, D. (2009). « Sportbetrug » und Strafrecht: Notwendige Differenzierung und kriminalpolitische Überlegungen. In Stefan Niebl, Nils Kassebohm, & Hans Lilie (Eds.). *Festschrift für Volkmar Mehle* (pp. 567–579). Baden-Baden: Nomos.

Rössner, D. (2011). Der Sport im Strafrecht und Strafprozessrecht. In J. Adolphsen (Ed.), *Sportrecht in der Praxis* (pp. 399–427). Stuttgart: Kohlhammer.

Rost, P. (2006). *The whistleblower: Confessions of a healthcare hitman*. New York: Soft Skull Press.

Rudolph, H. (2009–2010). Horse sense and high competition: Procedural concerns in equestrian doping arbitration. *Kentucky Journal for Equine, Agriculture, and Natural Resources Law, 2(1)*, 47–80.

Ryan, B. (2011). *Italian judge set to decide if 32 named in Mantova doping investigation should go on trial*. Retrieved from http://www.cyclingnews.com/news/italian-judge-set-to-decide-if-32-named-in-mantova-doping-investigation-should-go-on-trial

Sansa, F. (2011). Bentornati nel porto delle nebbie. *Il Fatto Quotidiano*. Retrieved from http://www.ilfattoquotidiano.it/2011/08/16/bentornati-nel-%E2%80%9Cporto-delle-nebbie%E2%80%9D/151406/

Savulescu, J., Foddy, B., & Clayton, M. (2004a). Why we should allow performance enhancing drugs in sport. *British Journal of Sports Medicine, 38*, 666–670.

Savulescu, J., Foddy, B., & Clayton, M. (2004b). Why we should allow performance enhancing drugs in sport. *British Journal of Sports Medicine, 38*(6), 666–670.

Savulescu, J. B., ter Meulen, J. R., & Kahane, G. (Eds.). (2011). *Enhancing human capacities*. Oxford: Wiley.

Scarpino, V. A., Arrigo, G., Benzi, S., Garattini, C. L., Vecchia, L. R., Bernardi, G., et al. (1990). Evaluation of prevalence of "doping" among Italian athletes. *Lancet, 336*, 1048–1050.

Schlink, L. (2011). Mafia big threat for 2012 London Olympics. *The Telegraph*. Retrieved from http://www.dailytelegraph.com.au/sport/more-sports/mafia-big-threat-for-2012-london-olympics/story-e6frey6i-1226013990795

Schnädelbach, D. (2010). Tipologie di medicinali contraffatti: Molte forme diverse, lo stesso pericolo. In Domenico Di Giorgio (Ed.), *Farmaci contraffatti. Il fenomeno e le attivitá di contrasto* pp. (31–35). Milano: Tecniche nuove.

Schneider, A., & Butcher, R. (2001). An ethical analysis of drug testing. In W. Wilson & E. Derse (Eds.), *Doping in elite sports*. Champaing, IL: Human Kinetics.

Seccombe, R. (1995). Squeezing the balloon: International drugs policy. *Drug and Alcohol Review, 14*(3), 311–316.

Senaat. (2005, March 9). De problematiek van de doping in de sport: Vaststellingen en *aanbevelingen. Text approved by the Commission for Social Affairs. Hearings* 2004–2005. Retrieved from http://www.senate.be/www/?MIval=/publications/viewPubDoc&TID=50340939&LANG=nl

Severino, P. (2012). Relazione del guardasigilli sull'amministrazione della Giustizia nell'anno 2011: Anno 2012. Retrieved from http://www.giustizia.it/giustizia//it/mg_6_9.wp?contentId=NOL57984

Simon, P. (2010). Faktenauflistung und Thesen für den Sportausschuss des Deutschen Bundestages, Session of November 10.

Simon, P. (2011, September 12–14). How many athletes dope? doping and prevalence. Presentation made at the symposium internationales symposium "Sportmedizin und Doping in Europa", Freiburg.

Simon, P., Striegel, H., Aust, F., Dietz, K., & Ulrich, R. (2006). Doping in fitness sports: Estimated number of unreported cases and individual probability of doping. *Addiction, 101*(11), 1640–1644.

Simpson, S. S. (2010–2011). Making sense of white-collar crime: Theory and research. *Ohio State Journal of Criminal Law, 8*, 481–502.

Singler, A. (2011). *Dopingprävention—Anspruch und Wirklichkeit*. Shaker: Aachen.

Singler, A. (2012). *Doping und Enhancement. Interdisziplinäre Studien zur Pathologie gesellschaftlicher Leistungsorientierung*. Göttingen: Cuvillier.

Singler, A., & Treutlein, G. (2001). *Doping. Von der Analyse zur Prävention—Vorbeugung gegen abweichendes Verhalten in soziologischem und pädagogischem Zugang.*. Aachen: Meyer & Meyer.

Singler, A., & Treutlein, G. (2010). *Doping im Spitzensport. Sportwissenschaftliche Analysen zur nationalen und internationalen Leistungsentwickung* (5th ed.). Aachen: Meyer & Meyer.

Sjöqvist, F., Garle, M., & Rane, A. (2008). Use of doping agents, particularly anabolic steroids, in sports and society. *The Lancet, 371*(9627), 1872–1882.

Smargiassi, M. (1996, April 21). Il professore in bici vola a quaranta all' ora. *La Repubblica, 3*. Retrieved from http://ricerca.repubblica.it/repubblica/archivio/repubblica/1996/04/21/il-professore-in-bici-vola-quaranta-all.html

Smith, D., Jr. (1975). *The Mafia mystique*. New York: Basic Books.

Smith, I. (2012). *Why WADA should not ban athletes for recreational drug use*. Retrieved from http://www.asser.nl/default.aspx?site_id=11&level1=13910&level2=13974&level3=&textid=35960

Soek, J. (2006). *The strict liability principle and the human rights of athletes in doping cases*. The Hague: Asser.

Sottas, P. E., Robinson, N., Fischetto, G., Dollé, G., Alonso, J. M., & Saugy, M. (2011). Prevalence of blood doping in samples collected from Elite Track and Field Athletes. *Clinical Chemistry, 57*(5), 762–769.

Spezia, L. (2001, March 16). Guandalini condannato a due anni. *La Repubblica, 1 of the Bologna section*. Retrieved from http://ricerca.repubblica.it/repubblica/archivio/repubblica/2001/03/16/guandalini-condannato-due-anni.html

Spezia, L. (2009, March 29). Maxi-inchiesta sul doping Verzelli di nuovo arrestato, *7 of the Bologna section*. Retrieved from http://ricerca.repubblica.it/repubblica/archivio/repubblica/2009/03/26/maxi-inchiesta-sul-doping-verzelli-di-nuovo-arrestato.html

Spitzer, G. (1998). *Doping in der DDR. Ein historischer Überblick zu einer konspirativen Praxis*. Köln: Strauss.

Sportausschuss des Deutschen Bundestages. (2011). Wortprotokoll, *34*. Sitzung. Retrieved from http://www.jensweinreich.de/wp-content/uploads/2011/10/34-SpA-Protokoll.pdf

Stevens, A. (2011). *Drugs, crime and public health: The political economy of drug policy*. London: Routledge.

Stewart, J. (1992). *Den of thieves*. New York: Simon and Schuster.

Stirling, A. E. & Kerr, G. A. (2006). Perfectionism and mood states among recreational and elite athletes. *Athletic Insight. 8(4)*, 13–27. Retrieved from http://www.athleticinsight.com/Vol8Iss4/PerfectionismPDF.pdf

Striegel, H., Simon, P., Frisch, S., Roecker, K., Dietz, K., Dickhuth, H. H., et al. (2006). Anabolic ergogenic substance users in fitness-sports: A distinct group supported by the health care system. *Drug and Alcohol Dependence, 81*, 11–19.

Striegel, H., Ulrich, R., & Simon, P. (2010). Randomized response estimates for doping and illicit drug use in elite athletes. *Drug and Alcohol Dependence, 106*(2–3), 230–232.

Sutherland, E. H. (1945). Is white-collar crime? *American Sociological Review, 10*(2), 132–139.

Sutherland, E. H. (1983). *White-collar crime: The uncut version*. New Haven: Yale University Press. (Original work published in 1948)

Swedish National Institute of Public Health. (2010). *Doping in Sweden—An inventory of its spread, consequences and interventions*. Östersund: Swedish National Institute of Public Health. Retrieved from http://www.fhi.se/PageFiles/10951/R2010-21-Doping%20in%20Sweden-webb.pdf

T.M.C. Asser Instituut. (2010). The implementation of the WADA code in the European Union. Report commissioned by the Flemish Minister responsible for sport in view of the Belgian Presidency of the European Union in the second half of 2010. Retrieved from http://www.asser.nl/upload/documents/9202010_100013rapport%20Asserstudie%20%28Engels%29.pdf

Tappan, P. W. (1947). Who is the criminal? *American Sociological Review, 12*, 96–102.

Taylor, P., & Gratton, C. (2000). *The economics of sport and recreation: An economic analysis*. London: Routledge.

taz. (2011, April 23). "Die Angst fährt im Hintergrund immer mit." Retrieved from http://www.taz.de/1/archiv/digitaz/artikel/?ressort=hi&dig=2011%2F04%2F23%2Fa0029&cHash=cf04ad32b6

Teetzel, S. (2004). 'The Road to Wada', Seventh International Symposium for Olympic Research, October, pp. 213–24. If you want you can add "quoted in Hanstad, D. V., A. Smith and I. Waddington. 2008. The Establishment of the World Anti-Doping Agency: A Study of the Management of Organizational Change and Unplanned Outcomes. *International Review for the Sociology of Sport*, 227–249.

Teetzel, S. (2011). Rules and reform: Eligibility, gender differences, and the Olympic games. *Sport in Society, 13*(3), 386–398.

Teitler, S., & Ram, H. (2008). Analyzing the new world anti-doping code: A different perspective. *The International Sports Law Journal*, 1–2. Retrieved from http://findarticles.com/p/articles/mi_m2ABX/is_1-2/ai_n42367138/?tag=content;col1

The Economist. (2011a, February 16). Silvio Berlusconi and the law: Back in the dock. Retrieved from http://www.economist.com/blogs/dailychart/2011/02/silvio_berlusconi_and_law

The Economist. (2011b, October 13). Raj Rajaratnam's insider trading: Away with you. *The Economist*. Retrieved from http://www.economist.com/blogs/schumpeter/2011/10/raj-rajaratnam%E2%80%99s-insider-trading

The Economist. (2011c, June 9). *Renaissance men*. Retrieved from http://www.economist.com/node/18780841

The Economist. (2011d, October 15). *Tipping the scales: The fight against crooked trading gathers pace*. Retrieved from http://www.economist.com/node/21532280

The Economist. (2012, January 18). *Seven down, many more to go*. Retrieved from http://www.economist.com/blogs/schumpeter/2012/01/insider-trading

The New York Times. (1994, August 23). *Olympic drug tests ignored*. Retrieved from http://www.nytimes.com/1994/08/23/sports/sports-people-olympics-olympic-drug-tests-ignored.html?n=Top%2fReference%2fTimes%20Topics%2fSubjects%2fT%2fTests%20and%20Testing

The Sunday Times. (October 28). *When the lying had to stop*. Retrieved from http://www.sunday-times.co.uk/news/pages/Sunday-Times/frontpage.html?2387908

The Telegraph. (2001). *Davids and Couto hit with FIFA bans*. Retrieved from http://www.telegraph.co.uk/sport/football/international/3006500/Davids-and-Couto-hit-with-FIFA-bans.html

The Telegraph. (2011, June 17). *International Cycling Union to ban dopers from team staff*. Retrieved from http://www.telegraph.co.uk/sport/othersports/cycling/8582665/International-Cycling-Union-to-ban-dopers-from-team-staff.html

The Telegraph. (2013, January 18). *Lance Armstrong's interview with Oprah Winfrey: The transcript*. Retrieved from http://www.telegraph.co.uk/sport/othersports/cycling/lancearmstrong/9810801/Lance-Armstrongs-interview-with-Oprah-Winfrey-the-transcript.html

Thevis, M., Geyer, H., Thomas, A., & Schänzer, W. (2011). Trafficking of drug candidates relevant for sports drug testing: Detection of non-approved therapeutics categorized as anabolic and gene doping agents in products distributed via the Internet. *Drug Testing and Analysis, 3*(5), 331–336.

Thevis, M., Sauer, M., Geyer, H., Sigmund, G., Mareck, U., & Schänzer, W. (2008). Determination of the prevalence of anabolic steroids, stimulants, and selected drugs subject to doping controls among elite sport students using analytical chemistry. *Journal of Sports Science, 26*, 1059–1065.

Thiblin, I., Kristiansson, M., & Rajs, J. (1997). Anabolic androgenic steroids and behavioural patterns among violent offenders. *Journal of Forensic Psychiatry, 8*, 299–310.

Thiblin, I., & Parlklo, T. (2002). Anabolic androgenic steroids and violence. *Acta Psychiatrica Scandinivica Supplementum, 412*, 125–128.

Thiblin, I., & Petersson, A. (2005). Pharmacoepidemiology of anabolic androgenic steroids: A review. *Fundamental and Clinical Pharmacology, 19*(1), 27–44.

Thiblin, I., Runeson, B., & Rajs, J. (1999). Anabolic androgenic steroids and suicide. *Annals of Clinical Psychiatry, 11*(4), 223–231.

Thomas, A., Geyer, H., Kamber, M., Schänzer, W., & Thevis, M. (2008). Mass spectrometric determination of gonadotrophin-releasing hormone (GnRH) in human urine for doping control purposes by means of LC–ESI-MS/MS. *Journal of Mass Spectrometry, 43*, 908–915.

Tirrò, S., & Valvo, L. (2010). Tipologie di medicinali contraffatti: Molte forme diverse, lo stesso pericolo. In Domenico Di Giorgio (Ed.), *Farmaci contraffatti. Il fenomeno e le attivitá di contrasto* (pp. 27–30). Milano: Tecniche nuove.

Todd, J., & Todd, T. (2001). Significant events in the history of drug testing and the Olympic movement, 1960–1999. In W. Wilson & E. Derse (Eds.), *Doping in elite sport: The politics of drugs in the Olympic movement* (pp. 65–126). Champaign: Human Kinetics.

Toti, G. (2002, March 7). Caso GH, tre sport nel mirino. *Corriere della Sera, 44*. Retrieved from http://archiviostorico.corriere.it/2002/marzo/07/Caso_tre_sport_nel_mirino_co_0_0203075649.shtml

Toti, G. (2003, March 26). Caso Conconi, indietro tutta. *Corriere della Sera, 46*. Retrieved from http://archiviostorico.corriere.it/2003/marzo/26/Caso_Conconi_indietro_tutta_co_0_030326239.shtml

Tranfaglia, N. (Ed.). (2001). *La sentenza Andreotti. Politica, mafia e giustizia nell'Italia contemporanea*. Milano: Garzanti.

Transparency International. (2011). *Corruption perceptions index*. Retrieved from http://cpi.transparency.org/cpi2011/results/

Travaglio, M. (1998, August 21). Provette sparite, un blitz al Coni. *La Repubblica, 46*.

Travaglio, M. (2005, October 6). Viva Storace—bananas. *L'Unità, 12*. Retrieved from http://cerca.unita.it/ARCHIVE/xml/175000/171330.xml?key=marco+travaglio&first=1461&orderby=1
Travaglio, M. (2007, June 1). Doping: fu un disegno criminoso. *La Repubblica, 54*. Retrieved from http://ricerca.repubblica.it/repubblica/archivio/repubblica/2007/06/01/doping-fu-un-disegno-criminoso.html?ref=search
Travaglio, M. (n.d.). *La Cronistoria di Tangentopoli*. Retrieved from http://files.meetup.com/213341/La%20Cronistoria%20di%20Tangentopoli_Marco%20Travaglio.pdf
Traversi, A. (2001). *Diritto penale dello sport*. Milan: Giuffré.
Tribunale di Bologna. (2000). Ordinanza di custodia cautelare nei confronti di P.B. + altri.
Tribunale di Bologna. (2004, October 1). Sentenza nei confronti di Ferrari Michele + 3. No. 2997/97 R.G. notizie di reato.
Tribunale di Ferrara. (2003, November 19). Sentenza nei confronti di Conconi Francesco + altri. No. 893/99 RGNG.
Tribunale di Forlì. (2009). Ordinanza di custodia cautelare nei confronti di V.M. + altri. No. 3870/07 RGNR.
Tribunale di Milano. (1998, September 29). *S*entenza nella causa penale a carico di M.B.+ 2.
Tribunale di Ravenna. (2004). Ordinanza applicative di misure cautelari nei confronti di M.A. + 73. N. 619/2003 21 R.G.N.R.
Tribunale di Rimini. (2011). Ordinanza di custodia cautelare nei confronti di V.E. B. + 4. No. 2898. RGNR.
Tribunale di San Remo. (2005). Sentenza a seguito di rito abbreviato nel procedimento penale nei confronti di D.P. D. + altri. Sentenza n. 362/05., N. 2336/03 RGNR.
Tribunale di Siracusa. (2010). Ordinanza di custodia cautelare nei confronti di A.G. + altri. Proc. n. 857807/07 RGNR e Proc n. 16/2010 RGGGIP.
Tribunale di Torino. (1994). Ordinanza di custodia cautelare in carcere nei confronti di B.S. + altri.
Tribunale di Torino. (2004, November 26). Sentenza nei confronti di Gribaudo Antonio + 1. N. 63/00 R.G. notizie di reato.
Tribunale di Torino. (2009). Sentenza nei confronti di A.C. + 2 . Proc. 2115/06 RGNR.
Tribunale di Torino. (2012a, July 16). Ordinanza di applicazione di misura cautelari nei confronti di V.G. + 5. N. 4654/10 RGNR.
Tribunale di Torino. (2012b, June 23). Sentenza nei confronti di A.G. + 1. No. 63700 R.G. notizie di reato.
Tribunale di Torino. (2012c, July 6). Sentenza nei confronti di + S.V. + 8. 4471/06 R.G. notizie di reato.
Tropeano, L. (2005, October 18). Olimpiadi: La guerra del doping. *La Stampa, 35*.
U.S. Anti-Doping Agency. (2012a). Anti-doping rules violations. Letter sent by U.S.ADA on June 12 to Mr. Johan Bruyneel and others.
U.S. Anti-Doping Agency. (2012b, July 10). Members of the United States Postal Service Pro-Cycling Team Doping Conspiracy, Dr. Garcia Del Moral, Dr. Ferrari And Trainer Marti Receive Lifetime Bans For Doping Violations. Retrieved from http://www.usada.org/media/sanction-usps7102012
U.S. Anti-Doping Agency. (2012c). Report on Proceedings under the World Anti-Doping Code and the Usada Protocol: United States Anti-Doping Agency, Claimant, v. Lance Armstrong, Respondent. Reasoned Decision of the United States Anti-Doping Agency on Disqualification and Ineligibility. Retrieved from http://cyclinginvestigation.usada.org/
U.S. Drug Enforcement Administration. (2005). News Release. International Internet Drug Ring Shattered—E-Traffickers Arrested: Indian/Costa Rican/Canadian Cyber Criminal Alliances Shut Down. Retrieved from http://centrostudi.gruppoabele.org/doping/?q=node/187
U.S. Drug Enforcement Administration. (2007). *DEA announces largest steroid enforcement action in U.S. History*. Retrieved from http://www.justice.gov/dea/pubs/pressrel/pr092407.html
U.S. Drug Enforcement Administration. (2012). *Stride data*. Retrieved from http://www.justice.gov/dea/stride_data.html
U.S. Government Accounting Office. (2005). *Anabolic steroids are easily purchased without a prescription and present significant challenges to law enforcement officials*. GAO-06-243R Anabolic Steroids. Retrieved from http://www.gao.gov/new.items/d06243r.pdf

U.S. Senate. (1951).m *Third interim report of the special committee to investigate organized crime in interstate commerce (Kefauver Committee).* 81st Congress, 2nd session. Washington, DC: U.S. Government Printing Office.

U.S. Senate, Judiciary Committee. (1957). *Investigations on improper activities in the labor or management field.* Hearings. Washington, DC: U.S. Government Printing Office.

UK Antidoping. (2011, February 17). *Future of anti-doping is in intelligence says WADA President.* Retrieved from http://www.ukad.org.uk/news/article/anti-doping-press-conference

UNESCO. (2007, January 5). *International Convention against Doping in Sport: 41 States will take part in first Conference of States Parties.* Retrieved from http://portal.unesco.org/en/ev.php-URL_ID=36311&URL_DO=DO_TOPIC&URL_SECTION=201.html

UNICRI. (2007). *Counterfeiting: A global spread, a global threat.* Retrieved from http://www.unicri.it/news/2007/0712-3_counterfeiting_crt_foundation/UNODCCP

United Nations General Assembly. (1994, December 2). *Report of the world ministerial conference on organized transnational crime.* A/49/748. Retrieved from http://www.imolin.org/imolin/en/naples.html

United Nations General Assembly. (2000, November 2). *Report of the Ad Hoc Committee on the elaboration of a convention against transnational organized crime on the work of its first to eleventh session.* A/55/383. Retrieved from http://www.undcp.org/palermo/convmain.html

United Nations General Assembly Special Session. (1997). Political Declaration of the General Assembly. A/S-20/4 chapter V, Section A, clause 19. Retrieved from http://www.un.org/ga/20special/poldecla.htm

United Nations Office for Drug Control and Crime Prevention. (2001a). *Global illicit drug trends.* New York: United Nations.

United Nations Office for Drug Control and Crime Prevention. (2001). *Global illicit drug trends 2001.* N.p. United Nations.

United Nations Office on Drugs and Crime. (2005). *2005 World drug report.* New York: United Nations.

United Nations Office on Drugs and Crime. (2010). *World drug report 2010.* New York: United Nations.

United Nations Office on Drugs and Crime. (2012). *World drug report 2012.* New York: United Nations.

Van der Beken, T., & Kilchling, M. (Eds.). (2000). *The role of the public prosecutor in the European criminal justice systems.* Brussels: Koninklijke Vlaamse Academie van België voor Wetenschappen en Kunsten.

Van Duyne, P. (1997). Organised crime, corruption, and power. *Crime, Law and Social Change, 26*, 201–238.

VeloNews.com. (2011, June 17). UCI to ban doping violators from team staff positions. Retrieved from http://velonews.competitor.com/2011/06/news/uci-to-ban-doping-violators-from-team-staff-positions_179000

Vinton, N. (2005, October 29). Olympics; I.O.C. ends opposition to Italy's doping laws. *The New York Times.* Retrieved from http://select.nytimes.com/gst/abstract.html?res=F00C16F7355B0C7A8EDDA90994DD404482

Voet, W. (2000). *Prikken en slikken: 30 jaar doping in de wielersport.* Baarn: De Fontein.

Waddington, I. (2000). *Sport, health and drugs.* London: E&FN Spon.

Waddington, I. (2011). Client control and the limits of professional autonomy: Or why do sports physicians dope athletes? Paper presented at the symposium: "Doping and Sports medicine", Freiburg, 12–14 September.

Waddington, I., & Smith, A. (2009). *An introduction to drugs in sport.* Milton Park: Routledge.

Wanjek, B., Rosendahl, J., Strauss, B., & Gabriel, H. H. (2007). Doping, drugs and drug abuse among adolescents in the State of Thuringia (Germany): Prevalence, knowledge and attitudes. *International Journal of Sports Medicine, 28*, 346–353.

Wassink, H., Coumans, B., & De Hon, O. (2010). *Gezondheidsrisico's illegale doping via internet.* Dopingautoriteit, Capelle a/d IJssel.

Watermann, Y. (2012). Turin: The largest asbestos trial ever. *Catherine Higgings Law Firm*. Retrieved from http://www.chigginslaw.co.uk/2012/02/turin-the-largest-asbestos-trial-ever/

Weinreich, J. (2012, July 13). Blatter wusste von Schmiergeldzahlungen. *Neue Zürcher Zeitung*. Retrieved from http://www.nzz.ch/aktuell/sport/fussball/brisante-sachverhalte-1.17347808

Wiener Zeitung. (2011). *Doping-Prozess: Walter Mayer verurteilt*. Retrieved from http://www.wienerzeitung.at/nachrichten/sport/doping/390055_Doping-Prozess-Walter-Mayer-verurteilt.html

Wiesing, U. (2011). Should performance-enhancing drugs in sport be legalized under medical supervision? *Sport Medicine, 41*(2), 167–176.

Winnipeg Free Press. (2006, September 9). World cycling chief declares "unconditional war" on doping. Retrieved from http://www.winnipegfreepress.com/historic/31775524.html

Woerdeman, J., de Hon, O., Levi, M., & de Ronde, W. P. (2010). Anabolic androgenic steroids in amateur sports in the Netherlands. *Nederlands Tijdschrift voor Geneeskunde*, *154*, A2004.

World Anti-Doping Agency. (2009a). *2008 adverse analytical findings and atypical findings reported by accredited laboratories—Overview of results*. Retrieved from http://www.wada-ama.org/Documents/Science_Medicine/Anti-Doping_Laboratories/WADA_LaboStatistics_2008.pdf

World Anti-Doping Agency. (2009b, May 9). Minutes of the WADA Executive Committee Meeting, Montreal. Retrieved from http://www.wada-ama.org/Documents/About_WADA/ExecutiveCommittee_Minutes/WADA_ExecutiveCommitteeMinutes_200905_EN.pdf

World Anti-Doping Agency. (2009c). *World anti-doping code*. Retrieved from http://www.wada-ama.org/Documents/World_Anti-Doping_Program/WADP-The-Code/WADA_Anti-Doping_CODE_2009_EN.pdf

World Anti-Doping Agency. (2010a). *2009 adverse analytical findings and atypical findings reported by accredited laboratories—Overview of results*. Retrieved from http://www.wada-ama.org/Documents/Science_Medicine/Anti-Doping_Laboratories/WADA_LaboStatistics_2008.pdf

World Anti-Doping Agency. (2010c, May 8). Minutes of the WADA executive committee meeting, Montreal. Retrieved from http://www.wada-ama.org/Documents/About_WADA/ExecutiveCommittee_Minutes/WADA_ExCo_Minutes_2010May8_Final_ENG.pdf

World Anti-Doping Agency. (2010d, November 20). Minutes of the WADA executive committee meeting, Montreal. Retrieved from http://www.wada-ama.org/Documents/About_WADA/ExecutiveCommittee_Minutes/WADA_ExCo_Minutes_20Nov2010_EN.pdf

World Anti-Doping Agency. (2010e, November 21). Minutes of the WADA foundation board meeting, Montreal. Retrieved from http://www.wada-ama.org/Documents/About_WADA/FoundationBoard_Minutes/WADA_FB_Minutes_21Nov2010_EN.pdf

World Anti-Doping Agency. (2011a). *2010 Adverse analytical findings and atypical findings reported by accredited laboratories—Overview of results*. Retrieved from http://www.wada-ama.org/Documents/Resources/Statistics/Laboratory_Statistics/WADA_2010_Laboratory_Statistics_Report.pdf

World Anti-Doping Agency. (2011b, May 14). *Minutes of the WADA executive committee meeting*. Retrieved from http://www.wada-ama.org/Documents/About_WADA/ExecutiveCommittee_Minutes/WADA_ExCo_Minutes_2011_14May_EN.pdf

World Anti-Doping Agency. (2011c, November 19). *Minutes of the WADA executive committee meeting*. Retrieved from http://www.wada-ama.org/Documents/About_WADA/ExecutiveCommittee_Minutes/WADA_ExCo_Minutes_19Nov2011_ENG_FINAL.pdf

World Anti-Doping Agency. (2011d, June 27). *WADA and WCO sign ground-breaking partnership*. Retrieved from http://www.wada-ama.org/en/News-Center/Articles/WADA-and-WCO-sign-ground-breaking-partnership/

World Anti-Doping Agency. (2011e, May 15). *WADA releases guidelines for investigations and evidence sharing*. Retrieved from http://www.wada-ama.org/en/News-Center/Press-release/WADA-Releases-Guidelines-to-Improve-Investigation-Cooperation-and-Intelligence-Sharing/

World Anti-Doping Agency. (2012a). *2011 laboratory testing figures reported by accredited laboratories*. Retrieved from http://www.wada-ama.org/Documents/Resources/Testing-Figures/WADA-2011-Laboratory-Testing-Figures.pdf

World Anti-Doping Agency. (2012b). *The 2012 prohibited list–international standard.* Retrieved from http://www.wada-ama.org/Documents/World_Anti-Doping_Program/WADP-Prohibited-list/2012/WADA_Prohibited_List_2012_EN.pdf

World Anti-Doping Agency. (2013a). *A brief history of anti-doping.* Retrieved from http://www.wada-ama.org/en/About-WADA/History/A-Brief-History-of-Anti-Doping/

World Anti-Doping Agency. (2013b). *Contributions to WADA's Budget 2012.* Retrieved from http://www.wada-ama.org/Documents/About_WADA/Funding/WADA_Contributions_2012_update_EN.pdf

World Anti-Doping Agency. (2013c). *Funding.* Retrieved from http://www.wada-ama.org/en/About-WADA/Funding/

World Anti-Doping Agency. (2013d). *Investigations and trafficking.* Retrieved from http://www.wada-ama.org/en/Anti-Doping-Community/Governments/Investigation--Trafficking/

World Anti-Doping Agency. (2013f). *Priorities.* Retrieved from http://www.wada-ama.org/en/About-WADA/History-Mission-Priorities-and-Strategic-Plan/Priorities/

World Anti-Doping Agency. (2013f). *Questions & answers on the athlete biological passport.* Retrievedfromhttp://www.wada-ama.org/en/Science-Medicine/Athlete-Biological-Passport/Q--A-on-the-Athlete-Biological-Passport/

World Anti-Doping Agency. (2013g). *Strategic plan.* Retrieved from http://www.wada-ama.org/en/About-WADA/History-Mission-Priorities-and-Strategic-Plan/Strategic-Plan/

World Anti-Doping Agency. (2013h). *Therapeutic use exemption.* Retrieved from http://www.wada-ama.org/en/Science-Medicine/TUE/

World Health Organization. (2012). *General information on counterfeit medicines.* Retrieved from http://www.who.int/medicines/services/counterfeit/overview/en/

Wright, V. (2010). *Deterrence in criminal justice: Evaluating certainty vs. severity of punishment.* Retrieved from http://www.sentencingproject.org/doc/Deterrence%20Briefing%20.pdf

Yesalis, C. E., & Bahrke, M. S. (2005). Anabolic steroid and stimulant use in North American Sport between 1850 and 1980. *Sport in History, 25*(3), 434–451.

Yesalis, C. E., Kennedy, N. J., Kopstein, A. N., & Bahrke, M. S. (1993). Anabolic-androgenic steroid use in the United States. *Journal of the American Medical Association, 27*, 1217–1221.

Zambardino, V. (1993a, November 28). Controlli a pioggia sugli atleti padovani. *La Repubblica, 26.* Retrieved from http://ricerca.repubblica.it/repubblica/archivio/repubblica/1993/11/28/controlli-pioggia-sugli-atleti-padovani.html

Zambardino, V. (1993b, December 1). La verità di Francesca. *La Repubblica, 30.* Retrieved from http://ricerca.repubblica.it/repubblica/archivio/repubblica/1993/12/01/la-verita-di-francesca.html

Zambardino, V. (1994, August 11). Benvenuti e i casi di doping 'Sospeso a vita chi sbaglia'. *La Repubblica, 32.* Retrieved from http://ricerca.repubblica.it/repubblica/archivio/repubblica/1994/08/11/benvenuti-casi-di-doping-sospeso-vita.html

Zhao, J., Stockwell, T., & Macdonald, S. (2009). Non-response bias in alcohol and drug population surveys. *Drug and Alcohol Review, 28*(6), 648–657.

Zinser, L. (2006, February 20). 2006 Olympic Winter Games—Police Action; Used syringes among items seized in raid. *The New York Times.* Retrieved from http://select.nytimes.com/gst/abstract.html?res=F50B17FA3A5A0C738EDDAB0894DE404482

Zollkriminalamt. (2012). Gewinnspannen. Mimeo.

Zunino, C. (2007, December 21). Camorra, l'ippodromo in ostaggio. "Qui adesso comandiamo noi". *La Repubblica.* Retrieved from http://www.repubblica.it/2007/12/sezioni/cronaca/ippodromo-malavita/ippodromo-malavita/ippodromo-malavita.html?ref=search

Zunino, C. (2009, November 23). Sperperi e illegalità così l' ippica italiana è diventata un debito. La Repubblica, 21. Retrieved from http://ricerca.repubblica.it/repubblica/archivio/repubblica/2009/11/23/sperperi-illegalita-cosi-ippica-italiana-diventata.html

Index

L. Paoli and A. Donati, *The Sports Doping Market: Understanding Supply and Demand, and the Challenges of Their Control*, DOI 10.1007/978-1-4614-8241-3,

W

CPSIA information can be obtained at www.ICGtesting.com
Printed in the USA
LVOW01*1151130414

381496LV00002B/287/P